Ethnic Challenges to the Modern Nation State

Edited by

Shlomo Ben-Ami
Professor of Modern History
Tel Aviv University
and
Member of the Knesset
Minister of Public Security, Government of the State of Israel

Yoav Peled
Senior Lecturer in Political Science
Tel Aviv University

and

Alberto Spektorowski
Lecturer in Political Science,
Tel Aviv University

First published in Great Britain 2000 by
MACMILLAN PRESS LTD
Houndmills, Basingstoke, Hampshire RG21 6XS and London
Companies and representatives throughout the world

A catalogue record for this book is available from the British Library.

ISBN 0–333–79283–1

 First published in the United States of America 2000 by
ST. MARTIN'S PRESS, INC.,
Scholarly and Reference Division,
175 Fifth Avenue, New York, N.Y. 10010

ISBN 0–312–23053–2

Library of Congress Cataloging-in-Publication Data
Ethnic challenges to the modern nation state / edited by Shlomo Ben-Ami,
Yoav Peled and Alberto Spektorowski.
p. cm.
Includes bibliographical references and index.
ISBN 0–312–23053–2 (cloth)
1. Nationalism. 2. Ethnic Groups—Political activity. I. Ben-Ami, Shlomo.
II Peled, Yoav. III. Spektorowski, Alberto, 1952–

JC311 .E85 2000
320.54 21; aa05 10-01—dc99
                                                                                    99–049537

10   9   8   7   6   5   4   3   2   1
09   08   07   06   05   04   03   02   01   00

Printed and bound in Great Britain
by Antony Rowe Ltd, Chippenham, Wiltshire

To Morris Curiel, a friend and a mentor, and to the memory of the late Norma Moreno Curiel.

Contents

Acknowledgements

This volume originated in an international conference organized by the Editors and held at the Morris E. Curiel Center for International Studies at Tel Aviv University in 1995. We wish to thank the participants in that conference, those whose papers are included in this volume as well as those who were not able to contribute to it, for their insightful and stimulating papers. One contributor to the volume, Gema Martin-Munoz, did not participate in the conference, and we thank her especially for allowing us to include her paper, which deals with the very important topic of the political-religious struggle in Algeria.

At the Morris E. Curiel Center, headed at the time by Shlomo Ben-Ami, we were fortunate enough to work with gifted and dedicated staff members, whose tireless efforts made the conference the success that it was and made this volume possible: Yael Levite, Yael Friedman, Allon Berkowitz and Tallie Graf. Elie Bar-Navi, who succeeded Ben-Ami as Director of the Center, was generous in his support during the time that this volume was being edited. Additional financial support for the production of this book was received from the Gershon Gordon Faculty of Social Sciences and from the Department of Political Science at Tel Aviv University, and we are thankful to them. Special thanks are due also to the two copy editors who worked on the typescript and were able to forge a coherent text out of fifteen disparate papers: Nik John at the Curiel Center and Janey Fisher for Macmillan.

Finally, we wish to thank Morris E. Curiel, whose generosity made the conference and this volume possible. We dedicate the book to him and to the memory of the late Norma Moreno Curiel as a token of our appreciation.

List of Contributors

Shlomo Ben-Ami, Tel Aviv University, Israel

José Brunner, Tel Aviv University, Israel

Alain-G. Gangon, McGill University, Quebec, Canada

Eric Herrán, Instituto Tecnologico Autonomo de Mexico (ITAM)

Rebecca Kook, Ben-Gurion University, Israel

Will Kymlicka, Queens University, Ontario, Canada

Gema Martin Muñoz, Autonomous University of Madrid, Spain

Benyamin Neuberger, Tel Aviv University, Israel

Stanley G. Payne, University of Wisconsin, USA

Ahmad H. Sa'di, Ben-Gurion University, Israel

Yoav Peled, Tel Aviv University, Israel

Gershon Shafir, University of California, San-Diego, USA

Ornit Shani, Cambridge University, England

Alberto Spektorowski, Tel Aviv University, Israel

Oren Yiftachel, Ben-Gurion University, Israel

Moshe Zuckerman, Tel Aviv University, Israel

1
Introduction

Shlomo Ben-Ami

In an essay on nationalism, Isaiah Berlin wondered about the failure of great thinkers to predict the central role that nationalism was to occupy in modern life. He attributed that failure to the much vilified Whig historiography with its vision of an enlightened and optimistic world of progress. Instead of appreciating the immanent forces of nationalism, he argued, the Whigs, like Lord Acton, preferred to dismiss them as 'forces of moral destruction'. A century later, Elie Kedourie, in his book on nationalism, was still strongly committed to this morally dismissive attitude to the phenomenon, as if by denouncing it we can do away with it. Marxists were, of course, no less blind to the power of nationalism.

Modern nationalism tends to have a 'bad press'. 'Collective egoism', 'a paranoid individualism of the masses', 'a malignant fantasy' – these are only a few of the adjectives it has attracted. We should not forget, however, that modern European nationalism was, in its early stages, closely linked with liberal and democratic movements. Nor would it be fair to ignore the fact that nationalism inspired important revolutions in this century and offered the only serious resistance to all forms of imperialism.

However we refer to it, whether we choose the definition of nationalism as 'a community of communication' or as 'an integrated existence within a system of messages', or prefer to dwell on the immigrant's nostalgia or on the xenophobic culture of regional self-government in Europe, the case of nationalism's thousand faces should not be dismissed even in the age of total media and the global village. In fact, nationalism may be sometimes a defensive reaction by small communities who see their identity challenged by the onslaught of the unifying culture of world media. Although not automatically adaptable to the era of MTV, the precepts of national education as laid down by Rousseau are not exactly anachronistic today:

> ... an education that must give souls a national formation, and direct their opinions and tastes in such a way that they will be patriotic by inclination, by passion, by necessity. When first he opens his eyes, an infant ought to see the fatherland, and up to the day of his death he ought never to see anything else.[1]

Indeed, nationalism is one of the most persistent forces in history – in modern history, one should perhaps say – although to speak of nationalism and modernity may sound redundant, since nationalism is a product, indeed a concomitant, of modernity. As a concept or practice, nationalism was unknown to the ancient or Christian medieval world. It was born out of the crisis of modernity in the eighteenth century: it came into existence with the breakdown of traditional structures and was forged through Etatism. Napoleon's wars of conquest throughout Europe taught a lesson that remains as relevant today as it was to the humiliated Germans of the age of Fichte, or to the Spaniards of the Guerrilla and the Constitution of Cadiz: occupation by an external force has frequently been the trigger for the emergence of nationalist reaction.

But Ernest Gellner's claim, that nationalism is a strictly political creature,[2] is hardly sustainable. Its mythological roots, the weight of common history, memory, religion, language, and the collective genius which Herder saw expressed in legends, myths and cathedrals, are as important as modernity. However, Meinecke's distinction between 'cultural' and 'political' nations may be too schematic. It is the encounter between 'culture' and 'politics', between a 'people defined in ethnic terms' and the crisis of modernity that is, as it were, the ideal mix; and when 'culture' is missing it sometimes needs to be invented.

Contemporary Europe's quest for unity and for the creation of a quasi-confederal structure is presumably an essay in curbing the malignant potentialities of nationalism of which two world wars had given sufficient proof. However, the European Union should not be seen as proof of the decay of nationalism or the nation-state as such; it may indeed be proof of its resilience – a system which cloaks national self-interest in the mantle of collective will. The nation-state and nationalism die hard.

Europe's immediate challenge now seems to be that of reconciling the community's natural diversity and the inevitable emphasis of its components on cultural and political self-determination, on the one hand, and the search for a unifying ethic, on the other. The European idea – or any other transnational endeavor, for that matter – can be sustained only if it avoids a descent into tribalism and intolerance. We have seen in Europe the shattering of the old postwar coalitions of mass parties into smaller groupings of parties – from libertarians and greens to regional separatists like the Lombard League in Italy or Henri Batasuna in Spain. The tension between the need for cultural-ethnic distinctiveness and integrative tendencies is related to what Jürgen Habermas identified as the West's 'legitimation crisis', that is the gap between what Edmund Burke called in his *Reflections*, 'the inns and resting places of the human spirit' (day-to-day existence, ethnic, religious and community ties) and the distant bureaucracy and universal values. The greatest European vice has been that of racial repression. We have seen the racist grasp for identity associated with Le Pen, the Austrian neo-fascists and the right-wing parties of North-Rhine Westphalia in Germany. Stopping the slide toward tribalism remains a major challenge for Europe.

This is, indeed, an ambiguous age. It is the age of global systems and quasi-federal structures, what Habermas called 'the age of post-national identity', but it is also the age of self-determination brought to its extreme. The challenge is to reconcile the two, which is easier said than done. Cases like that of Basque nationalism in Spain or French and English nationalism in Europe may simply be insoluble. Identity complexes die hard, if at all. They may even emerge and be consolidated in regions whose encounter with modernity was as successful as it could be, regions that are not exactly cases of economic backwardness or neo-colonialism, such as are the cases of Flandria, Croatia, Slovenia, Lombardy, Catalonia, and the Basque country.

But Europe teaches us another lesson too, and that is that nationalism, if respected, can become a responsible force and can be made into a benign basis for broader international cooperation. It only degenerates into cultural and ethnic narcissism when denied its fundamental aspirations. This is a lesson for the Middle East as well.

What we have to appreciate, however, is that no lofty dreams about a new Middle East or any other enterprise about a new regional order is possible without first coming to terms with nationalist sentiments. A future of regional cooperation in any region can be installed only after the satisfaction of national rights, not before and certainly not as a substitute thereof.

In some of the more visionary projects for the future of the Middle East we are told that the quest for national sovereignty is anachronistic, that the future lies not in borders but in new relations between peoples, and that markets are more important than states. Many of the more progressive minds among us would perhaps readily subscribe to such a vision, but we should avoid the fallacy. There is not going to be a new Middle East before the political and national cleavages in the area are solved. No nation, be it a majority or a minority nation, will accept the benefits of a market economy and the temptations of a regional common market as substitutes for what they conceive of as their national rights. Nor will they accept a new regional order that will not be sensitive to the need to reconcile tradition – ethnic, national, religious – with modernity. Thus, conceived as a neo-colonialist discourse, entirely alien to cultural and historical sensibilities, the slogan of a New Middle East is not always perceived by the Arab world as a contribution to peace based on the dignity of its partners.

The challenge of cooperation with the enemies of yesterday should not be seen, however, only in economic or even political terms; fundamentally, it is a cultural challenge, a question of identity. Common markets or even common strategic spaces cannot be built on deep cultural cleavages and hostility. The European Union is a good example; it is an alliance of democratic political systems institutionally synchronized with each other. The nations of the common European space share the same religion, a similar attitude to leisure, a common musical and artistic tradition, an affinity with the common European literary heritage, and similar habits of cultural consumption. Historical mythologies and memories are shared, traditional routes of pilgrimage have united the nations of the continent in common religious bonds throughout history, and now they all share the same market.

Israel and the nations of the Arab world, more particularly the Palestinians, do not constitute a common cultural and institutional space upon which a solid economic or political integration can be built. We hear voices from the Palestinian side and also from within Israel, especially and naturally among the *Mizrachim*, that Israel has to redefine its cultural identity if it is to build a solid peace with its neighbors based on cooperation. Israel, they say, should be more 'Oriental', and abandon its illusion of becoming a little America or Europe here on the eastern shores of the Mediterranean. The cultural abyss that exists between Israel and the Palestinians is a major handicap for reaching a settlement, they say, and it may also be the reason that once peace has been reached it will be spiritless and sterile.

I must admit that this argument is not very convincing. There is no denying, of course, that cultural confrontation is hardly a recipe for economic and political cooperation. But, there is nonetheless a kernel of paternalism in asking Israel to redefine its cultural identity if it wants real integration in this area. To begin with, no political imperatives, compelling and strong as they may be, can change cultural identity; this is the consequence of irresistible currents of history, tradition and religion. Israel can legitimately be asked to give up territory, not history. Secondly, and no less importantly, that very Palestinian elite that frequently, with the help of Cartesian and Kantian logic, asks Israel to be 'Oriental' as the ultimate price of peace, is hardly purely and neatly 'Oriental' itself. It is rather in the midst of a process of Westernization. A nation of Diaspora, the Palestinians ought to know better than other Arab nations the irresistible impact of history on the cultural identity of peoples. The Palestinians are not the pure Orient, nor are Israelis the pure West. We are both syntheses of traditions; our characters have been shaped by the vicissitudes of history, sometimes in surprisingly similar ways. Rather than Israel being compelled to become Oriental, and the Palestinians to embrace unconditionally Western culture, we should both let our natural constitutions, syncretic and mixed, develop spaces of cooperation. With the re-encounter between Diaspora and statehood, the Palestinians may still discover that they share with the Jews similar dilemmas of identity.

Themselves a nation of Diaspora, Jews have traditionally suffered from nationalism. Nationalist narcissism is the enemy of every national or religious group bent on salvation through the good will of states, cosmopolitan sentiments and the spirit of universality. Albert Einstein might have been right when he defined nationalism as 'an infantile sickness, the measles of the human race'. But Jews have learned their lesson the hard way. The normalization of Jewish existence could only be expressed through the move to national self-determination. It was Moses Hess, a Jewish Marxist *avant la lettre*, who was among the first not only to predict the future strength of nationalism, but also the inevitability that Jewish distinctiveness would be embodied in a national state. In the process Jews helped to create Palestinian nationalism, and today we are gradually and painfully coming to terms with the necessity to satisfy their quest for self-determination as a prerequisite for peace, and for a just and moral order in this region.

Perhaps, if and when peace is established between Israel and the Arab world, we shall have to face the dilemma we insistently postponed and removed from our agenda: is religious, ethnic Jewish nationalism going to give way to a modern nation-state, a state of and for its citizens – Jews and Arabs alike – a state whose expression and embodiment are its institutions, rather than, or at least not exclusively, its ethnic uniqueness?

Israel is an interesting case, for it reflects the tensions between three traditional concepts of nationalism:

1 civil nationalism that is being increasingly advocated by some progressive minds among us, who believe that the move from war to peace will require an institutional, civil brand of national integration to replace the mythological ethic of confrontation;
2 the ethnic concept of nationalism; and
3 the pluralistic, multi-ethnic and multi-cultural concept presumably more adaptable to the nature of immigrant societies such as the USA, Argentina, Canada, Australia and, perhaps in some future time, Israel as well.

Today these three concepts and practices of nationalism probably remain the major poles around which some of us, the laymen in the field, still prefer to conduct the discussion. Those who, like myself, were brought up in the tradition of *Nos ancestres les gaulois*, still carry an ideal image of French civil nationalism, the nation as a community of citizens, a legal community bent on imposing a 'civil religion' through a centralized system of education. But, the ethnic nationalism – that of *Nations before Nationalism* to use Armstrong's expression – of heroes, saints and wise men – has gained strength in recent years as a defensive reaction against rapid and global changes. This is true also in the West, where the ethnic nationalism of Irish, Basques and others continues to be a force to reckon with.

The pluralist concept of nationalism provides a synthesis of sorts, for it accepts the idea that the national state consists of cultural and ethnic communities with a degree of institutional and cultural autonomy. Although better adaptable to immigrant societies, it is clear that much of the tension in traditional European nation-states is the result of the erosion of the old pedagogic myths about national identity and a call for a more balanced presence in national life of a growing number of minority groups. It remains to be seen how long the old Jacobin nationalism of the *republique une et indivisible* will resist the pressure.

What is clear, however, is that the frequent and absolute condemnation *tout court* of nationalism is vague and vacuous. It produces a sense of *déja vu*; hence it leads nowhere. What we need perhaps, as Anthony Smith has suggested, is to adopt some criteria for the evaluation of nationalism that will enable us to draw a distinction between the more benign forms of nationalism and its pathological brands. But this requires coming ever closer to an understanding of the phenomenon, which is what volumes like this one are all about: an attempt to define the state of the question in academic research.

This volume is based on a conference organized by the Maurice E. Curiel Center for International Studies at Tel Aviv University in 1995. In a world of 'post' everything – post-modernity, post-communism, post-colonialism, and here in Israel even post-Zionism – the organizers of that conference felt that what might be termed the 'post-national' ethnic challenge to modernity and the state should be examined from various disciplinary angles and in various parts of the world. The contributors to this volume, most of whom participated in the conference, come from the disciplines of political science, philosophy, history, sociology and geography, and their contributions take as their case studies societies located in Europe, Asia, North America and Africa.

The volume is divided into four sections. The first section deals with identity and citizenship in the modern state, focusing on the complex of issues raised by the debates over multiculturalism. Two of its three chapters, by Will Kymlicka and by Yoav Peled and José Brunner, address the question of multiculturalism in the liberal state, a question that has become so prominent because of Kymlicka's extensive work on it. The third chapter in this section, by Rebecca Kook, introduces a skeptical note into the discussion of minority language rights, using Israel's Palestinian citizens as a case study. The second section deals with ethnic strife in Western Europe, with chapters by Stanley Payne on Catalan and Basque nationalism, by Moshe Zuckermann on Germany and by Alberto Spektorowski on the ethnic dimension of political movements of the 'new right' in Western Europe. The third section deals with ethnic minorities in settler societies, with two chapters, by Ahmad S'adi and Oren Yiftachel on Israel's Palestinian citizens, by Gershon Shafir on the transition to non-racialism in South Africa, by Alain Gagnon on Quebec and by Eric Herrán on the Zapatista rebellion in the Chiapas region of Mexico. The fourth and final part deals with post-colonial societies, with a chapter by Ornit Shani on Hindu radicalism in India, a chapter by Benyamin Neuberger on Black Africa and a chapter by Gema Martin Muñoz on Islamic radicalism in Algeria.

As the studies presented in this volume make evident, there is almost no type of state and no region of the world that is immune to the national or ethnic challenge. In James Joyce's *A Portrait of the Artist as a Young Man* we read:

> When the soul of a man is born in this country there are nets flung at it to hold it back from flight. You talk to me of nationality, language, religion. I shall try to fly by those nets.[3]

'Those nets', however, are persistent and resilient, and their encounter with the changing challenges of modernity form the subject matter of this volume.

Notes

1   J.J. Rousseau, *Political Writings*, tr. and ed. Frederick Watkins (New York: Nelson, 1953), p. 176.
2   E. Gellner, *Nations and Nationalism* (London: Cornell University Press, 1983) p. 1.
3   J. Joyce, *A Portrait of the Artist as a Young Man* (New York: the Viking Press, 1964 [1916]), p. 203.

PART ONE

Collective Identity, Individual Freedom and the Modern State: Theoretical Considerations

2
Modernity and National Identity

Will Kymlicka

Introduction

Virtually every recent discussion of nationalism has begun by emphasizing that the resurgence of nationalism was not predicted by theorists of modernization. National identities were supposed to fade in importance, replaced either by a supra-national cosmopolitan identity, or by a post-national civic or constitutional identity. This prediction has been proven clearly wrong. But while this failure has often been noted, we do not yet have a clear diagnosis of why and where modernization theorists went wrong.

In this chapter, I want to suggest that there were two separate errors at work. The first concerns the role of the state in supporting and perpetuating ethnocultural identities. Theorists argued that just as the modernization process had led to the depoliticization of religious identities, so a similar process would ultimately lead to the depoliticization of ethnocultural identities. Just as liberal democracies had achieved a separation of state and church, so there would be a separation of state and ethnocultural groups.

However, this analogy between religion and culture is flawed, I will argue. The state is inevitably involved in recognizing and reproducing particular ethnocultural groups, and so the politicization of cultural identities is, to some extent, inevitable.

The second error concerns the relationship between cultural identity and individual freedom. Modernization liberates people from fixed social roles and traditional identities, and fosters an ideal of autonomous individuality that encourages individuals to prefer choice and mobility over traditional ascriptive identities. Modernization theorists argued that this ideal of autonomous individuality conflicts with a deep attachment to one's cultural group, particularly in the case of smaller nations or national minorities. These smaller groups face strong economic and political pressures to assimilate into larger nations, and theorists assumed that the members of these groups would accept this process, rather than fight to maintain their cultural identity at the price of economic well-being or social mobility. To resist assimilation would require an irrational attachment to an ascriptive group identity that was inconsistent with the modern ideal of autonomous individuality.

However, this assumption that a deep attachment to one's cultural identity reflects an irrational and illiberal attitude is mistaken, I will argue. The modern desire for freedom and autonomy, far from weakening people's commitment to their own cultural identity, has in many cases strengthened it. People who value their autonomy also value their national culture, since their national culture provides the most important context within which people develop and exercise their autonomy.

I believe that these two errors continue to affect our ability to understand and evaluate nationalism. The first persists in the myth of a culturally neutral state, and in confused accounts of 'civic nationalism'; the second persists in the view of nationalism as an inherently illiberal and primordial phenomenon.

I will explore these two mistakes in more detail in the rest of the chapter. However, I must make one important qualification. I am focusing on the relationship between modernization and nationalism in the West, and hence on national identities and nationalist movements within Western liberal, democratic, secular, industrialized countries. I am particularly interested in nationalist sentiments amongst minority groups within Western democracies, such as the Québécois in Canada, the Flemish in Belgium, or Catalan in Spain. The mistakes I have just outlined have seriously impeded our ability to understand these movements.

Some of the trends I discuss in the West are also occurring elsewhere, as more and more countries undergo 'modernization'. But the process of modernization in Africa or Asia is very different from that in Western Europe or the Anglo-American democracies, and so the impact of modernization on nationalism might be very different as well. However, I want to leave that as an open question.

States and cultures

The first issue, then, involves the relationship between states and cultures. Some theorists argue that modern governments can and should

avoid supporting any particular societal culture or ethnonational identity. Indeed, some theorists argue that this is precisely what distinguishes liberal 'civic nations' from illiberal 'ethnic nations'. Ethnic
nations take the reproduction of a particular ethnonational culture and
identity as one of their most important goals. Civic nations, by contrast, are 'neutral' with respect to the ethnocultural identities of their
citizens, and define national membership purely in terms of adherence
to certain principles of democracy and justice. On this view, civic
nations treat culture in the same way as religion – that is, as something
which people should be free to pursue in their private life, but which is
not the concern of the state (so long as they respect the rights of
others). Just as liberalism precludes the establishment of an official religion, so too there cannot be official cultures which have preferred
status over other possible cultural allegiances.

For example, Michael Walzer argues that liberalism involves a 'sharp
divorce of state and ethnicity'. The liberal state stands above all the
various ethnic and national groups in the country, 'refusing to endorse
or support their ways of life or to take an active interest in their social
reproduction'. Instead, the state is 'neutral with reference to language,
history, literature, calendar' of these groups. He says the clearest
example of such a civic nation is the United States, whose ethnocultural neutrality is reflected in the fact that it has no constitutionally
recognized official language.[1]

But this is misleading. The fact is that the American government very
actively promotes a common language and societal culture. Thus it is a
legal requirement for children to learn the English language and
American history in schools; it is a legal requirement for immigrants (over
the age of 50) to learn the English language and American history in
order to acquire American citizenship; it is a *de facto* requirement for
employment in government that the applicant speak English; court pro-
ceedings and other government activities are typically conducted only in
English; and the resulting legislation and bureaucratic forms are typically
only provided in English. All levels of American government – federal,
state and municipal – have insisted that there is a legitimate governmental interest in promoting a common language, and the Supreme Court
has repeatedly affirmed that claim in upholding laws that mandate the
teaching and use of English in schools and government functions.
Indeed, as Gerald Johnson put it, 'it is one of history's little ironies that
no polyglot empire of the old world has dared to be so ruthless in imposing a single language upon its whole population as was the liberal republic "dedicated to the proposition that all men are created equal"'.[2]

In short, the United States has deliberately promoted integration into what I call a 'societal culture' which is based on the English language. I use the word *societal* to emphasize that it involves a common language and social institutions, rather than common religious beliefs, family customs or personal lifestyles. Societal cultures within a modern liberal democracy are inevitably pluralistic, containing Christians, Jews and Muslims; heterosexuals as well as homosexuals; urban professionals as well as rural farmers; conservatives as well as socialists. Such diversity is the inevitable result of the rights and freedoms guaranteed to liberal citizens, particularly when combined with an ethnically diverse population.

So a societal culture is a territorially concentrated culture, centered on a shared language which is used in a wide range of societal institutions, in both public and private life (schools, media, law, economy, government, and so on). Participation in such societal cultures provides access to meaningful ways of life across the full range of human activities, including social, educational, religious, recreational and economic life, encompassing both public and private spheres.

The American government has deliberately promoted integration into such a societal culture – that is, it has encouraged citizens to view their life-chances as tied up with participation in common societal institutions that operate in the English language. Nor is the United States unique in this respect. Promoting integration into a societal culture is part of a 'nation-building' project which all liberal democracies have engaged in, although as I discuss later, some countries have tried to sustain two or more societal cultures.

Obviously the sense in which the English-speaking Americans share a common 'culture' is a very thin one, since it does not preclude differences in religion, personal values, family relationships or lifestyle choices. But while this sort of common culture is thin, it is far from trivial. On the contrary, as I discuss below, attempts to integrate people into such a common societal culture have often been met with serious resistance. Although integration in this sense leaves a great deal of room for both the public and private expression of individual and collective differences, some groups have nonetheless vehemently rejected the idea that they should view their life-chances as tied up with the societal institutions conducted in the majority's language.

So the American government was not 'neutral' with respect to language and culture. Nor could it have been. The idea that the government could have been neutral with respect to ethnocultural groups is clearly false. Whether Americans would integrate into an English,

German or Spanish societal culture was necessarily determined by government policy.

One of the most important determinants of whether a culture survives is whether its language is a language of government – that is, whether its language is used in public schooling, courts, legislatures, welfare agencies, health service and so on. When the government decides the language of public schooling, it is providing what is probably the most important form of support needed by societal cultures, since it guarantees the passing on of the language and its associated traditions and conventions to the next generation.

Conversely, it is very difficult for languages to survive in modern industrialized societies unless they are used in public life. Given the spread of standardized education, the high demands for literacy in work, and widespread interaction with government agencies, any language which is not a public language becomes so marginalized that it is likely to survive only amongst a small elite, or in a ritualized form, or in isolated rural areas, not as a living and developing language underlying a flourishing culture. Government decisions about the language of public schools and public services are in effect decisions about which societal cultures will be able to exist within the country. And in the United States, a conscious decision was made to support only an anglophone societal culture.

Decisions regarding immigration and naturalization also affect the viability of societal cultures. Immigration can strengthen a national group, so long as the numbers are regulated and immigrants are encouraged (or required) to learn the nation's language and history. But if immigrants in a multination state integrate into the majority culture, then national minorities will be increasingly outnumbered and so increasingly powerless in political life. Moreover, states often encourage immigrants (or migrants from other parts of the country) to settle in lands traditionally held by national minorities, reducing them to a minority even within their historic territory.

For example, consider the American southwest. When the southwest was incorporated into the United States in 1848, there were very few anglophones. They were vastly outnumbered by the Chicanos and Indian tribes who had been residing in the area for centuries. Had the Chicanos controlled immigration into the region, they surely would have adopted a policy which encouraged or compelled immigrants to integrate into their societal culture, and thereby preserved their dominant status in the region. (For example, they might have sought immigrants from Mexico, rather than Europe.) Had this happened, the southwest today would be like Quebec or Catalonia – a region dominated by a linguistically distinct national minority. However, the American federal government had the opposite desire. Its aim was to establish the dominance of the anglophone societal culture throughout the territory of the southwest. And so it encouraged massive immigration into the area, and required the settlers and immigrants to learn English. We can debate the merits of this decision, but the important point is that a deliberate decision had to be made, one way or the other, about which societal culture would be dominant in the area. A decision had to be made about how many immigrants would be allowed into the area, and about what language they would be required to learn – decisions which have profound effects on the viability of the various societal cultures.

One could multiply the number of examples of public policy decisions which implicitly or explicitly support particular ethnocultural groups. For example, decisions about public holidays and school curriculum typically reflect and help perpetuate a particular national culture. Similarly, the boundaries of political sub-units can be drawn in such a way as to empower national minorities, by creating regional or municipal units in which they form a majority; or they can be drawn in such a way as to disempower minorities, by ensuring that the dominant group forms a majority within all sub-units. Again, we can debate the merits of various boundary decisions, but there is no 'neutral' way to avoid deciding whether or not to allow ethnocultural groups to form a majority within particular jurisdictions.[3]

This shows that the analogy between religion and culture is mistaken. It is possible for a state not to have an established church. But the state cannot help but give at least partial establishment to a culture when it decides which language is to be used in government; what language and history children must learn in school; what language and history immigrants must learn to become citizens; whether sub-units will be drawn to create districts controlled by national minorities; and so on. These political decisions directly determine the viability of societal cultures.

So the idea that 'civic nations' are neutral between ethnocultural identities is mythical. What then distinguishes civic from ethnic nations? One basic difference involves the terms of admission into the nation. 'Ethnic' nations, like Germany, define membership in terms of shared descent, so that people of a different racial or ethnic group (for example, Turkish guest-workers in Germany) cannot acquire citizenship no matter how long they live in the country.[4] 'Civic' nations, like the United States, are in principle open to anyone who lives in the territory, so long as they learn the language and history of the society. They define membership in terms of participation in a common societal culture, open to all, rather than on ethnic grounds. So ethnic nationalism is exclusive, civic nationalism is inclusive. That is a crucially important difference. But both involve the politicization of ethnocultural groups; both construe national membership in terms of participating in a common societal culture; and both use public policy to uphold and perpetuate that societal culture. The use of public policy to promote a particular societal culture is an inevitable feature of any modern state.

The choice of integration or self-government

So there are many ways that government decisions play a crucial role in sustaining national cultures. This is not to say that governments can only promote *one* societal culture. It is possible for government policies to encourage the sustaining of two or more societal cultures within a single country – indeed, as I discuss below, this is precisely what characterizes multination states.

However, historically, virtually all liberal democracies have, at one point or another, attempted to diffuse a single societal culture throughout all of their territory. This should not be seen purely as a matter of cultural imperialism or ethnocentric prejudice. This sort of nation-building serves a number of important and legitimate goals. For example, a modern economy requires a mobile, educated and literate workforce. Standardized public education in a common language has often been seen as essential if all citizens are to have equal opportunity to work in this modern economy. Also, participation in a common societal culture has often been seen as essential for generating solidarity within modern democratic states. The sort of solidarity required by a welfare state requires that citizens have a strong sense of common identity and common membership, so that they will make sacrifices for each other, and this common identity is assumed to be facilitated by a common language and history. Sharing a common language also makes it easier for citizens to engage in political debate with each other, and so has been seen as a precondition for creating a genuinely 'deliberative democracy'. In short, promoting integration into a common societal cultures has been seen as essential to social equality and political cohesion in modern states.

So all states have engaged in this process of 'nation-building' – that is, a process of promoting a common language, and a sense of common membership in, and equal access to, the social institutions based on that language.[5] Decisions regarding official languages, core curriculum in education, and the requirements for acquiring citizenship, were all made with the express intention of diffusing a particular culture throughout society, and of promoting a particular national identity based on participation in that societal culture.

Because these 'nation-building' projects can be seen, not merely as ethnocentric prejudice, but rather as extending freedom and equality to all citizens, they have not always been resisted by minority groups. Some ethnocultural groups have accepted the call to integrate. And in some countries, the result of these 'nation-building' programs has been to extend a common societal culture throughout the entire territory of the state. These are the paradigmatic 'nation-states' – for example, England, France, Germany.

But in other countries, territorially concentrated minorities have resisted integration into the dominant societal culture. In such 'multination states' – like Belgium, Canada, Switzerland, and Spain – one or more national minorities, with their own distinct languages and separate institutions, exist alongside the dominant societal culture.

Understanding these nation-building projects provides the first steps towards an explanation of the rise of nationalist movements amongst minority cultures. For, as Taylor notes, the process of nation-building inescapably privileges members of the majority culture:

> If a modern society has an 'official' language, in the fullest sense of the term, that is, a state-sponsored, -inculcated, and -defined language and culture, in which both economy and state function, then it is obviously an immense advantage to anyone if this language and culture is theirs. Speakers of other languages are at a distinct disadvantage.[6]

This means that minority cultures face a choice. If all public institutions are being run in another language, minorities face the danger of being marginalized from the major economic, academic, and political institutions of the society. To avoid perpetual marginalization, therefore, minorities must either integrate into the majority culture, or seek the sorts of rights and powers needed to maintain their own societal culture – that is, to create their own economic, political and educational institutions in their own language.

Faced with this choice, ethnocultural groups have responded in different ways. Some have accepted integration. This is particularly true of immigrant groups. By contrast, non-immigrant minorities have strongly resisted integration, and instead fought for self-government. By non-immigrant minorities I mean historically settled, territorially concentrated and previously self-governing cultures whose territory has somehow become incorporated into a larger state. I will call these groups 'national minorities' or 'incorporated minorities'. Such groups include the Québécois and Puerto Ricans in North America, and the Flemish and Catalans in Europe.

Why have immigrants accepted integration? One reason is that immigrants have already voluntarily left their own culture with the expectation of integrating into another national society. That is exactly what it means to become an immigrant. If they had found the idea of integrating into another culture repugnant, they would not have chosen to become immigrants.[7] Moreover, since they typically emigrated as individuals or families, rather than as entire communities, immigrants lack the territorial concentration or corporate institutions needed to form a linguistically distinct society alongside the mainstream society. To try to recreate such a distinct parallel society would require tremendous support from the host society – not only in terms of language rights, but also in terms of settlement policy, and even the redrawing of boundaries so as to enable some form of self-government – support which no host government is inclined to offer. So the nationalist option is neither desirable nor feasible for immigrants.

This is not to say that integration is a simple or uncontroversial process, or that immigrants are not raising important political demands, often under the rubric of multiculturalism. It is clear that immigrants today reject total assimilation, and seek instead some accommodation of their distinctive identities and practices, and I discuss these demands elsewhere.[8] But this has not taken the form of nationalism. Indeed there are very few (if any) examples in the modern world of immigrant groups forming nationalist movements for self-government or secession.[9]

Immigrants rarely object to the imposition of a common language, since they have already chosen to leave their old culture behind, and since the option of recreating a culturally distinct society alongside the existing national culture is not feasible. For incorporated national minorities, however, the imposition of the majority language threatens their existing culturally distinct society. Their language and historical narratives are already embodied in a full set of social practices and institutions, encompassing all aspects of social life, which are now threatened by the majority's efforts to diffuse a common societal culture. Such groups almost inevitably resist integration, and seek official recognition of their language and culture. Indeed, Walker Connor goes so far as to suggest that few, if any, examples exist of recognized national groups in this century having voluntarily assimilated to another culture, even though many have had significant economic incentives and political pressures to do so.[10]

This demand for official recognition needn't take the form of a secessionist movement for a separate state. It could instead take the form of demanding some form of local autonomy, perhaps through a system of federalism, and/or a system of official bilingualism. But, whatever the exact form, it typically involves the demand for the sorts of legal rights and legislative powers necessary to ensure the survival of a culturally distinct society alongside the majority society.

Such nationalist movements are a distinctly modern phenomenon, not only in the sense that they are a natural concomitant to the modernizing project of nation-building, but also in the sense that they are themselves a form of nation-building. Nationalists in Quebec or Catalonia also believe in the importance of diffusing a common culture and language throughout their society so as to diminish class and regional differences; and they use the same tools that the majority nation uses in its program of nation-building – that is, standardized public education, official languages, including language requirements for citizenship and government employment, and so on.

So nationalist movements by national minorities are not rejecting the dynamic of modernization and nation-building. They accept the idea that a modern economy and democratic community requires a diffused common culture. They are simply arguing that they form their own distinct economy and society within the boundaries of the larger state. They are arguing that some countries are not nation-states, but are multination states, containing two or more national societies.

In short, faced with the choice between integration or fighting to maintain a distinct societal culture, it seems that immigrant groups are likely to choose the former, while national minorities are likely to choose the latter. Of course, I have over-simplified the contrast. The extent to which immigrant groups have been allowed or encouraged to integrate varies considerably, as does the extent to which national minorities have been able to maintain a separate culture. And there are many ethnocultural groups which do not fit neatly into either of these categories.[11] But as a general rule in Western democracies, dominant cultures have had far less success integrating national groups than immigrant groups.[12] In multination states, national minorities have resisted integration into the common culture, and instead sought to protect their separate existence by consolidating their own societal cultures. It appears that the capacity and motivation to form and maintain such a distinct culture is character- istic of national groups, not immigrant groups.[13]

The value of cultural membership

So far, I have simply been describing the actual historical practices of liberal democracies towards ethnocultural groups. Virtually all Western democracies have followed the same basic pattern: the majority national group has attempted to diffuse its language and culture throughout the entire territory of the state; immigrant groups have typically accepted integration into this common culture, while national minorities have typically resisted integration and fought instead to maintain their status as separate and self-governing cultur- ally distinct societies.

But *why* are smaller national groups so keen to maintain themselves as distinct societal cultures, rather than integrating into a larger nation? This leads us to the second problem in modernization theory. According to modernization theorists, this commitment to cultural maintenance reflects an illiberal preference for ascriptive group iden- tity over individual choice – a preference which is incompatible with the modern ideal of autonomy.

This, I believe, is a profoundly mistaken interpretation. However, the mistake is not the emphasis on autonomy. On the contrary, I whole- heartedly share the assumption that a central feature of modernization is the diffusion of ideals of individual autonomy. Citizens of the modern world may not use the word 'autonomy', but they do demand the right to decide for themselves how to lead their lives. In particular, they demand the right to question the value of the traditions and prac- tices they have inherited from their parents or community leaders, and to judge for themselves whether these practices are worth continuing. We can of course find examples of groups (particularly conservative ethno-religious groups) desperately trying to discourage or inhibit the exercise of this sort of autonomy, but I think that the diffusion of autonomy is a powerful trend in modern societies which can only be temporarily deflected, not stopped or reversed. Indeed, I think that any social or political movement which thwarts the desire for individual autonomy will have trouble gaining or maintaining adherents, and so will have only limited numbers and marginal influence in the modern world.

Modernization theorists were mistaken, not in emphasizing individual autonomy, but rather in assuming that a commitment to minority nationalism involves abandoning the quest for individual autonomy. In reality, if we examine cases of minority nationalism in the Western democracies, we often find that nationalists have also been liberal reformers. That is, they have fought to gain greater self-government rights for their group while simultaneously fighting to liberalize their group so as to increase the individual freedom of group members.

Why were these liberal reformers also nationalists? Because they believed that participation in a national culture, far from inhibiting individual choice, is what makes individual freedom meaningful. On this view, freedom involves making choices amongst various options, and one's societal culture not only provides these options, but also makes them meaningful to one. Hence the gradual erosion of one's societal culture – a prospect which confronts national minorities who lack strong self-government rights – leads to a gradual erosion of one's individual autonomy.

I believe that this view of the connection between individual freedom and cultural membership is essentially correct, although difficult to articulate. I shall not explore it in detail here, since I have tried to do so elsewhere.[14] The basic idea is that modernity is defined (in part at least) by individual freedom of choice. But what does individual choice involve? People make choices about the social practices around them, based on their beliefs about the value of these practices; and to have a belief about the value of a practice is, in the first instance, a matter of understanding the meanings attached to it by our culture. I noted earlier that societal cultures involve 'a shared vocabulary of tradition and convention' which underlies a full range of social practices and institutions.[15] To understand the meaning of a social practice, therefore, requires understanding this 'shared vocabulary' – that is, understanding the language and history which constitute that vocabulary. Whether or not a course of action has any significance for us depends on whether, and how, our language renders vivid to us the point of that activity; and the way in which language renders vivid these activities is shaped by our history, our 'traditions and conventions'. Understanding these cultural narratives is a precondition for making intelligent judgments about how to lead our lives. In this sense, our culture not only provides options, it also 'provides the spectacles through which we identify experiences as valuable'.[16] The availability of meaningful options depends on access to a societal culture, and on understanding the history and language of that culture – its 'shared vocabulary of tradition and convention'.[17] For meaningful individual choice to be possible, individuals need to have not only access to information, the capacity to reflectively evaluate it, and freedom of expression and association. They also need access to a societal culture.[18]

For this reason, the foundational liberal commitment to individual freedom can be extended to generate a deep liberal commitment to the ongoing viability and flourishing of societal cultures. In multination states, this helps to explain the persistence of minority nationalisms – that is, the demand for language rights and self-government powers. These rights and powers ensure that national minorities are able to sustain and develop their societal cultures into the indefinite future.

This picture of the relationship between individual freedom and membership in a national culture is explicitly developed by various recent writers – Yael Tamir, Joseph Raz, Charles Taylor, David Miller.[19] But it is also implicit, I believe, in most contemporary liberal theorists, such as Dworkin or Rawls. Consider Rawls's argument about why the right to emigrate does not make political authority voluntary:

> [N]ormally leaving one's country is a grave step: it involves leaving the society and culture in which we have been raised, the society and culture whose language we use in speech and thought to express and understand ourselves, our aims, goals, and values; the society and culture whose history, customs, and conventions we depend on to find our place in the social world. In large part, we affirm our society and culture, and have an intimate and inexpressible knowledge of it, even though much of it we may question, if not reject. The government's authority cannot, then, be freely accepted in the sense that the bonds of society and culture, of history and social place of origin, begin so early to shape our life and are normally so strong that the right of emigration (suitably qualified) does not suffice to make accepting its authority free, politically speaking, in the way that liberty of conscience suffices to make accepting ecclesiastical authority free.[20]

Because of these bonds to the 'language we use in speech and thought to express and understand ourselves', cultural ties 'are normally too strong to be given up, and this fact is not to be deplored'. Hence for the purposes of developing a theory of justice, we should assume that 'people are born and are expected to lead a complete life' within the same 'society and culture'.[21]

I agree with Rawls's view about the difficulty of leaving one's culture.[22] But his argument has implications beyond those which he himself draws. Rawls presents this as an argument about the difficulty of leaving one's political community. But his argument does not rest on the value of specifically political ties (for example, the bonds to one's government and fellow citizens). Rather it rests on the value of cultural ties (for instance, bonds to one's language and history). And cultural boundaries may not coincide with political boundaries. For example, someone leaving East Germany for West Germany in 1950 would not be breaking the ties of language and culture which Rawls emphasizes, even though she would be crossing state borders. But a francophone leaving Quebec City for Toronto, or a Puerto Rican leaving San Juan for Chicago, would be breaking those ties, even though she would be remaining within the same country.

According to Rawls, then, the ties to one's culture are normally too strong to give up, and this is not to be regretted. We cannot be expected or required to make such a sacrifice, even if some people voluntarily do so.

Why are the bonds of language and culture so strong for most people? Commentators offer a number of reasons. Margalit and Raz argue that membership in a societal culture (what they call a 'pervasive culture') is crucial to people's well-being for two reasons. The first reason is the one I have discussed above – namely, that cultural membership provides meaningful options, in the sense that 'familiarity with a culture determines the boundaries of the imaginable'. Hence if a culture is decaying or discriminated against, 'the options and opportunities open to its members will shrink, become less attractive, and their pursuit less likely to be successful'.[23] But why can't the members of a decaying culture simply integrate into another culture? According to Margalit and Raz, this is difficult, not only because it is 'a very slow process indeed', but also because of the role of cultural membership in people's self-identity. Cultural membership has a 'high social profile', in the sense that it affects how others perceive and respond to us, which in turn shapes our self-identity. Moreover, national identity is particularly suited to serving as the 'primary foci of identification', because it is based on belonging not accomplishment:

> Identification is more secure, less liable to be threatened, if it does not depend on accomplishment. Although accomplishments play their role in people's sense of their own identity, it would seem that at the most fundamental level our sense of our own identity

depends on criteria of belonging rather than on those of accomplishment. Secure identification at that level is particularly important to one's well-being.[24]

Hence cultural identity provides an 'anchor for [people's] self-identification and the safety of effortless secure belonging'. But this in turn means that people's self-respect is bound up with the esteem in which their national group is held. If a culture is not generally respected, then the dignity and self-respect of its members will also be threatened. Similar arguments about the role of respect for national membership in supporting dignity and self-identity are given by Charles Taylor [25] and Yael Tamir.[26]

Tamir also emphasizes the extent to which cultural membership adds an 'additional meaning' to our actions, which become not only acts of individual accomplishment, but also 'part of a continuous creative effort whereby culture is made and remade'. She argues that where institutions are 'informed by a culture [people] find understandable and meaningful', this 'allows a certain degree of transparency that facilitates their participation in public affairs', which in turn promotes a sense of belonging and relationships of mutual recognition and mutual responsibility.[27] Other commentators make the related point that the mutual intelligibility which comes from shared national identity promotes relationships of solidarity and trust.[28] James Nickel emphasizes the potential harm to valuable intergenerational bonds when parents are unable to pass on their culture to their children and grandchildren.[29] Benedict Anderson emphasizes the way national identity enables us to transcend our mortality, by linking us to something whose existence seems to extend back into time immemorial, and forward into the indefinite future.[30]

No doubt all of these factors play a role in explaining people's bond to their own culture. I suspect that the causes of this attachment lie deep in the human condition, tied up with the way humans as cultural creatures need to make sense of their world, and that a full explanation would involve aspects of psychology, sociology, linguistics and the philosophy of mind. But whatever the explanation, this bond does seem to be a fact, and, like Rawls, I see no reason to regret it. I should emphasize, again, that I am only dealing with general trends. Some people seem most at home leading a truly cosmopolitan life, moving freely between different societal cultures. Others have difficulty making sense of the cultural meanings within their own culture. But most people, most of the time, have a deep bond to their own societal culture, and see their individual liberty as intimately tied up with the options available within that culture.

Thus the desire of national minorities to maintain themselves as distinct societal cultures does not conflict with the aspiration to individual freedom, but rather provides its context. We can put the same point another way. The liberal ideal is a society of free and equal individuals, but what is the relevant 'society'? For most people it seems to be their nation. The sort of freedom and equality they most value, and can make most use of, is freedom and equality within their own societal culture. And they are willing to forego a wider freedom and equality to ensure the continued existence of their nation.

For example, few citizens in liberal democracies favor a system of open borders, where people could freely cross borders and settle, work and vote in whatever country they desire. Such a system would dramatically increase the domain within which people would be treated as free and equal citizens. Yet open borders would also make it more likely that people's own national community would be overrun by settlers from other cultures, and that they would be unable to ensure their survival as a distinct national culture. So we have a choice between, on the one hand, increased mobility and an expanded domain within which people are free and equal individuals, and, on the other hand, decreased mobility but with a greater assurance that people can continue to be free and equal members of their own national culture. Most people in liberal democracies clearly favor the latter. They would rather be free and equal within their own nation, even if this means they have less freedom to work and vote elsewhere, than be free and equal citizens of the world, if this means they are less likely to be able to live and work in their own language and culture.

And most theorists in the liberal tradition have implicitly agreed with this. Few major liberal theorists have endorsed open borders, or even seriously considered it. They have generally accepted – indeed, simply taken for granted – that the sort of freedom and equality which matters most to people is freedom and equality within one's societal culture. Like Rawls, they assume that 'people are born and are expected to lead a complete life' within the same 'society and culture', and that this defines the scope within which people must be free and equal.[31]

In short, liberal theorists have generally, if implicitly, accepted that cultures or nations are basic units of liberal political theory. In this sense, as Tamir puts it, 'most liberals are liberal nationalists'[32] – that is, liberal goals are achieved in a liberalized societal culture or nation.

Liberal nationalism versus communitarianism

It may seem paradoxical for liberals like Rawls to claim that the bonds to one's culture are 'normally too strong to be given up'. What has happened to the much vaunted liberal freedom of choice? But Rawls's view is in fact common within the liberal tradition. The freedom which liberals demand for individuals is not primarily the freedom to go beyond one's language and history, but rather the freedom to move around within one's societal culture, to distance oneself from particular cultural roles, to choose which features of the culture are most worth developing, and which are without value.

Some readers may still think that this reflects an illiberal or irrational attitude towards one's ascriptive group, even if the attitude runs deep in the historical liberal tradition. Viewing national bonds as 'normally too strong to be given up' may seem to reflect a primordial commitment to ascriptive groups that is ultimately inconsistent with the commitment to individual autonomy which characterizes modernity.

We can see why this is a mistake by comparing the sort of liberal nationalism I am defending from more 'communitarian' views of the self, which really do question the modernist commitment to autonomy. 'Communitarianism' can refer to many positions, but one strand of communitarianism is defined by its rejection of the liberal view about the importance of being free to revise one's ends. These communitarians deny that we can 'stand apart' from (some of) our ends. According to Michael Sandel, a leading American communitarian, some of our ends are 'constitutive' ends, in the sense that they define our sense of personal identity.[33] It makes no sense, on his view, to say that my ends might not be worthy of my allegiance, for they define who I am. Whereas Rawls claims that individuals 'do not regard themselves as inevitably bound to, or identical with, the pursuit of any particular complex of fundamental interests that they may have at any given moment',[34] Sandel responds that we are in fact 'identical with' at least some of our final ends. Since these ends are constitutive of people's identity, there is no reason why the state shouldn't reinforce people's allegiance to those ends, and limit their ability to question and revise these ends.

I believe that this communitarian conception of the self is mistaken. It is not easy or enjoyable to revise one's deepest ends, but it is possible, and sometimes a regrettable necessity. New experiences or circumstances may reveal that our earlier beliefs about the good are mistaken. No end is immune from such potential revision. As Dworkin puts it, it is true that 'no one can put everything about himself in question all at once', but it 'hardly follows that for each person there is some one connection or association so fundamental that it cannot be detached for inspection while holding others in place'.[35]

Some people may think of themselves as being incapable of questioning or revising their ends, but in fact 'our conceptions of the good may and often do change over time, usually slowly but sometimes rather suddenly', even for those people who think of themselves as having constitutive ends.[36] No matter how confident we are about our ends at a particular moment, new circumstances or experiences may arise, often in unpredictable ways, that cause us to reevaluate them. It is not possible to predict in advance when the need for such a reconsideration will arise. A liberal society does not compel people to revise their commitments – and many people will go for years without having any reason to question their basic commitments – but it does recognize that the freedom of choice is not a one-shot affair, and that earlier choices sometimes need to be revisited.

Since our judgments about the good are fallible in this way, we have an interest not only in pursuing our existing conception of the good, but also in being able to assess and potentially revise that conception. Our current ends are not always worthy of our continued allegiance, and exposure to other ways of life helps us make informed judgments about what is truly valuable.

The liberal nationalist view is quite different, therefore, from the communitarian one, although both views claim that we have a deep bond to a particular sort of social group. The difference is partly a matter of scope. Communitarians typically talk about our attachment to sub-national groups – churches, neighborhoods, family, unions, and so on – rather than to the larger society which encompasses these subgroups. But this difference in scope reflects an even deeper divergence. Communitarians are looking for groups which are defined by a shared conception of the good. They seek to promote a 'politics of the common good', in which groups can promote a shared conception of the good, even if this limits the ability of individual members to revise their ends. They believe that members have a 'constitutive' bond to the group's values, and so no harm is done by limiting individual rights in order to promote shared values.

As communitarians are the first to admit, this 'politics of a common good' cannot apply at the national level. As Sandel puts it, 'the nation proved too vast a scale across which to cultivate the shared self-understandings necessary to community.'[37] The members of a modern nation rarely share moral values or traditional ways of life. They share a language and history, but often disagree fundamentally about the ultimate ends in life. A common national identity, therefore, is not a useful basis for communitarian politics, which can only exist at a more local level.

The liberal nationalist view I am defending insists that people can stand back and assess moral values and traditional ways of life, and should be given not only the legal right to do so, but also the social conditions which enhance this capacity (for example, a liberal education). Liberal nationalists object to communitarian politics at the subnational level. To inhibit people from questioning their inherited social roles can condemn them to unsatisfying, even oppressive, lives.[38] And at the national level, the very fact which makes national identity so inappropriate for communitarian politics – namely, that it does not rest on a shared conception of the good – is precisely what makes it an appropriate basis for liberal politics. The national culture provides a meaningful context of choice for people, without limiting their ability to question and revise particular values or beliefs.

Dissolving the 'paradox' of liberal nationalism

So far, I have argued that modernization theorists misjudged the persistence of minority nationalisms within Western democracies because they (a) misjudged the extent to which modern liberal states are inevitably involved in maintaining and reproducing societal cultures, and (b) misjudged the extent to which participation in one's societal culture provides the primary context for the exercise of individual freedom. Recognizing these mistakes helps to explain why minority nationalisms have persisted, rather than diminished, in modernized democracies.[39]

However, this seems to raise an important paradox, which I wish to discuss and help to dispel. The argument that I have just given presupposes that people have a strong attachment to their own culture, and that this attachment is not inconsistent with the desire for individual freedom, and hence for the liberalization of one's culture. Many commentators are puzzled that people would have a strong attachment to a liberalized culture. After all, as a culture is liberalized – and so allows members to question and reject traditional ways of life – the resulting cultural identity becomes both 'thinner' and less distinctive. That is, as a culture becomes more liberal, the members are less and less likely to share the same substantive conception of the good life, and more and more likely to share basic values with people in other liberal cultures.

Why then do the members of national minorities remain so committed to their own societal culture? The Québécois provide a nice illustration of this puzzle. Before the Quiet Revolution, the Québécois generally shared a rural, Catholic, conservative and patriarchal conception of the good. Today, after a rapid period of liberalization, most people have abandoned this traditional way of life, and Québécois society now exhibits all the diversity that any modern society contains – for example, atheists and Catholics, gays and heterosexuals, urban yuppies and rural farmers, socialists and conservatives, and so on. To be a 'Québécois' today, therefore, simply means being a participant in the francophone society of Quebec. And francophones in Quebec no more agree about conceptions of the good than anglophones in the United States. So being a 'Québécois' seems to be a very thin form of identity.

Moreover, the process of liberalization has also meant that the Québécois have become much more like English-Canadians in their basic values. Liberalization in Quebec over the last 30 years has been accompanied by a pronounced convergence in personal and political values between English- and French-speaking Canadians, so that it would now be

difficult to identify consistent differences in attitudes on issues such as moral values, prestige ranking of professions, role of the government, workers' rights, aboriginal rights, equality between the sexes and races, and conception of authority.[40]

In short, liberalization in Quebec has meant both an increase in differences amongst the Québécois, in terms of their conceptions of the good, and a reduction in differences between the Québécois and the members of other liberal cultures. This is not unique to Quebec. The same process is at work throughout Europe. The modernization and liberalization of Western Europe has resulted both in fewer commonalities within each of the national cultures, and in greater commonalities across these cultures. As Spain has liberalized, it has both become more pluralistic internally, and Spaniards have become more like the French or Germans in terms of their modern, secular, bureaucratic, industrialized, democratic and consumerist civilization.

This explains why so many theorists have assumed that liberalization and modernization would displace any strong sense of national identity. As cultures liberalize, people share less and less with their fellow members of the national group, in terms of traditional customs or conceptions of the good life, and become more and more like the members of other nations, in terms of sharing a common civilization. Why then would anyone feel strongly attached to their own nation?

Faced with this puzzle, two responses are possible. One is to avoid the paradox by assuming that minority nationalisms must, after all, be illiberal. On this view, the apparent shift in Quebec political culture towards secular liberal pluralism is simply skin-deep, and the demand for greater autonomy reveals a deeper, covert desire to retreat from modernity and recreate a more closely-knit and intense communal life, based on shared ethnicity, history and religion. This view denies that a truly liberal nationalism is possible – the desire for national recognition and autonomy by Quebec proves that they do not in fact share the liberal values of other Canadians.

The other response is to accept that the paradox of liberal nationalism is real, and will not go away. This view accepts that Quebec nationalism is fundamentally driven by a forward-looking conception of Quebec as a pluralistic, liberal modern society, rather than a backward-looking communitarian or conservative ideology.

I believe that the evidence clearly supports this latter view. The evidence is overwhelming that the members of liberal cultures *do* value their cultural membership. Far from displacing national identity, liberalization has in fact gone hand in hand with an increased sense of nationhood. Many of the liberal reformers in Quebec have been staunch nationalists, and the nationalist movement grew in strength throughout the Quiet Revolution and afterwards. The same combination of liberalization and a strengthened national identity can be found in many other countries. For example, in Belgium, the liberalization of Flemish society has been accompanied by a sharp rise in nationalist sentiment. Likewise, the liberalization of Spanish society has been accompanied by a strengthening of nationalist sentiment in Catalonia and the Basque Country.[41] The fact that their culture has become tolerant and pluralistic has in no way diminished the pervasiveness or intensity of people's desire to live and work in their own culture.

This sort of attachment seems deeply 'paradoxical' to many commentators, a paradox which can only explained in terms of an irrational 'narcissism of minor differences'.[42] But this is only paradoxical if one starts with the assumption that people's commitment to their national culture is illiberal. If one assumes that the value of national identity is that it provides one with ascribed roles and goals, then valuing a liberal culture is paradoxical. But if instead one assumes that individuals find meaningful autonomy by exploring the options and practices available in their own societal culture, then the combination of increasing internal diversity and decreasing external differentiation that one finds in Quebec or Catalonia is precisely what one would expect.

Autonomous individuals value their national identity not *in spite* of its thinness, but rather *because* of it – that is, because a thin national culture provides the context within which individuals can develop and exercise their autonomy. The idea of a deep attachment to a thin cultural identity is not a paradox of liberal nationalism, but rather is part of the very definition of liberal nationalism. If such a thing as liberal nationalism exists, it can only be in this form of a deep attachment to a thin identity.

If 'the cause of liberty' finds 'its basis in the autonomy of national groups', as Ernest Barker put it,[43] then one would expect to see both greater diversity within national cultures, in terms of the range of ways of life they contain, and greater commonality across national cultures, in terms of a shared commitment to the same basic liberal democratic principles of social organization. The fact that the members of national minorities demand self-government even as their national identity has become both thinner and less distinctive is not evidence of an illiberal attachment. On the contrary, it is evidence of how fully national minorities have joined modernity, and adopted the modern commitment to individual autonomy.

The persistence of minority nationalism may still seem puzzling to some people, and I am painfully aware that I have not really explained why the members of national minorities are so attached to their national culture. Nor do I know what would count as an adequate explanation. But for those who remain sceptical, I offer one final reminder. It would be a mistake to rephrase the question as 'Why are minorities so attached to their national identity?', as if this were a feature only of minority national groups, and not also of majority ones. If we phrase the question this way, we are inclined to look for attributes which distinguish minorities from majorities – for example, a sense of defensiveness, or resentment. But in reality, there is no evidence that the members of majorities are any less attached to their freedom to live and work in their societal culture than the members of national minorities. And in so far as this is true, then fairness seems to require accommodating these deep attachments, whatever the exact explanation for them. It may be a mystery about why people in general value their national identity, but there is nothing puzzling about the fact that *minorities* do so – they do so for the same reason as the members of majority nations.[44]

Illiberal groups

So far, I have tried to show that nationalist movements for self-government within Western democracies often reflect a concern for, and commitment to, individual freedom. Of course, some nations and nationalist movements are deeply illiberal. Some cultures, far from enabling autonomy, simply assign particular roles and duties to people, and prevent people from questioning or revising them. Other cultures allow this autonomy to some, while denying it to others, such as women, lower castes, or visible minorities. This is rarely true of nations in the West, although there are some exceptions. Clearly, these sorts of cultures do not promote liberal values.

It is clear from this that liberals cannot endorse cultural membership uncritically. Indeed, if the liberal commitment to respecting national identity flows from its role in enabling autonomy, should we not encourage or compel the members of illiberal cultures to assimilate to more liberal cultures? But again this ignores the way people are bound to their own cultures. The aim of liberals should not be to dissolve non-liberal nations, but rather to seek to liberalize them. This may not always be possible. But it is worth remembering that all existing liberal nations had illiberal pasts, and their liberalization required a prolonged process of institutional reform. To assume that any culture is inherently illiberal, and incapable of reform, is ethnocentric and ahistorical. Moreover, the liberality of a culture is a matter of degree. All cultures have illiberal strands, just as few cultures are entirely repressive of individual liberty. Indeed, it is quite misleading to talk of 'liberal' and 'illiberal' cultures, as if the world was divided into completely liberal societies on the one hand, and completely illiberal ones on the other. The task of liberal reform remains incomplete in every society, and it would be ludicrous to say that only purely liberal nations should be respected, while others should be assimilated.

So, as a general rule, liberals should not prevent illiberal nations from maintaining their societal culture, but should promote the liberalization of these cultures. The issue of how to promote liberalization, and more generally how liberal states should treat nonliberal minorities, is a large topic, which I pursue at length elsewhere.[45]

Why do some nationalist movements develop in a liberal way, while others do not? The answer will obviously depend on many specific historical factors, but one particular factor is worth emphasizing. The extent to which a nationalist movement is liberal seems largely to depend on whether or not it arises within a country with long-established liberal institutions. Flemish, Scottish and Quebec nationalisms are liberal, because Belgium, Britain and Canada are long-standing liberal democracies. Any nationalist movement which sought to impose illiberal practices on a population accustomed to the benefits of liberal governance would not acquire any popular support. By contrast, Serb, Ukrainian and Slovak nationalisms are illiberal, because they emerged in illiberal states. Nationalist movements, then, tend to take their cue from the political culture around them.

Conclusion

In this chapter, I have outlined two mistakes which help explain why modernization theorists underestimated the likelihood of the persistence of nationalism: a) a failure to recognize the inevitable role of the state in upholding particular ethnocultural groups; and b) a failure to recognize the role of national identity in upholding individual autonomy. These two mistakes continue to inhibit a clear understanding of nationalism in the West.

It is surprising, I think, that the first mistake continues to be made, since it is a glaring error which is obvious to anyone who actually examines the organization and function of modern states. The second is a more understandable mistake, however, since as we've seen, there is something paradoxical about the importance of national identity to individual freedom, given that the effect of liberalization is to make ethnocultural groups more diverse internally, and less distinctive *vis-à-vis* other groups.

However, I have argued that people's membership in their own societal culture does play an important role in enabling meaningful individual choice and in supporting self-identity. While the members of a (liberalized) nation no longer share moral values or traditional ways of life, they still have a deep attachment to their own language and culture. Indeed, it is precisely because national identity does not rest on shared values – as Tamir puts it, national identity lies 'outside the normative sphere'[46] – that it provides a secure foundation for individual autonomy and self-identity. Cultural membership provides us with an intelligible context of choice, and a secure sense of identity and belonging, that we call upon in confronting questions about personal values and projects. And the fact that national identity does not require shared values also explains why nations are appropriate units for liberal theory – national groupings provide a domain of freedom and equality, and a source of mutual recognition and trust, which can accommodate the inevitable disagreements and dissent about conceptions of the good in modern society.

If I am right that national identity and individual autonomy are intimately connected, and that the state is inevitably involved in determining which societal cultures can sustain themselves, we can safely predict that nationalism is likely to remain an enduring feature of modernity. The myth that the state can simply be based on democratic principles, without supporting a particular national identity or culture, has made it impossible to see why national minorities are so keen on forming or maintaining political units in which they are a majority. Indeed, as Ernest Gellner noted, once we recognize the inevitable links between states, cultures and individual freedom, the question is not so much why nationalist movements arise, but why there aren't more of them.[47]

Notes

1 Walzer, Michael, 'Comment', in Amy Gutmann (ed.), *Multiculturalism and the 'Politics of Recognition'* (Princeton University Press, Princeton 1992), pp. 99–103. Ignatieff, Michael, *Blood and Belonging: Journeys into the New Nationalism*, (Farrar, Straus and Giroux, New York 1993). Pfaff, William, *The Wrath of Nations: Civilization and the Furies of Nationalism* (Simon and Schuster, New York 1993).
2 Johnson, Gerald, *Our English Heritage*, (Greenwood Press, Westport 1973). p. 119.
3 For a more detailed discussion of this point, see Kymlicka, 1997.
4 This is changing somewhat. A recent change to Germany's naturalization law makes it easier for non-Germans between the ages of 16 and 24 to acquire citizenship, if they have lived in Germany for at least 8 years.
5 For the ubiquity of this process, see Gellner, 1983; Anderson, 1983.
6 Taylor, Charles, 'Nationalism and Modernity', in R. McKim and J. McMahan (eds), *The Morality of Nationalism* (Oxford University Press, New York 1997), p. 3.
7 Obviously this does not apply to refugees. However, the feasibility constraints which I go on to discuss do apply equally to refugees.
8 Kymlicka, W., *Finding Our Way: Rethinking Ethnocultural Relations in Canada*, (Oxford University Press, Toronto, 1998) Chapters 1–4.
9 I should emphasize that I am speaking here of immigrant groups within those liberal democratic countries where there is a tradition of welcoming immigrants, and where it is easy for immigrants to become full citizens regardless of their race, religion or ethnic origin. Under these circumstances, immigrant groups have not demanded group self-government. Of

course, in many parts of the world – including some Western democracies – immigrants are much less welcome, and it is far more difficult for them to acquire equal citizenship. Where immigrants are subject to severe prejudice and legal discrimination – and hence where full equality within the mainstream society is unachievable – it is more likely that immigrants will seek to create a separate and self-governing society, alongside the mainstream society. For example, insofar as the German government persists in refusing to grant citizenship to long-term Turkish residents (and their children and grandchildren), one would expect Turks to press for greater powers of self-government, so that they can create and perpetuate a separate and self-governing society alongside the German society to which they are denied entry. But this is not the preference of the Turks, whose main goal, like immigrants in other liberal democracies, is to become full and equal participants in German society. And while I cannot argue the point here, I believe that any plausible account of liberal justice will insist that long-term immigrants should be able to acquire citizenship. In short, the historical record suggests that quasi-federal forms of self-government will only be sought by immigrant groups within liberal democracies if they face unjust barriers to their full integration and participation in the mainstream society.

10 Connor, 1972:350–1; 1973:20. For a more recent survey of ethnonational conflicts around the world, which shows clearly the important differences between immigrant groups and incorporated national groups, see Gurr, 1993.

11 For a more extended typology, see Kymlicka, 1998a.

12 This generalization is borne out by the American experience. The tendency for American immigrants to integrate is well-known, and the idea of the American 'melting-pot' is often celebrated. Less well-known is the tendency for American national minorities to resist integration. These national minorities include the American Indians, Alaskan Eskimos, Puerto Ricans, the descendants of Mexicans (Chicanos) living in the southwest when the United States annexed Texas, New Mexico and California after the Mexican War of 1846–8, native Hawaiians, the Chamoros of Guam, and various other Pacific islanders. These groups were all involuntarily incorporated into the United States, through conquest, colonization or imperial cession. As they were incorporated, most acquired a special political status. For example, Indian tribes are recognized as 'domestic dependent nations' with their own governments, courts, and treaty rights; Puerto Rico is a 'Commonwealth'; and Guam is a 'protectorate'. Each of these peoples is federated to the American polity with special powers of self-government. These groups also have rights regarding language and land use. In short, national minorities in the United States have a range of group rights intended to reflect and protect their status as distinct cultural communities, and they have fought to retain and expand these rights. It is often said that the American constitution only recognizes individual rights. This is simply inaccurate – national minorities in the United States do have significant group rights. Indeed, the American government has not been markedly more successful than any other Western democracy in integrating its national minorities into a common culture. For surveys of the rights of national minorities in the US, see O'Brien, 1987; Resnik, 1989; Aleinikoff, 1994.

13 This connection is confirmed from another direction, by studies of nationalism. Most analysts of nationalism have concluded that the defining feature of nations is that they are 'pervasive cultures', 'encompassing cultures', or 'organizational cultures' (for example., A. Smith, 1986:2; Margalit and Raz, 1980:444; Tamir, 1993; Poole, 1993). In short, just as societal cultures are almost invariably national cultures, so nations are almost invariably societal cultures.

14 Kymlicka, W., *Multicultural Citizenship: a Liberal Theory of Minority Rights*, (Oxford University Press, Oxford 1995), Chapter 5.

15 Dworkin, R., *A Matter of Principle*, (Harvard University Press, London 1985). p. 231.

16 Ibid., p. 228.

17 Ibid. pp. 228, 231.

18 Some theorists accept this view, but deny that the members of a national minority need access to their *own* culture (see, for example, Binder, 1993:253–5; Buchanan, 1991:54–5; Waldron, 1992; Tomasi, 1995, Nickel, 1994, Lenihan, 1991). I agree that integrating into another culture is rarely an impossibility. However, for most people it has unacceptably high costs – costs which it is unfair to impose on people (unless they voluntarily accept them). Or so I argue in Kymlicka, 1995: Chapter 6.

19 For related arguments about the dependence of freedom on national culture, see Taylor, 1985; Tamir, 1993: Chapter 1–2; Margalit and Raz, 1990; Miller, 1995.

20 Rawls, John, *Political Liberalism*, (Columbia University Press, New York 1993) p. 222.

21 Ibid., p. 277.

22 It's worth remembering that while many immigrants flourish in their new country, there is a selection factor at work. That is, those people who choose to uproot themselves are likely to be the people who have the weakest psychological bond to the old culture, and the strongest desire and determination to succeed elsewhere. We cannot assume *a priori* that they represent the norm in terms of cultural adaptability.

23 Margalit, Avishai and Joseph Raz, 'National Self-Determination', *Journal of Philosophy*, Vol. 87/9, 1990, p. 449. Reprinted in Will Kymlicka (ed.), *The Rights of Minority Cultures*, (Oxford University Press, 1995), pp. 79–92.

24 Ibid., 447–9.

25 Taylor, Charles, 'The Politics of Recognition', in Amy Gutmann (ed.), *Multiculturalism and the 'Politics of Recognition'*, (Princeton University Press, Princeton 1992), pp. 25–73.

26 Tamir, Yael, *Liberal Nationalism*, (Princeton University Press, Princeton 1993). pp. 41,71–3.

27 Ibid., pp. 72, 85–6.

28 Miller, David, 'In Defense of Nationality', *Journal of Applied Philosophy*, Vol. 10/1, 1993, pp. 3–16.; Barry, Brian, 'Self-Government Revisited' in *Democracy and Power: Essays in Political Theory I*, (Oxford University Press, Oxford 1991), pp. 174–5.

29 Nickel, James, 'The Value of Cultural Belonging: Expanding Kymlicka's Theory', *Dialogue*, Vol. 33/4, 1994, pp. 635–42.

30   Anderson, Benedict, *Imagined Communities: Reflections on the Origin and Spread of Nationalism*, (New Left Books, London 1983).
31   Rawls 1993:*op. cit.*, p. 277. Of course, once that national existence is not threatened, then people will favor increased mobility, since being able to move and work in other cultures is a valuable option for some people under some circumstances. For liberal defenders of open borders – all of whom see themselves as criticizing the orthodox liberal view – see Ackerman, 1980:89–95; Carens, 1987; Hudson, 1986; King, 1983; Bader, 1995.
32   Tamir, Yael, *op. cit.* p. 139.
33   Sandel, Michael, *Liberalism and the Limits of Justice* (Cambridge University Press, Cambridge 1982). pp. 150–165; MacIntyre, Alasdair, *After Virtue: a Study in Moral Theory* (Duckworth, London 1981), chapter 15; Bell, Daniel, *Communitarianism and its Critics* (Oxford University Press, Oxford 1993), pp. 24–54.
34   Rawls, 1974, *op. cit.* p. 641.
35   Dworkin, 1989: *op. cit. p.* 489.
36   Rawls, 1985: *op. cit.* p. 242.
37   Sandel, Michael, *Liberalism and the Limits of Justice* (Cambridge University Press, Cambridge 1982), p. 93; MacIntyre, Alasdair, *After Virtue: a Study in Moral Theory* (Duckworth, London 1981) p. 221; Miller, David, 'In What Sense Must Socialism Be Communitarian?', *Social Philosophy and Policy*, Vol. 6/2, 1988–9 pp. 51–73.
38   The danger of oppression is exacerbated by the fact that many traditional roles and practices were defined historically on the basis of sexist, racist, classist and homophobic assumptions. Some social roles are so compromised by their unjust origins that they should be rejected entirely, not just gradually reformed (D. Phillips, 1993).
39   Of course, this is only a partial explanation for any particular nationalist movement, which would also require examining the particular historical, economic, demographic and political circumstances of the society. My aim here is not so much to explain why nationalist movements arise, but rather to explain why modernization theorists were wrong to suppose that modernization would inhibit nationalist mobilization.
40   Dion, Stéphane, 'Le Nationalisme dans la Convergence Culturelle', in R. Hudon and R. Pelletier (eds), *L'Engagement intellectuel: mélanges en l'honneur de Léon Dion* (Les Presses de l'Université Laval, Sainte-Foy 1991). p. 301. Dion, Stéphane, 'Explaining Quebec Nationalism', in R. Kent Weaver (ed.), *The Collapse of Canada?* (Brookings Institute, Washington 1992). p. 99. The only significant difference Dion notes concerns openness to immigration, a difference that is understandable in the light of Francophone fears as a minority.
41   Peterson, W., 'On the Subnations of Europe', in Nathan Glazer and Daniel P. Moynihan (eds), *Ethnicity: Theory and Experience* (Harvard University Press, Cambridge, 1975); Hennessy, Alistair, 'The Renaissance of Federal Ideas in Contemporary Spain', in Murray Forsyth (ed.), *Federalism and Nationalism* (Leicester University Press, Leicester, 1989); Payne, Stanley G., 'Catalan and Basque Nationalism: Contrasting Patterns', in this volume, Chapter 5.
42   Ignatieff, Michael, *Blood and Belonging: Journeys into the New Nationalism* (Farrar, Straus and Ginoux, New York, 1993), p. 21; Dion, *La Nationalisme*.

43 Barker, Ernest, *National Character and the Factors in its Formation* (Methuen, London, 1948), p. 248.
44 Minorities tend to be more self-conscious about this attachment, since conscious efforts are often needed to protect their societal culture. Majorities, whose culture is less vulnerable, can take their national identity for granted. But if the majority's culture ever becomes threatened, then they, as much as minorities, will come to its defense. As George Bernard Shaw once put it, 'A healthy nation is as unconscious of its nationality as a healthy man of his bones. But if you break a nation's nationality, it will think of nothing else but getting it set again.'
45 See Kymlicka, 1995: Chapter 8.
46 Tamir, Yael, *op. cit.*, p. 90.
47 Gellner, Ernest, *Nations and Nationalism*, (Blackwell, Oxford, 1993).

References

Ackerman, Bruce (1980), *Social Justice in the Liberal State*. (Yale University Press, New Haven).

Aleinikoff, Alexander (1994), 'Puerto Rico and the Constitution: Conundrums and Prospects', *Constitutional Commentary*, Vol. 11, pp. 15–43.

Anderson, Benedict (1983), *Imagined Communities: Reflections on the Origin and Spread of Nationalism* (New Left Books, London).

Bader, Veit (1995), 'Citizenship and Exclusion: Radical Democracy, Community and Justice', *Political Theory*, Vol. 23/2, pp. 211–46.

Barker, Ernest (1948), *National Character and the Factors in its Formation* (Methuen, London).

Barry, Brian (1991), 'Self-Government Revisited' in *Democracy and Power: Essays in Political Theory I*, (Oxford University Press, Oxford), pp. 156–86.

Bell, Daniel (1993), *Communitarianism and its Critics* (Oxford University Press, Oxford).

Binder, Guyora, (1993), 'The Case for Self-Determination', *Stanford Journal of International Law*, Vol. 29, pp. 223–70.

Buchanan, Allen (1991), *Secession: the Legitimacy of Political Divorce* (Westview Press, Boulder).

Carens, Joseph (1987), 'Aliens and Citizens: the Case for Open Borders', *Review of Politics*, Vol. 49/3, pp. 251–73. Reprinted in Will Kymlicka (ed.), *The Rights of Minority Cultures* (Oxford University Press, 1995), pp. 331–49.

Connor, Walker (1972), 'Nation-Building or Nation-Destroying', *World Politics*, Vol. 24, pp. 319–55.

Connor, Walker (1973), 'The Politics of Ethnonationalism', *Journal of International Affairs*, Vol. 27/1, pp. 1–21.

Dion, Stéphane (1991), 'Le Nationalisme dans la Convergence Culturelle', in R. Hudon and R. Pelletier (eds), *L'Engagement Intellectuel: Melanges en l'honneur de Léon Dion* (Les Presses de l'Université Laval, Sainte-Foy).

Dion, Stéphane (1992), 'Explaining Quebec Nationalism', in R. Kent Weaver (ed.), *The Collapse of Canada?* (Brookings Institute, Washington).

Dworkin, R. (1985), *A Matter of Principle* (Harvard University Press, London).

Dworkin, R. (1989), 'Liberal Community', *California Law Review*, Vol. 77/3, pp. 479–504.

Gellner, Ernest, (1983), *Nations and Nationalism* (Blackwell, Oxford).

Gurr, Ted (1993), *Minorities at Risk: a Global View of Ethnopolitical Conflict* (Institute of Peace Press, Washington).

Hennessy, Alistair (1989), 'The renaissance of federal ideas in contemporary Spain', in Murray Forsyth, (ed.), *Federalism and Nationalism* (Leicester University Press, Leicester), pp. 11–23.

Hobsbawm, E.J. (1990), *Nations and Nationalism since 1780: Programme Myth and Reality* (Cambridge University Press, Cambridge).

Hudson, James (1986), 'The Philosophy of Immigration', *Journal of Libertarian Studies*, Vol. 8/1, pp. 51–62.

Ignatieff, Michael (1993), *Blood and Belonging: Journeys into the New Nationalism* (Farrar, Straus and Giroux, New York).

Johnson, Gerald (1973), *Our English Heritage* (Greenwood Press, Westport).

King, Timothy (1983), 'Immigration from Developing Countries: Some Philosophical Issues', *Ethics*, Vol. 93/3, pp. 525–36.

Kymlicka, W. (1989), *Liberalism, Community, and Culture* (Oxford University Press, Oxford).

Kymlicka, W. (1995), *Multicultural Citizenship: a Liberal Theory of Minority Rights* (Oxford University Press, Oxford).

Kymlicka, W. (1997), 'Is Federalism a Viable Alternative to Secession?', in Percy Lehning (ed.), *Theories of Secession* (Routledge, London), pp. 110–49.

Kymlicka, W. (1998a), 'Ethnocultural Minority Groups', in Ruth Chadwick (ed.), *Encyclopedia of Applied Ethics* (Academic Press).

Kymlicka, W. (1998b), *Finding Our Way: Rethinking Ethnocultural Relations in Canada* (Oxford University Press, Toronto).

Lenihan, Donald (1991), 'Liberalism and the Problem of Cultural Membership', *Canadian Journal of Law and Jurisprudence*, Vol. 4/2, pp. 401–19.

MacIntyre, Alasdair (1981), *After Virtue: a Study in Moral Theory* (Duckworth, London).

Margalit, Avishai and Joseph Raz (1990), 'National Self-Determination', *Journal of Philosophy*, Vol. 87/9, pp. 439–61. Reprinted in Will Kymlicka (ed.), *The Rights of Minority Cultures* (Oxford University Press, 1995), pp. 79–92.

Miller, David (1988–89), 'In What Sense Must Socialism be Communitarian?', *Social Philosophy and Policy*, Vol. 6/2, pp. 51–73.

Miller, David (1993), 'In Defense of Nationality', *Journal of Applied Philosophy*, Vol. 10/1, pp. 3–16.

Nickel, James (1994), 'The Value of Cultural Belonging: Expanding Kymlicka's Theory', *Dialogue*, Vol. 33/4, pp. 635–42.

O' Brien, Sharon (1987), 'Cultural Rights in the United States: a Conflict of Values', *Law and Inequality Journal*, Vol. 5, pp. 267–358.

Peterson, W. (1975), 'On the Subnations of Europe', in N. Glazer and D. Moynihan (eds), *Ethnicity: Theory and Experience* (Harvard University Press, Cambridge).

Pfaff, William (1993), *The Wrath of Nations: Civilization and the Furies of Nationalism* (Simons and Schuster, New York).

Phillips, D.Z. (1993), *Looking Backward: a critical appraisal of communitarian thought* (Princeton University Press, Princeton).

Poole, Ross (1993), 'Nationalism and the Nation State in Late Modernity', *European Studies Journal*, Vol. 10/1, pp. 161–74.

Rawls, John (1974), 'Reply to Alexander and Musgrave', *Quarterly Journal of Economics*, Vol. 88/4, pp. 633–55.

Rawls, John (1985), 'Justice as Fairness: Political not Metaphysical', *Philosophy and Public Affairs*, Vol. 14/3, pp. 223–51.

Rawls, John (1993), *Political Liberalism* (Columbia University Press, New York).

Reitz, Jeffrey and Raymond Breton (1994), *The Illusion of Difference: Realities of Ethnicity in Canada and the United States* (C.D. Howe Institute, Ottawa).

Resnik, Judith (1989), 'Dependent Sovereigns: Indian Tribes, States, and the Federal Courts', *University of Chicago Law Review*, Vol. 56, pp. 671–759.

Sandel, Michael (1982), *Liberalism and the Limits of Justice* (Cambridge University Press, Cambridge).

Smith, Anthony (1986), *The Ethnic Origins of Nations* (Blackwell, Oxford).

Steinberg, Stephen (1981), *The Ethnic Myth: Race, Ethnicity, and Class in America* (Atheneum, New York).

Tamir, Yael (1993), *Liberal Nationalism* (Princeton University Press, Princeton).

Taylor, Charles (1985), *Philosophy and the Human Sciences: Philosophical Papers 2* (Cambridge University Press, Cambridge).

Taylor, Charles (1992), 'The Politics of Recognition', in Amy Gutmann (ed.), *Multiculturalism and the 'Politics of Recognition'* (Princeton University Press, Princeton), pp. 25–73.

Taylor, Charles (1997), 'Nationalism and Modernity', in R. McKim and J. McMahan (eds), *The Morality of Nationalism* (Oxford University Press, New York).

Tomasi, John (1995), 'Kymlicka, Liberalism, and Respect for Cultural Minorities', *Ethics* Vol. 105/3, pp. 580–603.

Waldron, Jeremy (1992), 'Minority Cultures and the Cosmopolitan Alternative', *University of Michigan Journal of Law Reform*, Vol. 25/3, pp. 751–93. Reprinted in Will Kymlicka (ed.), *The Rights of Minority Cultures* (Oxford University Press, 1995), pp. 93–119.

Walzer, Michael (1992), 'Comment', in Amy Gutmann (ed.), *Multiculturalism and the 'Politics of Recognition'* (Princeton University Press, Princeton), pp. 99–103.

3
Towards the Rehabilitation of 'Nation-Building' and the Reconstruction of Nations

Rebecca Kook

Introduction

The discourse surrounding multi-culturalism has focused attention on a central institution of democracy, namely, citizenship. In the light of centuries of racial and gender discrimination in such bastions of democracy as the United States, Canada and the United Kingdom, so-called cultural pluralists have suggested a reconceptualization of the institution of citizenship, and its capacity as a mechanism of integration.[1] They propose that democratic society incorporate individuals on a group basis in addition to the individual basis, and that the state recognize collective cultural rights. In effect, this notion challenges the hegemony of the classic liberal notion of an individualistically based political community.

The idea of collective cultural rights is not confined, however, to issues of race and gender in the West. Clearly, the resurgence of ethnic and national conflict in south-eastern Europe and the former Soviet Union, along with the partial resolution of age-long ethno-national conflicts in South Africa and the Middle East, have rendered the notion of collective cultural rights extremely appealing. Whether from the empowerment of previously disenfranchized populations (such as in South Africa, Israel), increased political representation of alien residents (for example, France and Germany), and the search for a common basis of shared national sovereignty in eastern Europe and in northern Ireland, it appears that political communities, world wide, are undergoing a process of either de- or re-construction. Despite the vast diversity, however, all these efforts share a common dilemma: should minority ethno-national or religious groups be incorporated into society on the basis of group identity, or solely on an individual basis?

Moreover, in the context of this type of fragmentation, what could then provide the basis for unity?

In this chapter I question the efficacy of recognizing collective cultural rights as a mechanism for stabilizing ethno-nationally fragmented societies. I argue that this type of strategy, which I identify as *differentiation*, when applied to contexts of ethnic or national fragmentation, often perpetuates discrimination and inequality rather than eliminating it.

The plan of the chapter is as follows. In the first part I discuss the evolution of the notion of collective cultural rights. I argue that the idea of differentiated citizenship is the conceptual heir to the critique generated by the concept of nation-building. This critique, however, was fundamentally misconceived in so far as it failed to recognize the compatibility of different levels of identity, and equated cultural identity with political loyalty. The contemporary concept of collective cultural rights is premised on the same assumptions, and hence assumes differentiation to be the appropriate strategy for culturally plural societies. In the second part I illustrate how differentiation often fails as an appropriate strategy in the type of reconstructed societies mentioned above, that is, societies which have recently undergone ethnic or national conflict. To this end, I examine a specific case of cultural rights, namely language rights, and demonstrate how the granting of such rights can serve as a mechanism of control rather then liberation. My discussion of language rights is backed up by an empirical examination of the official language policy in Israel, and its impact upon the Israeli Palestinian national minority.

Alternative strategies for stabilizing fragmented societies

Conceptually, the idea of collective cultural rights emerged as a means of stabilizing ethnically, religiously or nationally fragmented societies.[2] With variations, two fundamental strategies have been suggested. The first is integration, which posits that the proper way to stabilize fragmented societies is to provide and then maintain a common basis of identity – through shared values, symbols, and so on. Implicit in this approach is the notion that social fragmentation is inherently unstable, and that stability requires a unified political community. The second strategy can be loosely termed 'differentiation', and it essentially argues for the institutionalization of differences. This approach seeks a way to stabilize society through the recognition of the primacy of the identity of the different groups. Collective cultural rights emerge as one of the central political manifestations of the differentiation strategy.

Integration

While the search for integration has been an inherent aspect of many political theories, the concept most closely associated with integration has been that of nation-building. As a concept, nation-building developed within modernization theory. It emerged in the mid-1950s as a response to the dilemmas posed by the newly established states of the third world.[3] Not really a theory in itself, the concept promoted the idea of an integrated political community as both a precondition for the development of modern democratic polities, and as its outcome. In other words, such an 'integrated community' was seen as both an ends and a means.

While the 'nation-builders' did not employ the term 'nation' consistently, preferring in many cases that of political community (or at times national identity),[4] undoubtedly the denotation was to the liberal, inclusive and integrative notion of 'nation'.[5] Accordingly, the concept of nation-building was premised on two assumptions:

1 The idea of an integrated nation as a *precondition* for modernization (and hence for democracy) argued that for democracies to remain stable, they require a basis of shared values and a set of common interests and goals. As primarily western theorists, a shared national identity seemed to them to be the 'natural' choice for a framework from which this common basis was to be generated and then maintained. It was this equation, of modern democracy and national-civic-political identity, which then generated the hypothesis that any other sub-national identity (ethnic, tribal, religious) is incompatible with modernity and democracy.

2 A common national identity was also seen as an inevitable *outcome* of modernization, in so far as modernization led to increased mobilization and industrialization. These two processes, in turn, were perceived as promoting the creation of an integrated *state-bound* community through the extension of communication networks and common educational facilities and curricula. Such a community would, it was argued, eventually lead to the disintegration of sub-national identities on the one hand, and to the promotion of an all-national identity on the other.

Thus, this national identity was seen to be not merely integrative, but assimilating, inasmuch as former identities would eventually become obsolete, and blend almost naturally into the new identity. Accordingly, in the epistemological and ideological climate of the late 1950s and the 1960s, ethnic or tribal identities were seen as not merely 'traditional' but actually inferior in their political status as well as somehow less sturdy in terms of personal development.[6]

As the preferred strategy for achieving stable democracy in fragmented societies, integration remained an implicit preference in most of the post-modernization theories as well. In addition to being central to political culture theories,[7] integration became the preferred strategy for some of the anti-modernization theories as well. Thus while dependency theory, for example, might have attacked nation-building on ideological grounds (and was in fact not particularly interested in questions of national identity as such), it accepted the fundamental tenet that development (and ultimately democracy) required the maintenance of a unified or integrated community, whether the basis of that community be religious, ethnic, tribal or national.[8]

Differentiation

Nonetheless, the legacy of development studies in general and of nation-building in particular has been an ambivalent one. Despite the persistence of the belief in the necessity of some type of unified community to maintain a stable developed polity, disillusionment with the empirical development of the third world generated a cycle of critique of the entire modernization and nation-building discourse. Walker Connor, for example, as early as 1972, pointed out that far from generating assimilation, mobilization and modernization tend to exacerbate ethnic conflict, rather than to minimize it. Therefore, particularistic ethnic identities should not be taken lightly, and should not be relegated to an inferior political status.[9]

This line of criticism dominated the understanding of ethnicity and nationalism in the third world for the best part of the following two decades.[10] As explanatory variables the centrality accorded to identity spilled over into studies of the industrial countries, as numerous studies of the resurgence of ethnic identity in the west illustrate.[11] Comparative democratic theory reflected this legitimization of 'identity' with the growing popularity of consociationalism, which is actually based on a procedural interpretation of collective cultural rights.[12] Thus, 'identity' – cultural, ethnic or religious – was elevated in both its epistemological as well as political status, and its expression, manifestations and potential needs came to be seen as both morally and politically legitimate.

One of the clearest and most ardent defenses of the primacy of identity is to be found in the multi-culturalism discourse, which focuses on the status of racial, gender and ethnic identities within liberal democracies. Initiated and then fueled by the perceived legacies of racial and gender discrimination in the established western democracies, so-called multi-culturalists seek to remedy current discriminatory practices as well as to compensate for past discrimination by according disadvantaged racial and gender groups distinct rights *as groups*. The notion of acknowledging group rights within liberal society has also been applied to ethnicity, and has generated a debate around the compatibility of liberalism with collective cultural rights.[13] Within this debate, the concept of differentiated citizenship has emerged as the preferred strategy for reconciling collective cultural rights with a unified body of citizens.[14]

Traditionally citizenship was seen ' ... as a shared identity that would integrate previously excluded groups within ... society and provide a source of national unity',[15] and hence actually defined by integration. Indeed, the recent argument for differentiation emerged as a critique of this integrative capacity. Within this context, the so-called 'cultural pluralists' contend that the institution of citizenship has failed in its integrative or inclusionary task by systematically discriminating against 'different' groups – where the difference is defined on the basis of race, gender, or more generally culture (which usually includes ethnicity and religion). Therefore, integration into the 'common culture' (or institution of citizenship) can truly occur only if the state adopts a conception of 'differentiated citizenship.' Accordingly, integration occurs not merely on an individual basis, but on a group basis as well. Hence, to be consistently democratic and inclusive, the state must recognize *in addition to* equal individual rights, certain group rights as well.

Two fundamental justifications are offered for this institution of differentiated citizenship: the first is that culturally excluded groups have often suffered from inequality in the political sphere. The solution to this disadvantage 'lies at least in part in providing institutionalized means for the explicit recognition and representation of oppressed groups'; the second reason is that often culturally distinct groups have distinct needs which can only be met through group-differentiated policies. These types of policies include, among other things, language rights, land rights and reproductive rights, libel laws, publicly funded schools for religious minorities, exemption from laws that interfere with religious worship, animal slaughtering legislation, and so on.[16]

The misconceived legacy of nation-building

The main critique of the integration strategy attacked the two basic assumptions mentioned above: that nation-building was both a precondition for modernization, and an outcome of various forces of modernization. Modernization, it was contended, did not lead in fact to assimilation, and in any case ethnic or other sub-national identities were inherently non-assimilable.

This critique was both empirical and conceptual. Empirically it rested upon evidence which showed that in various African states, rapid mobilization and industrialization tended to exacerbate ethnic conflict. Conceptually, it argued for the primacy of ethnic, tribal and religious identities. These two notions, of the primacy of identity and the impact of industrialization upon ethnic conflict, were related in a curious way. Connor makes these arguments explicitly, and due to the impact of his articles, they are worth expanding upon. He argues that cultural awareness, that is, awareness of one's own identity and that of other members of one's own cultural milieu, by definition exact conflictual attitudes and relations with other cultural identities or groups. Increased cultural awareness is an inevitable outcome of political mobilization, extension of communications networks, and in short, the elimination of cultural isolation:

> ... the substantial body of data which is available supports the proposition that material increases in what Deutsch termed social communication and mobilization tend to increase cultural awareness and to exacerbate inter ethnic conflict.[17]

The fact that indeed Connor (and his colleagues) imputed an inherently conflictual nature to ethnic awareness and identity is substantiated by his discussion of the delay in ethnic awareness in Europe:

> With fewer and poorer roads ... local radio rather than state-wide television...lower levels of education ... ethnic complacency could be maintained: Britanny's culture appeared safe from French encroachment, Edinburgh felt remote and isolated from London, most Waloons and Flems seldom came into contact ... with members of the other group.[18]

In short, complacency about one's own identity can occur only in isolation.

This particular, and indeed central, criticism of nation-building laid the groundwork for the introduction of the notion of the primacy of identity. Thus, the defense of differentiation as the preferred strategy for stabilizing fragmentation is, in a fundamental sense, the heir to the nation-building critique. Indeed, the defenses of differentiated citizenship – that integration failed despite industrial and technological advances, and that cultural groups embody distinct needs – are both premised upon this assumption of the primacy of cultural identity: that the distinct cultural identities are neither assimilable nor were they ever truly integrated.

Hence, the legacy of ethnic and communal conflict which resulted, partially, from the modernization and nation-building efforts of the west, led many theoreticians to the conclusion that cultural identity is inherent, and hence unassimilable. Moreover, posited against the oppressive policies and intents of colonial and post-colonial imperialism, the non-assimilable character of particular cultural identities has become a normative tenet as well;[19] particularist cultural identities – be they ethnic, religious or other – have emerged as a more legitimate focus for the development of communities. The main question which should thus be asked is the following: is differentiated citizenship, a strategy originally conceived for cases of racial and gender discrimination in the liberal west, appropriate for ethnically fragmented societies in non-liberal states? Kymlicka, in his discussion of the different types of collective rights demands, distinguishes between two fundamental categories: the first includes demands for special political representation, and for culture-related policies. These demands insist either on compensation for cases of distinct political discrimination, as, for example, affirmative action in the United States, or on the accommodation of cultural groups, such as allowing certain religious attire in public schools, and accommodating cultural habits in the work place.[20] These types of rights can and should be granted because the demands are aimed, in the long run, at the integration of the group within the larger society. The second category includes the types of rights demanded by ethnic or national groups and are aimed at different levels of cultural or political autonomy. These types of rights pose a more difficult dilemma for the state since ultimately they are aimed not at integration, but rather at the break up of the state and society. Ironically, then, even the more ardent proponents of differentiation, such as Kymlicka, use integration as the fundamental yardstick with which to judge the appropriateness of the strategy.

However, it is precisely these types of demands that are actually or potentially made in the newly fragmented contexts mentioned above, and for this reason, any recognition by the state of these demands, would be made with great caution. One must not neglect the fact that in the cases of fragmentation and reconstruction characteristic of such diverse societies as South Africa, Israel and south-eastern Europe, the state plays a primary role, much greater in scope and degree of involvement than it does in the west. Hence, in any assessment of preferred strategies, the role of the state cannot be ignored. Newly democratizing governments like the one in South Africa would be very reluctant to formulate policies which are aimed, ultimately, at the disintegration of the society which they are just now establishing. Accordingly, policies supposedly aimed at granting such rights should be analyzed by the observer with great caution.

Language rights

Clearly, then, acknowledging and granting collective cultural rights is reflective of the general strategy I have termed differentiation. Presumably, the underlying rationale is that stability (in societies which generate demands for cultural rights, that is, fragmented societies) can be achieved only through recognition of the primacy of the identity of the parts over or at least as equal *to* the identity of the whole. Furthermore, groups which demand these rights presume that a state, and hence society, which distributes such rights will be a more equitable one, and that their status, both as a group and as individuals, will consequently improve. This, however, may not always be the case. To explain the impact of collective cultural rights upon the status of a given group, an analysis of the right to language will be employed. Indeed, the right to language, understood as the right of the community to communicate within their own language, and, most importantly, to educate their children in their own original or authentic language – which is distinct (as is their entire cultural identity) from that of the rest of society – is one of most prominent rights commonly demanded by collectivities.[21]

Language is of rudimentary and fundamental importance to both individuals and collectives. It lies at the core of national identity, and hence at the center of nation-and state-building. Symbolically, language is seen to embody the spirit of nations; it is the vehicle through which members of the nation express their relationship to their past, present and future fellow nationals – and hence, is the cement of that imagined community called the nation. On a more technical level, it is the basis for all political, economic and social interaction. Without a common language there is no society. Through a shared language, members of a political or national community communicate, interact, and share their lives. The promotion of a hegemonic language is therefore seen as one of the central tasks of nation- and state-building. Historically, states have promoted hegemonic languages first and foremost through the establishment of a public educational system, and the maintenance of a primary language of instruction. Indeed, the establishment of such schools, and the process of standardization of language were necessary conditions for the development of a national bureaucracy which presents the foundation for all modern state organizations.[22]

Hence, the power to determine which language functions as the official one, as well as control over the primary channels of language distribution, is one of the most important components in the state power structure. Put simply, language is power and, hence, control. As the vehicle *par excellence* of cooperation and communication, language functions as the basis of any political community. Therefore, political control over language is tantamount to control over one of the main membership criteria in the political community. The primary manifestations of these criteria are first and foremost the official public language of instruction; and secondly, the official language of government communication (government office communication and the language of official national symbols such as currency, street and other signs, postal stamps and so on) and, like all mechanisms of control, this mechanism embodies both an inclusive as well as exclusive capacity.

In their inclusive capacity official languages serve all the above-mentioned purposes. By providing a basis for communication and interaction, they allow for the assimilation of individuals into the political economic and social mainstay of society. As all immigrants to new societies will quickly attest, acquiring the national language is the first task and hurdle to overcome in the long line of hurdles towards assimilation and integration into the host society.

This same inclusive capacity serves also to exclude, willy nilly, those who do not speak – or have difficulties in acquiring – the official language. Clearly, then, control over language distribution enables the state a certain degree of leverage in exclusion of those minorities perceived as undeserving of membership in the political community. Moreover, intrusive state structures have the capacity both to make the acquisition of such language skills difficult and competitive, and to make those skills all the more essential for advancement and acceptance; often, socio-economic status is mirrored in differential levels of language proficiency. Hence, economic, political and social structures of discrimination often manifest cultural hierarchies within society, which result in an overlapping of kinds between lower socio-economic strata, consistently discriminated against, and cultural marginality. Indeed, this exclusionary aspect of language policy frequently provides the basis of minority group accusations against the state of discrimination, and hence the basis for various types of cultural autonomy demands. The right to language, though prominent, is but one in a series of several such demands.

The exclusive capacity of state control over language, coupled with the explosive symbolic content of language in terms of all collective and primarily national identities, renders demands for language rights particularly potent. Minority groups will then often demand a right to language so as to serve two functions: first, to allow them to overcome discrimination which results from the exclusionary outcomes of state control over language, and second, to satisfy their own collective identity. The extent and the way in which these two demands interact differ from case to case, but both are almost universally present.

Cases wherein these demands are denied are seen as classic instances of the enforcement of language control. Thus, withholding the right to language (and on a more general level, all or any collective rights) is commonly and indeed intuitively seen as a manifestation of the state's enforcement of the mechanism of control. Closer examination reveals, however, that this is equally true when the state *grants* these rights.

Distribution of rights – individual and collective – ought to be assessed in its political context, for within the modern centralized state, it is the state, and the state alone, which ultimately determines who gets which right. Thus, while within democracies the decisions which lead to the granting (or withholding) of rights clearly result from intense negotiation on different levels and between different actors, when all is said and done, it is the state which has the right to give. This monopolistic capacity of the state as rights-distributor is, of course, one of the central attributes of political sovereignty, as well as a primary means of control and regulation of membership within civic, political and national communities.

If we limit our discussion of rights to the legal sense, and take rights to describe 'a type of institutional arrangement in which interests are guaranteed legal protection'[23], then receipt of a right can be seen as embodying two levels of significance: the first is symbolic and represents membership within the community of citizens, and/or the national community; the second is practical, and enables individuals to further satisfy their interests, and to realize their life goals and plans.

For the right to be of any consequence, both levels require a network of institutional and legal guarantees.

Within this context of rights distribution, what are, then, the consequences of granting the right to language? On the whole, groups will demand that the right to language satisfy two needs: a) to be a symbol of identity, and b) to overcome discrimination. Hence, the potential benefits of the right should be assessed in terms of their capacity to help overcome, or at least minimize, the perceived discrimination against the group. The decision to grant the right to language to a given group has tremendous symbolic import: it is tantamount to acknowledging the highest level of collective identity, and, by implication, the somewhat incohesive nature of the primary political community. Hence, symbolically, the granting of the right in and of itself is sufficient to satisfy the group's need for self-identity – with or without a network of supporting institutions. On a practical level, however, for the right to be enforced, and for perceived discrimination to be minimized, a network of appropriate institutions need be established – or subsidized – by the state.

Clearly, then, for the right to language to benefit the minority group, a minimum set of institutions must be provided. These include adequate educational facilities for the instruction of the language, and the potential for a bilingual bureaucratic and government institutional network which would enable communication between members of the group and the state institutions. Lacking such institutional guarantees, the right to language will remain a symbolic right – perhaps potent in its symbolism, but impotent in its practical impact.[24]

Hence, the extent to which the right indeed benefits and helps the group achieve its goals (that is, asserting their identity and minimizing discrimination), is dependent upon the extent to which the state provides institutional and legal guarantees. In so far as these types of guarantees present themselves as *costs* to the state, their continued provision will involve continuous negotiation between the group and the state, and thus the inherent perpetuation of the state's ability to control – both potentially and actually – the quality of life of the members of the group, and the extent to which they are discriminated against. Hence, the granting of the right of language can potentially function as much as a mechanism of control as does the withholding of this right.

An important assumption must be underscored. As with all other political distributions, rights provision takes place under conditions of scarcity: the amount and scope of rights which the state decides to distribute are limited, and hence there is always a cost attached to the right provided. Within liberal democracies, where rights are usually distributed on an individual level, the costs are embedded within the social contract and the institution of citizenship (rights are granted in exchange for fulfillment of the various civic duties). For collective rights, however, lacking any general arrangement for compensation, the give and take, cost and benefit associated with the provision of the right is more direct. In other words, the price tab is attached individually to every collective right granted. The group provides the state with continued allegiance, and the state provides distinct institutions. The continued dependence of the group upon state provision of these institutions does not significantly lessen, therefore, the control of the state over the group.

It follows therefore, that given the choice made by the state, the political dynamic of granting the right to language differs from case to case, depending on a wide variety of variables – amongst which of great importance is the perception of the state of the potential threat the said group represents to its sovereignty and hence to the prospects for stability.

Official languages in Israel

The State of Israel has never passed a law designating official languages. Designation of the official languages in Israel is rooted in Article 82 of the Mandatory Palestine Order-in-Council, of 1922. In this article, three official languages were designated – English, Arabic and Hebrew. Although the article itself was never revoked, section 15(b) of the Law and Government Ordinance, 1948, repeals the status of English. Israel thus formally recognizes two official languages: Hebrew and Arabic.[25]

Nonetheless, it is widely acknowledged that for all intents and purposes, Hebrew is the primary official language of the state, and hence the status of official languages is, in Israel – to quote Amnon Rubinstein, a leading constitutional expert and the Minister of Education (1993–5) – 'problematic'.[26] Indeed, the problematic nature of the status of official languages in Israel mirrors that of Israel's non-Jewish, or Palestinian, citizens in general. With the establishment of the state in 1948, and the decision to impose citizenship upon those Palestinians who remained within the territory of the Israeli state, the government laid the basis for the contradictory policy which characterizes its attitude towards this population up until today: on the one hand it formally granted this population autonomy in the spheres of religion and culture, and attributed to them the label of 'Arab' nationality in the official identity cards. At the same time, however, it actually refused to acknowledge any political or national content to their collective identity. This refusal was a natural outcome of Israel's fundamental perception of this population as an integral part of the larger Arab/Palestinian nation with whom it was at war. Any expression of Palestinian or Arab nationalism was thus seen as a direct threat to the sovereignty and integrity of the Israeli state. Because of the essentially intertwined nature of culture and nationalism, any cultural expression was also by definition suspect as an expression of nationalism.[27]

In terms of religious autonomy, Moslem and Christian Palestinians have control over their own religious affairs. However, the notion of cultural autonomy was, from the outset, fuzzy. Cultural autonomy thus manifested itself primarily in the formal 'right to language' and in the establishment of a separate, parallel educational system. But even these two manifestations, because of the clearly national aspect of the phenomenon, have been implemented in an inconsistent fashion.

The official status of Arabic demands by law, for example, that all laws and regulations must be, upon request, translated into Arabic; that all correspondence with government offices may be conducted in Arabic; that letters may be addressed in Arabic; that Arabic may be used in the parliament.[28] However, few of these regulations are enforced. Arabic is also inconsistently applied to official national symbols – although used on postal stamps, and currency, it is absent from the Israeli passport, and from most plaques on official monuments. The use of Arabic on street signs exists, but is entirely inconsistent, and can be found only in cities with a significant Arab population. Thus for example, none of the street signs in Tel Aviv have their name written in Arabic (they are written in English and Hebrew) and even in Haifa, which is a bi-ethnic or bi-national city, one can find street signs in areas which are almost exclusively Jewish written only in Hebrew. In areas populated primarily by Palestinians, the signs are in both languages.[29] Indeed, the sole area in which the official status of Arabic is enforced consistently seems to be in education, which, of course, is of intense significance. Israel maintains three parallel public educational systems: the first, which is the main one, is geared towards the secular Jewish population; the second is geared towards the religious Jewish population; and the third is aimed at the Palestinian-Arab population. In the first two systems, the main language of instruction is Hebrew. There Arabic is taught as a second and third language, along with English and sometimes French. In the latter system, Arabic is the main language of instruction, and Hebrew is taught as a second language.

Thus, within both the primary and secondary schools of the majority of the Palestinian population in Israel, the language of instruction is Arabic: all subjects including history, mathematics, geography and so on are taught in Arabic. In addition, Arabic language and literature and Hebrew language and literature are taught.[30] Thus, for the first 18 years of their lives, Palestinian citizens of Israel primarily speak Arabic: this is the language of instruction, the language of socializing, and the language at home. Although in recent years the number of hours allocated to the study of Hebrew has increased, and the level at which instruction of Hebrew commences was lowered from the sixth to the third grade, on the whole the proficiency of Palestinians in Hebrew is far lower than their Israeli-Jewish counterparts at the age of graduation from high school.

The particularly difficult, and also the most central, issue for the Palestinians themselves concerns the state regulation of the curricula and of the hiring of educational personnel. Declarations made by the Israeli authorities that the educational system should be used as a vehicle for transmitting Jewish history and for 'deepening the knowledge of the Jewish identity ...' have caused deep resentment on the part of the Palestinians.[31] Because of the aforementioned tie between cultural and national sentiment, the curricula committees were reluctant to allow the teaching of any Palestinian body of literature for fear of encouraging a sense of Palestinian identity. What resulted was the paradoxical situation wherein the maintenance of a parallel educational system, and the employment of Arabic as the official language of instruction were implemented as part of a plan of cultural autonomy, but any attempt to introduce authentic cultural elements – in the form of literature or history – were barred for fear of the political ramifications.

A more significant paradox, however, is that while Arabic is maintained as the official language of instruction in recognition of the fact that cultural context is central to the realization of one's potential, this in fact hampers the development of the Palestinians, and perpetuates their marginal status within Israeli society. For although Arabic is the official language of school instruction, the mainstay of Israeli life – economic, political and social – is conducted in Hebrew. This is true for both the public and private spheres. Affairs in all government offices – including all bureaucratic offices such as social security, welfare services, the ministry of education and the like – are conducted in Hebrew. The language of instruction in the institutions of higher learning is Hebrew, and finally, the economy – businesses and industry – is dominated almost exclusively by Hebrew. In the economic sphere one should add that while Arab-run business and industry is conducted in Arabic, due to the marginal status of this population in the general socio-economic structure of society, these represent a very small percentage of the country's economic structure. In short, the state fails to provide adequate institutional and legal guarantees of the right to language.

Hence, as a result, the prospects for the successful advancement of Palestinians within Israeli society are minimized. Palestinian citizens of Israel are, as a result of their lack of proficiency in the main language of society, among other reasons, systematically marginalized within society. The right to language granted to the national minority serves not to enhance their life opportunities, but rather to perpetuate their marginal position within Israeli society. Since the right to language essentially allows them no alternative but to become educated in what has become a peripheral language in Israeli society, they are destined to remain a marginal minority.

This is reflected most clearly in their difficulties in the institutions of higher learning, where fluency in Hebrew is a necessary condition for success,[32] and perhaps less directly, but nonetheless as importantly, in their ability to advance in other channels of life: business, social and other. To a large extent, Hechter's model of internal colonial domination – wherein economic peripheral status creates cultural peripheral status resulting in, ultimately, a distinct national identity – operates here in a slightly different causal interaction: economic and cultural peripherality serve to complement each other, resulting in a distinct national/cultural and economic identity.[33] Amongst other cultural markers which have developed as a result of this peripheralization and marginalization, one cannot help but remark upon the distinct Arabic accent which most Palestinians have in Hebrew which, as opposed to the stark racial differences between Blacks and Whites, or other indigenous and colonial populations, enables quick distinction between two ethnic groups which are otherwise externally indistinguishable from one another.

In light of the inconsistent fashion in which cultural autonomy is granted to the Palestinian citizens of Israel, and in light of the marginalizing effect that designation of Arabic as an official language has upon this population, one can only wonder about the motives of the Israeli government when they decided to grant this right to language. In a representative speech to the parliament in 1952, in response to a suggestion made by then Herut member of parliament Raziel, Ben Gurion stated:

... we will not forbid [the Arabs] the use of their language in any way ... to be sure, this is not the way the issue is handled in most of the parliaments of the world, but we do not have to learn everything from others. There are a number of important things which we taught the world and we can be an example of a humane attitude toward the language of the minority. ... the state must see to it that Hebrew be [not only] an official language, but must provide the means for imparting the knowledge of Hebrew to immigrants and to all the residents of Israel, *without depriving the Arab minority of the right to its own language.*[34]

The fact that the content of the curricula approved for both primary and secondary schools was clearly designed in such a way as to obliterate any cultural/national, or even cultural/ethnic, identity stands in stark contradiction to the contention that the designation of Arabic as an official language of education resulted from the respect of the Jewish leadership for the collective cultural/national identity of this population. Indeed, it is quite curious that in the context of military rule over this population, during which all activities – ranging from sports, through education and ending with politics – were closely regulated and controlled, that the right to language was so keenly observed and granted.

Hence, the proposition that the right to language was intentionally granted as an additional mechanism of control deserves some attention.

Conclusion

This discussion of language rights makes one point extremely clear: a debate concerning strategies for stabilizing fragmented societies should include an assessment of the role of the state. Clearly, as the case of Israel demonstrates, the failure (or refusal) of the state to provide adequate institutional guarantees may render any collective cultural right a potential mechanism of control and discrimination. While it may be argued that, in the case of Israel, the relationship of conflict which exists between Israel and the Palestinian minority renders any state mechanism a vehicle of control, one must not forget that in contexts in which the right to language is demanded we should assume a somewhat confrontational relationship between the state and the minority requesting the right: indeed, within harmonious cultural-ethnic relationships no such demands will arise. Hence, given this context, the potential for manipulation of that right by the state is ever-present and its possible consequences should be considered.

Similarly, as was noted in the first section of this chapter, ethno-cultural demands are ultimately not aimed at integration, and as has been evidenced often throughout history, the road leading from cultural autonomy to demands for political independence may be a short and slippery one. Hence, one would be hard pressed to find governments which would willingly grant a minority both the rights and the institutional guarantees with which to develop a basis for ever-larger autonomy. Since the granting of rights without the necessary institutions may potentially serve as a mechanism of control, and the granting of the rights along with the necessary institutions may lay the ground-work for a competing focus of political loyalty and sovereignty, the notion of collective cultural rights does not necessarily emerge as an appropriate strategy for reconciling minority demands and democratic stability. Thus, the discussion of language rights may possibly suggest the appropriateness of the integration strategy, through a rehabilitation of sorts of the notion of nation-building.

The basis for one of the central criticisms of the traditional model of nation-building was that, in essence, cultural proximity promotes cultural conflict, and that by eliminating cultural isolation, the rapid processes of nation-building actually promoted violent conflict and the disintegration of society. It would appear that the problem with nation-building is not that it minimized cultural isolation, but that it perceived non-national identities as inherently competitive with national identity, and, therefore, as somehow embodying values that contradicted the essence of modernity. However, much in the same way as in Europe, for example, Welsh identity did not develop merely due to contact with the English, but clearly as a result of oppressive and violent policies, it is the extent to which this identity allows for other identities to coexist within its political framework which is the key to its potential success. Once one recognizes that identity does not *ipso facto* translate into political loyalty, it is possible to devise a national identity which allows for the integration (rather then assimilation) of a variety of ethnic, religious and linguistic identities.

Indeed, it would appear that the distinction between integration and assimilation might provide the key to a renewed interpretation of the notion of nation-building and the idea of the construction of political communities. Despite the rather fashionable usage of the idea of 'construction of communities,' communities are not constructed from thin air, but merely represent a new hierarchy of formerly existing identities. Within these new hierarchies, the political identity is constructed around a set of values and symbols shared by all distinct cultures. Thus, separate cultural identities coexist, but are not attributed with political power. Similarly, it is possible to integrate distinct cultures without assimilating them into one dominant one. The task which remains is assembling that set of shared values and symbols which would serve as a unifying basis.

Ironically, despite the fact that both the nation-building critique, as well as the critique of integrative citizenship, rest, at least in part, upon the accusation of particular ideological inclinations, they themselves seem to have fallen prey to the most prominent ideological assertions of nationalist ideology, namely, the primacy of ethnicity, and the equation of individual freedom with collective self-determination. Indeed, nationalism, when it appeared on the political scene in the late eighteenth century, was innovative in precisely these two points: it added an additional dimension to individual liberty by proclaiming that an individual is only truly free if and only if he or she can express his or her collective national identity, and that the ultimate guarantee of such freedom is the ability to live within a polity controlled by members of one's own nationality. Much of the defense of cultural pluralism, and the arguments for collective cultural rights rest upon this assumption: that true freedom for the group and its members is gained only through the ability to exercise their culture freely, and that the ultimate guarantee of that freedom is attained *through the political recognition and institutionalization* of these cultural attributes. If modern history has taught us anything, it has taught us the folly and fallacy embedded in these assumptions: while national self-determination might enhance freedom, it does not do so by definition. Expressions and manifestations of culture, as the discussion above demonstrated, do not necessarily gain advantage from political institutionalization. Hence, both state planners, as well as collective group leaders, might be well advised to reconsider the engineering of a national political community, one which will allow for other identities, over the construction of a fragmented community, which might ultimately cause the destruction of other identities.

Notes

1 Young, Iris Marion, *Justice and the Politics of Difference* (Princeton University Press, Princeton, 1990); Kymlicka, Will, *Multicultural Citizenship* (Oxford University Press, Oxford, 1995); Phillips, Anne, *The Politics of Presence* (Oxford University Press, Oxford, 1995).
2 Kukathas, Chandran, 'Are There Any Cultural Rights?' *Political Theory*, 20/1, pp. 105–39.
3 Almond, Gabriel, and Bingham Powell Jr., *Comparative Politics; a Developmental Approach* (Little, Brown, Boston, 1966). Almond, Gabriel and

James S. Coleman, (eds), *The Politics of Developing Areas* (Princeton University Press, Princeton, 1960). Jacob, Philip E., and James V. Toscano, *The Integration of Political Communities* (Lippincott, Philadelphia, 1964). Apter, David, *The Politics of Modernization* (University of Chicago Press, Chicago, 1965). Bendix, Reinhart, *Nation-Building and Citizenship* (University of California Press, Berkeley, 1968).

4   Sorting through the usage of terms would demand an entire study. Some theorists, such as Deutsch, use the term 'nation' and 'national identity' in a similar way to theorists of nationalism. Others however, for example Bendix, use the term 'national identity' yet never really refer to the nation, but only to the state. Still others, most notably Huntington, use the term 'political community' in a very similar way to the way in which 'nation' is used by nationalism theory. Finally, theorists such as Apter, use the term 'civil religion' – but in their definitions are closely akin to those used by Huntington for 'political community'. See Apter (1965); Bendix (1968); Huntington (1968); Deutsch (1953, 1966).

5. Smith 1994.

6   Ricci, David, *The Tragedy of Political Science* (Yale University Press, New Haven, 1984).

7   Almond, Gabriel, and Sidney Verba, *The Civic Culture: Political Attitudes and Democracies in Five Nations* (Princeton University Press, Princeton, 1963). Pye, Lucien, *Aspects of Political Development* (Little, Brown, Boston, 1966). Inglehart, Ronald, *Culture Shift in Advanced Industrial Society* (Princeton University Press, Princeton, 1990). Eckstein, Harry, *Regarding Politics; Essays on Political Theory, Stability and Change* (University of California Press, Berkeley, 1992).

8   Wiarda, Howard J. (ed.), *New Directions in Comparative Politics* (Westview Press, Boulder, 1991).

9   Connor, Walker, 'Nation-Building or Nation-Destroying?' *World Politics,* 24, 1972, pp. 319–55.

10 Esman, Milton, and Itamar Rabinovitch *(*eds*)*, *Ethnicity, Pluralism and the State in the Middle East* (Cornell University Press, Ithaca, 1988). Enloe, Cynthia, *Ethnic Conflict and Political Development* (Little, Brown and Co., Boston, 1973).

11 Tiryakian, Edward A. and Ronald Rogowski (eds*)*, *New Nationalisms of the Developed West *(Allen and Unwin, London, 1985). Esman, Milton (ed.), *Ethnic Conflict in the Western World* (Cornell University Press, Ithaca, 1980). This line of inquiry was paralleled by similar cycles in the study of nationalism in general. If the late 1960s and early 1970s witnessed major studies of nationalism emphasizing its essential modernity (Kedourie, 1966; Gellner, 1971), the late 1970s and 1980s generated a new wave of studies which sought to illustrate the historical and 'ethnic' origin of nations (Smith, 1981, 1985; Armstrong, 1981). As is the case in all classifications, exceptions merely prove the rule. The noted exception is Benedict Anderson's *Imagined Communities,* published for the first time in 1983. In my analytical schema he belongs to the first category.

12 Lijphart, Arendt, *Democracies: Patterns of Majoritarian and Consensus Government in 21 Countries* (Yale University Press, New Haven, 1977). Rae, Douglas and Michael Taylor (eds), *The Analysis of Political Cleavages* (Yale University Press, New Haven, 1978).

13 Taylor, Charles, 'The Politics of Recognition', in Amy Gutman (ed.),*Multiculturalism and 'The Politics of Recognition* (Princeton University Press, Princeton, 1992).

14 Young, Iris Marion, *Justice and the Politics of Difference* (Princeton University Press, Princeton, 1990).

15 Kymlicka, Will, *Multicultural Citizenship* (Oxford University Press, Oxford, 1995). Marshall, T.H., *Class Citizenship and Social Development* (Anchor, New York, 1965).

16 Parekh, Sunita, 'Britain and the Social Logic of Pluralism,' in G. Andrews (ed.), *Citizenship* (Lawrence and Wishart, London, 1991). Modood, T., 'Establishment, Multiculturalism and British Citizenship', *Political Quarterly,* 65, 1994, pp. 53–73.

17 Connor, Walker, 'Nation-Building or Nation-Destroying?' *World Politics,* 24, 1972, pp. 319–55.

18 Ibid., p. 330.

19 Gellner, Ernest, *Nations and Nationalism* (Blackwell, Oxford, 1983). Said, Edward, W., *Culture and Imperialism* (Vintage Books, New York, 1993).

20 Kymlicka, Will, *Multicultural Citizenship* (Oxford University Press, Oxford, 1995).

21 Van Dyke, *Human Rights, Ethnicity and Discrimination* (Greenwood Press, Conn. 1985). O'Barr, William, and Jean F. O'Barr (eds), *Language and Politics* (Mouton, the Hague, 1976). Chiswick, Barry, R. (ed.), *Immigration, Language and Ethnicity: Canada and the U.S.* (the AEI Press, Washington D.C., 1992).

22 Laitin, David, Carlota Sole and Stathis N. Kalyvas, 'Language and the Construction of States: the Case of Catalonia in Spain', *Politics and Society* 22, 1994, pp. 5–29.

23. Miller, 1991, p. 231.

24 Noted that it is assured that for the right to language to have anything besides a symbolic import, the right must involve provision, by the state, of state monies to subsidize adequate institutions. There are, of course, cases where the state acknowledges the right of a minority to its own language, but fails to supplement this acknowledgment with any financial or institutional support. Then indeed, the right itself may have some symbolic significance, but nothing apart from that.

25 Kretzmer, David, *The Legal Status of the Arabs in Israel* (Westview Press, Boulder, 1990).

26 Rubinstein, Amnon, *Constitutional Law of the State of Israel* (5th edition), (Schoken Press, Tel Aviv, 1996).

27. Lustick, Ian S., Arabs in the Jewish State (University of Texas Press, Austin, Texas), 1980.

28 Landau, Jacob, *The Arab Minority in Israel 1967–1991* (Clarendon Press, Oxford, 1993).

29 Fisherman, Haya, and Joshua A. Fishman, 'The "Official Languages" of Israel: their Status in Law and Police Attitudes and Knowledge Concerning Them,' in Jean-Guy Savard and Richard Vigneault (eds), *Multilingual Political Systems; Problems and Solutions* (Les Presses de L'Universite Laval, Quebec, 1975), pp. 505–30.

30   Al-Haj, Majid, *Education, Empowerment, and Control: the case of the Arabs in Israel* (State University of New York, Albany, 1995).
31   Ibid.
32   An interesting aspect of this paradox is afforded by a close examination of the psychometric exams instituted by the Israeli universities as a main entrance criterion. Recently, the supervisory committee of Arab education has voiced a complaint that these exams serve to discriminate against the Arab students and bar their entry into the more selective faculties of law and medicine. (Only 5.8 per cent of the national student body are Palestinians; 6 per cent of the law students; 8 per cent of the medicine students; 5 per cent of social science students – despite the fact that they are close to 20 per cent of the population.) Indeed, although the sole language of instruction in the universities is Hebrew, the universities conduct psychometric exams in both Hebrew and Arabic. Furthermore, the universities provide extra tutoring to all immigrants whose mother tongue is not Hebrew – for instance, Russians and Ethiopians – but not for Palestinians. The supervisory committee, based on relative performance of Palestinian students compared with Jewish students on these exams, and on testimonies by numerous Palestinian students, contend that the level of Arabic proficiency required by this exam is far higher then the level of Hebrew proficiency required by the Hebrew exam. In addition, the Arabic exam requires knowledge of three languages (Arabic, Hebrew and English) while the Hebrew exam requires knowledge of only two. Furthermore, the language section in the Arabic exam is more extensive then that in the Hebrew exam, at the expense of the analytic sections. A final paradoxical element is added if one assesses the outcome *vis à vis* the Druze students who, as opposed to the Palestinian students, usually arrive in the university following three years of military service during which they speak Hebrew. They are then expected to complete an exam in archaic Arabic (Interview with Ziad Assad, representative of the Druze students at Haifa University, 5 May 1995; *Ha'aretz*, 16 April 1995).
33   Hechter, Michael, *Internal Colonialism* (Routledge and Kegan Paul, London, 1975).
34   Emphasis my own, quoted in Fisherman and Fishman, '*The "Official Languages" of Israel*', p. 505.

References

Al-Haj, Majid, *Education, Empowerment, and Control: the case of the Arabs in Israel* (State University of New York, Albany, 1995).
Almond, Gabriel and James S. Coleman (eds), *The Politics of Developing Areas* (Princeton University Press, Princeton, 1960).
Almond, Gabriel and Sidney Verba, *The Civic Culture; Political Attitudes and Democracies in Five Nations* (Princeton University Press, Princeton, 1963).
Almond, Gabriel and Bingham Powell Jr, *Comparative Politics; a Developmental Approach* (Little, Brown, Boston, 1966).
Apter, David, *The Politics of Modernization* (University of Chicago Press, Chicago, 1965).
Bendix, Reinhart, *Nation-Building and Citizenship* (University of California Press, Berkeley, 1968).

Benziman, Uzi and Atallah Mansour, *Subtenants: the Arabs in Israel; their Status and Government Policy Towards Them* (Keter, Jerusalem, 1992), in Hebrew.

Chiswick, Barry R., (ed.), *Immigration, Language and Ethnicity: Canada and the U.S.* (The AEI Press, Washington DC, 1992).

Connor, Walker, 'Nation-Building or Nation-Destroying' *World Politics*, 24, 1972, pp. 319–55.

Eckstein, Harry, *Regarding Politics; Essays on Political Theory, Stability and Change* (University of California Press, Berkeley, 1992).

Enloe, Cynthia, *Ethnic Conflict and Political Development* (Little, Brown and Co., Boston, 1973).

Esman, Milton, (ed.), *Ethnic Conflict in the Western World* (Cornell University Press, Ithaca, 1980).

Esman, Milton and Itamar Rabinovitch, (eds), *Ethnicity, Pluralism and the State in the Middle East* (Cornell University Press, Ithaca, 1988).

Fisherman, Haya, and Joshua A. Fishman, 'The "Official Languages" of Israel: Their Status in Law and Police Attitudes and Knowledge Concerning Them,' in Jean-Guy Savard and Richard Vigneault (eds), *Multilingual Political Systems; Problems and Solutions* (Les Presses de L'Universite Laval, Quebec, 1975), pp. 505–30.

Gellner, Ernest, *Nations and Nationalism* (Blackwell, Oxford, 1983).

Hechter, Michael, *Internal Colonialism* (Routledge and Kegan Paul, London, 1975).

Inglehart, Ronald, *Culture Shift in Advanced Industrial Society* (Princeton University Press, Princeton, 1990).

Jacob, Philip E., and James V. Toscano, *The Integration of Political Communities* (Lippincott, Philadelphia, 1964).

Jiryis, Sabri, *The Arabs in Israel* (Monthly Review Press, New York, 1975).

Kretzmer, David, *The Legal Status of the Arabs in Israel* (Westview Press, Boulder, 1990).

Kukathas, Chandran, 'Are there any Cultural Rights?' *Political Theory*, 20/1, pp. 105–39.

Kymlicka, Will, *Multicultural Citizenship* (Oxford University Press, Oxford, 1995).

Laitin, David, Carlota Sole and Stathis N. Kalyvas, 'Language and the Construction of States: the Case of Catalonia in Spain,' *Politics and Society* 22, 1994, pp. 5–29.

Landau, Jacob, *The Arab Minority in Israel 1967–1991* (Clarendon Press, Oxford, 1993).

Lijphard, Arendt, *Democracies: Patterns of Majoritarian and Consensus Government in 21 Countries* (Yale University Press, New Haven, 1977).

Marshall, Tang H., *Class Citizenship and Social Development* (Anchor, New York, 1965).

Miller, David, *et al.*, (eds), *The Blackwell Encyclopedia of Political Thought* (Blackwell Publishers, Oxford, 1994).

Modood, Tarig, 'Establishment, Multiculturalism and British Citizenship', in *Political Quarterly*, 65, 1994, pp. 53–73.

O'Barr, William, and Jean F. O'Barr, (eds), *Language and Politics* (Moulton, The Hague, 1976).

Parekh, Sunita, 'Britain and the Social Logic of Pluralism', in G. Andrews (ed.), *Citizenship* (Lawrence and Wishart, London, 1991).

Phillips, Anne, *The Politics of Presence* (Oxford University Press, Oxford, 1995).

Pye, Lucien, *Aspects of Political Development* (Little, Brown, Boston, 1966).

Rae, Douglas and Michael Taylor, (eds), *The Analysis of Political Cleavages* (Yale University Press, New Haven, 1978).

Ricci, David, *The Tragedy of Political Science* (Yale University Press, New Haven, 1984).

Rubinstein, Amnon, *Constitutional Law of the State of Israel* (Hebrew, 5th edition), (Schoken Press, Tel Aviv, 1996).

Said, Edward, W., *Culture and Imperialism* (Vintage Books, New York, 1993).

Taylor, Charles, 'The Politics of Recognition', in Amy Gutman (ed.), *Multiculturalism and 'The Politics of Recognition'* (Princeton University Press, Princeton, 1991).

Tiryakian, Edward A., and Ronald Rogowski, (eds), *New Nationalisms of the Developed West* (Allen and Unwin, London, 1985).

Van Dyke, *Human Rights, Ethnicity and Discrimination* (Greenwood Press, Conn. 1985).

Young, Iris Marion, *Justice and the Politics of Difference* (Princeton University Press, Princeton, 1990).

4
Culture is not Enough: a Democratic Critique of Liberal Multiculturalism

Yoav Peled and José Brunner[1]

Introduction

What rights should be accorded minority cultures within a liberal society? Can minorities legitimately demand special rights, such as state protection from infringement by the majority culture which dominates the public sphere? Are distinctions that can be drawn between different types of minorities – such as immigrants versus indigenous groups – relevant to a liberal stance towards the allocation of cultural rights to these groups?

The most far-reaching effort to raise such questions in a systematic fashion, and formulate comprehensive liberal answers, has been undertaken by Will Kymlicka.[2] His liberal multiculturalism is based on the claim that a congenial cultural context is a necessary prerequisite for making autonomous individual choices about a life-plan. This claim has been subject to various kinds of criticism on the part of other liberal thinkers.

Kymlicka's liberal critics have generally assumed that the problem with his project is that it is based on the value of autonomy; hence they have sought to substitute for it other values taken from the arsenal of liberalism. But as we have shown elsewhere,[3] the various attempts undertaken by his critics to base a multicultural framework on liberal principles also run into dead-ends. For the problem with Kymlicka's project, as we will argue, is not its grounding in individual autonomy, but rather that he conceives of autonomy in a limited and somewhat formalistic manner, such as suggests itself in liberal discourse. Thus, while we agree with Kymlicka's critics that his notion of autonomy is bound to lead his multiculturalism into contradictions, we do not wish to replace it by another liberal notion. We prefer to suggest that the solution to Kymlicka's problems has to be sought in a redefinition of autonomy. Therefore we wish to lead the debate away from formal definitions of autonomy, rights and liberties towards the conditions of freedom, that is, to the *material* and *institutional* means necessary for an effective exercise of a person's private and public autonomy. The presence in a society of any disadvantage in access to such enabling conditions of action makes some people less capable of realizing autonomous choices, and therefore them and their society less free.

Our concern, then, is with the actual practice of freedom by individuals, not only with the existence of a legally protected social space in which they can potentially act without being hindered. Following Amartya Sen we value a person's ability to function as an autonomous agent above his or her legal rights. We value, that is, capabilities or competence. For in our view, this is the meaning of valuing individual freedom.[4] This, then, is the angle from which we formulate our critique of Kymlicka. We proceed in four steps: first we present the way in which Kymlicka seeks to provide a defense of universal, liberal principles of freedom, while taking note of the cultural embeddedness of individuals. In the second section we present a four-pronged critique of Kymlicka. We show that he has uncritically accepted Rawls's unfounded claim that a stable cultural context is needed to ensure individual autonomy. We point to the problems of his strict distinction between national minorities – to whom he is ready to accord full minority rights – and immigrant minorities, who in his view neither wish nor deserve them. We demonstrate that he has vacillated between limiting the authority of illiberal groups over their members (as distinguished from their autonomy *vis-à-vis* the larger society) and allowing such groups at least some leeway in infringing the rights of their members. In addition, he has invested a great deal of hope in the noncoercive liberalization of illiberal groups. In this he has failed, we argue, to realize fully that liberalization would be tantamount to the same cultural attrition from which he had sought to protect these groups. In general, as we explain, the problem with Kymlicka's work is that it is based on narrow and limited conceptions of its central categories, such as cultural embeddedness, power, coercion, free will, and individual autonomy.

In section three we seek to point to the most crucial issue in which the narrow boundaries of Kymlicka's multiculturalism vitiate his aim of promoting individual autonomy. His discussion of multiculturalism remains restricted to two domains – culture and politics – and their interrelation. Of course, multiculturalism deals with the politics of culture; but to ensure individual autonomy and freedom, as Kymlicka seeks to do, multicultural theorists also have to consider the complex relationships between culture, politics and the domain of material – that is, economic – goods. Thus, we argue that Kymlicka's aim of furthering individual autonomy and liberty by means of a multicultural framework can only be pursued by placing both politics and culture within a broader, socio-economic approach.

In outlining the contours of such a socio-economically oriented, or democratic, multiculturalism our main argument is, that only a shift of focus, from a liberal conception of rights to social practices, could make it possible to assess the effects of specific cultural practices on the capabilities of individual members of a minority group. We contend that individual capabilities cannot adequately be assessed by a limited examination of access to and control of cultural goods, such as language. Rather, the value of specific cultural proficiencies in terms of their contribution to individual freedom and autonomy have to be evaluated in terms of their socio-economic effects. At issue, we claim, are not only cultural rights and their effects on self-respect and the like but, no less importantly, the socio-economic structure faced by members of minority groups and the set of practices available to them, which allow them to take advantage of the opportunities presented to them. Hence we support Nancy Fraser in her demand that multiculturalism broaden its concern from exclusively cultural issues and demands for recognition, to issues of economic and social well-being in general, which have to do with the redistribution of material goods.[5]

Finally, in the fourth section of this chapter we provide a sketchy analysis of Israel as a multicultural society. We do this in order to illustrate the problems of the liberal approach, that concentrates exclusively on cultural rights, and contrast it with the materialist approach we advocate. Our materialist approach considers the economy as well, and its concern is with individual capabilities for social, political and economic practices, rather than with formal rights only. It is for this reason that we found it apt to characterize it as 'democratic multiculturalism'.

1 Kymlicka's liberal multiculturalism

The political theory of liberalism is based on an individualist moral ontology that regards individuals as fundamentally equal and as the exclusive ultimate bearers of political and social rights. Therefore, liberal theorists seek to support and enhance the individual autonomy of all, in other words the capacity of all persons to make their own choices and develop their own individual life-plans, by granting them equal civil rights and liberties.

Because they value autonomy, liberal thinkers are committed to tolerating a wide variety of individual life-plans, whether they like them or not. In their view the purpose of the state is to facilitate the varied projects of its citizens, rather than to impose ends of its own, and to restrict them only when they infringe on one another's freedom. The hero of liberal theory is the deliberative, rights-bearing individual, who entered the stage of political discourse in the West during the seventeenth century, and took up a place in its limelight in the wake of the revolutions of 1776 and 1789.

In contrast to classical liberals such as John Locke, modern liberals do not adhere to simplistic and atomistic individualism. They acknowledge that their hero is a product of an historical process and of a particular form of culture, which is Western, modern, capitalist, pluralist, science-oriented, tends towards secularism, and values individual choice. Moreover, they also are cognizant of the fact that individuals seek the company and recognition of others. Finally, they assume that the liberal hero respects the law since he or she can only live in a law-governed community, whose regulations safeguard his or her autonomy by imposing obligations on others. In other words, modern liberal theorists are keenly aware that the autonomous individual is socially constructed and embedded – by means of education, laws and social conventions – and can only live an autonomous life in a society that provides for appropriate forms of social interaction.

Kymlicka's work has become the most widely discussed endeavor to reconcile this brand of liberalism with special minority rights. His aim is to articulate a new, multiculturalist version of liberalism. This multiculturalist liberalism

(a) recognizes the social embeddedness of individuals and hence the importance of culture for human autonomy

(b) acknowledges the ethnic and cultural plurality of all societies, including modern, Western ones; and

(c) validates non-Western cultures too as providing resources for individual choice.

The question Kymlicka poses himself is: 'How can we defend minority rights within liberalism, given that its moral ontology recognizes only individuals, each of whom is to be treated with equal consideration?'[6] He seeks to ground collective rights in those of the individual by arguing that a person's capacity to make autonomous choices about a preferred way of life is culture-dependent. Thus, he makes the existence of a congenial cultural environment a prerequisite for the exercise of the individual right of autonomous or free choice. As Kymlicka puts it: 'only through having a rich and secure cultural structure ... people can become aware, in a vivid way, of the options available to them, and intelligently examine their value'. Hence, concern for cultural structure 'accords with, rather than conflicts with, the liberal concern for our ability and freedom to judge the value of our life-plans'.[7]

As a result, Kymlicka's multicultural liberalism acknowledges the right of pre-modern and non-Western cultures to protection – rather than just tolerance – within the general framework of modern, liberal societies. Like modern liberalism, multicultural liberalism proclaims itself an ideal capable of universalization, but it does so, somewhat ironically, because it entails special rights for illiberal, pre-modern and non-Western cultures.

Kymlicka has argued that the 'old' – or modern – abstract liberal concept of equal citizenship perpetuates inequalities between groups and individuals. In his view it privileges those who conform to the underlying and for the most part unspoken norms of society, which have been defined and imposed as 'normal' by the dominant group – Western, white, heterosexual, property-owning men – in accordance with their own interests and values. Hence, Kymlicka seeks to reconcile liberal tenets of equality and autonomy with the attribution of special rights to ethnic and national minorities. In fact, he argues that his conception of cultural rights as a primary good was implicitly recognized by John Rawls and could easily be added to his list of primary goods. In his words: 'Rawls's own argument for the importance of liberty as a primary good is also an argument for the importance of cultural membership as a primary good'.[8]

Kymlicka stresses that the primary good being recognized 'is the cultural community as a context of choice, not the character of the community or its traditional ways of life, which people are free to endorse or reject'.[9] He uses the term 'culture' to denote a community of belonging, a social framework in which one can experience membership. His argument is that an individual needs to be part of a 'societal culture' in order to acquire the tools necessary for autonomous choice, such as self-respect, a selection of valuable options and different ways of life, a sense of history, personal capacity, agency and identity. In his view, while the specific values, beliefs and rituals of a given culture may change over time, it is important that it continues to exist as 'a viable community of individuals with a shared heritage'.[10]

Like Rawls, Kymlicka stresses that individuals do not decide on their life-plans from scratch, but rather rely on models and ways of life of those who have preceded them.[11] Therefore, individuals cannot take their decisions on how to lead their lives in a social and cultural vacuum. In one way or another, the range of options they consider is embedded in their cultural heritage, that is, in the form of life or ethos into which they are born and which determines their sense of who they are to a large degree. Individuals are situated in cultural narratives of various kinds: they live through, and inherit memories of, culturally specific individual and collective life-experiences which suggest what is worthwhile and valuable, and how they are to choose their ends.[12] He claims that the ability of members of a minority culture to make choices – that is, make rational life-plans and decide what is worthwhile – might be seriously impaired if their cultural heritage and standards of excellence are denigrated or marginalized by a dominant and exclusionary standard of civic virtue, and if their access to role models, cultural norms and values, and participation in the common good are denied. Hence he argues that '[r]espect for the autonomy of the members of minority cultures requires respect for their cultural structure, and that in turn may require special linguistic, educational, and even political rights for minority cultures'.[13]

Kymlicka argues for special cultural rights as part of a liberal theory of equality, claiming that while the culture of the majority is not endangered, the cultural frameworks of traditional minority groups such as aboriginal peoples, are in peril of disintegration if they do not get special protection.[14] In order to grant their members the same primary good of autonomy, he deems it necessary to infringe upon the rights of members of the majority culture. Hence he supports aboriginal demands to restrict the property rights of whites in aboriginal land and impose restrictions on migrant workers.[15]

As a whole, Kymlicka is ready to accord three types of rights to the groups he considers national minorities:

(a) self-government rights, in other words some sort of political autonomy or territorial jurisdiction, as well as a veto right over legislation affecting crucial aboriginal interests;[16]

(b) polyethnic rights (which Kymlicka is ready to grant also to immigrant ethnic groups, whom he does not regard as national minorities), that is state support for special educational institutions, associations and festivals; and

(c)   special representation rights – mechanisms that guarantee group representation in order to ensure a voice for minorities and a fair hearing of their concerns in the state's decision-making procedures.[17]

Of course, it is possible to claim that by advancing an ideal of equality among cultures, as Kymlicka does, this multicultural liberalism also promotes a form of Eurocentrism. For by protecting a pluralism of cultures in the name of individual autonomy, self-criticism, skepticism as to absolutes and ultimate values, rational and secular discourse in matters of politics and society, as well as a readiness to see Western values through the eyes of others and vice versa, Kymlicka preaches the liberal Enlightenment ideals of religious tolerance, individualism and self-reflection. This position, as Leszek Kolakowski has pointed out, maintains 'tacitly or explicitly, that a culture capable of expressing these ideas in a vigorous way, defending them and introducing them, however imperfectly, into its life, is a superior culture'.[18]

Still, in spite of its paradoxes and shortcomings, to be elaborated further below, Kymlicka's work constitutes the most serious attempt so far to articulate principles of multicultural politics in a distinctly liberal key. In many ways he can be said to have stretched the project of liberal multiculturalism to its limit. Precisely for this reason it is necessary and fruitful to analyze his work critically in order to reveal the impasses immanent in this project.

2   Four limitations of Kymlicka's multiculturalism

In our view, Kymlicka's argument is composed of four highly questionable components:

(a)   a universalistic assumption concerning the necessity of a stable cultural context for the development of the individual's autonomous capabilities, which is presented without any empirical or historical support;

(b)   a rather simplistic, dichotomous distinction between two types of minority groups – immigrants and national minorities;

(c)   a conceptualization of the relations between state and minority groups that exhibits a limited understanding of the dynamics of power involved; and

(d)   a concern for the freedom of individuals that reveals an equally shallow view of the power relations between the group and its members.

As evidence for the claim that autonomy (the capacity to revise one's life-plan by subjecting one's received values and assumptions to critical reflection) is contingent upon membership in a stable culture, Kymlicka refers his readers to Rawls. Neither Kymlicka nor Rawls, however, support their sweeping generalization with any sociological, psychological or historical data. Moreover, neither theorist makes too much of the fact, of which they are clearly aware, that not all cultures foster the ability of individuals to appraise and revise received wisdoms and values critically. More has to be said on the fact that some cultures, however rich they may be, not only fail to do so, but regard the development and use of such critical faculties as a transgression and a threat to the community. Thus, it is not entirely clear on what basis Rawls and Kymlicka present their claims in a universalistic fashion.

As John Tomasi has argued, no less persuasively, 'a certain degree of cultural instability – including an instability that affects the deep sources of people's beliefs about value' is a precondition of personal experimentation and critical thinking.[19] Moreover, as numerous famous examples have shown, being an outsider to one's own culture as well as to that of the majority, in other words being marginalized or exiled, may cause many problems, but is not necessarily disadvantageous for individual autonomy as understood by Kymlicka. Pace Rawls and Kymlicka, Jewish intellectuals who have transposed themselves from an orthodox environment into their surrounding secular, non-Jewish societies, as well as a number of prominent postcolonial intellectuals, have exalted marginality, hybridity, the diaspora, liminality, exile and even nomadism, as cultural conditions that they consider empowering for critical thinking. Similarly, many of these intellectuals have severely criticized approaches that regard societal cultures as primordial 'givens' that deserve protection.[20]

Kymlicka's drastic differentiation between national minorities and immigrant ethnic minorities, which marks his work from its beginnings to his most recent contributions to the debate on Canadian ethnic politics, reflects some of the difficulties he has in coming to terms with the complexities of social life. His concern with cultural rights is directed exclusively at minorities that he declares to be 'nations', by which he means previously self-governing, historical communities sharing a distinct culture and living together on a given territory.[21] Kymlicka's argument is that such national minorities deserve special minority rights if their incorporation into a larger state has been involuntary, as is the case in conquest or colonialism. Thus, some of his discourse focuses on the rights of indigenous groups, such as the Inuit and other native peoples of the Americas.

In contrast, Kymlicka regards migration as a voluntary act, claiming that immigrants have willingly forsaken their home cultures and have implanted themselves in foreign lands. This act signifies, for Kymlicka, lack of interest on the part of these groups in continuing to belong to their original cultures and a declaration of intent to integrate into the new one. Thus he denies special cultural rights to immigrants and other minority groups, who arrived as latecomers in a country into which they migrated, rather than having been conquered. He argues that the receiving societies are only under a moral obligation to allow the immigrants to integrate; they are not obligated to enable them to preserve their cultures of origin.[22] The only exception to this rule Kymlicka is willing to consider is in the case of long-settled groups who had been allowed to carry on their illiberal practices for generations.[23]

Of course, Kymlicka realizes that a great number of immigrant groups differ decisively from the example of a middle-class American emigrating to Sweden[24] and acknowledges that immigration is often a result of circumstances which threaten the cultural or physical survival of the emigrating group. But, strangely enough, he continues to refer to immigrant groups as minorities who have freely chosen their fate. As he recently put it: 'my approach focuses on two paradigmatic cases – voluntary immigrants and incorporated national minorities – whose histories, current characteristics, and future aspirations are very different'. He acknowledges, however, that as a result of this dichotomous perspective, his framework of analysis fails to provide adequate categories for ethnic minorities such as guest workers in Europe who are prevented from naturalization, or African Americans in the United States. For while African Americans arrived in America after the white settlers, it is evident that their migration was anything but voluntary.[25]

Ultimately, Kymlicka holds that immigrant minorities do not have to be granted special rights since they do not actually demand self-government as national minorities do.[26] In addition, he argues that the wealthy countries of the world have a moral obligation to redistribute their wealth to the poorer countries, and that such a redistribution would eliminate the need for labor migration.[27]

There seem to be a number of fundamental contradictions vitiating the logic of this argument. First, while Kymlicka uses free will as a criterion for the distinction between two types of minority groups or the allocation of cultural rights, he realizes that this criterion does not actually distinguish the groups he wishes to separate from one another. Second, he claims that the cultural rights he does not wish to grant to immigrants have not been claimed by them anyway, thus shifting his focus from the *need* of minority cultures for legal protection to the absence of an expressed *wish* or preference for special rights.[28] Finally, he makes policy suggestions as to how one might solve the problem of immigrant minorities on the global level, a question that has no bearing on the issue of rights, the issue that he initially raised.

We take Kymlicka's twists and turns as symptoms of the fact, that while he has an astute perception of the problems raised by the attempt to construct a liberal multiculturalism, he lacks the conceptual tools necessary to cope with these problems. His effort is hampered by a limited understanding of power relations, coercion, free will and the inextricable intertwining of economic and cultural dimensions in social questions.[29]

According to Kymlicka's liberal premises, the group as such has no inherent right to self-preservation or perpetuation. Its importance lies exclusively in its function as a facilitator of individual autonomy.[30] On the one hand, Kymlicka postulates that liberal neutrality is incapable of guaranteeing the existence of a pluralistic political framework that can provide all people with a range of options for meaningful individual choice. The achievement of liberal aims requires, therefore, the protection of minority cultures 'as an essential component of liberal political practice'.[31] On the other hand, however, Kymlicka is also aware that the individual's right freely to choose a way of life may be endangered by the very cultural environment which makes this choice possible in the first place.

Initially, at least, Kymlicka's concern for the protection of cultural rights stopped at the point where a group sought to dictate a way of life to its members:

> A liberal theory can accept special rights for a minority culture against the larger community so as to ensure equality of circumstances between them. But it will not justify (except under extreme circumstances) special rights for a culture against its own members.[32]

In other words, his concern was to protect 'special' cultural rights, but not 'group' rights. Thus Kymlicka insisted that the valid claims of a minority culture to protection from external social forces did not entail the right to limit the autonomous moral choices of its members.[33]

In line with this reasoning, Kymlicka has stated that 'finding a way to liberalize a cultural community without destroying it is a task that liberals face in every country once we recognize the importance of a secure cultural context of choice'.[34] However, there are reasonable logical, as well as historical-empirical, grounds to assume that the liberalization of a culture which is based on illiberal principles may lead to its dissolution as a stable social framework. This means that, from their own perspective, multicultural liberals play with fire when they attempt to liberalize illiberal cultures, since they may always discover *ex post factum* that they have undermined, rather than reinforced, the necessary conditions for individual autonomy.

Trying to find a way out of this dilemma, Kymlicka seems to have shifted his ground recently. He now argues that while liberals should identify and make known their preferences to illiberal groups in their midst, liberal states should not *impose* their liberal values on these groups. To support this position, Kymlicka draws a very unlikely analogy between illiberal domestic minorities and foreign sovereign states. Just as in the case of foreign illiberal states liberals would not advocate imposing liberal values by force, except under the most extreme circumstances, so in the case of illiberal 'national minorities', he argues, the liberal state should do no more than try to liberalize them by non-coercive persuasion.[35]

As Geoffrey Brahm Levey has pointed out, however, it is out of respect for sovereignty that intervention in the affairs of other states is considered illegitimate,[36] whereas the entire problem of cultural rights arises only because national minorities are not sovereign. Thus claiming that minorities should be treated 'as if' they were sovereign when they violate individual rights of their members seems absurd. Kymlicka's analogy challenges the very conception of the sovereign state as it has developed in modern political theory over the past three centuries. Rather than providing a solution to the contradictions of liberal multiculturalism, this analogy testifies to Kymlicka's inability to resolve it. For his argument results in the paradoxical conclusion that a government can, or must, refuse to protect some of its citizens from infringements upon their autonomy, if this infringement is caused by the conventions of an illiberal minority culture that had been given the right to self-government. Non-intervention in the face of illiberal practices violating individual autonomy can thus be justified as a measure of protection for individual autonomy, because it safeguards the cultural context of those citizens whose autonomy has been violated.

Furthermore, Kymlicka's advocacy of using state power to convince rather than coerce displays a certain *naïveté* concerning the nature of political and cultural exchanges and negotiations. Such transactions allow no clear-cut distinction between agreement, persuasion and coercion, since they take place between very unequal partners and involve the allocation of, and access to, a wide range of powerful material and cultural resources. For instance, no outright coercion is involved in the use of modern technology for the dissemination of global fantasies of upward mobility and success, such as are mass-produced by American television programs. Kymlicka advocates 'temporary measures' to restrict and control the intrusion of Western media into aboriginal cultures, so as to prevent the latter's collapse under the onslaught of Western resources. In fact, he uses some of his strongest language in defense of short-term, illiberal restrictions on liberties for the sake of protecting stable cultural membership.[37]

However, Kymlicka's support of isolated temporary measures does not do justice to the global, structural imbalance between modern and traditional cultures and the immense power exercised by Western mass media. Traditional minority cultures all over the world feel exposed to an incessant impingement of Western symbolic force. Together with poverty and deprivation, this intrusion is one of the causes of illiberal, fundamentalist backlashes which attempt to install emergency measures of defense against what is perceived as symbolic violence inflicted by the West.[38]

Kymlicka's limited understanding of the dynamics of cultural and social power downplays not only the difficulties faced by cultural minorities, but also the problem of freedom for individuals *within* these groups. His concern that a person should be able to choose freely an individual way of life, uncoerced by the group, completely ignores the problematic nature of the formation of choice within *any* social context. Coercion is the means of last resort for any social body seeking to induce conformity in its members. Much more significant is the very structuring of the self and its socialization through the prevailing norms of the group, a process that takes place throughout a person's life, and not only at the moment one is about to make a particular choice.

Kymlicka views individual freedom through the 'negative' perspective articulated by Isaiah Berlin, that is, as free choice in the absence of external constraints. This conception of freedom relies on what Steven Lukes has called the 'one-dimensional view' of power.[39] Thus Kymlicka fails to see that, as a rule, social and cultural domination does not only occur where there is actual, observable conflict, and does not imply necessarily tangible impediments and means of direct coercion. Instead, as Lukes has pointed out, various forms of social and cultural domination proceed by 'shaping [people's] perceptions, cognitions and preferences in such a way that they can see or imagine no alternative to it'.[40] This more complex view of social domination guided John Stuart Mill in his explanation of why Mormon women consented to polygamy. Mill claimed that only 'the common ideas and customs of the world, which, teaching women to think marriage the one thing needful, make it intelligible that many a woman should prefer being one of several wives to not being a wife at all'.[41]

Through the control of access to means of action and conditions of self-development, such as education, employment and political participation, social groups – or rather, their elites – can deny recalcitrant members the means of realizing socially or culturally deviant choices without having to strip them of their free will or capacity of choice.[42] Under such conditions it seems unlikely that one can ensure the ability to make autonomous choices by adding a modern conception of civil rights onto traditional social structures and cultural forms.

3   From negative to positive freedom

Some of Kymlicka's liberal critics believe that the problem with his project is its grounding in the value of autonomy. Hence they seek to substitute for it other values taken from the liberal arsenal, such as tolerance or respect for the choices of others.[43] As we mentioned above, however, we do not believe that the alternatives offered by Kymlicka's liberal critics can solve the problems of multicultural liberalism with which he grapples.

In our view, the problem with Kymlicka's project is not that it is based on the value of individual autonomy. The problem is, rather, that he conceives of autonomy in a limited and formalistic manner, such as suggests itself in liberal discourse. Thus, we propose that the solution to Kymlicka's problems has to be sought in a broader view of autonomy and, therefore, we wish to lead the debate away from formal definitions of autonomy, rights and liberties and towards the conditions of freedom, that is, the *material* and *institutional* means necessary for an effective exercise of a person's private and public autonomy. The presence in a society of any disadvantage in access to such enabling conditions of action makes some people less capable of realizing autonomous choices, and, therefore, the society less democratic.

Our concern then is with the actual *practice* of freedom by individuals, not only with the existence of a legally protected social space in which they can potentially act without being hindered. Following Amartya Sen, we value a person's ability to function as an autonomous agent rather than his or her formal rights. We value, that is, *capabilities* or *competence*, for in our view, this is the meaning of valuing individual freedom. As Sen has pointed out, '[t]he capability to function is the thing that comes closest to the notion of positive freedom, and if freedom is valued then capability itself can serve as an object of value and moral importance'.[44]

Berlin, of course, vigorously condemned the positive notion of freedom, arguing that it would lead those who are guided by it down the slippery slope to authoritarianism and coercion, and – despite good intentions – would transform the idea of freedom into a notion that sanctions oppression and violence.[45] But as Charles Taylor has pointed out, Berlin's attack is directed at an extreme, caricatural variant of the family of positive conceptions.[46] For this family includes all those views of modern political life that owe something to the classical republican tradition, and that imply 'that freedom involves at least partially collective self-rule'.[47] In fact, it has been argued that even classical and modern liberal theorists such as John Locke and John Stuart Mill had important elements of positivity in their conceptions of freedom.[48]

The main problem with the negative conception of freedom is that 'the concept of restraint will not capture the ways that people can be manipulated and conditioned in relation to the very makeup of desires and powers'.[49] Thus, the legal protection of the right to choose between different life-plans is not a sufficient guarantee of freedom, because the very formulation of the alternatives may be unfree in two important ways: First, people may be influenced by 'improper socialization'[50] in such a way that they cannot rationally comprehend the different courses of action open to them. Second, those courses of action may be themselves unduly limited, for example, by the way resources are distributed in the society. For instance, in certain cultures that do not formally prohibit women from pursuing an education, many women may still 'choose' not to do so, either because they are tacitly discouraged by their culture (through the diminution of marriage prospects, for example), or because the opportunities for acquiring education are too scarce or too expensive, or both.[51]

In lieu of the negative conception of freedom we propose the positive conception of 'freedom as self-development' as recently restated by Gould.[52] On this conception, freedom consists of three distinct elements, that include the negative notion, but cover a much broader territory and are thus not open to the objections outlined above: (a) choice or intentionality, (b) the development of personal capabilities, and (c) achievement of a person's long-term goals.[53] Gould's own formulation is worth citing at some length:

> This conception, like that of negative freedom, also presupposes that people have the capacity for free choice and for acting to realize their purposes. However, the concept of positive freedom ... emphasizes that in order to effect such choices concretely a wide range of actual options need to be available to people, for only through such activity is self-development possible. Thus this conception stresses the importance of the availability of the objective conditions – both material and social – without which the purposes could not be achieved. Among the material conditions are the means of subsistence as well as the means for labor and for leisure activity. The social conditions include cooperative forms of social interaction, reciprocal recognition of each one's free agency, and access to training, education, and various social institutions.[54]

Since Gould's definition of freedom is not procedural, like the negative definition, but rather 'consequence-sensitive',[55] if not positively consequentialist, it raises all kinds of problems of standards, evaluations and measurements.[56] It is not our purpose to contend with these issues in this essay. What we wish to argue here, is only that (a) Gould's positive conception of freedom could serve as a basis for a more coherent treatment of the issue of cultural rights than the negative one, and (b) Kymlicka himself has implicitly adopted a partially positive conception in his own analysis.

Gould does not directly address the question of groups, minority or otherwise, because her discussion is focused on individuals as the ultimate bearers of moral value. But the positive conception of freedom, it has been famously claimed, necessarily leads to collectivist conclusions. While, with Gould, Sen, Christman, and others, we do not feel that the positive conception of freedom must lead to *moral* collectivism, we do believe that this conception importantly draws our attention to the inevitable social context of all human purposive activity. Again, in Gould's words:

> [Self-developing] individuals are not isolated, but rather are social individuals. That is, they express who they are and become who they want to be in large part through their relations with others. Moreover, many of their actions are such that they are essentially

social, that is, they are joint actions that could not be carried out by individuals alone. To this degree, their own self-development depends on these social relations and ... on the extent to which these others are themselves self-developing.[57]

The implications of Gould's arguments for the issue of cultural rights are quite obvious. Like Kymlicka, she is cognizant of the value of culture, and of social relations in general, for the possibility of individual freedom. Since her conception of freedom is much richer than Kymlicka's, however, her interest is not limited to cultural matters, but is directed at social and economic issues in general. This, together with the notion of freedom as self-development, provides us with more adequate tools than Kymlicka's for dealing with the problem of illiberal minority groups.

In fact, Kymlicka had already transgressed Berlin's strict boundaries of negative liberty when he conflated autonomy with recognition. Furthermore, in his debate with Kukathas over what constitutes a 'substantial' right of exit from illiberal minority groups, Kymlicka has specifically noted that there are 'preconditions for making a meaningful choice', referring primarily to adequate education.[58] Moreover, in exceeding the bounds of negative liberty, Kymlicka may have been following in Rawls's footsteps. Sen has pointed out that, without acknowledging it, Rawls's theory of primary goods has an implicit notion of capabilities. For a primary good is something that *enables* people to actualize their capacity for reasonable, autonomous choice, and thus refers to positive freedom or capabilities.[59] Thus, we agree with Joseph Carens that 'Kymlicka's books ... provide the materials for a more satisfactory position than the one he himself adopts'.[60]

Contours of a democratic multiculturalism

Because Kymlicka has not consciously transcended the negative conception of freedom, his liberal multiculturalism can address the issue of minority groups' participation in the political sphere solely as a legal and political measure, designed for the collective, cultural self-protection and self-preservation of minorities. Extrapolating from Kymlicka's position, but transgressing its liberal limitations, we would like to propose an alternative approach – which we term 'democratic multiculturalism' – with a much broader concern. Focusing on the extent to which individuals belonging to different cultural groups are capable of equal and meaningful participation in all spheres of social activity, our concern is with the quality of *citizenship* enjoyed by all members of the society, rather than with rights as such.[61]

This conception of democratic multiculturalism derives from a positive notion of freedom that, as we have pointed out, is implicit in Kymlicka's work but remains unacknowledged and undeveloped because of his liberal commitment. As we understand it, democratic multiculturalism refers to actual cultural, social and political capabilities and practices rather than to formal procedures and principles. Thus, the perspective of democratic multiculturalism is participatory; it cannot be satisfied with the self-protective view of citizenship characteristic of liberal thinking.

A focus on the positive dimension of freedom also draws attention to the intertwinement of culture and economy. By limiting himself to national or ethnic culture as the only relevant social context of individual choice, and marginalizing or ignoring all other cultural contexts – such as social classes, urban neighborhoods or professional communities of discourse[62] – as well as the effects of economic conditions, Kymlicka has severed the question of freedom and autonomy from the real world. For most minority groups suffer not only from cultural marginalization, but also, and perhaps more basically, from economic exploitation and deprivation, to which the perspective of liberal, pluralist political science tends to turn a blind eye.[63]

Recently, Nancy Fraser has issued a call 'to link the struggle for recognition to the struggle for redistribution' stressing that '*cultural differences can only be freely elaborated and democratically mediated on the basis of social equality*'.[64] She opposes what she calls 'the pluralist version of multiculturalism' from a socialist perspective, suggesting, instead, to 'develop an alternative version that permits us to make normative judgments about the value of different differences by interrogating their relation to inequality ... A plausible slogan or watchword for this project is "No recognition without redistribution"'.[65] Fraser presents us with the intellectual and practical challenge of, as she puts it: 'developing a *critical* theory of recognition, one which identifies and defends only those versions of the cultural politics of difference that can be coherently combined with the social politics of equality'.[66]

Aware of the fact that cultural and economic demands inextricably interpenetrate each other, but that demands for cultural recognition cannot be reduced to those of redistribution, or vice versa, Fraser aims to 'develop a more general overarching conception of justice that can encompass both distribution and recognition'.[67] In our view, an approach which refers to autonomy in terms of positive, rather than negative freedom can provide the basis for such a conception. Of course, such an approach is not tied to the liberal form of multiculturalism, although it does not necessarily require one to exceed the bounds of liberal theorizing. It does demand, however, the continuous problematization of the relationships between culture and economy, and a consideration of their interrelatedness in each specific case in which claims to cultural rights are made.

From this angle it becomes possible to consider a number of important questions which are involved in the issue of minority rights, but which cannot be conceptualized within the terms of an economy-blind approach. Only by interrelating economy and culture can one evaluate, for instance, whether the effects of certain cultural rights – such as particular regulations concerning education and language, as well as land rights – are economically and socially empowering for those who are supposed to benefit from them, or whether they disempower them in socio-economic terms, and hence are detrimental to individual autonomy. Similarly, only such a vantage point allows one to contemplate what Wesley Cooper has called the 'culture vulture' problem, that is, the question whether a certain minority culture might not be 'so different and expensive to maintain that its flourishing would require sacrifices on the part of the majority culture that could not be justified by appeal to justice'.[68]

However, we wish not only to endorse Fraser's suggestion, but to take it a step further. Rawls and Kymlicka speak of 'rich' cultures in the metaphoric sense, without explicating what this richness consists in. Inspired by the work of Pierre Bourdieu, we propose to adopt an economic perspective on the *riches of a minority culture*, examining its *currency*, as it were, and its *rate of exchange* with the cultural currency of the majority, as well as with other values such as material or social capital.[69]

From this Bourdieu-inspired perspective, minority cultures are seen as social fields which are located in a wider socio-economic space that structures the available strategies for the definition of cultural identities and the constraints and opportunities faced by members of minority cultures. Thus, if a minority culture fails to train its members to cope with the demands of modern life and instills types of knowledge and attitudes that alienate them from the surrounding society, they equip their members with cultural currencies that cannot be 'exchanged' outside the narrow confines of the minority group. Though such a culture may be rich in its own terms, that is, possess a long and diverse tradition, it leaves its members poor in terms of capabilities for autonomy.

Thus, under certain circumstances, speaking a 'rich' language which is of no use outside the minority culture may impoverish an individual, that is, not enhance his or her autonomy, but rather inhibit it. One set of circumstances that comes to mind here is when economic opportunities within the minority group are limited and people are forced to seek their livelihood in the larger society. In such a case, being highly educated in the 'rich' minority culture, at the expense of having some basic proficiency in the majority language, can prove a great liability for a person's quest for autonomy. As Carens has pointed out,

> no aboriginal person can routinely expect to communicate with doctors, lawyers, dentists ... in her native language, much less to find employment in that language in the economy outside the reserve. There is a deep tension, which aboriginal people experience daily, between secure access to their societal culture ... and access to other primary goods like income, wealth, opportunities, and power.[70]

In fact, it may even be in the interest of the majority to limit the minority's access to the resources available in the larger society by granting it cultural autonomy. If members of minority cultures are educated in their own language, rather than in the majority language, they may be disadvantaged in competing for educational and employment opportunities. In other words, in certain situations cultural autonomy may function as a form of economic and cultural segregation.[71]

To sum up: democratic multiculturalism postulates that when culture is checked for its effects on individual autonomy, it has to be examined in terms of the social, economic and political capabilities it provides for individuals and thus in terms of the social, economic and political practices it enables, furthers or prevents. Therefore, democratic multiculturalism situates culture within a wider social framework that includes the economy, and *vis-à-vis* the cultural currency that is used in the majority culture. As against all forms of segregation, democratic multiculturalism endorses group representation for the purpose of creating a *diversified common culture*, which allocates minorities a place in the shared public sphere.[72] Rather than the legal protection of certain minority *rights*, the aim of democratic multiculturalism is the construction of a plural, participatory, common culture based on equal and meaningful *citizenship* for all.

4   Israel as a multicultural society

To illustrate the differences between liberal and democratic multiculturalism we will briefly review now the situation of four cultural
minority groups in Israel – Palestinian-Arab citizens, *mizrahim* (Jews
originating in Moslem countries), *haredim* (ultra-orthodox religious
Jews) and national-religious Jews (moderately orthodox and nationalist) – and assess how their respective situations would be evaluated by
the two perspectives. We use 'minority' in the sociological sense, as
mizrahim are hardly a minority in Israel in a numerical sense.
Moreover, we are aware that in Kymlicka's terms only the rights of the
Palestinians, who are an indigenous group, should be of concern to
liberal multiculturalists. *Mizrahim*, like all other Jews, are immigrants to
Israel, while the two religious groups do not differ *ethnically* from the
dominant Jewish majority, but only in terms of their greater religiosity.

However, rather than being constrained by Kymlicka's dichotomous
analytic framework, that divides all ethnic groups into immigrant latecomers, who neither deserve nor wish for national rights, and conquered, prior inhabitants who are entitled to them, we wish to expose
its limitations. For Kymlicka's framework that, by his own admission,
excludes African-Americans, guest workers, and many other groups, is
problematic even in the Canadian context.[73] Moreover, Kymlicka's
dichotomy can be legitimately ignored in our case, since we invoke the
Israeli example for one purpose only: to illustrate the limitations of a
purely cultural outlook that is blind to the intertwining of economic,
cultural and social factors in the question of minority rights.

Israel's Palestinian *citizens* (as distinguished from the non-citizen
Palestinians residing in the occupied territories and in the areas under
the control of the Palestinian National Authority) possess, formally at
least, equal liberal citizenship rights as individuals. As a group,
however, they are barred from participation in determining the
common good of society, which is still highly Jewish and communitarian in orientation. In certain areas, primarily religion and education,
Israel's Palestinian citizens enjoy limited autonomy, the most important aspect of which is that Palestinian children are educated in separate state schools and in their own language, Arabic, up to the end of
their secondary education.[74]

As Rebecca Kook argues in this volume, and as can be attested by many
faculty members in Israel's colleges and universities, graduates of the separate Palestinian school system suffer from a lack of sufficient proficiency
in Hebrew, the majority language used in business, government and

higher education. Since fully half of the Palestinians are employed in the larger, that is Jewish, labor market, this handicap affects their chances of success and is among the important reasons, although by no means the only one, for their social and economic inferiority.[75] Thus, while the state could be said to recognize the cultural rights of Palestinians, this recognition functions as a tool of cultural and economic exclusion and of political domination. (It could be, and has been argued, correctly, that Palestinian citizens do not control their separate school system, and that the system is seriously underfinanced, relative to its Jewish counterpart.[76] It is doubtful, however, whether the rectification of these injustices would significantly enhance the capacity of the graduates of these schools to function in the larger, Jewish society.)

Mizrahim are not accorded any cultural autonomy as such, and state policy towards them has been culturally assimilationist and politically and economically exclusionary. While *mizrahim* have bitterly complained about the denigration of their culture, and some efforts have been made to preserve and enhance it, initially they sought not cultural autonomy but integration into the mainstream of society, as individuals, on better terms than those offered them by the dominant *ashkenazi* (European) Jews. This attitude was consonant with Kymlicka's expectations from immigrant groups. And indeed, the culturally assimilationist and selectively cooptative policy of the state has enabled about one third of the *mizrahim* to integrate into the mainstream, economically and politically. The others, and especially the lower third, in socio-economic terms, have launched a very successful effort in recent years to organize themselves autonomously on the model of the *haredim*.[77]

Haredim have total control over their own communal affairs, most importantly their educational systems, that are financed by the state without being subject to state supervision. In order to help them further to preserve their culture, which had been nearly destroyed in the Holocaust, *haredim* have been granted other privileges as well, such as exemption from military service for women and deferment for *yeshiva* (Talmudic academy) students. The latter provision has made all *haredi* males of draft age enroll in *yeshivot*, causing the number of *yeshiva* students to exceed anything ever known in Jewish history.

The deferment from military service, which is granted only to full-time *yeshiva* students, and becomes an exemption at the age of 41, has created a situation of prolonged dependency of young *haredi* males on their communal religious authorities. Since they cannot join the labor market or receive secular education or occupational training until the age of 41, these young men depend on state subsidies administered by their religious elders (and on their wives' earnings) for their livelihood. The *yeshiva* authorities also have to certify that a person is indeed enrolled there, which gives them added power over their students. These powers are used to ensure conformity with communal codes and prevent exit from the community into the larger society.[78]

Finally, the national-religious (religious Zionist) community also enjoys educational autonomy within a special system of state schools it effectively controls. These schools, however, teach secular, as well as religious subjects, and their male graduates are not exempted from military service. Graduates who go on to *yeshivot* have a special arrangement whereby they can combine higher religious studies with a shortened military service, which some of them do in their own separate units. Since this community prepares its youth for life in a modern secular society, and belonging to it does not confer any special privileges, other than cultural preservation, the communal authorities have no power, except religious ideology, over their members and cannot prevent their exit into the larger society.

If we evaluate these four types of arrangements from the two perspectives we juxtapose here, we will arrive at strikingly different judgments. Both liberal and democratic multicultural perspectives will agree that the rights granted the national-religious community are the most satisfactory, since they combine cultural preservation with the development of individual capacity. But this is the easiest case, since the cultural divergence of the national-religious from the larger society which, like them, is Jewish and *ashkenazi*-dominated, is the smallest. Beyond that, from a liberal perspective of cultural preservation, the autonomy granted the *haredim* must be judged a striking success. For *haredi* culture has not only been preserved but has experienced an astonishing revival. However, such an assessment would have to ignore the fact that the autonomy granted the *haredim* has seriously harmed the capabilities of their individual members to function as productive citizens in the larger society.

From Kymlicka's perspective even the 'autonomy' granted to citizen Palestinians must be judged better than the assimilationist policies adopted towards *mizrahim*, although, individually, the latter are much more capable of functioning successfully in the society than the former. Alternatively, Kymlicka could consider the *mizrahim* to be immigrants and approve of their assimilation. This would be an awkward, if factually correct choice, in a society where all Jews are immigrants, and would also contradict the current effort of many *mizrahim* to set up autonomous institutions.

Kymlicka's liberal multiculturalism proves to be of little value, then, in rendering a coherent moral evaluation of the arrangements made with regard to cultural minorities in Israel, a society that, with some straining, could be considered a Western liberal democracy. From a democratic multiculturalist perspective, the situation of all minority groups in Israel, save the national-religious, will be found wanting, although in varying degrees. Democratic multiculturalists would like to see all minority groups granted the means to establish autonomous cultural institutions on a *voluntary* basis. However, forcing members of minority groups into separate institutions, whether by law as in the case of the Palestinians, or by excessive privileges as in the case of the *haredim*, and thus harming their ability to function in the larger society, is anti-participatory, and hence a condemnable practice. From this perspective, denigrating a minority culture and denying its members the means to establish autonomous institutions, while allowing significant numbers of its members to integrate into the mainstream of society, is not to be recommended, but is still preferable to forcibly keeping all of them in separate autonomous institutions.[79]

Democratic multiculturalism, we realize, does not provide clear, universalizable policy guidelines that can be relied upon in every instance. But it does draw our attention to two important points neglected by Kymlicka's doctrine: the need to consider people's overall life-chances when discussing their personal autonomy; and the importance of involving all members of society in the democratic process of shaping its culture and way of life. At the very least, democratic multiculturalism cautions us against reifying 'culture' and attributing a higher moral value to forms of consciousness than to the actual human beings who carry these forms of consciousness in their heads.

Conclusion

Liberal multiculturalism is beset by serious problems when it comes to consider the proper attitude that should be taken by the liberal state towards illiberal minorities in its midst. If, as Kymlicka has argued, group cultural rights are justified only because, and hence only to the extent that, they enhance individual autonomy, then groups that discourage autonomy, namely, most minority groups in the real world, should not be granted these rights. If they are granted these rights, as Kymlicka thinks they should be, how can individual members be protected from encroachment by the group against their autonomy? Non-coercive liberalization, Kymlicka's most coherent answer, doubly defeats his purpose: it can cause the groups to disintegrate, while failing to protect their individual members in the process.

At the root of the problem, we have argued, is the liberal commitment to the negative conception of freedom, that restricts the understanding of autonomy even of liberal thinkers, such as Rawls and Kymlicka, whose thought may contain unacknowledged elements of the positive conception. If we openly adopt a broader, positive notion of freedom, however, a notion that stresses capabilities, rather than lack of restraints, as the key standard of liberty, then we may be able to evaluate the extent to which various cultural practices enhance or inhibit individual freedom, and hence what cultural practices should be protected and encouraged by a liberal democratic state.

Once we begin to think in terms of capabilities and practices it becomes clear that culture is only one of many socio-economic conditions that affect individual freedom and autonomy. No less important are the economic opportunities that are available in any particular society. Since democratic multiculturalism, the alternative we favor, is not constricted by the narrow, negative conception of freedom, it can take all relevant factors into account when considering which minority cultural practices deserve to be protected and which do not.

Furthermore, as we have pointed out, the orientation of democratic multiculturalism towards minority cultures is participatory, rather than protective. It is concerned not only with the negative task of preservation, but with the positive ability of members of minority groups to be productively involved in the economic and cultural life of the larger society. If guided by democratic multiculturalism, the outcome of this involvement should not be the assimilation of minority cultures but rather the development of a richer, pluralistic culture encompassing the society as a whole.

Notes

1   No senior author.
2   Will Kymlicka, *Liberalism, Community and Culture* (Oxford: Oxford University Press, 1989); 'Liberal Individualism and Liberal Neutrality', *Ethics*, Vol. 99 (1989), pp. 883–905; 'Individual and Community Rights', in J. Baker (ed.), *Group Rights* (Toronto: University of Toronto Press, 1994); *Multicultural Citizenship* (Oxford: Clarendon Press, 1995); 'Do We Need a

Liberal Theory of Minority Rights?', *Constellations* Vol. 4 (1997), pp. 72–87; *Finding Our Way: Rethinking Ethnocultural Relations in Canada* (Toronto: Oxford University Press, 1998); 'Modernity and National Identity', in this volume, Chapter 2.

3 José Brunner and Yoav Peled, 'Das Elend des Liberalen Multikulturalismus: Kymlicka und seine Kritiker', ['The Poverty of Liberal Multiculturalism; Kymlicka and his Critics'] *Deutsche Zeitschrift für Philosophie*, 3/1998, 'On Autonomy, Capabilities and Democracy: a Critique of Liberal Multiculturalism', in Menachem Mautner, Avi Sagi and Ronen Shamir (eds), *Multiculturalism in a Democratic and Jewish State* (Tel Aviv, Ramot, 1998) (in Hebrew).

4 See Amartya Sen, 'Rights and Capabilities', in T. Honderich (ed.), *Morality and Objectivity* (London, Routledge and Kegan Paul, 1985), p. 138.

5 Nancy Fraser, 'From Redistribution to Recognition? Dilemmas of Justice in a "Post-Socialist Age"', *New Left Review* 212 (1995), pp. 68–93.

6 Kymlicka, *Liberalism, Community and Culture*, p. 162.

7 Ibid., pp. 165, 167.

8 Ibid., p. 166; see also p. 178.

9 Ibid., p. 172.

10 Ibid., p. 168.

11 Ibid., p. 178; John Rawls, *A Theory of Justice* (Oxford: Oxford University Press, 1971), pp. 563–564.

12 Kymlicka, *Liberalism, Community and Culture*, p. 165; see also Joseph Raz, 'Multiculturalism: a Liberal Perspective', *Dissent*, Vol. 41 (1994), p. 71.

13 Kymlicka, 'Liberal Individualism and Liberal Neutrality', p. 183; see also José Brunner and Yoav Peled, 'Rawls on Respect and Self-Respect: An Israeli Perspective', *Political Studies,* Vol. 44 (1996), pp. 287–302.

14 Kymlicka, 'Liberal Individualism', p. 189.

15 Kymlicka, *Multicultural Citizenship*, p. 43.

16 Kymlicka, *Liberalism, Community and Culture*, p. 147.

17 Kymlicka, *Multicultural Citizenship*, pp. 26–33, 75–151.

18 Leszek Kolakowski, 'Looking for the Barbarians: the Illusions of Cultural Universalism', in *Modernity on Endless Trial* (Chicago: University of Chicago Press, 1990), p. 22.

19 John Tomasi, 'Kymlicka, Liberalism, and Respect for Cultural Minorities', *Ethics*, Vol. 105 (1995), p. 591.

20 See, Edward Said, *Representations of the Intellectual: the 1993 Reith Lectures* (London: Vintage, 1993); Fred Dallmayr, 'The Politics of Nonidentity: Adorno, Postmodernism – and Edward Said', *Political Theory*, Vol. 25 (1997), pp. 33–56.

21 Kymlicka, *Multicultural Citizenship*, pp. 10–11.

22 Ibid., pp. 95–8.

23 Ibid., p. 170.

24 Ibid., p. 99.

25 Kymlicka, 'Do We Need a Liberal Theory of Minority Rights?', pp. 77–9.

26 Kymlicka, *Multicultural Citizenship*, pp. 11, 15.

27 Ibid., p. 99.

28 See M. Galenkamp, 'The Rationale of Minority Rights: Wishes Rather than Needs?', in J. Raikka (ed.) *Do We Need Minority Rights?* (The Hague, Martinus Nijhoff, 1996).

29 Cf. Geoffrey Brahm Levey, 'Equality, Autonomy, and Cultural Rights', *Political Theory*, Vol. 25 (1997), pp. 218–219.

30 Bhikhu Parekh, 'Dilemmas of a Multicultural Theory of Citizenship', *Constellations*, Vol. 4 (1997), p. 56.

31 Kymlicka, *Liberalism, Community and Culture*, p. 164.

32 Will Kymlicka, 'The Rights of Minority Cultures: Reply to Kukathas', *Political Theory*, Vol. 20 (1992), p. 142.

33 Kymlicka, *Liberalism, Community and Culture*, pp. 195–8.

34 Ibid., p. 170.

35 Ibid., pp. 163–70.

36 Levey, 'Equality, Autonomy, and Cultural Rights', p. 227.

37 Kymlicka, *Liberalism, Community and Culture*, p. 170.

38 Benjamin R. Barber, *Jihad vs. McWorld: How Globalism and Tribalism are Reshaping the World*, New York: Ballantine, 1995.

39 Steven Lukes, *Power: a Radical View* (London: Macmillan, 1974), pp. 11–15.

40 Ibid., p. 24.

41 John Stuart Mill, *On Liberty* (Harmondsworth, Penguin, 1984 [1859]), p. 161.

42 See Carol Gould, *Rethinking Democracy: Freedom and Social Cooperation in Politics, Economy, and Society* (Cambridge, Cambridge University Press, 1990), p. 43.

43 Chandran Kukathas, 'Are there any Cultural Rights?, *Political Theory*, Vol. 20 (1992), pp. 105–139; 'Cultural Toleration', in Ian Shapiro and Will Kymlicka (eds) *Ethnicity and Group Rights* (New York and London: New York University Press, 1997); Yael Tamir, 'Two Concepts of Multiculturalism', *Journal of Philosophy and Education*, Vol. 29 (1995), pp. 161–72, respectively.

44 Sen, 'Rights and Capabilities', p. 138.

45 Isaiah Berlin, 'Two Concepts of Liberty', in *Four Essays on Liberty* (Oxford, Oxford University Press, 1969[1958]), pp. 132–33.

46 Charles Taylor, 'What's Wrong With Negative Liberty', in *Philosophy and the Human Sciences: Philosophical Papers II* (Cambridge, Cambridge University Press, 1985), p. 211.

47 Ibid., p. 214.

48 S.J. Heyman, 'Positive and Negative Liberty', *Chicago-Kent Law Review*, Vol. 68 (1992), pp. 81–9; cf. Mill's discussion of Mormon women, above.

49 J. Christman, 'Liberalism and Individual Positive Freedom', *Ethics*, Vol. 101 (1991), p. 344.

50 Carol Gould, *Rethinking Democracy*, p. 56.

51 See ibid., pp. 36–8.

52 Gould, *Rethinking Democracy*.

53 Ibid., pp. 46–8.

54 Ibid., p. 41.

55 Sen, 'Rights and Capabilities', p. 136.

56 See Martha Nussbaum and Amartya Sen (eds), *The Quality of Life* (New York, 1993).

57 Gould, *Rethinking Democracy*, p. 49.

58 Kymlicka, *Multicultural Citizenship*, pp. 234–5 n18; 'The Rights of Minority Cultures: Reply to Kukathas', p. 143.

59 Sen, 'Rights and Capabilities', p. 142.

60 John H. Carens, 'Liberalism and Culture', *Constellations*, Vol. 4 (1997), p. 44;

61 cf. Rainer Forst, 'Foundations of a Theory of Multicultural Justice', *Constellations*, Vol. 4 (1997), pp. 67–8.

62 See Brian Walker, 'Plural Cultures, Contested Territories: A Critique of Kymlicka,' *Canadian Journal of Political Science*, Vol. 30 (1997), pp. 211–34; Andre Marmor, 'Equality and Minority Cultures', Paper Presented at the International Conference on 'Multicultural Democracy', Ramat Gan, 1998.

63 Cf. Walker, 'Plural Cultures, Contested Territories'.

64 Nancy Fraser, "Multiculturalism and Gender Equity: The U.S. 'Difference' Debates Revisited", *Constellations*, Vol 3 (1996), p. 71 (original emphasis).

65 Ibid., p. 72.

66 Ibid., p. 69.

67 Nancy Fraser, 'A Rejoinder to Iris Young', *New Left Review*, 223 (1997), p. 127.

68 W.E. Cooper, 'Culture Vultures and the Re-Enchantment of Citizenship', in J. Raikka)ed.) *Do We Need Minority Rights?* (The Hague, Martinus Nijhoff, 1996), p. 26.

69 Pierre Bourdieu, *Language and Symbolic Power* (Cambridge, Polity, 1991), pp. 229–31.

70 Carens, 'Liberalism and Culture', p. 43.

71 See Rebecca Kook, 'Towards The Rehabilitation Of "Nation Building" and the Reconstruction of Nations', Chapter 3 in this volume.

72 Iris MarionYoung, *Justice and the Politics of Difference* (Princeton, Princeton University Press, 1990); 'Deferring Group Presentation', in Ian Shapiro and Will Kymlicka (eds), *Ethnicity and Group Rights* (New York, New York University Press, 1997); 'A Multicultural Continuum: a Critique of Will Kymlicka's Ethnic-Nation Dichotomy', *Constellations*, Vol. 4 (1997), pp. 48–53.

73 Carens, 'Liberalism and Culture'; Walker, 'Plural Cultures'.

74 Sammy Smooha, *Israel: Pluralism and Conflict* (Berkeley, University of California Press, 1978); 'Minority Status in an Ethnic Democracy: the Status of the Arab Minority in Israel', *Ethnic and Racial Studies*, Vol. 13 (1990), pp. 389–413; Yoav Peled, 'Ethnic Democracy and the Legal Construction of Citizenship: Arab Citizens of the Jewish State', *American Political Science Review*, Vol. 86 (1992), pp. 432–43.

75 Noah Lewin-Epstein and Moshe Semyonov, *The Arab Minority in Israel's Economy* (Boulder, Westview Press, 1993).

76 Majid Al-Haj, *Education, Empowerment and Control: the Case of the Arabs in Israel* (Albany, NY, SUNY Press, 1995).

77 Smooha, *Israel: Pluralism and Conflict*; Hannah Herzog, 'Ethnicity as a Product of Political Negotiation: The Case of Israel', *Ethnic and Racial Studies*, Vol. 7 (1984), pp. 517–33; Shlomo Swirski, *The Oriental Majority* (London, Zed, 1989); Yoav Peled, 'Ethnic Exclusionism in the Periphery: the Case of Oriental Jews in Israel's Development Towns', *Ethnic and Racial Studies*, Vol. 13 (1990), pp. 345–67; 'Towards a Redefinition of Jewish Nationalism in Israel? The Enigma of *Shas*', *Ethnic and Racial Studies*, Vol. 21 (1998), pp. 703–27; Yinon Cohen and Yitzhak Haberfeld, 'Second-

Generation Immigrants in Israel: Have the Ethnic Gaps in Schooling and Earning Declined?' *Ethnic and Racial Studies*, Vol. 21 (1998), pp. 507–28.

78 Stuart Cohen, '*The Scroll or the Sword? Dilemmas of Religion and Military Service in Israel* (Harwood, 1997), pp. 85–101.

79 Cf. Yossi Yonah, 'Fifty Years Later: the Scope and Limits of Liberal Democracy in Israel', *Constellations*, Vol. 6, No. 3 (1999), pp. 411–28.

PART TWO

Ethnic Strife and the State in Western Europe

5

Catalan and Basque Nationalism: Contrasting Patterns

Stanley G. Payne

Since the end of the Franco dictatorship, the two 'peripheral nationalisms' of the Catalans and Basques have become the strongest stateless nationalisms in western Europe. Though chronologically roughly parallel phenomena in modern Spain, there are deep differences between the two in terms of their history, culture, structure and politics, and in the roles of the two regions in the history of Spain during the past millennium.

Though the Spanish state is very old, the history of modern nationalisms in Spain – and even of a Spanish nation – is necessarily much shorter. The historic Trastámara-Habsburg monarchy of the fifteenth through seventeenth centuries, which created the first all-Spanish state, in key respects remained traditionalist in form. It established a single dynasty for a monarchist confederation of the institutionally distinct states of Aragon, Catalonia, Valencia, Navarre and Castile (with the Basque provinces a separate territory under the crown of Castile). The first generally unified system of state and administration was introduced by the Bourbon dynasty after 1700. The separate legal and constitutional systems of Aragon, Catalonia and Valencia were abolished, so that the only particularist structures remaining were those of the three Basque provinces and Navarre. By the reign of Carlos III (1759–88), the Spanish state had begun to exert increasing pressure against them as well, and the modern polemic regarding Basque *fueros* (legal privileges and exemptions) began to take shape.[1]

A form of modern nationalism was first introduced in Spain by early-nineteenth-century liberalism. The liberals were determined to unify Spain through classic liberal constitutionalism and anticlericalism, and to centralize the state and administration on the French model. This produced enormous resistance and conflict, especially in the two principal

Carlist wars of the 1830s and 1870s. Liberal/traditionalist conflict stretched altogether from the first antiliberal *golpe de Estado* of 1814 down to the conclusion of the final Carlist war in 1876, the most protracted such contest anywhere in the world during the nineteenth century.

Liberals did not make nationalism *per se* their principal cause, but they introduced common use of the term *nación* and were clearly dedicated to a modern and unified administration, church-state reform, modern education and a liberal constitutional system. This was based on a general belief in the historic identity and unity of Spain from the early days of the kingdom of Asturias and the reconquest through the rise of Castile and the formation of the Spanish state. Castile and the Castilian language formed the core of a kind of Spanish/Castilian essentialism common to the majority of liberals and expressed above all in nineteenth-century liberal historiography, such as Modesto Lafuente's 30-volume *Historia de España*.

Spanish liberalism experienced profound internal fragmentation, however, and devoted much of its energy to internal conflict. It largely failed to advance education rapidly or to promote accelerated economic development, so that its modernization and nation-building projects achieved at best only limited success. Faithful to classic tenets of nineteenth-century economic liberalism, it proved weak in implementing concerted national strategies, and in the longer term relinquished overtly nationalistic politics, taking common Spanish unity and identity for granted.[2]

The place of Catalonia and the Basque provinces within Spain and the attitudes of Catalans and Basques toward modernization differed substantially during most of the eighteenth and nineteenth centuries. Particularist Catalan institutions completely disappeared in 1716, Spanish becoming the official language of the region even though Catalan was still universally spoken at home. During this same period, the Catalan economy began to profit much more than ever before from the all-Spanish and colonial economic framework, leading the process of recovery from the profound seventeenth-century decline. By the middle decades of the eighteenth century Catalonia – and especially Barcelona – was the leader of modernization in Spain, a position which it held throughout the following century as well.

In the early nineteenth century Catalans began to play a leading role among the advocates of modern political and institutional change, but Catalan liberals sought to promote liberalism for all of Spain, and differed from other Spanish liberals primarily in their search for some

degree of decentralization. The role of Catalans was especially prominent in the short-lived Federal Republic of 1873–4, which attempted,
but failed, to introduce drastic decentralization. Catalan political and
economic leaders nonetheless sought to implement greater economic
development and political change within the common framework of
modern Spain, even though concern mounted during the second half
of the nineteenth century that Catalan interests were not being adequately defended.

The situation in the Basque provinces was quite different. There the
last phase of the Old Regime was a time of severe economic crisis.
Though Vizcaya and Guipuzcoa may have then had the greatest population density of any Spanish provinces, per capita income may have
been below the Spanish average. Society was becoming divided between
modernizers and liberals (who sought political change, liberal capitalist
institutions and greater integration with Spain) and the traditionalist
majority, who clung to the particularist institutions of the *fueros* that
provided self-government through a kind of corporate elite, and fiscal
military and tariff exemptions. This situation helps to explain the broad
and deep support for Carlist traditionalism in the Basque provinces and
Navarre. Though Carlism was generally a popular cause – in contrast to
elitist, capitalist liberalism – with supporters all over Spain, nowhere
else was this support so mobilized and extensive, all the more mobilized
thanks to the self-governing particularist institutions of these four
provinces.[3] The first main Carlist conflict was ended in a compromise in
1840, by which the Basque *fueros* were largely preserved as an exception
to the central legal administrative structure of Spain. They were not
abolished until the end of the final Carlist war in 1876, and even then
the Basque provinces and Navarre were allowed to retain highly advan-
tageous separate *conciertos* for taxes.[4]

The 'peripheral nationalisms' which developed in the final years of
the century were almost simultaneous, Catalanism taking form in the
1880s and 1890s, and the Basque Nationalist Party (PNV) being organized in 1895–7. Each drew on a cultural renascence, though that which
took place in the Basque Country was expressed almost exclusively in
Castilian and altogether lacked the literary vigor and cultural diversity
of the Catalan '*Renaixença*.'[5] The tone of the two nationalisms was
vastly different. Catalanism was solidly based on the modernizing
Catalan bourgeoisie and propounded regional autonomy within a
more modern, reformist and progressive Spanish system, within which
the Catalanists hoped to play an even more leading role in the future.[6]
The Basque nationalism defined by Savino de Arana Goiri was quite

different. Limited at first to a small and mostly petit-bourgeois intelligentsia, it was consciously archaicizing. Whereas Catalan nationalism rode comfortably on the wave of Catalan modernization, Basque nationalism developed as a kind of reaction against the beginning of rapid industrialization in Vizkaya from approximately 1880 onwards, and was spurred by antipathy to the workers who moved in from other parts of Spain, virtually for the first time in Basque history. It demanded complete separation from Spain, which was demonized in a paranoid manner, and insisted on the literal restoration of the fifteenth-century *fueros*. Arana's program also stressed a distinct and superior racial and cultural identity, and called for a virtual theocracy in a future Basque state, all of whose laws were to be adjusted to the strictest Catholicism.[7] Whereas Catalanism was modern, industrializing, liberal and pledged to cooperation with Spain, Basque nationalism was inherently post-Carlist, archaicizing, anti-industrialist, clerical and in some respects even reactionary.

The first Catalanist political organization, the *Unió Catalanistam*, formed in 1891, was followed by the *Lliga Regionalista*, which increasingly dominated parliamentary politics in Catalonia during the next two decades. After World War I, however, it was challenged by the petit-bourgeois, left-democratic *Acció Catalana*, which defeated the *Lliga* in 1923, while farther to the left formed the radical federalist *Estat Català*, organized by Francesc Macià between 1919 and 1922. By the time of the Primo de Rivera dictatorship and the beginning of the Second Republic, the leadership of Catalanism had been taken over by populist, left-democratic and radically federalist forces which did not seek separation from Spain but insisted on more complete autonomy than did the conservative-liberal *Lliga*, and were much more self-absorbed in Catalan affairs.

While Catalanism had moved from the right-center to the left-center, Basque nationalism slowly moved from the far right to the right-center and center. The early death of Arana Goiri and the entry into the Basque Nationalist Party of a small sector of more liberal, somewhat secular-minded and pro-industrialist capitalists, led by Ramón de la Sota, gave the movement a more cooperative, less reactionary cast. Even before the death of Arana in 1903, it accepted the need to cooperate with the Spanish liberal system and to work for a broad structure of autonomy within Spain. The more moderate post-Arana leaders expelled the sizeable radical sector of the party in 1921, leading to an open political division not overcome until the reunification of the party ten years later.

Because of the radical anticlericalism of the Spanish Republic in 1931, Basque nationalists entered the first phase of Republican politics on the far right, but soon moved toward the center in order to cooperate in establishing a system of autonomy. Three different draft statutes for autonomy between 1931 and 1934 nonetheless failed, and on the eve of the Civil War the PNV refused to ally itself either with the proto-authoritarian electoral alliance of the Spanish right or the leftist and anticlerical Popular Front. The outbreak of civil war divided the movement, more conservative Basque nationalists in Alava and Navarre joining the right-wing Spanish insurgents, while the main sectors of the PNV in Vizcaya and Guipuzcoa sought to bargain with the Popular Front Republican government, distasteful as they found the latter. This finally produced a statute of Basque autonomy in October 1936, though by that time only the province of Vizcaya remained in Republican hands. Cooperation with the geographically non-contiguous central Republican government proved difficult, and the PNV to a certain extent maintained an independent domestic and foreign policy, both before and after the collapse of Basque resistance in June 1937.[8] The Civil War proved to be an especial trauma because it was also a civil war between Basques, badly divided by the issues of 1936.

In Catalonia the left-democratic federation of *Esquerra Republicana de Catalunya*, led by Estat Català, dominated Catalan politics during the Republican period, and gained a broad but not complete system of autonomy late in 1932. Dissatisfied with the way the new system functioned and strongly opposed to the right-center coalition that took over Spanish government late the following year, the *Esquerra* leadership joined the ill-fated revolutionary insurrection of October 1934, leading to the virtual annulment of autonomy for the next 16 months. The *Esquerra* regained control after the Popular Front elections of February 1936, but in the Civil War that soon followed lost power over much of Catalonia to the revolutionary anarchosyndicalists, and then, after May 1937, found its authority increasingly restricted by the wartime central Republican government which had taken up residence in Barcelona. The politics and policies of radical Catalanism thus ended in complete defeat by 1939.

Though both peripheral nationalist movements had failed completely during Spain's early-twentieth-century epoch of accelerated development and expanded conflict, major differences persisted. Catalan nationalism was divided between a majority sector of lower-middle class radicals and progressives and a large minority of more conservative bourgeois liberals, but – thanks in part to the abstentionism of working-class anarchosyndicalists – had in one form or another dominated Catalan politics for most of the early twentieth century. While Basque nationalism was united, with the exception of one small sector, behind the PNV, it had remained a minority force in its region, whose political representation under the Republic had been triangulated between parties of the Spanish left, Spanish right and Basque nationalists.

Both peripheral nationalisms were rigorously repressed by the Franco regime, under which limited expressions of culture in the vernacular only became possible – with very limited previous exceptions – in the 1960s. Both Catalonia and the Basque provinces, especially the latter, expanded economically under the dictatorship, and for twenty years peripheral nationalism seemed relatively dormant, especially in the Basque Country. This changed only late in the 1960s, when radical unrest – both political and social – became more salient in the latter than in Catalonia, so that the last years of Francoism were a time of growing repression and polarization in the Basque provinces.

The responses of the two movements in 1977 to the willingness of the new democratic monarchy to begin restoration of autonomy differed markedly. Josep Tarradellas, president of the *Catalan Generalitat* (regional government) in exile, quickly accepted an invitation to return to Barcelona and help preside over a cooperative process of democratization and autonomy. As in the nineteenth century, Catalans put their shoulders to the wheel and strongly supported the democratic transition, applauding the new constitution and the new system of autonomy which eventually became somewhat broader than the Republican structure which had preceded it. Jordi Pujol, leader of the liberal democratic *Convergencia i Unió* coalition, then defeated the parties of the Spanish left in the first regular regional Catalan elections in 1980, and has dominated Catalan government and politics ever since. Since 1993, he has indirectly dominated part of Spanish affairs as well, providing the necessary votes in Madrid to keep in power the minority governments first of the Socialists (to 1996) and then of the Spanish conservatives, in the process exercising crucial influence on policy and winning new concessions for Catalonia and the other regional autonomies in Spain.[9]

The case of Basque nationalism has been profoundly different. A new revolutionary movement known from its acronym as ETA (Basque Land and Liberty) seized the initiative during the 1960s and 1970s, emerging as one of the most active terrorist movements in the world after the death of Franco, now in opposition not to the dictatorship but to the new Spanish democracy. The PNV nonetheless retained most nationalist votes until it broke in two in 1986, but dragged its feet on cooperating with the new democratic system, insisting on the integral restoration of the late-medieval *fueros*. The Basque provinces were thus the only region in Spain in which most of the electorate failed to ratify the new democratic Spanish constitution of 1978. Party structure and political opinion in the Basque provinces were highly fragmented,[10] and only briefly were the semi-moderate nationalists of the PNV able to govern the new regional system on their own. Both the PNV, and the *Eusko Alkartasuna* party which split from it, demanded eventual independence, while ETA and its political front organization, *Herri Batasuna* (United Land), call for revolutionary separatism. All this occurred amid the serious decline of superannuated Basque heavy industry, once the backbone of the regional economy, and has produced more than a little fear and demoralization. Meanwhile the Catalan economy has navigated industrial reconversion more successfully, and has regained its lead over the Basque economy.

The greater success and creative stability of Catalan nationalism can be readily interpreted in terms of Catalonia's lead in modernization, and the fact that nationalism has been directed by elites concerned to advance such a process in a practical way. Most of a large middle class has been effectively mobilized during the twentieth century to support such policies, and Catalan nationalism has rarely been tempted by the negatively reactive policies of much of Basque nationalism, even though left progressive nationalism was momentarily led astray amid the convulsions of 1934–6.

The extremism of Basque nationalism, on the other hand, has presented something of a puzzle. The initial character of Arana Goiri's movement of the 1890s may be explained by reference to the trauma of nineteenth-century modernization in the Basque provinces, first in the great liberal-Carlist civil wars and later by the sudden spurt of new industrialization. The pathology of the last quarter of the twentieth century has been more difficult to understand. The two most common explanations refer to a) the repression exercised by the Franco regime; and b) the manifold traumas inflicted by 'late modernity' in the 1960s and 1970s, which involved hyperindustrialization and hyperurbanization, accompanied by the permanent loss of ancestral farmsteads, sudden secularization within a strongly Catholic society, and bewildering cultural change. It is often alleged that the most challenging aspect of late modernity was the largest immigration of Spaniards into the Basque Country in history, provoking a new Basque identity crisis.

There is some truth to both explanations, yet neither is fully adequate. Basque nationalism, and political expression generally, were certainly repressed by the Franco regime, yet the repression was at first no more severe than in Catalonia and in other parts of Spain. Indeed, the physical repression in terms of imprisonment and political executions seems to have been somewhat milder than in some other regions. Repression was in fact most severe in the strongholds of the left, which the Basque provinces proportionately were not. It was generally accepted by Franco's court-martials that Basque nationalists had not been involved in *delitos de sangre* (blood crimes), and thus the execution rate was low. After Spanish Nationalists conquered the province of Barcelona, more than 2 500 political executions took place.[11] The equivalent figure for Vizcaya may have been no more than 350, a figure which, even when adjusted for the lower population compared with Barcelona, was nonetheless much smaller.[12] Indeed by the 1950s and early 1960s nationalist resistance had become largely inactive in the Basque provinces, showing fewer signs of life than Catalanism. Obviously, the long life of the dictatorship eventually became a factor in mobilizing resistance, but that resistance only reached significant proportions long after the harshest repression had eased. Economically, the politics of the Franco regime at first clearly aided the Basque economy more than that of Catalonia, protecting and stimulating Basque heavy industry and helping the Basque provinces to achieve the highest per capita income in Spain. This situation was the very reverse of economic discrimination.

The effect of aspects of the 'crisis of late modernity' is equally or more convincing. Immigration into both regions of peripheral nationalism reached unprecedented rates in the 1950s and 1960s, amounting in the former decade to 174 per thousand in the Basque Country compared with 123 per thousand in Catalonia. Corresponding figures for the 1960s were 160 for the Basque provinces and 158 for Catalonia, in both cases falling significantly in the succeeding decade.[13] There is no question that, given the small geographic area of the two main Basque provinces of Vizcaya and Guipuzcoa, the broad expansion of industrialization and urbanization engulfed more of the remaining culturally semi-traditionalist countryside than was the case in Catalonia. Moreover, Catalan society was more sophisticated and secularized compared with that of the Basques, so that the profound religious and cultural changes of the 1960s had proportionately less impact. It is very difficult to measure the significance of psychological transfer from religion to holistic and millenarian secular politics in the Basque provinces during those years, but it seems to have played some role.[14]

The religious issue in fact cut both ways. If traditional religiosity grew weaker, its emotional commitment sometimes transferred to nationalism, and the latter was nonetheless still strongly supported by the Basque clergy, who during the late twentieth century have tended to make of it a kind of spiritual fetish verging on idolatry, accompanied by rather weak protests against its terrorist manifestations.[15]

A recent interpretation which sheds further light on the problem is the 'structural conduciveness' theory advanced Juan Díez Medrano.[16] This refers not so much to the social and economic structures of the two regions *per se* as to the structures of political mobilization and activity which developed during the reburgeoning of political activity in the last phase of the Franco regime. Díez Medrano emphasizes the range and diversity of Catalan nationalist political mobilization from that time on, involving very broad sectors of the middle classes, and thus producing a great diversity of movements and ideological expressions ranging from Catholic moderate conservatism to the extreme left. This broad mobilization eventually coalesced primarily around moderate leadership, and was of course facilitated by salient aspects of society and culture, such as the greater size of the Catalan middle classes, and their lesser economic dependence on big business and large banks than was the case in the Basque Country. Similarly, the common use of Catalan and the larger Catalan intelligentsia, bolstered by the strength of Catalan literature and culture and the presence of one of the most important universities in Spain, enhanced this situation. Consequently Catalanism could not be dominated by any small extremist sector. Under democracy, relative consensus has been achieved through the leadership of moderate middle-class Catalanism on the one hand and, to a lesser degree, of moderate working-class socialism on the other.

The situation in the Basque Country was more bleak. Basque big business and the socio-economic elite were more intensely interconnected with and dependent on the central Spanish economy and its government than was the case in Catalonia. The PNV, on the other hand, felt 'burnt' by its earlier relationship with revolutionary Republicanism. During World War II its leadership came to look to the United States for an ultimate resolution of European (and Spanish) problems. José Antonio de Aguirre took a firmly anti-communist and anti-left stance, and hoped to see the short-lived outbreak of leftist and nationalist militancy in the Basque Country in the years immediately following World War II followed up by strong American pressure. The Cold War realignment dashed such hopes, and by the 1950s the PNV, like most of the Spanish opposition, was left without a viable strategy. During the 1950s and early 1960s, Basque elite society was a bastion of conservatism, and nationalism appeared quiescent. As of 1960, every indication was that nationalism – and even separatism – was weaker in the Basque Country than in Catalonia.

In this climate of weakness, demobilization and perceived *entreguismo*, ETA was born in the 1960s. It was heavily influenced by the general mood of political radicalization in the western world during that decade, and especially by the national liberation struggles, real or imagined, in Cuba, Algeria and various Third World countries. These provided an ideology of Marxism-Leninism combined with revolutionary nationalism and terrorism which ETA sought to apply to Basque-Spanish relations. By the end of the decade ETA appeared to be the only effective champion of Basque interests, especially when compared with its semi-quiescent parent movement, the PNV. It is generally agreed that the enormous publicity which attended the 'Burgos trial' of 1970, combined with the intermittent waves of repression which assailed the Basque Country because of ETA between 1968 and 1975, greatly enhanced the organization's image and gave it prestige among pronationalist Basques. After the death of Franco this dialectical relationship intensified. The nationalist minority grew into a plurality and then at last a bare majority for the first time, while the influence and prestige of the right-wing pro-Basque bourgeois elite declined precipitously. The entire political debate in the Basque Country was radicalized. Under democracy, the moderate sector of the PNV did regain a position of some hegemony by 1980, but the PNV was itself less moderate than a generation earlier and for nearly a decade seemed to want to take advantage of the pressure generated by terrorist nationalism. In 1986 the PNV split yet again, the somewhat more radical, more pro-separatist sector forming a smaller second party, *Eusko Alkartasuna*. Though only about 13 per cent of the electorate voted for *Herri Batasuna*, the political arm of ETA, this was ten times the support provided for the revolutionary Catalanist splinters of FAC, PSAN or *Terra Lliure* in Catalonia. Such support in Basque society fostered a strong infrastructure for the terrorist *comandos* through the mid-1990s. Thus Díez Medrano's theory of 'structural conduciveness' does assist in providing an explanation for the degree and persistence of violent, revolutionary nationalism, in terms of winning prestige and sympathy, and through processes of secondary socialization building an infrastructure of support that would endure for an entire generation.

Though support for direct separatism is comparatively limited even in the Basque Country, present conditions of autonomy and strong nationalist acculturation indicate even greater strength for peripheral nationalism in Spain in the future, and this is consistent with the salience of smaller group and regional identity in other parts of Europe. In the Basque case, this process has rested on unique and particularist historical institutions, the persistence of semi-traditional religion and culture, and economic 'overdevelopment'. Díez Medrano argues that the latter is particularly influential, and even radicalizing, because of the Basque specialization in capital goods, as contrasted with consumer goods, which heightened economic concentration, dependency on the Spanish state, and intra-regional social and economic division.

The radicalization of Basque nationalism can be explained not so much by Spanish oppression (though that existed, and paradoxically was comparatively more extreme, or perceived as more extreme, during the later 'liberal' period of Francoism), as by the persistence of an older anticapitalist political culture whose youthful militants experienced the full effects of the crisis of late modernity as outlined above. Díez Medrano is also correct in emphasizing that political and other conditions in the Basque Country were structurally much more conducive to enhancing support for radicalization, compared with those in Catalonia.

Comparative analysis has been further enriched by the more recent study of Daniele Conversi, who accepts the structuralist and socio-economic interpretations of Díez Medrano but adds to them in important ways. Conversi emphasizes the role of language, culture and ethno-symbolic functions of nationalism (as originally defined by his mentor, Anthony D. Smith), stressing the importance of language as a major unifying factor in Catalonia, as contrasted with the absence of any core agreement over the use of language and other cultural or ideological values in the Basque movement. Thus he has achieved the fullest and most complete analysis of the differences between these two peripheral nationalisms.[17]

Conversi synthesizes the sources of these differences in terms of six explanations dealing with basic elements of culture, economics, class, history, politics, and anthropology. The anthropological and cultural or 'popular' explanations refer to specific differences in local culture and language and more broadly in distinct historical cultures or 'national characters.' The economic and class explanations parallel those of Díez Medrano, concerning the differences in economic structure and the diverse roles and attitudes of the leading sectors. The chief historical-institutional difference has to do with the complete historical absence of any Basque state, while Conversi's chief political explanation lies in the greater repressiveness of the Francoist state in the Basque Country in its final years. The latter argument is, of course, somewhat circular, since the reason that the Spanish dictatorship wielded a heavier hand in the Basque provinces was simply because more political and social opposition was expressed there and more vigorously.

Conclusion

The Catalan and Basque movements have for some time clearly been the strongest stateless movements of peripheral nationalism in western Europe, yet the differences between the two movements are profound. Though both look toward the broadening of a 'post-modern' confederal inter-relationship between the major regions of western Europe to the detriment of the authority of the classic modern states, Catalan nationalism is politically better adjusted to cope with either this or a more limited outcome. Basque nationalism remains more divided, and in part still wedded to violence. Profound historical, cultural and structural differences between these two regions can account for the deep asymmetry of the two movements. Basque extremism still poses a major problem for the Spanish state and, despite the general success of democratization and decentralization in Spain, the two major peripheral nationalisms still constitute by far the most serious challenge to the country's political system.

Notes

1   See particularly J. Fernández Sebastián, *La génesis del fuerismo: Prensa e ideas políticas en la crisis del Antiguo Régimen* (País Vasco. 1750–1840), (Madrid, 1991).

2   The literature on nineteenth-century liberal nationalism in Spain is growing. See *Nationalism and the Nation in the Iberian Peninsula*, C. Mar-Molinero and A. Smith (eds) (Oxford-Washington DC, 1996), especially J. Alvarez Junco, 'The Nation-Building Process in Nineteenth-Century Spain,' pp. 89–106; I. Fox, *La invención de España* (Madrid, 1997); C. Boyd, *Historia Patria* (Princeton, 1997); 'Nations: Nationalismes et Questions Nationales,' *Ibérica*, 4 (1994); 'Estudios sobre nacionalismo español contemporáneo,' *Studia Historica*, 12 (1994); and various studies in *Nationalism in Europe Past and Present*, J.B. Beramendí, R. Maíz and X.M. Núñez (eds) (Santiago de Compostela, 1994), 2 vols.

3   Alfonso Bullón de Mendoza, *La primera guerra carlista* (Madrid, 1992); José Extramiana, *Historia de las guerras carlistas* (San Sebastian, 1980); and Vicente Garmendia, *La ideología carlista* (1868–1876) (Zarautz, 1984).

4 Manuel Montero, *La construcción del País Vasco contemporáneo* (San Sebastian, 1993), presents the best recent analytical synthesis of these developments in the nineteenth century.
5 See Jon Juaristi, *El linaje de Aitor: La invención de la tradicion vasca* (Madrid, 1987), and J.M. Sánches-Prieto, *El imaginario vasco: Representaciones de una conciencia históica, nacional y política en el escenario europeo 1833–1876* (Barcelona, 1993).
6 The best brief survey is Albert Balcells, *El nacionalismo catalán* (Madrid, 1991), which includes a full bibliography.
7 The equivalent work for Basque nationalism is F. García de Cortázar and J.M. Azcona, *El nacionalismo vasco* (Madrid, 1991).
8 F. de Meer, *El Partido Nacionalista Vasco ante la guerra de España (1936–1937)* (Pamplon, 1992).
9 The chief political biography is J. Antich, *El Virrey* (Barcelona, 1994).
10 The most penetrating analysis of the division of opinion in the Basque Country is J.J. Linz, *Conflicto en Euskadi* (Madrid, 1986).
11 J.M. Solé i Sabaté, *La repressió franquista a Catalunya, 1938–1953* (Barcelona, 1985).
12 Here I follow the data of R. Salas Larrazabal, *Perdidas de la guerra* (Barcelona, 1977), pp. 286–90. Cf. the more general remarks of A. de Blas Guerrero, *Sobre el nacionalismo español* (Madrid, 1989), pp. 95–114.
13 These data are drawn from Table 10, Chapter 7 of J. Díez Medrano, *Divided Nations: Class, Politics, and Nationalism in the Basque Country and Catalonia* (Ithaca, 1995).
14 Here see the discussion in P. Waldmann, *Militanter Nationalismus in Baskenland* (Frankfurt, 1990), pp. 61–139.
15 Concerning 'idolatry' among the Basque clergy, see the scathing remarks by the Jesuit historian García de Cortázar and by Azcona in their *Nacionalismo vasco* pp. 161–6, and also in García de Cortázar and J.P. Fusi, *Política, identidad e iglesia en el País Vasco* (San Sebastian, 1988).
16 In the work cited above in footnote 13.
17 Daniele Conversi, *The Basques, the Catalans and Spain. Alternative Routes to Nationalist Mobilisation* (London, 1997).

6
Ethnicity, Multiculturalism and Society in Germany

Moshe Zuckermann

Fundamentally different from the civic orientation underlying the development of French national identity in modern times, German nation building relied rather on ethnically oriented modes of self-determination. It seems that the values of *Volk* had a more profound impact on the crystallization of German political culture than the normative institutions of (bourgeois) civil society. The catastrophic results of this evolution in the twentieth century led, during the 1960s, to a radical change in the German socio-political discourse: against the background of an ever-growing immigration of foreign workers (*Gastarbeiter*) into post-war West Germany, and the revolt of the student movement, emphatically questioning the hitherto prevailing values of the German society and the views of the older generation (a revolt that had its dominating share in democratizing the German public sphere), a different dimension of ethnicity – resulting in various *life-worlds* and an expanding multiculturalism – began to 'reshape' the structure and texture of German society. Nevertheless, it seems that the potential socio-political success of this new development still depends to a large extent on the stability of the German economy.

The development of the German concept of the 'national' relied, from its early beginnings in the late eighteenth century and the first decades of the nineteenth century, on a major ethnic component of far-reaching implications: the concept of folk (*Volk*). The latter, which served initially to denote a social reality, and even contained, up to a certain point in time – at least, as far as Enlightenment thinkers like Johann Gottfried Herder are concerned – a certain cosmopolitan element, was soon abandoned in favor of a basically irrational and chauvinistic

108

notion, essentially reactionary, though perfectly anti-feudalistic and anti-absolutistic in its intents.[1] This pattern, the vague association between 'bourgeois-progressive' and 'restaurative' tendencies, typical of the first two decades of nineteenth century Germany, and – to a lesser degree – even of the Vormärz-period, corresponded very well with the 'real social conditions' in Germany, where no self-aware bourgeois class with firm social-economic interests and corresponding political convictions had yet emerged. Thus, as Wolfgang Emmerich has put it, the fact that not the democratic tendency (weak as it may have been in any case), but the 'restaurative-chauvinistic' notion of the national movement established itself as the 'predominant ideology', had to do with a basic pattern prevailing among leading figures of the national movement – people like Adam von Müller, Görres, Arndt, or Jahn – who, in patriotically opposing French imperial politics, were at the same time fighting against 'the land of the bourgeois revolution, of modern civilization, and of capitalism'. They intended to restore the 'class harmony of the corporative state', in which the capitalistic mode of production could be perceived as nothing more than a 'disturbing factor in social life'. From then on, Emmerich claims, national differences were not explained by the 'materialistic history of the peoples, but by elements belonging to the super-structure, like poetry, or – even more irrational – by the concept of "Volkscharakter" ("the personality of the people"), which, since Ludwig Friedrich Jahn, has been promoted to *Volkstum*'[2] – an even more obscure conception, that may be translated as 'national character'.

In his major work, *Prelude to Nation-States*, which deals with the French and German experience between 1789 and 1815 as a kind of historic paradigm of the two major competing manifestations of national development in Europe, Hans Kohn pointed to the immediate implications of transforming the universalistic Enlightenment ideals of the national to the concept of a folk-oriented nation. His exemplary reference is to Heinrich Luden, a famous professor of history at the University of Jena, who, since 1806, 'no longer stressed the community of Europe or of mankind, but the diversity and peculiarity of each nation, regarding the division into nations as a beneficial and eternal work of nature'. He taught that all manifestations of culture and life 'are invested in each people with a unique character which belongs only to this people'. Thus, not only did he praise the competitive struggle among nations – 'the fierce and ambitious battle for survival and domination' – as an 'iron law of nature', but this conviction led him to subscribe to a nationalism 'skeptical about the rights of man and lukewarm over parliamentary liberties'. Luden maintained that 'only a state built upon the ethnic principle can be a true fatherland, that state and nation must coincide'. He accepted from Jahn and Fichte the emphasis on folk, on purity of language and descent, and 'the faith that the Germans were purer in race and more original in their language than other people, especially the French, and therefore superior to them'. But, as Kohn explicitly points out, more important was his insistence, not yet shared by Fichte, that 'political and ethnic frontiers must coincide, and that only a fatherland which united the whole nationality could provide a truly human life, culture, and happiness. Where folk and state were not identical, where a state included various nationalities or language groups, there, Luden was convinced, only misery, half-heartedness, and split personalities – "Halbheit, Zerrissenheit, Unlust und Jammer" – could exist'.[3] It is not without reason that Wolfgang Emmerich maintains that 'the idiosyncrasy against anything out-landish, against being swamped by foreign influences, which is charac-teristic for the later chauvinism', is already to be found in these kind of early nationalistic attitudes.[4]

The overlapping of ethnical authenticity and cultural originality thus became a major ideological device of German nationalism. The socio-genetic sources of this peculiar notion were indicated by Norbert Elias. He convincingly showed how, in the second half of the eighteenth century, the concept of 'culture' (*Kultur*) gradually became a kind of political slogan, by which the German bourgeois class – a social stratum almost completely excluded from the realm of politics, and paradigmatically represented here by its frustrated intelligentsia – distinguished itself from German aristocracy, on one hand, and from the French nation, on the other: 'culture' (*Kultur*), the sphere of practice of intellectuals and artists, was emphatically monopolized against both – the good-for-nothing superficiality of the aristocracy, which is not able to 'produce', let alone 'achieve', anything, as well as the revolutionary agitation, the socio-political practice, and the corresponding spiritual production of the French bourgeois elite, the results of which can be apprehended as nothing more than the contemptible fruits of a shallow 'civilization' (*Zivilisation*), differing essentially from the depth of works produced by them, the true protagonists of the German 'nation of culture' (*Kulturnation*).[5]

These ideological patterns should be kept in mind in view of the later developments of German history, especially in face of their cat-astrophic culmination in the events of the twentieth century. The so-called 'German Sonderweg' – the anti-revolutionary, and in many ways authoritarian path of what has been referred to by Helmuth Plessner as 'the belated nation' (*die verspätete Nation*[6]) – confirms *a posteriori* the potential dangers inherent in the peculiar constellation of the apolitical cultural inwardness and the non-emancipatory struggle for ethnical unity that determined the evolution of German political culture for many decades. Nevertheless, this somewhat finalistic point of view does not adhere to a rigid deterministic notion, according to which any historical outcome, in any historical phase, was *inevitably* (and one-dimensionally) programmed by the antecedent conditions of previous phases. Yet, there is good reason for the question whether Hitler's ideological concept of *Volksgemeinschaft* did not find ground prepared in the all-too-well established elements of the ethnically, or even race-oriented *völkische Weltanschauung* (folkish view of the world), as well as in the essentially anti-modernistic and anti-civilisatoric notion of *Gemeinschaft*, as opposed to the (admittedly threatening in its own way) concept of modern *Gesellschaft* – the so-called 'civil society'. The ideological (in other words consciousness-blinding) dimension of this act of adaptation strikes one even more, as the highly indus-trialized and bureaucratized German society in the period of National Socialism was nothing less than a corporative *Gemeinschaft* in any traditional sense; it has even been argued that it is, paradoxi-cally, exactly this totalitarian period in Germany's contemporary history that has 'pushed' German society, once and for all, into modernity.

Anyway, these catastrophic results of Germany's unique socio-political development since the times of the French Revolution, gave way, after the Second World War, to an extensive debate and major rethinking of the *Sonderweg*, especially of the ideological peculiarities of German political culture, as being a significant part of it. To be more exact, and taking into account the prevailing restorative climate of the Adenauer era in the 1950s, one may argue that the real turning-point in this respect did not actually occur until the late 1960s. It is rather symptomatic of this that in 1968, some 54 per cent of the West German public still maintained that no criticism of one's fatherland, expressed by foreigners, should be tolerated; yet, only 7 per cent of the students held this opinion.[7] Both data are significant: the first in its revelation of the idiosyncrasy, which still saturated the German public discourse and general self-awareness; the second for the rising critical approach to be found within some parts of the younger generation. Indeed, as Wolfgang Mommsen has put it,

> the so-called "student revolution" in the late sixties was, at least in its beginnings, determined by a rebellion of the younger generation against the short-winded pragmatism, which was revealed, in the sixties, by all dominating strata of west-German society, without exception. The students' protest was directed – though in an extremely vague and confused way – against the inability of the older generation to confront society with moral aims, and against its silence about its own involvement in the events of the younger German past.[8]

The general mental predisposition of most members of the student movement may best be described by the words of the philosopher Peter Sloterdijk, who said, reflecting upon himself in 1989, that 'to be born so close to the horror, meant – if not for the whole generation, at least for those who are about forty today – to have been brought into a world, in which people have not yet learned to be responsible for themselves and for each other.'[9]

Still, notwithstanding the psychological matrix and moral aspects of the students' revolt, one should point out the immense impact it had on the German political culture in the long run – confused and agitated as this revolt may have been at times. In fact, I would go so far as to maintain that it was the students' rebellion (in connection with other, mostly cultural, activities of the leftist intelligentsia) which actually politicized the German public sphere in the post-war era, imbuing it with democratic impulses – an achievement that cannot be overestimated in view of the traditional German public realm, which had been known for its authoritarian structure and essentially a-political patterns.

This turned out to be all the more important, as the Federal Republic became – very soon after its constitution, and even more so as a result of the so-called 'German economic miracle' (*deutsches Wirtschaftswunder*) – a land of extensive immigration. What have been described euphemistically as *Gastarbeiter* ('guest workers'), were nothing less than the relatively cheap labor force imported from abroad, being a much needed component in the development of the emerging German economy at this time. Hence, the persisting wave of ever more immigrating foreigners – Italians, Spaniards, Yugoslavs and Turks, to name just the biggest groups – became a major factor in ethnifying German society; as a matter of fact, it gave ethnicity in Germany a whole new dimension. By saying so, I do not claim that the ethnic factor – meaning the establishment of *foreign* communities – was wholly new to the German society. The beginning of Germany's gradual ethnific-ation dates from the last decades of the nineteenth century, a process which was interrupted only by the catastrophic measures undertaken by the National Socialist regime. New in the 1960s, however, was a unique constellation of factors: the objective economic need for a foreign labor force; a sort of 'new (democratic) page' in the political culture of the land; and the actual mass arrival of large ethnic groups and their establishment in society.

As for the economic necessity: it may suffice to mention that, a few years ago, one of Germany's most prominent politicians (Heiner Geißler) still had to declare that 'we need the foreigners ... in order to secure Germany's future'. The political scientist Claus Leggewie has commented on this statement by rightly maintaining that 'sublimi-nally, the sober calculation of cost and profit has long ago turned to be an existential question', as 'the economic rationality of the import of labour force shows an eventually demographic clue': the immigrants are 'a kind of "supply of fresh blood" for the west-German welfare state, which suffers, more than any other, from a natal deficit'.[10] As for the so-called 'new page' opened in Germany's political culture: it would be naive to assume that it cancelled – at once! – the long-lasting impact of previous political traditions; however, it cannot be denied that this very confrontation, despite the occasional minor setbacks, opened the way for the liberal establishment of a steadily growing democratic political culture. And as for the ethnification of society itself, there can be no doubt that – as was presented above – it con-cerned one of the sorest points in German socio-political history. Exactly because of the notorious ethnic component, embedded in the old folkish idea of the nation-state, it could not at all be taken for granted that the German society would be able to absorb foreign ethni-cal populations. Looked upon from this point of view, the fact that 'after the war, both German states had their extreme difficulties in han-dling immigration',[11] as Leggewie claims, had its deep historic, cultural roots.

Yet, as the ever-growing immigration actually took place, it was, from a certain point in time, not any more a question of *if*, but rather a problem of *how* to handle the changing of society, the evolving multi-tude of cultural practices and real diversity of the ethnic life-worlds. This new reality may be perceived as a *general* 'challenge to the ability

for evolution', issued to *all* late-capitalist societies, the ethnical plural-
ization of which is indeed striking (though not entirely new, of
course).[12] On the conceptual level, this gave the main impulse for
developing the 'fascinating idea' of multiculturalism, an ideal
described by Leggewie as follows:

> A society, which incorporates foreigners, without violating them by
> monopolization, into a political community, that is capable of han-
> dling social conflicts, resulting from the plurality of the ways-of-life,
> in peaceful-civil forms, without demolishing, by the very practice of
> the intervention, the total difference and obstinacy [of the foreign-
> ers]. This means, then, integration without brutally uniforming the
> citizens (as in the individualistic conception of human rights in the
> French Revolution), and autonomy without ignorant relativism on
> the side of those determining themselves (as in the contradicting
> model of the horizontal ethnic-groups-Apartheid).[13]

This concept – a combination of the modern idea of the socially generated emancipation of the individual, and the postmodern criticism of
the formal, or essentially abstract, emancipation of the citizen, being
the 'true' result of modernistic development – has, of course, its theoretical merits. But, as Leggewie himself realistically points out, 'within
the existing immigration societies, such a program comes close to the
achievement of the impossible'.[14] Thus, his emphatic plea for a contemporary German society, which is not based on a 'community of
blood and fate [*Bluts-und Schicksalsgemeinschaft*]' any more, but on 'a
"Kulturnation" [nation of culture] in the postmodern sense',[15] can be
interpreted at best as some sort of regulative idea; but it still is – despite
all good intentions – ideological in essence. This is clearly revealed,
when Leggewie maintains that 'anti-racism must become an habitual
matter of course, a civilizatoric gesture *comme il faut* – in the offices, in
the subways, and in the discos of the countryside', and he adds his
comment that 'only then injustice, effected by immigration, and social
conflicts evolving from it can be moderated, though never completely
eradicated'.[16]

The ideological dimension of this general line of argument has been
stressed lately by Berndt Ostendorf, who, in referring to the situation in
the USA, claimed that 'ethnicity, being a crucial category of political difference, has suppressed the perception of class differences'.[17] Ostendorf
expresses the view that 'the discourse world of the intellectuals and
ethnic lobbies, dealing with the politics of difference, has become "ide-

ological" (in the classical sense)', that it is 'parochial', and has indeed 'only little to do with the political reality'.[18] He asserts that the deconstruction of the so-called 'Dead White Males' has 'multiculturally opened the definition of universalism', but the consumption of this highly cultural political world still remains determined by class. Moreover, he maintains that there is a real dichotomy between the protagonists of this ethnical discourse: 'an academically trained middle class, which is able to afford principles', as opposed to 'an illiterate low class, that cannot even guarantee its own survival'. Hence, Ostendorf argues that, in view of the catastrophic prospects of this social abyss, it is, at least at the moment, much more important 'to start with the economic differences between poor and rich', a task that, in his opinion, cannot be approached through the prevailing chauvinistic propaganda of ethno-nationalistic self-determination, that is by ethnically narrowing the scope of the issue, but only within a big 'multicultural, maybe even transnational coalition'.[19]

This is, of course, not exactly the situation in Germany. But in view of the new economic discrepancy between Germans in east and west, effected by the political unification of the two German states; in view of the prevailing resentment between '*Wessis*' and '*Ossis*', as they significantly call each other; in view of the brutal atrocities performed by organized extremist right-wing youth gangs against foreigners and *Gastarbeiter*; and in view of the mere fact that Germany has become one of the most attractive immigration countries within the new big 'migration of peoples' of the Third and Second worlds into the rich First – one should be at least cautious about idealizing this complex socio-economic reality by simply evoking its exotic multiculturalism. Without the proper economic infrastructure, ethnical multitude can easily become a multicultural hell.

Ethnicity is a *particularistic*, essentially pre-modern mode of orientation towards society, aiming at the essential detachment from foreign collectivities, on one hand, and at the actual segregation of varying groups within the same collectivity – though denounced as 'artificial' – on the other. Multiculturalism is a *pluralistic*, essentially modern (or, if you will, postmodern) way of thinking about the shape and texture of current social collectivities. Both ethnicity as well as multiculturalism, which prevail in economically developed societies based on the capitalistic mode of production, are *identity*-oriented. Given the fact that they strive for autonomy (in the case of ethnicity) or equality (in the case of multiculturalism), it is the very inner logic of capitalism, resulting in inevitable structural dependencies and socio-economic inequalities, that may objectively turn the emancipatory notion of ethnical self-determination within multicultural, democratic modern societies into an ideology in the classical sense: a false consciousness about the *real* social mechanisms of segregation, inequality, resentment and forced 'identity'.

Notes

1 Wolfgang Emmerich, *Zur Kritik der Volkstumsideologie* (Frankfurt/M, 1971), p. 48.
2 Ibid., p. 46.
3 Hans Kohn, *Prelude to Nation-States* (New Jersey Toronto London Melbourne, 1967), pp. 226f.
4 Emmerich, (cf. Note 1), p. 43.
5 Norbert Elias, *Über den Zivilisationsproze?* (Frankfurt/M, 1976), pp. 1–50.
6 Helmuth Plessner, *Die verspätete Nation* (Frankfurt/M, 1974).
7 Martin und Sylvia Greiffenhagen, *Ein schwieriges Vaterland* (Frankfurt/M, 1981), p. 298.
8 Wolfgang J. Mommsen, 'Eine "deutschere" Geschichte', in Heidi Bohnet-von der Thisen (ed.), *Denkanstöße '92* (München – Zurich, 1991), p. 109.
9 Peter Sloterdijk, *Versprechen auf Deutsch* (Frankfurt/M, 1990), p. 17.
10 Claus Leggewie, 'Deutschland in den United Colors of Benetton', in Arthur Heinrich & Klaus Neumann (eds), *Alles Banane. Ausblick auf das endgültige Deutschland* (Köln, 1990), pp. 89f.
11 Ibid., p. 96.
12 Ibid., p. 93.
13 Ibid., p. 95
14 Ibid.
15 Ibid., p. 96.
16 Ibid., p. 101.
17 Berndt Ostendorf, 'Der Preis des Multikulturalismus', *Perspektiven*, 23, (1995), p. 5.
18 Ibid., p. 1.
19 Ibid., p. 5.

7

The New Right and the Intellectual Elaboration of Ethnic Europe: from Racism to the Politics of Differentialism

Alberto Spektorowski

Introduction

The controversy over the demands of Islamic schoolgirls in France to don veils in public schools evolved from a local debate concerning the propriety of displaying cultural distinctions in public into a larger, theoretical issue focusing on the principle of tolerance in liberal society.[1] On the one hand, France's particular tradition of national republicanism and its integrationist notions of citizenship could hardly be defined as liberal. On the other hand, liberalism itself is ambiguous on the question of ethnic demands in the public sphere. In fact, the liberal tradition rests on a secular concept of citizenship and a clear division between the public and private spheres.[2] Several theories of radical democratism have tried to demonstrate the incompetence of liberal democracy to deal with ethnic demands.[3]

However, the issue I undertake to examine here deals with the question of ethnicity and citizenship from a rather unexpected perspective. This is through the 'differentialist' approach, advanced by one of the most sophisticated right-wing anti-liberal movements in Europe, the French New Right. This perspective, as I shall try to prove, challenges not only liberal and republican theories of citizenship, but also shifts the political discourse of right-wing racism from ethnophobia to ethnophilia, whose results, as I will try to address in this chapter, are actually the same. At first glance, the suggestion of a communion between radical right ideologies and movements usually associated with political violence, narrow nationalism and racism, with pluralism and the rights of ethnic groups seems implausible, even ridiculous. Nonetheless, the idea of challenging the concept of a liberal republican tradition of citizenship by means of a pluralist, anti-liberal view of '*la*

117

difference' appears to be one of the most distinctive innovations ema-
nating from a group of neo-fascist intellectuals commonly recognized
as the European New Right.[4] Although representing a whole European
intellectual movement, the New Right is basically a French movement
concentrated in research institutes such as GRECE (*Groupement de
Recherche et d'Etude pour la Civilization Européen*), or linked to cultural
journals like *Nouvelle Ecole* (founded in 1968), *Elements*, and *Krisis*.
GRECE was the logical alternative for young French nationalist militants after the dissolution of the *Jeune Nation* movement in 1958, the
disbanding of the OAS, and the defeat of the *Rassemblement Européen de
la Liberté* (REL) in the 1967 legislative elections. This latest group continued the ideological line of the *Movement Nationaliste du Progres*
(MNP), the political expression of the nationalist intellectuals working
for the journal *Europe Action* and of the students' organization FEN.
Both the MNP and *Europe Action* reached the conclusion that, in order
to have a discernible influence, the extreme right would have to
abandon the violence, infighting and sterile doctrinal quarrels that had
characterized the extreme right in the 1940s and 1950s. Differently
from other right-wing movements world wide, the New Right focused
on a 'meta-political' struggle and its members defined themselves as
'Gramscians of the Right'. Its basic concern was to gain re-legitimiza-
tion and adapt a right-wing ideological and intellectual tradition to
modern times, in order to provide intellectual ammunition to right-
wing political movements of regionalist or nationalist character.
However, in contrast to the discredited old racial and chauvinist thesis
of the old radical right the New Right provides a new theory of 'cultural differentialism', which paradoxically appears, at first sight, to fit
contrasting interests: those of radical rightists' demanding a Europe
'free of immigrants'; as well as a theory of cultural emancipation for
Third World countries.

In this chapter, then, I shall deal with a new type of radical right-
wing ideology which, in contrast to 'old right wing views' on racial
supremacy, relates the idea of racism precisely to the liberal republican
tradition and its integrationist zeal. Indeed, the social-Darwinist
counter-revolutionary tradition of the past became the theoretical basis
for a new theory of cultural and ethnic emancipation which accordingly permits European, as well as non-Western cultural identities, to
free themselves from the cultural imperialism of liberalism. However,
as noted, the New Right's advocacy of the right to '*la difference*' does
not support the coexistence of distinct ethnic communities under the
same roof. In other words, the New Right call for 'other cultures' ethnic

pride, does not imply, in the long run, a multicultural society, but rather the opposite, namely a multicultural world in which each culture develops its own moral code, and its own political framework. Therefore, by upholding the right of ethnic cultures to maintain distinct identities, the New Right reinforces European culture's right to preserve its own ethnic purity. Furthermore, by upholding the right of other cultures to abandon liberalism and the morality of universal rights, the New Right supports Europe's own search for political authenticity, which also implies the abandonment of foreign 'Judeo-Christian' democratic egalitarianism and liberalism. In other words, Europe should hark back to its prehumanist roots, abolishing all political models of statehood and citizenship that would allow for the reception and integration of immigrants. The Europe envisaged by the New Right is an ethnically pure national-socialist entity exercising world dominance. In contrast to previous models, however, this new national-socialist order would be achieved without war and bitter repression, on a legitimate basis of mutual respect rooted in moral and cultural relativism.

Therefore, the main aim of this paper is to present, from a theoretical perspective, the past and present development of the counter-revolutionary traditional opposition to French republicanism, and through it to analyze the new critiques of the idea of democratic citizenship and immigrant integration in the European community.

Citizenship, ethnocentrism, and the republican tradition

Tzvetan Todorov stresses the impossibility of distinguishing between ethnocentric and non-ethnocentric universalism. The former consists in the unwarranted establishment of the specific values of one's own society as universal values – a caricature of universality. The latter seeks a rational basis for preferring certain values to others.[5] This spirit was preserved in the ideals of French nationalism and citizenship that were introduced by the French Revolution. Since then, national consciousness and the enlightened humanist tradition have been more or less conflated into a single category.

The principles invoked by the 1789 French Declaration of the Rights of Man and of the Citizen are the heart of the French view of citizenship as simultaneously universalistic, integrative, and particularistic. Historically, however, the French resolution of the national question goes back to the republican synthesis, whose central tenets are an austere secular morality to replace that of the church, an active citizenry educated in public schools, a highly centralized, majoritarian government, and a homogeneous culture achieved through both national education and a slow war of attrition against signs of diversity.[6] In the words of Ernst Renan, the French

> traditionally thought as a universal nation ... .[T]he French nation-state is constructed according to a certain number of principles ...of which one of the primary ones is that forgetting the diversity of [one's] origins is a requisite in order to belong to a 'homogeneous' national group.[7]

The French pursued this goal during the 1880s by making primary education (under Jules Ferry) free, compulsory, secular, and intensely nationalistic. The army, too, which had been reorganized on the basis of universal conscription, was conceived as the school of the nation.[8]

In both the domestic and colonial spheres, the Jacobean ideology was dominated by the ideal of assimilating immigrants and the colonized nations overseas into the French community. Several parliamentary debates at the end of the nineteenth century reflected the immense republican zeal exhibited by advocates of the naturalization and integration of immigrants in French society. In fact, these parliamentary debates were the first signs of the confrontation between the supporters of *jus solis* and the supporters of *jus sanguinis*.[9] Although the preference for *jus sanguinis* during the 1880s remained limited and superficial, it reflected the incipient ethnicization of self-image that would later be translated into a radical version of organic anti-liberal nationalism.

The philosophical values invoked by the supporters of *jus solis* served the goal of nationalizing immigrants. Legislation passed in 1889 gave enduring form to the rules governing the attribution of citizenship. This traditional assimiliationism informed the initial shaping of the citizenship law during the Revolutionary and Napoleonic periods; it informed the extension of *jus solis* to third-generation immigrants in 1851; it informed the liberal 1927 law of naturalization; and it informed the major post-war citizenship law reforms of 1945 and 1986–7. Subsequent major revisions of that law – in 1927, 1945, and 1973 – modified provisions concerning naturalization, the effect of marriage on citizenship, and the attribution of citizenship *jus sanguinis*, but did not affect the principle of *jus solis* for second-generation immigrants.[10]

The republicans also advocated granting France's colonial subjects the rights and duties of French citizenship. Accordingly, in 1848, after the abolition of slavery, the subjects of the colonies inherited from the *ancien regime* were made citizens. In 1946, the first Constituent Assembly of the Fourth Republic extended French citizenship to the residents of the more recently conquered territories (excluding the protectorates). Nonetheless, France's self-confidence in its civilizing mission hindered its ability to understand the values of different moral codes. Alien cultures were scorned, and seen as inferior peoples requiring civilization. A naval officer in Cochinchina noted that '[t]his generous nation, whose opinions rule civilized Europe, has a higher mission … the call to enlightenment and liberty of the races and peoples still the slaves of ignorance and despotism'.[11] Unlike their European rivals, the French believed they were achieving an industrial civilization without losing sight of basic spiritual and moral values.[12] This explains why even early rebellions against French rule were not understood as a demand for independence from France. Despite local independence uprisings in Tunisia, Morocco and Algeria which were suppressed with brutal force, De Gaulle's colonial humanism, discussed at the Brazzaville conference, conferred voting rights on Algerian Moslems, extended civil and political liberties, and introduced administrative and political decentralization. These reforms, assimilationist in spirit, were limited in impact by the government's clear insistence on continued French dominance.

It should be noted that, for the most part, the advocates and opponents of French colonial rights had the same principles. They shared a similar conceptual background, which filtered the colonial aspiration to emancipation through the heritage of French political and philosophical experience. Right-wing imperialists adjusted their imperialism to the French civilizing tradition, while liberal anticolonialists were not necessarily anti-imperialists.[13] They wanted to improve conditions in the colonies, and, in some cases, considered self-rule, because they were convinced that the colonies would yearn to remain under French cultural and economic influence.

The Algerian revolution was a turning point in French intellectual attitudes to the question of the colonies. The Algerian crisis helped left-wing intellectuals to understand the major socio-economic changes the country was undergoing in those years, and played a crucial role in easing the transition away from the previous attachment to France's universalistic projections.[14] Intellectuals from both the right and the left attempted to redefine France's position in the world in the light of new attitudes towards the colonies. Supporters of *Realpolitik*, such as Raymond Aron and Raymond Cartier, believed that France should free itself of Algeria. France's *'grandeur,'* according to Cartier, was obstructed by its special attachment to its colonial policies.

For left-wing radical intellectuals such as Sartre and Fanon, the French Revolution's universalistic message of popular sovereignty, filtered through the Marxist perspective, was at the heart of the attack on French colonial imperialism. As some critics pointed out, however, Sartre's Hegelian belief that history had only one meaning prevented him from attaching importance to the differentialist Islamic currents (by that time in the minority) of the Algerian revolution.[15] Via the theories of Levi Strauss – which had already been extensively documented and analyzed – left-wing ideologues began to be critical of the universal and ethnocentric values of western concepts of modernity.[16] Less well-known, however, is how New Right ideologues rehabilitated racist ideologies in order to criticize French national universal ethnocentrism. In other words, how was it possible to use the ideological roots of right-wing nationalism and aggressive national-socialist ideology as the basis for radical anti-imperialism? Moreover, what are the implications of this new approach for the elaboration of new ideas on European citizenship? What seems to be clear however, is that a proliferated intellectual tradition, associated with the right, provides an important ideological basis to current theories of cultural relativism and of resistance to the idea of republican citizenship and integration.

Moral relativism, ethnicity, and the intellectual rebellion against ethnocentric modernity

Old and new radical right-wing ideologies all use the concepts of race, ethnicity and nationalism for political goals. While the intellectual basis of liberal society, its universalism and rationalism, had to be demolished on account of their being the source of cultural decadence, the real forces of authenticity expressed through the images of the warrior and the worker, the organic nation or the ethnic group, should be rescued, because they are the basis for European cultural resurrection. All of them coincide with Carl Schmitt's belief that,

> [t]he concept of humanity is an especially useful ideological instrument of imperialist expansion, and in its ethical humanitarian form it is a specific vehicle of economic imperialism. Here one is reminded of a somewhat modified expression of Proudhon's: whoever invokes humanity wants to cheat. To confiscate the word humanity, to invoke and monopolize such a term ... denies the

enemy the quality of being human, declaring him to be an outlaw to humanity ...[17]

Under the influence of this 'anti-humanism', complemented by a social Darwinist content, the positivist creed began to shed its rationalist features: 'heredity' and 'environment' replaced conscious, logical choice as the main determinants of human action.[18] These conclusions would change the basic understanding of nationalism, transforming it from its liberal, humanitarian incarnation into an organic, aggressive one.

This transformation was made possible from the end of the nineteenth century by the advent of new scientific justification for old historical tenets, such as the unconscious birth of the nation and the romantic notion of the popular soul.[19] Thus, while up until the 1860s nationalist movements were viewed first as national-liberation movements expressing a universal message against tyranny, and second as vehicles of a particular ethnic character, during the last decades of the century the priorities changed. Indeed, during the Second Empire a mood of critical dissatisfaction with the 'French tradition' was articulated by Ernst Renan and H. Taine. In the aftermath of the military defeat by Germany, however, the ethnic aspect predominated. This intellectual development did not imply a purely racial approach. In fact, after the nineteenth century, the concept of race made a substantive transition from the physical to the cultural plane. Although the celebration of race determinism was not abandoned, its cultural realm was accentuated.[20] Writers like Ernest Renan, for example, attempted to neutralize the impact of social Darwinism. Nonetheless, although Renan believed in the future intermixing of cultures and in the triumph of humanity and universal reason, the basic association of environment and cultural development as a universal condition could hardly be discarded. The idea of cultural and scientific contingency limits the potential for improvement on the one hand, while cultural and moral relativism eliminate the necessity for improvement on the other.

Renan's legacy was radicalized by G. Le Bon, who dismissed the idea that 'non-advanced' peoples could be educated. In contrast to Enlightenment values, which assume that 'important social changes are to be wrought by legislative acts,' Le Bon argued that institutions were of extremely minor significance with respect to the evolution of civilization.[21]

Le Bon's indictment of unadvanced people could be interpreted as a basis for cultural and ethnic superiority. At the same time, however, it provided justification for the cultural pride of under-developed societies. Since different races or peoples could hardly think in the same ways, morals were relative. Le Bon believed that European education had no positive impact on non-European peoples, but actually corrupted them, since it destroyed what they had without putting anything in its place. Therefore, although education was used to spare a people these stages, all it actually did was to disturb the people's morals and intelligence, and to reduce 'it in the end to a level inferior to that it would have reached if it had been left to itself.'[22] This celebration of unschooled intelligence was accompanied by the conviction that a clear distinction existed between scientific truth and morality.

The correspondence between Gobineau and Tocqueville illustrates the theoretical implications of this debate. According to Gobineau, society might be amoral, but its knowledge is not; good stems from truth, and science provides an ethical code which everyone must obey.[23] Tocqueville, in contrast, noted the moral value of applying a scientific truth. 'What purpose does it serve to persuade people living ... under sub conditions that they can do "nothing to better themselves"?'[24] He could accept the proposition that human races were unequally endowed, but did not see that as a reason that they should not have the same rights.

As current critics of modernization would argue, a universal and egalitarian approach to human rights might be an unqualified effort to improve the conditions of groups subject to discrimination. Nevertheless, it is the only appropriate theoretical approach that will block the development of further discrimination. This point was clearly made by Tocqueville, when he predicted that Gobineau's ideas would be especially useful to Germany in the future: 'Your book is fated to return to France from abroad, especially from Germany. Alone in Europe the Germans possess the particular talent of becoming impassioned with what they take as abstract truths without considering their practical consequences'.[25] Tocqueville's prophecy did not foresee, however, that in France itself the principle of moral relativism would become a crucial concept for nationalist intellectuals.

In the Dreyfus affair, the principle of moral relativism had a decisive political applicability. Maurice Barres remarked: 'Never has the necessity of relativism been more strongly felt than in the Dreyfus affair, which is at bottom an orgy of "metaphysicians"'.[26] In other words, if there was any such thing as a universal concept of justice, then Dreyfus was innocent. If what mattered was France, however, then Dreyfus' innocence was irrelevant. Whatever the absolute truth of the matter,

French justice required that Dreyfus be condemned. On one hand, the national good and the collectivity, which had a clear priority over the individual, could not be challenged by universal values. On the other hand, Barres found more excuses for Dreyfus than a universalist would. In fact, according to Barres, Dreyfus could not be tried by French justice, because he himself acted according to the dictates of his race. Dreyfus could not become a true Frenchman because the individual cannot define his or her affiliation with a collective identity. For Barres, the living reflection of the general interest must be *'relier à notre terre et à nos morts ...'*.[27]

In other words, the real homeland differs from the legal. Dreyfus's legal homeland was France, by virtue of his French citizenship. However, his real, authentic feelings were determined by his true essence: that of a Jew, who cannot feel the land and the 'real' nature of France which is beyond human rational comprehension. Using the same criteria, Barres attacked those *'miserables qui veulent enseigner aux enfants la vérité absolute'*, because those children must learn *'la vérité française·'*.[28]

Maurice Barres' individualistic romanticism, his violent anti-rationalism and his cult of unconsciousness, completed his conception of man as defined by the collectivity. His irrational romanticism gave his nationalist zeal its aggressive side, while the collective and Darwinist determinism provided its scientific immutability. Both these aspects together were the basis of Barres's *'socialisme nationale'*, which some analysts have argued is the heart of fascist ideology.[29] Nowadays, however, Barres's relativism can be viewed from a different perspective. His anti-humanism in fact provides a strong theoretical argument for relativistic tolerance. As he himself wrote, 'if we were disinterested minds, instead of judging Dreyfus according to French morality and according to our justice, like a peer, we would recognize him as a representative of a different species.'[30]

Barres' importance, however, lies in the fact that he did not limit himself to criticizing bourgeois republicanism's lack of patriotism and flexibility. The Jacobinist tradition, as we have seen, represented the highest appeal to patriotism. Barres's idea of the nation, however, reflected a much deeper criticism of liberal society and rationalist philosophy. In his view, a society based on contract could not work and could not defend itself. No education, however good, could transform foreigners into French citizens. Although the nationalist and xenophobic tendencies of republican nationalism during the 1880s promoted the nationalization of the masses through school and the army, Barres believed that the basis of citizenship and national belonging could never depend on integrationist politics and educational policies. Like Michelet and Renan, Barres acknowledged that races no longer existed, but, unlike his predecessors, he saw this as cause for regret. For him, ethnic nationalism was a symbol of the decline of liberal society. At the same time, and more importantly, the moral relativism implied in the politics of ethnicity offered a new concept of emancipation for Europe, as well as for other cultures which had been co-opted and conquered by Western universal values.

The new Europeanist right and the self-emancipation of Europe

One of the most stunning achievements of the New Right is the transmutation of an ideology of radical nationalism and imperialism into an ideology of 'anti-imperialist' differentialism. In contrast to left-wing anti-imperialism, which is based on a universal conception of proletarian and human redemption, the New Right's anti-imperialism is an extension of its criticism of all ideologies of progress.

During the Cold War, the New Right called for an alliance between Europe and the Third World.

> Around 1905, the Third World turned towards Japan. Around 1930, it turned towards Germany ... . Today it is left with the possibility of turning towards Europe, which, itself seeking a third way, is the potential ally of all the countries in the world which seek to escape the ascendancy of the superpowers.[31]

The central thesis is based on the conviction that the process of decolonization is still in progress. Only with the end of 'moralism and universalism' can the Third World rest on a realistic foundation.[32] An example of total decolonization was the Iranian Moslem revolution, which was actually a cultural revolution that emancipated the Iranian people from the political conceptualizations of the West. According to the New Right, that revolution was not a clash between the totalitarian model of Islam, on one hand, and the totalitarian model of the West, on the other, but reflected a people's quest for cultural identity in the face of the totalitarianism of the West. The integralist Islam found a 'new vitality, a new dynamism, thanks to the fundamentalist mystique ... .'. This is an identity 'to which they are entitled, and which it is logical to recognize when one presses one's own right to cultural identity'.[33]

However, there is a direct and logical connecting line between the New Right's support of real decolonization, and even Third World anti-imperialism, and Europe's own redefinition of its cultural heritage under a different concept of communitarian membership. Rather than being integrated in Western societies, the Third World should be really emancipated. This cannot be done by means of the old Marxist-socialist revolutionary theories, which are at a loss to facilitate cultural emancipation in the non-Western world. Since 1980, the assumption has been that in the name of 'another Third World ... that would merge with an authentic differentialism ... it is wise to reject multiracial society and think of returning immigrants to their own countries'.[34] In other words, the development of a proud and emancipated Third World means the development of a proud and ethnically closed Europe.

An explanation for the metamorphosis from 'heterophobia' to 'heterophilia' can be found in the new cultural strategy employed by New Right ideologues. For Alain de Benoist, this process is rooted in the attitudes and writings of some neofascist intellectuals at the time of Algeria's decolonization. The Algerian experience convinced not only De Gaulle of the inconveniences of colonialism, but also some neofascists and ultra-nationalists. The debate centered on the question of colonialism and the nationalization of the colonial population. Groups such as *Jeune Nation* and the *Federation des Etudiants Nationalistes* came to the 'inescapable' conclusion that the worst thing for French nationalism would be a totally French Algeria.[35] Although the idea of conquest, expansion and dominion was part of the social-Darwinist legacy of French anti-liberal nationalists, the most important goal was felt to be the preservation of ethnic purity.

For the New Right, the logical conclusion of the French republican idea is the imperialism of the past and its current corollary, namely mass immigration. To restore France and Europe to their true identities, the liberal democratic nation-state and its companion concept of legal citizenship, incorporating the myth of integration, should be replaced by differential ethnic regional democracy. An 'ethnic' Europe focused on its peoples and its regions would in fact produce a different type of ethnic republicanism, one which is anti-integrationist and respects cultural 'otherness'. The sources of these new ideas of the New Right lie in radical regionalism and the Europeanism proposed by Jean Mabire and Dominique Venner. These two prominent rightist ideologues influenced Alain de Benoist and other right-wing intellectuals during their formative years. Jean Mabire, the editor-in-chief of *Europe*

Action, radicalized the concept of ultra-nationalist ethnicism. His vision of France was shaped by his Norman spirit. An admirer of Drieu La Rochelle, the antisemitic writer who extolled Norman ethnicity, Jean Mabire argued that the regionalist spirit could save France. Although Mabire's regionalism may appear to resemble that of the left, it is in fact permeated by the concept of *ethnisme enracin* which is the equivalent of *socialisme enracine*. *Socialisme enracine*, as opposed to 'universal socialism', was complemented by Dominique Venner's social Darwinism, and applied to Europe. In short, a European socialism essentially means restoring Europe to its own ethnic roots.

When Alain de Benoist joined the magazine *Europe Action*, his main belief was that Europe should defend the cause of the white race against the Third World. The magazine's political program in 1963, '*Qu'est-ce que le nationalisme?*', defined ethnocentric nationalism as the political expression of the West.[36] At the same time, the concept of a racial, Europeanist nationalism was extrapolated from the concept of French or German or Spanish nationalism. This Europeanist nationalism represented the political expression of white people's needs. As Jean Mabire said, 'For us Europe is the heart of Johannesburg, Quebec, Sidney and Budapest.'

The New Right recycled these ideas, adding a 'respectful' attitude towards Third World cultures. In the high-school manifesto '*Manifeste de la classe 60*' issued at the beginning of the 1960s, the future New Right intellectuals had already decided that the 'French ethnic group ... is the fundamental basis of our national existence, and its alteration by foreign relations would certainly cause it to disappear'.[37]

However, the healthy development of this French ethnic identity which differs from the Jacobinist idea of the French nation depends on a European union of ethnic groups. Rather than being integrated into Western societies or adopting Western organizational models, the Third World should really achieve emancipation through the adoption of its own political models. Accordingly, the New Right plan focuses not on the Third World but on Europe. Europe is to salvage its anti-liberal and anti-democratic roots, while the Third World should return to its own roots.[38]

The invention of European authenticity

Whether the celebration of common ethnic roots or a common culture has an authentic popular source or has been constructed for political purposes is a cardinal question. I believe, however, that the politicization of ethnicity in both the old and new rightist movements is a device to undermine the philosophical roots of liberal democratic society. The necessity of creating a common European cultural and ethnic myth, to unite the different flags and peoples of Europe with a sense of common destiny, is a central idea of the New Right. Moreover, this ethnic myth is meant to provide an alternative to democracy as a model of political organization.

In this respect, the discovery of the works of Georges Dumezil (1898–1986) at the end of the 1960s, allowed the New Right to redefine its European nationalism in terms of the communitarian origins of 'Indo-Europeanism', a concept guaranteeing the unity and specificity of a unique mentality and a unique political organization.[39] The name of Dumezil is usually associated with the Indo-European tripartite ideology, which assumes that Indo-European religion and mythology reflect pervasive structural patterns of the basic Indo-European social hierarchy, which consists in three functional classes: priests, warriors and producers.[40] This hierarchical distribution of society liberated Europe from the egalitarian spirit of the French Revolution, which was the logical conclusion of moral Christianity.

The Indo-European culture has its own historical conception, and its own particular values. In contrast to the egalitarian spirit of Christianity, the Indo-European spirit is reflected in Nietzsche's formula that 'everything goes, everything comes back, the road of existence turns eternally ... . At every moment existence begins ...'.[41] In this infinite or spherical conception, man is creator of his own destiny. In fact, the theories of amoral decisionism are rooted in this Indo-Europeanist racialism.

Ernest Renan himself attached the same semi-biological context of epistemological contingency, concluding that only a scientific-minded people could deal with science. Therefore, science could be mastered only by an Indo-European culture. Technology, decisionism, and the vitalism of life philosophy are all directly linked to the 'Indo-European' cultural genetic theory. In contrast to theories that sever the link between decisionism and national socialism, the New Right relates the philosophy that true political sovereignty is revealed in moments of emergency (*Ausnahmezustand*)[42] to the

> deep currents of our history that we want to restore. They are in fact evidence of the invincibility of the European mentality in the face of the attempts to enslave it spiritually or politically that have threatened it for two millennia, but also of its desire for power.[43]

A technological approach and decisionist vitality are in fact considered to be inherent in the European tradition.

> In Indo European societies, politics determines the modes of social and economic action. In modern (liberal democratic) societies, in contrast, politics is subordinated to social and economic factors. That means that the aspirations of the masses determine the decisions on power: The commercial class ... imposes its wishes on warriors and sovereigns.[44]

The 'Indo-European culture', on the other hand, which has provided the foundation for a new, vital, regenerative spirit in Europe, revives the concept of the political and its control over economics and civil society. This is, in fact, a new framework for a personalized, populist democracy that would replace the idea of liberal state legal citizenship.

National socialist Europe: the end of the international community and of the idea of legal citizenship

The theoretical background analysed above serves the European New Right as the intellectual framework for promoting two basic goals: the end of the idea of liberal citizenship, which encompasses the principle of integration; and the end of the European nation-state, which, according to the New Right, cannot deal with the new demands of world economic and political developments.

The two goals are interrelated, and their advancement implies an immigrant-free Europe and the development of the latter's inner economic and cultural strength. As noted elsewhere, this nationalist socialist Europe is for the New Right, paradoxically, the basis for a new model of ethnic plurality that contrasts with the assimilationist model of citizenship promoted by Jacobinist ideology.

'France tends to become a juridical space dominated by the ideology of the rights of men wherein civil society ... loses each day its wealth and density under the effect of economization and rationalization'.[45] This Habermasian thesis, adopted by Alain de Benoist, is completed by what the latter calls the defense of the communitarian model, which 'allows the preservation of diversity in harmony'. In contrast to that harmony, the supporters of an individualism which, ironically, promotes identical beings, strive for 'a general competition which leads to generalized exclusionism'.[46]

On the surface, it would appear that the New Right strives for a type of 'open communitarianism' which differs from both the assimilationist zeal of French republicanism and from the multiracial, apartheid society derived from multiculturalism.[47] Actually, the idea of open communitarianism implies a ghettoization of society based on community pride rather than force. The main point here is that this ghettoization of immigrants proud of their cultures, together with Europe's return to its own pre-liberal cultural and ethnic roots, would lead to a dissolution of the liberal nation-state. The latter promotes its integrationist zeal through centralization and redistributive policies which, according to the New Right, should no longer exist.

Thus, while on one hand, communitarian pluralism fosters acceptance of different cultural and ethnic groups, on the other hand, it dissolves the only basis for modernizing and technologizing ethnic communities. At the same time, the elimination of the concept of 'formal legality' inherent in integrationist policies leads to what the New Right most desires, namely a redefinition of Europe's own ethnic identity, based on a federation of 'its peoples'. A 'new' Europe can then be created on the basis of an ethnic federation between the most developed regions of the continent, the result being a national socialist Europe whose democratic foundations would be ethnically and culturally determined.

Moreover, while the contractual and individualistic basis of liberal society is projected on a national consciousness that, in Europe, was from the beginning permeated by an awareness of the wider international sphere, the politicization of ethnicity strives to deconstruct international politics. Theoretically, the national idea requires a reference beyond itself. This reference need not be something as abstract as 'man', but merely the notion of Europe, defined by Montesquieu, as a community of nation-states.[48] By this criterion, Europe could develop from a Europe of nation-states into a political and economic union, resting on the same philosophical basis that sustains both the autonomy of the individual and the nation-state that is theoretically posited on the primacy of the individual.

In juxtaposition to the concept of liberal Europe are the twin notions of an ethnic federation of peoples and of cultural differentialism as a radical expression of moral and political relativism. In this respect, both right-wing and left-wing intellectuals maintain that the European goal of political union has been developing independently of the tradition of cultural unity which initially brought it forth. This fact has introduced a sharp break between the new European community and

Europe as a historical and cultural entity. The revolutionary wars and Napoleon's campaign to achieve the armed conquest of Europe took place in what is usually known as 'the Europe of nationalities', for which the nineteenth-century blueprint was the Treaty of Vienna.[49] Against the European Union, the New Right advances the idea of an ethnic federation of the peoples of Europe. Obviously, this trend challenges the idea of France as a nation-state. As de Benoist wrote regarding the prospect of a new imperial Europe, 'the Republic – one and indivisible – would be replaced by a federal republic of French peoples',[50] which would be absorbed into an ethnic federation of the strongest and most developed peoples of Europe. This would save France's real identity, as expressed in the spirit of its provinces, and Europe, as a strong, dominant and productive conglomeration of peoples, would be culturally and economically hegemonic.

For the left and for radical democratic theorists, the idea of a federal 'Europe of the peoples' is closer to authentic, direct social democracy than the large unit of the nation-state is. Accordingly, in this respect, left-wing and right-wing intellectuals have revived the tradition of conflict initiated in France by the Proudhonian anarchical trend. The Proudhonian syndicates adopted a federal type organization and were reluctant to get involved in parliamentary politics. It was Proudhon's administrative decentralization that revived the life of the commune and the province, and that was most closely linked to the federalism supported by the 'third way' tradition in France, known as the federalist/personalist movement, and associated with the names of Alexandre Marc, Emmanuel Mounier, and Denis de Rougemont. This current was part of the French quest for a third road between capitalism and socialism, and it was drastically opposed to the nation-state. Thus, the New Right, like some left-wing thinkers, wants a federative ethnic European union, and opposes Maastricht's economic and political union, since Maastricht promoted an economic and juridical state that would merely be a transformation and enlargement of the bureaucratic state. Maastrich's premise is that the market creates the economic identity, which in turn is the basis for the 'European identity'. Under this formula, however, Europe will not only lose its authenticity, but will also create a market favorable to the United States. 'The paradoxical result is that the creation of that single market of 320 million inhabitants with their strong purchasing power will favor first of all not the Europeans, but their competitors.'[51]

In contrast to political and economical union, which blurs political borders and protects the rights of the individual, only an ethnic federation could provide the model for a closed, 'communitarian' Europe that could renew its cultural identity. In fact, for the New Right intellectuals, such a federation would be a barrier both against waves of immigration and against the liberal, materialistic values represented by the United States. Moreover, since a federated European union would include only the industrially developed peoples of Central Europe (the Indo-European stock with its innate industrial and technical gifts), the possibility of economic independence would seem much better founded than if an independent, autarkic, undeveloped region were to be contemplated. The New Right's idea of ethnicity is essentially racism, while the left looks more to cultural and historical roots, and is relatively open to new members. The New Right holds that only an ethnic federation can produce a closed 'communitarian' Europe that will recover its cultural identity and maintain a barrier against waves of immigration and against the liberal, materialistic values represented by the United States. Moreover, the New Right is well aware that Europe's political supremacy is only possible under an European union which is not political but technological and ethnical. In other words 'in order to create itself Europe requires a unity of political decision making. But this European political unity cannot be built on the national Jacobin model if it does not want to see the richness and diversity of all European components disappear. It also cannot result from the economic supra-nationality dreamt by Brussels' technocrats. [The alternative in fact, is the idea of empire] ..which is never a closed totality, as opposed to the nation ... . The Empire's frontiers are naturally fluid and provisional, which reinforces its organic character'.[52] In fact, the neo-fascist New Right envisions a new, national-socialist empire, not limited by bureaucratic legality but by its own ethnic cultural and technological spirit.

Conclusion

The purpose of this chapter was to prove, by means of a critical analysis of the New Right ideology in Europe, the continuity of a particular line of political thought which, not long ago, served as the theoretical basis for the most devastating ideologies of modern times. In contrast to other analyses of radical right movements and ideologies, this critical study strives to indicate the implications of this ideological tradition for current issues of political theory. Paradoxically, new political problems which the Enlightenment tradition found difficult to resolve are theoretically addressed by the New Right in a way similar to that adopted by some of the left-wing critics of modern liberalism. Thus, the importance of this analysis lies in the fact that it attempts to expose what I suggest will be the new theoretical discourse of the European neo-fascist right, especially regarding the issue of ethnic and minority group rights.

This is not intended to be a comprehensive analysis of the political ideology of the New Right, but it pinpoints one of the central issues it addresses in current discussions on political theory and on the future of a new Europe. Although on the surface the New Right would appear to deal with the republican idea and the concept of citizenship that has developed in France, its main message is based on what old radical right and fascist ideologues have theoretically and practically striven to destroy: liberal democratic society and the universalistic ideas of the Enlightenment.

There is a clear distinction between the Europeanist ideology of the New Right and the ideologies of other right-wing movements in France and elsewhere in the world. I suggest, indeed, that the cultural strategy of New Right intellectuals is to undermine nationalist ideologies like that expressed by Le Pen's *Front National* because, 'in France he is a professional supporter of the "indigenist" tradition of France, but he justifies colonialism in New Caledonia...'.[53] The New Right's cultural activities are designed to provide a common intellectual background for different separatist movements in Western and Eastern Europe. The real ideological implication and the theoretical importance of these new ideas, though, are that conflicts between different European regions could be resolved in the framework of a hierarchically organized ethnic federation, probably led by Germanic peoples. Obviously, however, there is no empirical evidence that Europe is moving towards such a federation. Furthermore, there is evidence that the regionalist movements, although far from liberal, are reluctant to accept any ideological guidance or hierarchy of any sort. These trends are highly variable, however.

Despite everything, there is a perverse logic in the New Right's 'libertarian' ideology, in which the parameters of a new Europe are determined by its 'authentic cultural role'. It must be understood that for the New Right, the only way to close Europe off to immigrants is by developing its own assertive identity. A strong Europe would indeed act as a powerful autarkic unit whose hegemony in world affairs would be clearly felt. In fact, the neo-fascist New Right envisions a national socialist Europe that would achieve its position not by the power of universalistic ideologies, but rather by blind 'power politics' based on technological superiority and ethnic and cultural cohesiveness.

What is striking about the New Right's political ideas, however, is that the same elements that would produce an aggressive, vital, healthy nationalist society are the essential ingredients for a continental cultural renaissance which, according to the 'ethnic plurality' argument, would protect emancipated Europe from foreign penetration, be it 'southern' immigration or American cultural and economic imperialism. Thus, ethnic democracy is the only possible basis for the true emancipation of Europe as well as of the Third World. The immigration issue is a problem that cannot be resolved either by integration or by multiculturalism, because 'it is not true that immigrants threaten French national identity. It is because France has lost its identity that immigration becomes such a problem'.[54]

In short, in order to strengthen nationalism, it is vital to strip the republican nation-state of its universalist and egalitarian values. The autonomous regional unit contains the spirit of hierarchically organized ethnic democracy. That ethnic democracy is in turn the basis for an ethnic federation of European peoples: namely, a national socialist Europe.

Halting mass Third World immigration and rescuing Europe's cultural and political world hegemony would be possible only through spiritual renaissance – a renaissance that directly depends on the elaboration of a different path to organic modernity, and on a new concept of European nationalism focusing on Europe's innate technological and decisionist capacities. In reviewing the New Right's political legacy, I have attempted to show that the rediscovery of authenticity, the politicization of ethnic values, and the focus on the vitality of the masses expressing their own will in a direct, unmediated way, all challenge the essence of political democracy.

Some post-modern left intellectuals are aware of the problems posed by New Right philosophy. Jacques Derrida, for instance, fears that,

> from everywhere in Europe ... in the name of identity, be it cultural or not, the worst violence, those that we recognize all too well without yet having thought them through, the crimes of xenophobia, racism, anti-semitism, religious or national fanaticism, are being unleashed, mixed up with each other.[55]

The New Right theorists are well aware of this trend. They understand the new relationship between fascist ideology, the ethnicization of politics and the theoretical deconstruction of the liberal state; and accordingly they strive for the new ethnic anti-liberal order, in some cases with the theoretical collaboration of left-wing and radical demo-

cratic intellectuals and ideologues (who probably have no clear understanding of the New Right ideology).

Notes

1 This question was analysed by A.E. Galeotti in 'Citizenship and Equality',
  Political Theory (1993). The principle of tolerance has inspired a policy of
  accommodating ethnic demands as well as other group demands involving
  the public sphere. In other words, if a social difference such as that of the
  schoolgirls in France is denied public visibility and political legitimacy, the
  group associated with it inevitably bears a social stigma, according to
  Galeotti (p. 597).

    This theoretical premise is shared by S. Benhabib, who concludes that
  'agreements in societies living with value pluralism are to be sought for not
  at the level of substantive beliefs but at the level of procedures, processes and
  practices for attaining and revising beliefs'. See S. Benhabib, 'Towards a
  Deliberative Model of Democratic Legitimacy', paper presented at the Legal
  Theory Workshop, Yale Law School (February, 1995). This essay appeared
  originally in Seyla Benhabib and Andrew Arato, eds, *Constellations. An
  International Journal of Democratic and Critical Theory* 1, No. 1 (Basil Blackwell,
  April, 1994).

2 Classic liberalism was based on an ideal of liberty that forbade the state to
  infringe upon the liberty of its citizens except to prevent them from
  harming others. This kind of liberalism was tolerant towards private concerns that had no public consequences. John Locke and John Milton
  argued, however, that tolerance should not be extended to the intolerant,
  since that would undermine the very possibility of a tolerant society.
  Joseph Raz presents a modern version of this thesis, giving priority to protecting the conditions of autonomy over the preservation and proliferation
  of the ways of life that individuals may autonomously decide to pursue.
  See Yael Tamir, *Liberal Nationalism* (Princeton University Press, 1992),
  p. 131.

    For liberals, differences can be reduced to individual claims, and plural-
  ism simply reflects different conceptions of the common good which can
  be promoted by rational discourse through conventional public channels.
  Hence, there is no legal impediment to the free development of ethnic
  communities. Even communitarian demands to control specific communal
  spheres could be met within the framework of the law.

    A difficulty arises, however, when a specific ethnic group demands that
  its difference be accepted as 'normal' in the public sphere, or when ethnic
  values are presented as equal to the 'normal' values of the country. Recent
  liberal theories which have attempted to deal with such demands suggest
  that a basic premise of liberal society should be the neutrality of the public
  sphere. Political neutrality 'is the central liberal ideal. It requires that constitutional principles and political decisions be justifiable without appeal to
  the presumed superiority of any controversial view of the good life'. See
  Charles Larmor, 'Liberal Neutrality. Patterns of Moral Complexity', *Political
  Theory* 17 (1989), p. 580.

For a broader analysis of this argument, see R. Dworkin, 'Liberalism', in *A Matter of Principle* (Harvard University Press, 1985), and Bruce Ackerman, *Social Justice in the Liberal State* (Yale University Press, 1980). These writers all maintain that liberalism must be associated with a strong ideal of state neutrality. In addition, they hold that state neutrality should be posited on philosophical neutrality, arguing that basic principles must themselves be neutral in terms of value judgements. This precludes any claims that one way of life may be intrinsically better than others.

Other writers, such as Will Kymlicka, accept state neutrality but not philosophical neutrality. See W. Kymlicka, *Contemporary Political Philosophy* (Oxford: Clarendom Press, 1989). State neutrality would be justified by some kind of utilitarian view. For a critique of Kymlicka's thesis, see Thomas Hurka, 'Kymlicka on Liberal Neutrality', *Journal of Political Philosophy* 3, No. 1 (March, 1995).

Communitarian critics of liberalism, however, have stressed the fact that liberal society is not neutral towards all the different conceptions of good because it is tailored to include only those conceptions native to the liberal polity and filters out those produced by alien cultures. In other words, the communitarian critique suggests that liberal democracy is ethnocentric.

3 Theories of radical democracy insist that interest groups and groups that are specially discriminated against – such as gender, ethnic provenance, and others – do not require a universalistic egalitarian approach, but rather special treatment. This requirement could be met by a 'semi-corporatist' view of society instead of a liberal-egalitarian one. On radical theories of democracy see Chantal Mouffe, as well as Iris Young, *Justice and the Politics of Difference* (Princeton University Press, 1990).

Slightly different in tone and style, some theories of deliberative democracy modify these radical views on democracy, which they describe as proceduralist, minimalist, and anti-substantive. The deliberative view attempts to bridge the gap between Kantianism and an ethical outlook that would not remove from the political agenda issues recognized as belonging to the private sphere. On the deliberative concept of democracy see Kenneth Baynes, 'The Liberal Communitarian Controversy and Communicative Ethics', *Philosophy and Social Criticism* 14, Nos. 3–4 (1988): 305, and S. Benhabib, *op. cit.*

4 On the New Right's communitarian, anti-nation-state ideology see my unpublished article 'The Neo-fascist New Right and the Deconstruction of Liberal Nation State' (1998).

5 T. Todorov, *On Human Diversity: Nationalism, Racism and Exoticism in French Thought* (Cambridge: Harvard University Press, 1993), pp. 1–2.

6 Mark Lilla, 'Europe Through a Glass Darkly', *Daedalus* 123, No. 2 (Spring, 1994): 153.

7 Alain de Benoist, 'Pluralisme ou assimilation?' *Elements* 77 (No. especial, 20 ans. 1972–92).

8 See E. Weber, *Peasants into Frenchmen: the Modernization of Rural France, 1870–1914* (Stanford: Stanford University Press).

9 Earlier, Napoleon's proposal of unconditional *jus solis* was based on state interests that supposedly necessitated a larger army. However, despite such pragmatic arguments for immigrant nationalization in France – notably the

demographic, military, and economic interests of the state – the extension of the French citizenship law was basically a response to republican idealism. In fact, the Tribunat rejected Napoleon's proposal because it believed that Napoleon's concept was too much concerned with the vertical dimension of citizenship and too little with its horizontal dimension: the bonds of nationhood, the ties to the land, and the links among people that make nationhood a substantial social reality. See Rogers Brubacker, *Citizenship and Nationhood in France and Germany* (Cambridge: Harvard University Press, 1992), p. 90. The policy of naturalization at the end of the century was based on France's refusal to accept that second-generation immigrants would not serve in the army. According to R. Brubaker, they were not particularly needed in the army, but for the republican ideology this 'discrimination' was intolerable.

10 *Citizenship and Nationhood*, p. 112.

11 Girardet Raoul, *L'idee coloniale en France de 1871–1962* (Paris: Table Ronde, 1972), p. 23.

12 P.C. Sorum, *Intellectuals and Decolonization in France* (Chapel Hill: North Carolina Press, 1977), p. 24.

13 There is a conceptual difference between anticolonialism and anti-imperialism; not all anticolonialists were anti-imperialists. The anticolonialists believed that the principle of French cultural protection should be upheld despite colonial independence. Liberal and left-wing anticolonialist intellectuals wanted to reform the system for the benefit of the colonial peoples, but not necessarily by putting an end to it. The common feeling was that the liberated countries should at least be part of a cultural commonwealth with France.

The writings of leftist intellectuals like Claude Bourdet, who edited *Combat*, Jean Rous, secretary-general of the Congress of Peoples Against Imperialism, Jean-Paul Sartre, Marleu Ponty, and Francis Jeanson, who wrote for *Les Temps Modernes*, combined a class-minded analysis with French political theory to support the colonies' demand for independence.

Jean Rous, a former colleague of Trotsky, showed in his *Tunisie..attention!* how the principle of popular democracy proclaimed by the French Revolution should be applied to the Tunisians. Unlike the French communists, who worried about the immediate consequences of independence, Rous and his Trotskyist colleagues, Daniel Guerin and Claude Lefort, endorsed unconditional self-determination. Sartre's essay on Algeria in *Les Temps Modernes* in March and April, 1956, entitled 'Colonialism Is a System', is a clear example of this argument. On one hand, he refuted the idea that colonialism could be reformed. On the other, his notions concerning colonial capitalism fit into the emerging body of opinion that independence was a prerequisite for political maturation and economic development. In fact, he wrote 'political independence is indeed the antechamber leading toward cultural economic development, towards prosperity and ... happiness'. See Jean Rous, *Cronique de la décolonization* (Paris: Editions Présence Africaine, 1965), pp. 290–1. In his view, decolonization did not have to mean the end of a 'legitimate cultural radiance', but rather quite the opposite.

Social Catholics like Ernest Mounier (writing in the journal *Esprit*) argued that after independence French colonies would remain under French

influence because it offered them a humanist path to modernity. The federative commonwealth promoted by Ernst Mounier in fact represented the
symbiosis between modernity and French nationalism.

Some moderate leftists, notably Servan Schreiver and Maurice Duverger,
doubted the colonies' ability to maintain their independence, and feared
that independence would foster the exploitation of the masses by a small
group of former subjects. Others, like Albert Camus, called for the extension
of full metropolitan political rights to many Moslems, in order to prove to
them that France desired 'to export to Algeria the democratic regime' that it
enjoyed itself. See Albert Camus, *Actuelles III Croniques Algeriennes, 1939–58*
(Paris: Gallimard, 1958), p. 103. He also believed that the Algerians would
be won over by political and social reforms. For a broader analysis of this
issue, see Paul Clay Sorum, *Intellectuals and Decolonization* in France
(University of North Carolina Press, 1977).

14 Tony Judt, *Past Imperfect*, pp. 285–7.
15 P.C. Sorum, *Intellectuals and Decolonization in France*, pp. 172–3. For criticisms of Sartre and Jeanson, see Crouzet, 'Bataille des intellectuels', *La Nef*
   12–13 (Oct., 1962–Jan., 1963), p. 54.
16 On Levi Strauss's attack on French ethnocentrism, see Todorov, *op. cit.*
17 Carl Schmitt, *The Concept of the Political*, trans. George Schwab (New Jersey:
   Rutgers University Press, 1976), p. 54. Carl Schmitt's argument could
   undoubtedly be used by the left as well. Both it and the decisionist theory
   influenced leftist intellectuals like Walter Benjamin and Otto Kircheimer in
   their criticism of the Weimar Republic. Carl Schmitt's influence on the left
   can be seen in 'Special Section on Carl Schmitt and the Frankfurt School',
   Telos 71 (Spring, 1987).
18 S. Hughes, *Consciousness and Society: the Reorientation of European Social
   Thought, 1890–1930* (Sussex: The Harvester Press, 1979), p. 38.
19 Zeev Sternhell, *Ni Droite ni Gauche, L'idéologie fasciste en France* (Paris: Ed.
   Seuil), p. 49.
20 Todorov, *op .cit.*, p. 153.
21 G. Le Bon, *The Psychology of Peoples (1894)* (New York: G.E. Stechert, 1912),
   p. XIX.
22 Ibid., p. 82.
23 Todorov, *op. cit.*, p. 126.
24 Alexis de Tocqueville, *The European Revolution. Correspondence with Gobineau*
   (Garden City, N.Y: Doubleday, 1959), pp. 228–9.
25 Ibid.
26 Maurice Barres, *Scenes et doctrines du nationalisme* (1902), 2 vols (Paris: Plon-
   Nourrit, 1925), Vol. I, p. 84. Cited in Tzvetan Todorov, *On Human Diversity.
   Nationalism, Racism and Exoticism in French Thought* (Cambridge: Harvard
   University Press, 1993), p. 57.
27 Maurice Barres, 'Le 2 novembre en Lorraine', in *Amori et Dolori Sacrum*
   (Paris: Plon), pp. 264–5.
28 Barres, *Scenes et doctrines du nationalisme*, Vol. I, p. 113.
29 Zeev Sternhell, *Maurice Barres*.
30 Barres, *Scenes*, p. 167.
31 Robert de Herte 'Europe-Tiers Monde, la nouvelle alliance', *Eléments*,
   No.48–9 (Winter 1983–4).

32   Robert de Herte 'Pour un autre tiers mundisme', *Eléments* No.48–9 (Winter 1983–4), p. 25.

33   Pierre Vial 'L'integrisme musulman:una vraie revolutuion culturelle', *Eléments*, No. 48–9, p. 82.

34   Guillaume Faye, 'La societe multiraciale en question', *Eléments*, No 48–9 (Winter 1983–4), p. 76.

35   Maurice Bardeche, one of the most prominent post-war neo-fascists, supported the OAS in its attack against French democracy and against De Gaulle. He could not, however, accept the thesis that French citizenship should be extended to Algerians. He was agreeable to the economic exploitation of the colonies, but not to their integration. 'I am convinced that colonization cannot last, that we must seek a new formula of association between France and Algeria, recognizing a certain form of independence for the latter which will still give France the benefits of a sort of alliance with Algeria and, at the same time, access to its natural riches'. J. Algazy, *La tentation neo-fasciste en France, 1944–1965* (Paris: Fayard, 1984), p. 213.

36   *Europe Action* 5, cited in Taguieff, p. 124.

37   J. Algazy, *La tentation neo-fasciste en France, 1944–1965*, p. 198.

38   Guillaume Faye, 'La societe multiraciale en question', *Eléments* No. 48–9 (Winter, 1983–4), p. 76. Alain de Benoist has been critical of the Front National since 1986. In July, 1992, de Benoist condemned the *Front National's* xenophobia in an interview with *Les Dossiers de l'Histoire*. In line with his solidarity with the Third World and his support of a Third World-Europe alliance, he proposed a new solidarity with immigrants. This, however, is actually a rather sophisticated way of attacking both liberals and nationalists, since his interpretation also envisages, ultimately, an immigrant-free Europe.

39   P.A. Taguieff, *Sur la nouvelle droite* (Paris: Descartes, 1994), p. 174.

40   E. Polome, 'Introduction', *Homage to Georges Dumezil, Journal of Indo-European Studies*, Monograph No. 3 (Washington, 1982), p. 7.

41   Cited in G. Hourdin, 'La Nouvelle Droite', in A.M. Duranton Crabol, *Visages de la Nouvelle Droite. Le GRECE et son histoire* (Presses de la Fondation Nationale des Sciences Politiques, 1988), p. 88.

42   See Seyla Benhabib, 'Democracy and Difference: Reflections on the Metapolitics of Lyotard and Derrida', *Journal of Political Philosophy* 2, No. 1 (1994), p. 4. According to Benhabib, certain formulations of Derrida and Lyotard bring them into the realm of 'decisionist' political theory. However, Benhabib correctly concludes that this does not mean they support reactionary conservative thought. I would add, they do not support reactionary conservative thought *consciously*.

43   *Eléments* 12, (Sept.-Nov., 1975), p. 42, cited in A.M. Duranton Crabol, Visages de la nouvelle droite; La GRECE et son histoire (Paris: Presses de la Fondation Nationale des Sciences Politiques, 1988), p. 91.

44   Alain de Benoist, *La Nueva Derecha*, Coleccion Tablero (Ed. Planeta, 1982), p. 87. Translated from the French *Les idees à l'endroit* (Ed. Livres Hallier, 1979).

45   Alain de Benoist 'Pluralisme ou assimilation', *Eléments* 77, p. 50.

46   Alain de Benoist, 'Le modele communautaire' *Eléments* 77, p. 58.

47   *Ibid.*

48 Michael Mosher, 'Nationalism and the Idea of Europe', *History of European Ideas* 19, No. 4–6 (1993).
49 Etienne Tassin, 'Europe: a Political Community?' in Charles Mouffe, *Dimensions of Radical Democracy: Pluralism, Citizenship and Democracy*, p. 171.
50 Alain de Benoist, 'Pluralisme et assimilation', *Eléments* 77, p. 52.
51 'L'Europe de 1992: Un mauvais conte de fées', *Eléments* 65 (Spring, 1980).
52 Alain de Benoist, 'The Idea of Empire', *Telos* 98–99 (Winter 1993–Spring 1994): pp. 93–97. Originally delivered as a lecture at GRECE's 24th National Congress, devoted to the topic 'Nation and Empire', Paris, 24 March 1991.
53 Alain de Benoist, 'Entretien avec Alain Rollat, May, 1992', cited in Taguieff, *op. cit.* p. 44.
54 *Ibid.*, p. 58.
55 J. Derrida, 'The Other Heading: Memories, Responses and Responsibilities', cited in 'The Other Heading: Reflections on Today's Europe', in Seyla Benhabib, *op. cit.* p. 3.

PART THREE

Ethnic Challenges in Settler States

8
Minority Protest and the Emergence of Ethnic Regionalism: Palestinian-Arabs in the Israeli 'Ethnocracy'
Oren Yiftachel

Introduction

The challenge posed by minorities to central state administrations has intensified in recent years, spawning a wave of research into the causes and consequences of ethnic protest.[1] The rich work on the subject has, however, only rarely focused on the influence of politico-geographical factors, such as planning and spatial policies and ethnic regionalism.

Given the above, the present chapter documents, analyses and interprets the evolution of public protest staged by an ethnic regional minority: the Palestinian-Arabs in Galilee, Israel. The analysis assesses the role of national and relative deprivation issues in generating Arab protest, but also pays special attention to the role of spatial factors in that process. In this way, the chapter attempts to make a geographical contribution to the study of ethnic protest and insurgency. The main argument advanced here is that Arab protest activity in Galilee points to the emergence of an ethnic regionalism, which locates Arab struggle and identity between local and state levels. The nature of Arab struggle derives from the discriminatory nature of the Israeli 'ethnocracy' which constrains meaningful Arab politics to specific spaces. This setting generates significant and parallel mobilization on three key issues: land rights, socioeconomic deprivation, and national (Palestinian) independence in the occupied territories.

The Galilee region was chosen as a case study because it forms the main regional concentration of Palestinian-Arab citizens in the bi-ethnic state of Israel. In 1996, the region accommodated some 490 000 Arabs, who formed 75 per cent of the region's population (Figure 8.1). Due to the overwhelming Arab character of the region, the Israeli government has continuously attempted to increase the region's Jewish

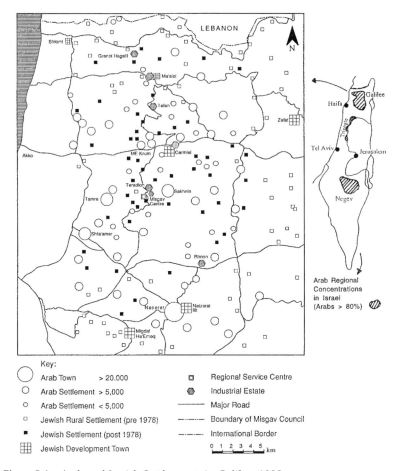

Figure 8.1   Arab and Jewish Settlements in Galilee, 1993

population. As such, the study of minority protest in Galilee can well illustrate the mutual relations between public policy, changing ethnic regional geography and political relations in a bi-ethnic (or binational) polity.

The chapter discusses previous studies on minority protest and the role of policy and geography, before presenting its detailed analysis of Arab protest. It builds on foundations provided by two previous works: a broad overview of Arab protest up to the mid-1980s[2] and the detailed raw data of protest in Galilee up to the late 1980s.[3] The term 'minority' is used in this chapter interchangeably with 'ethnic minority', denoting a culturally distinct group of people, united by a belief in a common past.[4] Likewise, the 'Arabs in Israel' and the 'Palestinians in Israel' are terms referring to the same group (the term 'Arabs' being generally used in this chapter in order to be unequivocally inclusive of sub-groups such as the Druze and the Bedouins). The 'state' is the agglomeration of institutions and authorities which formulate and implement public policies. 'Planning (or spatial) policy' deals with the combination of territorial, land, land-use, settlement and building matters.

Ethnic minority protest: some theoretical observations

Types of minority protest and violence

Minority protest is defined here as the combination of all anti-government and anti-majority acts of demonstration and violence staged by the minority group under study. Non-violent protest is one of the most commonly used vehicles for political change in open regimes. It ranges from rhetoric to illegal action. Clearly, a large part of societal protest rhetoric and activity is a legitimate ingredient of the 'tug and push game of policy making'.[5] However, persisting protest staged by an ethnic minority has been used as an indicator of potential political instability.[6] This has been the case in several bi-ethnic open regimes, such as Northern Ireland and Sri Lanka, where outbreaks of inter-ethnic violence were preceded by lengthy periods of minority demonstrations and protest.[7]

Grenier[8], Muller[9] and Hibbs[10] study types of political protest which include demonstrations, rallies, strikes and media campaigns. They define three types of protest activity which may challenge the structure of open regimes:

(a)   activities which are anti-government, anti-majority or anti-system in character;
(b)   activities which oppose the socio-political status quo;
(c)   activities which are collective, being staged on behalf of a substantial community, excluding purely local anti-government protest.

In addition to the above, acts of anti-government political violence (which are grouped in this chapter under the umbrella of 'protest') can pose a clear threat to political systems, particularly in democratic states. These acts include riots, assassinations, political deaths and injuries.[11] For violence to be considered as protest, it has to be anti-government or anti-majority in nature, have political significance and be conducted collectively. This excludes criminal violence or the use of force in intra-ethnic disputes. Unlike peaceful protest activity, however, all anti-government, anti-majority or anti-system violence is illegal, thereby possessing a greater destabilizing potential. The above classifications and definitions will guide the empirical study of regional ethnic protest in Israel, later in the chapter.

Explaining minority protest

There exist several competing theories on the causes for minority protest. Such protest activity is usually seen as a stage in the political mobilization of deprived ethnic minorities, and their challenge to discrimination and disparities in their respective states. As claimed by Gurr and Lichbach,[12] political protest is a key early indicator in the process of minority insurgence. As such, the study of protest is of critical importance for students of ethnic relations and for public policy makers.

1   Deprivation, policy and ethno-nationalism

Although the range of relevant theories is wide, the leading explanations of ethnic protest appear to fall either within the 'relative deprivation' or the 'ethnic nationalism-identity' schools of thought. A third approach links public protest and political mobilization to the 'mobilization of group resources', but it is less relevant to our case of a 'homeland' ethnic minority.[13] The relative deprivation school claims that persisting gaps and disparities between minority and majority create increasing tension between the groups, born out of a 'frustration-aggression' nexus.[14] Ethnic conflicts thus often revolve around the groups' shares of national resources. Ethnicity is perceived as instrumental, forming an effective core around which to mobilize support for civil struggles.[15] Accordingly, protest will be mainly staged over issues of *socio-economic deprivation*, and will generally not challenge the prevailing structure and character of the state.

Socio-economic deprivation is often the result of public policies. As such, protest against ethnic deprivation may frequently be directed against public policies in general, and the *distribution of public resources* in particular. In that context, Gurr,[16] in the most comprehensive study to date on global patterns of minority protest, finds a direct link between state policy, ethnic deprivation and levels of ethnic conflict, stating that in most democratic regimes, which have attempted reforms in ethnic relations, ethnic protest and violence was usually limited.[17] The relative deprivation account of ethnic protest and conflict has been observed to be particularly applicable for immigrant societies, where ethnic minorities are often categorized as 'ethno-classes'.[18]

On the other hand, the ethno-national approach (which appears in different guises such as 'ethnic phenomenon' or 'ethnic revival') claims that ethnic differences are intrinsically embedded in human group behavior, and that ethnic protest and political mobilization are first and foremost expressions of a permanent desire for ethnic self-determi-nation *vis-à-vis* dominant majorities and state administrations. This approach perceives ethnicity as primordial and even 'bio-social'[19] and sees ethnic protest as part of a global process of ethnic revival and ethno-national demarcation. Accordingly, ethnic protest is likely to focus increasingly on national, cultural and territorial issues, and less on socio-economic grievances.[20]

During the ethnic-nationalization process, protest may begin with local and general deprivation matters, and move later to territorial and self-determination demands. The national issues are likely to generate the most intense levels of protest, as occurred for example in Quebec, Northern Ireland and Sri Lanka. In such cases, ethnic protest may con-tinue to accelerate over long periods as part of a general process of ethnic political self-assertion. While ethnic nationalism and self-deter-mination demands have been expressed in all types of multi-ethnic societies, the processes described above have mostly been experienced by homeland ethnic minorities, which occupy peripheral positions in open societies.[21] Yet, three related factors which influence minority protest are underplayed by the on-going debate on the nature and reasons for ethnic protest. These are the role of planning policy, ethnic geography and ethnic regionalism.

2 *Planning policies*

A component of public policy which is of crucial importance for the explanation of protest by homeland ethnic minorities is the govern-ment's spatial planning policy. While the link between public policy and ethnic socio-economic deprivation has been studied widely, the impact of planning policies has remained relatively under-researched.[22] In multi-ethnic societies, particularly in 'deeply divided' states (those occupied by homeland, non-assimilating communities), governments have often used planning and territorial policies as a major tool in shaping ethnic relations. The ability to expropriate land for 'public purposes', to demarcate local authority and electoral boundaries, and to determine the location of key land uses (with their negative and positive externalities), have all become instruments in government attempts to establish a desired pattern of ethnic social and political relations within their states.[23]

In this context, the dynamics of regional settlement in general, and ethnic regional mix in particular, are critical to the understanding of ethnic regional behavior. Mixed regions are seldom created 'naturally', and are often the result of government planning and settlement policies, which attract majority populations to peripheral regions dominated by ethnic minorities.[24] These minorities are often subject to adverse government policies which reduce their land resources, change their cultural milieu, and dramatically alter the development process of their regions.[25] Such a process has occurred in the case of the Galilee region, as detailed below.

3   Ethnic geography and ethnic regionalism

Linked to the government's planning policies is the geography of ethnic relations, and the influence of such geography on levels of ethnic protest and conflict. Repeated studies have found a direct association between a minority's spatial concentration and its ability to mobilize political campaigns against state policies.[26] However, several geographical issues have not received sufficient attention, including the issue of mixed ethnic regions, and the impact of such mix on minority protest and insurgency. Most work of that nature focused on an urban scale,[27] leaving the consequences of ethnic regional mix relatively unknown. Some useful explorations of particular mixed regions in multi-ethnic societies were carried out by Anderson,[28] Coakely, Gradus, Rudolph and Thompson, and Murphy, all pointing to some problems in maintaining peaceful coexistence in such regions within open regimes. The events of recent years in the ethnically mixed regions/states of Croatia, Bosnia and Azerbaijan further stress the problematic nature of ethnic regional mix in the context of democratization.

In addition, despite several ground-breaking studies on the political-geography of ethnicity,[29] relatively little attention has been devoted to the association between ethnic regional protest and the emergence of ethnic regionalism. Ethnic regional protest often reflects the formation of ethnic regionalism, which is a distinct type of ethnic political orientation, lying between the two poles of the ethnic nationalism-relative deprivation dichotomy discussed above.

Ethnic regionalism denotes the mobilization of regional-ethnic interests and the crystallization of identity between the local and state levels. The aim of ethno-regional movements is to maximize benefits from public resources for the regional group, while maintaining, protecting and enhancing its distinct identity and territory.[30] Examples of such ethnic movements abound, including the Basques and the Catalans in Spain, the Waloons in Belgium, or the Scots in Britain. Such groups usually demand (and often receive) a large degree of ethnic autonomy, but differ from fully fledged national movements by their lack of explicit demands for full political independence.[31]

It is therefore postulated here that ethnic protest is often a surface expression of emerging ethnic regionalism. The process often reflects the formation of a group which is neither a fully fledged ethnic nation, nor a mere ethno-class vying for material resources. Accordingly, during the process of ethnic regionalism, protest is likely to focus on a relatively even mixture of national, territorial and socio-economic issues, without long-term dominance of any of the above.[32]

Previous studies on the political behavior of ethnic groups have highlighted a range of goals, from irredentism to assimilation. 'Autonomism' is usually highlighted as a point between these two poles,[33] but its links to ethnic geography in general, and to government planning policies in particular are seldom systematically explored. It is argued here, as claimed by Mikessel and Murphy,[34] that the combination of ethnic geography and government policies is critical to the understanding of ethnic insurgency, and its translation to the particular form of ethnic regionalism. It will be shown later that the Arabs in Israel's Galilee region can be classified as a case of a fledgling ethnic regional movement.

To conclude, then, existing theories postulate that ethnic protest is caused by ethno-national revival or group socio-economic deprivation. It is argued here, however, that a distinct third case exists, where protest by ethnic regional minorities exhibits neither an explicit push for national self-determination, nor a strong socio-economic focus. Such a case is ethnic regionalism which has three central, and fairly equal concerns: a) maintaining a national identity, b) protecting an ethnic territorial base, and c) improving the group's share of state resources. Accordingly, a full understanding of ethnic regional protest requires an analysis of two factors relatively neglected in previous studies: spatial policy and ethnic geography. These arguments will be explored below in the case of Israel's Galilee region.

The Palestinian-Arab minority: Israeli 'ethnocracy' and Galilee policy

Palestinian-Arabs in Israel

The Palestinian-Arab minority in Israel (within its pre-1967 borders) is a non-assimilating 'homeland' community. It constitutes 16 per cent of the state's population, residing in three main regional concentrations (of which Galilee is the largest) as well as several mixed cities (see Figure 8.1 page 146).

The historical and political background to Arab-Jewish relations in Israel is covered extensively elsewhere.[35] As a necessary background, it should be briefly noted that the evolution of these majority-minority relations has been strongly influenced by the Middle Eastern conflict in general, and the Jewish-Palestinian struggle for control over Palestine/Israel in particular.[36] Palestinian-Arabs who remained in Israel (on their own historical land) following the 1948 war, have been therefore considered by many Jews to be a 'hostile minority' in a context of on-going political and military tension between Arabs and Jews.

Despite a notable process of modernization, the Arabs in Israel and in Galilee have generally remained in their villages, which have become semi-urban. They have also experienced in recent decades an occupational change from peasantry to hired and self-employed labor,[37] a shift towards the political left,[38] and a rise in the influence and strength of Moslem movements.

The Arab minority in Israel has experienced some positive effects of residing within the Jewish state, especially a significant rise in living and educational standards, use of Israel's universal welfare services, and exposure to, and participation in, its open political culture.[39] However, mainly due to the on-going Arab-Jewish conflict, the Arab minority has also been subject to continuous policies of control and discrimination, including military rule from 1948 to 1966, a transfer of an estimated 65 per cent of their lands to the state through expropriations, and the persistence of socio-economic and power disparities between Arabs and Jews.[40]

The structural discrimination experienced by the Arabs in the self-declared 'Jewish State' points to the existence of a Jewish 'ethnocracy' in Israel. This is a regime type characterized by two key principles:

1   Despite several democratic features, ethnicity (and not territorial citizenship) is the main organizing logic for the allocation of state resources;

2   A dominant ethnic group appropriates the state apparatus and dictates the nature of most public policies.

Against this background, the Arabs have become in recent years increasingly organized, and have staged a campaign for civil equality.[41] This has caused, at least in the short term, some decline in the level of inequality,[42] especially under the Labor government that was in power between 1992 and 1996. The growing militancy of the Arab political campaign gave rise to two leading explanations:

(a) *politicization*, which claims that the growing assertion and militancy of the minority reflects, first and foremost, a struggle for better terms of Arab-Jewish coexistence in Israel, and an acceptance of life as an ethnic minority within a Jewish 'ethnic democracy';[43]
(b) *radicalization*, which argues that the strengthening Arab struggle for civil rights masks a deeper process of Palestinian nationalism, which is likely to lead towards Arab separatism.[44]

As regards the growing incidence and intensity of Arab protest, the politicization school is close to the 'relative deprivation' interpretation, claiming most Arab protest can be attributed to the gaps and disparities they experience *vis-à-vis* Israel's Jewish population; while the radicalization approach is closer to the 'ethnic nationalism' interpretation, postulating that the growing Arab protest is part of a global and powerful process experienced by minorities around the globe, regardless of their socio-economic position. Despite its importance and centrality to the understanding of Arab-Jewish relations in Israel, I have previously criticized the politicization-radicalization debate as presenting a false dichotomy,[45] and the analysis of Arab protest below will show that both politicization and radicalization of the Arabs are occurring concurrently.

Israel's policies and ethnic geography in Galilee

The Galilee region, which has had an Arab majority since Israel's independence in 1948, has been a target for continuous government policies aimed at increasing its Jewish population in order to create a 'better population balance' between Arabs and Jews.[46] These efforts (commonly known as the 'Judaization of Galilee' strategy) resulted in the establishment of several Jewish towns during the 1950s and 1960s, and assumed increasing urgency during the mid-1970s.[47] Subsequently, a Jewish settlement program was implemented in Galilee during the late 1970s and early 1980s, creating 62 new small Jewish settlements (known as *mitzpim*) and enlarging the existing Jewish towns. In addition, several industrial estates were created with a range of new industries, and a road network developed to serve the new settlements. The government continuously attempted to attract Jewish migrants and investors into the region with a range of financial benefits, and a promise of better quality of life.[48]

At the same time, the Arab population in the region was expanding rapidly, due to high rates of natural growth. Many small villages have grown into small and medium-size towns, and have increased their physical size dramatically, owing to a process of low-density suburbanization.[49] The two Arab cities – Nazareth and Shfa'amer – have also grown, forming the main administrative, economic and political centers for the Arabs in the region. The settlement geography in Galilee has therefore changed dramatically since 1948, and particularly since the late 1970s. The region currently consists of a complex mixture of Arab villages, towns and cities; a range of dispersed small Jewish *mitzpim* and agricultural settlements; three Jewish towns and two Jewish cities (see Figure 8.1 page 146). As shown below, this changing ethnic geography played an important part in shaping Arab regional protest.

Arab protest in Galilee, 1975–91

Methodology

The research methodology involved a detailed documentation of Arab protest activity in the Galilee, and an analysis of its temporal and locational association with policy initiatives, processes within the Arab sector and general political events in the Middle East. Data were collected for the 1975–91 period, during which a profound political mobilization of the Arab minority in Israel had started to occur.[50] As Lehman-Wilzig notes:[51] ' … prior to 1975, the annual number of Arab protest events could be counted on one hand …'. The study period therefore covers the emergence as well as development of Arab protest in the region.

According to the definitions of protest spelled out earlier (pages 147–8), only collective protest activity (as opposed to rhetoric) was included in the analysis. Protest was considered 'regional' only if it had participants from at least five of the region's Arab villages. Data were compiled from a search of seven newspapers, archives of Arab organizations, records of state authorities and personal interviews. Data on protest events were translated into an index of 'protest intensity'. The quantification of this index was based on the allocation of numerical values to three key features of protest activity:

(a) duration (measured by days);
(b) size (measured by number of participants); and
(c) strength (measured by level of violence, arrests or conflict with authorities).

This procedure follows the methods used by Grenier,[52] Gurr,[53] Hibbs[54] and Lehman-Wilzig[55] (with several small adaptations). In addition, as further explained below, Arab protest was broken down into the main protest issues, based on a systematic content analysis of newspaper reports and protest publications.

The evolution of protest

Figure 8.2 traces the evolution of Arab protest in the region on a six-monthly basis, in terms of number of events and their respective intensity. The main peaks in the graph denote the periods of most intense Arab protest which had usually culminated in the declaration of state-wide general strikes, during which business, work, municipal and educational activities in the Arab community ceased (although participation in the strikes was not always full). Eleven such strikes were called during the study period (in addition, of course, to many local and regional strikes). To facilitate the discussion below, the dates and names of these strikes are listed below in chronological order:

- March 1976: first Land Day (protesting against land expropriation)
- September 1982: strike in protest of the massacre in Sabra and Shatila (during the Lebanon War)
- June 1987: Equality Day (protesting against discrimination of Arabs in Israel)
- December 1987: Peace Day (striking in support of Palestinian uprising in occupied territories – the Intifada)
- March 1988: 13th Land Day (protesting over Israel's treatment of Palestinians during the Intifada)
- November 1988: Dwelling Day (protesting against the demolition of unauthorized dwellings and against Israel's planning and land policies)
- March 1989: 14th Land Day (protesting against discrimination in municipal financial allocations, land expropriation, and in support of Intifada)

156

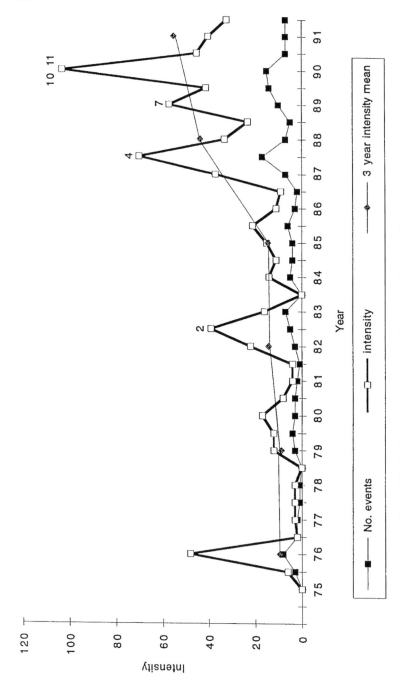

Figure 8.2 Arab protest in Galilee, 1975–91, by event numbers and intensity (six-monthly data)

- February 1990: strike against discrimination in municipal budgets
- March 1990: 15th Land Day (protesting over Intifada events and against land policy following arrival of mass Jewish migration from USSR)
- May 1990: strike in protest of killing of seven Arabs by a Jewish reserve soldier
- October 1990: two-day strike in protest over killing of 21 Arabs in Temple Mount, Jerusalem.

Although these general strikes constituted the peaks of Arab protest, it should be remembered that 156 other regional strikes and events had taken place alongside these state-wide strikes. Only the combination of state-wide activities (like the general strikes) and more local or sectoral events can truly portray the overall pattern of Arab protest in Galilee, as shown in Figure 8.2.

Further analysis of Figure 8.2 highlights three related trends.

1 First and foremost, it can be noted that during the study period, Arabs in Galilee have increasingly used political protest in an attempt to attain their goals in Israeli society. Given the relative lack of Arab protest in the period prior to 1976, it is obvious that since 1976 the Arabs have made a radical change in their political behavior, drawing on their numbers and on various methods of political protest as a strategic tool of the first order.

2 One can note a steady (if fluctuating) rise in the number of protest events: while in late 1970s, after the sudden burst of protest due to the first Land Day in 1976, the annual average was around 2–3 events, during the late 1980s and early 1990s this figure increased to between 14 and 20, with some decline in 1991. Beyond the research period, it may be of interest to note that the 1991 level was broadly maintained in 1992 and 1993, but a rise in the number of protest events was registered again in 1994.

3 A more consistent rise is notable in the intensity of Arab protest: the relatively small increase in the number of annual events is somewhat misleading when the notable rise in the intensity of protest is taken into account. In other words: Arabs in Galilee have staged longer, larger and more militant protest as time progressed. This longitudinal trend is further emphasized in Figure 8.2, where a three-year mean of Arab protest intensity is plotted. A consistent rise in regional protest intensity is clearly evident from 1975 throughout the study period.[56]

Arab protest has in general remained within the non-violent confines of the law. Given the years of frustration and discrimination in Israel, this is indeed a testimony to the incorporation of Arabs into Israel's democratizing and competitive political culture. However, limited violence has surfaced occasionally, especially in events linked to the Palestinian Intifada after its break-out in late 1987.

Some comparisons

In order to gain a better understanding of the rise in Arab regional protest activity, it may be useful to compare it with two key reference groups: Israeli Jews and world minorities. While such comparison is inevitably limited, due to constraints of data availability, some overall commonalities and differences can be traced.

Figure 8.3 compares Arab protest to state-wide Israeli-Jewish trends between 1955 and 1986.[57] In broad terms, Arab protest in Galilee has followed the development of Jewish protest around the country with a 5–10 year time-lag. This lends some support to Lehman-Wilzig's general claim that:[58] 'in most respects the evolution of Israeli Arab protest is markedly similar to that found among Israel's Jews.' The data also corroborate Smooha's[59] and Rouhana and Ghanem's[60] observation of the Arab minority in Israel undergoing processes of modernization, politicization and democratization. These processes entail, by their very nature, greater exposure to, and adoption of, a political culture where protest and demonstration strategies are commonly used. In other words, the political incorporation of the Galilee Arabs into the Israeli political system has undoubtedly influenced the development of their regional and national protest initiatives.

However, further analysis shows that several key differences do exist, of which two stand out. Most notable is the concentration of Arab protest on political-territorial issues, as opposed to a far more diverse range of protest issues by Jews. To illustrate, the data presented in this chapter show that 65 per cent of Arab protest was on national, political, territorial or land issues, as opposed to only 29 per cent of Jewish protest (until 1986).[61] Another important difference is the more common incidence of violence in Arab protest, as reported above. To illustrate, there has only been one Jewish-Israeli killed in a demonstration, while 11 Arabs have been killed in that manner (usually by the police), seven from Galilee. As Lehman-Wilzig notes:[62] 'Israeli (Jewish) public protest by and large is not violent and on only very rare occasions threatens the public order'. As already mentioned above, and

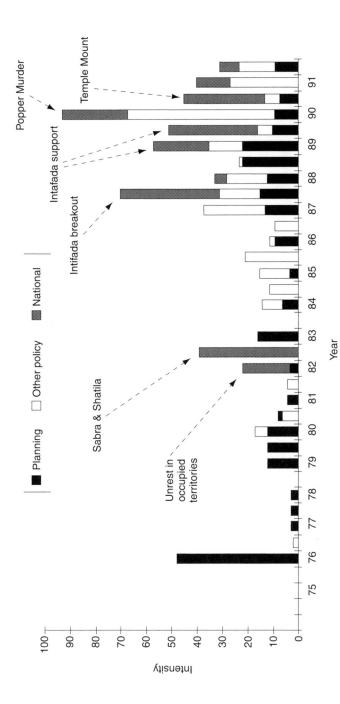

Figure 8.3 Protest issues and intensity by Arabs in Galilee, 1976–91 (showing main national events)

especially since 1987, this cannot be said about Arab protest in Israel and in Galilee.

Finally, the status of the Arabs as a 'hostile minority' within the Israeli ethnocracy, situated largely outside the boundaries of the Israeli-Jewish collective identity,[63] forms a critical difference between the bases of Arab and Jewish protest. Thus, while Jewish protest attempts, above all, to influence the redistribution of resources among Jewish groups within a Jewish state, Arab protest often entails a challenge to the very Jewish-Zionist character of the state. This explains the higher intensity and incidence of violence in Arab protest (as compared to Jewish protest), especially since the outbreak of the Intifada in late 1987, during which the most intense Arab protest was staged in support of the Palestinian struggle for self-determination.[64] Equivalent protest (on Jewish self-determination) is, naturally, non-existent among Jewish protesters.

Another useful comparison can be drawn between the protest staged by Arabs in Galilee and other regional minorities around the world. As Gurr shows,[65] there has been a general increase in the magnitude and intensity of minority protest in all regions of the world, and by all types of minorities during the post-war period, although some notable variations stand out here as well. Given Israel's geopolitical circumstances, the patterns of protest most similar to the case of Arabs in Galilee, are protest by minorities in North Africa and the Middle East, and – to a lesser extent – minorities in western democracies and Japan. In both cases there was an overall increase in protest, with a tapering down during the last decade or two. Here too, data from Galilee demonstrate a similar pattern, albeit with a five- to 15-year time-lag.

It should however be pointed out that several key differences also exist between the Arabs in Galilee and many other minorities studied in Gurr's world survey, and that comparisons should be made with caution. The main difference is caused by varying historical and political circumstances. The Arab community in Israel was all but shattered during the 1948 War, with 80 per cent of its members becoming refugees, including most of its social, economic and political leaders. It was placed under a military government until 1966, and has suffered a peripheral position in the Israeli economy and society ever since. Therefore, unlike many other minorities, the political development of the Arabs in Israel in general, and Galilee in particular, did not begin in earnest until the 1970s. This explains the time-lag evident in the evolution of Arab protest, as compared to most minorities in the western world and the Middle East.

Another significant difference is evident in the evolution of minority protest. As Gurr shows,[66] the intensity of protest by aggrieved minorities in most western democracies started to subside during the early 1970s after several decades of showing increasing levels. This decline has continued until the end of his study in 1989, mainly due to more accommodating public policies. Even allowing for the above-mentioned time-lag, the pattern of Palestinian protest in Israel has not followed that pattern, with a steady increase in protest intensity, with only minor fluctuations. This indicates that majority-minority relations in Israel have not yet reached a point of genuine dialogue and mutual compromise, as has been the case in most multi-ethnic democracies since the early 1970s. Let us return now to the role of relative deprivation, planning policy and ethnic geography in shaping Arab protest.

Key influences on Arab protest

As noted earlier, content analysis of the reporting of Arab protest and the material accompanying that protest (leaflets, press releases and interviews) showed that three overwhelming causes drove Arab protest:

(a) national issues (mainly pertaining to the Palestinians outside Israel);
(b) socio-economic deprivation; and
(c) land, territorial and building issues (hereafter termed 'planning' issues).

In the latter two categories, protest was mostly staged against Israel's policies in these areas.

Inevitably, this breakdown is somewhat artificial, because issues often overlap in their explicit and implicit use. When particular protest events were declared for more than one issue, the 'intensity score' allocated to that event was divided according to the assessed importance of the different issues in the particular event. Thus, while this methodology may obscure certain subtleties, it does represent the main thrusts of Arab protest and political mobilization.

(a)   National issues

Figure 8.3 demonstrates the breakdown of protest into the three main protest issues mentioned above, on a six-monthly basis. Quantitative analysis of protest issues (measured by their intensity score) shows that 35.1 per cent of Arab protest was over planning issues, 34.3 per cent

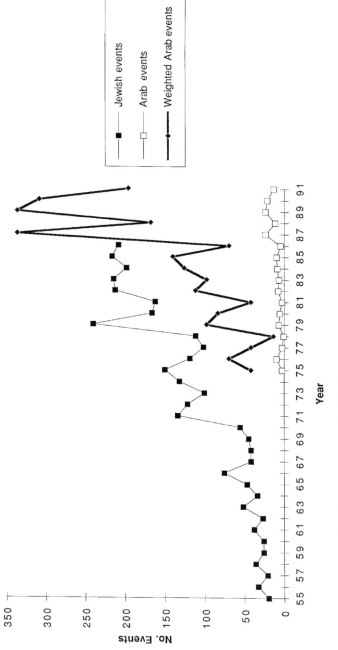

Figure 8.4   Jewish and Arab protest events (weighted)

over socioeconomic deprivation, and 30.6 per cent over national-Palestinian issues (see Appendix 8.1).

Delving further into this relatively even breakdown, it can be noted that protest has been most intense over national-Palestinian issues. As can be deduced from Appendix 8.1, the average mean of a protest event on national issues was 11.1 points, compared with 3.8 points on planning and land issues and 3.3 points on socio-economic deprivation. As illustrated in Figure 8.4, the importance of national issues was especially pronounced during events in the Lebanon War of 1982–3, and the Intifada (1987 onwards). This demonstrates the unparalleled power of national-ethnic issues to mobilize the Palestinian-Arab population in Galilee, as well as in the rest of Israel. Apart from the first Land Day in 1976, the most intense and violent protest events (Peace Day, the 13th and 14th Land Days, and the mourning over the victims of Sabra and Shatila) were all events of unambiguous national-Palestinian nature.

The fact that the events over which protest was staged occurred outside Israel, further illustrates the potency of the national cause to ignite ethnic protest, even from afar. This lends support to the 'ethnic nationalism' explanation discussed earlier. The mobilizing power of this issue was illustrated once more in February and March 1994, following the murder of 29 Palestinians in a sacred grave in Hebron, when the Arab minority in Israel staged a two-day general strike, accompanied by large-scale demonstrations and violence. However, as shown below, the national-Palestinian issue is far from being the only significant generator of Arab protest in Galilee.

(b) Relative deprivation and public policies

Beyond the pronounced impact of national issues on Arab protest, relative deprivation matters have also shaped Arab protest during the research period, together with matters of land and territory (Figures 8.4, 8.5). These issues are directly linked to Israel's planning and socio-economic policies in the region, which in most cases have caused or exacerbated the deprivation of the region's Arabs.

In order to understand better the adverse impact of Israel's policies on Arab life, and with the risk of some repetition, it may be useful to provide here a more detailed account of the implementation of these policies beyond the broad regional overview provided earlier. As mentioned, Israel's planning policies in Galilee have, in the main, eroded the land holdings and territorial control of Palestinian-Arabs in the

164

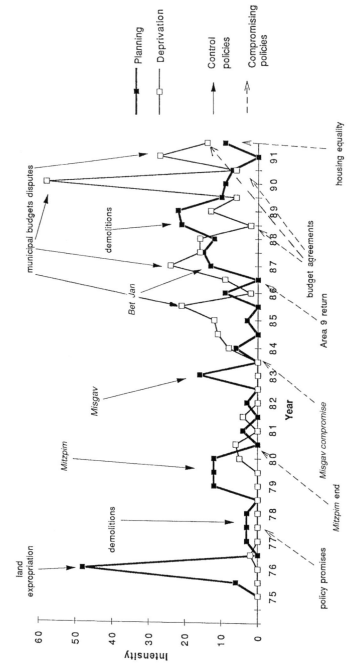

Figure 8.5 Intensity of protest on planning and socio-economic deprivation issues among Arabs 1975–91 (showing key policy events)

country. They have contained the expansion of Arab villages, shifted land resources from the ownership and municipal control of Arabs to the state and to Jewish local authorities, established many new Jewish settlements in order to break the territorial contiguity of Arab settlements, threatened and at times carried out the demolition of unauthorized dwellings, delayed the approval of village plans for Arab village across the country (without which all building approvals require special discretion), and excluded Arabs from a meaningful participation in decision-making processes.[67] Against this background, it is not surprising that Israel's planning policies have become a source of effective mobilization.

Israel's social and economic policies in the region (appearing in Figure 8.3 under 'other' policy) have been marked by neglect of the Arabs in Galilee. Very little government-initiated development of physical, economic and social infrastructure has occurred. The development that did occur, has seriously lagged behind the Jewish sector in both time and standard.[68] This has become a source of pronounced grievance, especially since the establishment of many (relatively well-serviced) Jewish towns and settlements in Galilee, in close proximity to the deprived Arab settlements. The single most important focus of Arab protest in this area of public policy has been over municipal budgets. Despite continuous promises for equality, Arab municipalities have been seriously underfunded by the government compared to their Jewish counterparts, with the ratios in funding ranging from 1:2 to 1:8 in favor of Jewish settlements, depending on size. In general, the disparity in municipal budgets has narrowed over the years, but still remains pronounced, and is a continuous source of Arab-Jewish tension.[69]

The temporal association between Israeli policies and Arab protest in the region is illustrated in Figure 8.5, with several notable peaks in Arab protest caused by opposition to 'control' policies. The periods of these peaks include:

- early 1976 with events surrounding Land Day and the intense Arab protest against widespread land expropriation;
- the late 1979 and early 1980 period with a combination of protest against the establishment of *mitzpim* (new Jewish settlements) in Galilee and against a lack of development in the Arab sector and financial discrimination against Arab villages;
- the 1985–6 period with intensive protest activity on the issue of local authority budgets;

- mid-1987 with the Equality Day general strike and broad Arab support for the struggle of the Bet Jan village to regain control over its lands; late 1988 with the Dwelling Day general strike;
- early 1989, late 1990 and early 1991 with waves of Arab protest against inequality in municipal budgets.

The timing of these peaks in Arab protest followed quite closely on the heels of policy initiatives by the government (usually with adverse impact on the Arabs), or periods of conflicts over the legacy of these control policies.

Like the peaks identified above, the troughs in Arab protest depicted in Figure 8.5 can also be related to the introduction of 'conciliatory' policies by the Israeli government. In 1977 and 1978, for example, no major new policies detrimental to the Arab minority were introduced and the government promised to initiate more positive programs in the Arab sector,[70] explaining the lull in protest action. Another trough is evident in late 1983 following a compromise and settlement of the Misgav conflict. Likewise the decline in protest activity in late 1986 followed the return of Arab land in Galilee known as 'Area 9' (near Sakhnin; See Figure 8.1) from army use to its original owners (Figure 8.5).

Finally, a relative decline in Arab protest intensity can be discerned during 1991 (even though the absolute level remained quite high). This, again, is a reflection of several policy-achievements of Arabs in Israel and Galilee, like repeated government promises to avoid as much as possible the expropriation of Arab land for the absorption of Jewish immigrants; the equalization of government housing assistance between Arabs and Jews; and – most significantly – a government decision in August 1991 to provide equal services in Arab and Jewish municipalities, and the subsequent transfer of funds to Arab local authorities (see Figure 8.5). Assisting the decline was a gradual 'banalization' of the Intifada in the occupied territories.

In general, then, while the growing importance of the national Palestinian cause in generating Arab protest is recognized, the above analysis also reveals a close temporal association between 'control' and 'conciliatory' policies and changes in levels of protest. This association, depicted graphically in Figure 8.5, clearly demonstrates the key role of public policies in determining the extent of minority deprivation, and – subsequently – levels of protest and violence. Because of the direct association between municipal, welfare and planning policies, and Arab relative deprivation in Israel (at least in their own eyes), the data lend some support to the relative deprivation approach.

(c)   Land and geography

Having demonstrated the important role of national, relative deprivation and public policy issues, in generating Arab protest, the analysis
will now move to a factor often neglected in protest analysis: the geography of ethnic relations and the emergence of ethnic regionalism.
Given Israel's geographical history and political circumstances, and the
settlement process of Jews in Galilee, it is clear that most protest events
in the region were influenced by geographical factors.

On a conceptual level, the Palestinian-Arabs in Galilee constitute a
homeland ethnic group, with a long tradition of rural living, and
strong bonds to their land.[71] Land is an important element in
Palestinian culture, illustrated by the use of a folk song named 'My
Land' as the Palestinian anthem, as well as many other land-related
images and titles in Palestinian public life.[72] Hence, policies which
deliberately threaten the Arabs' ties with the land are likely to be
strongly opposed.

On a more empirical level, the most obvious relation between geography and protest is the constant Arab opposition to, and protest
against, Israeli policies designed to contain and control Arab settlements, while at the same time to fill the region with many Jewish villages and towns. Israel has created a totally new ethnic geography in
the region (see Figure 8.1), transforming it from an Arab regional
enclave, into an ethnically mixed region. Many Arab acts of protest –
beginning with Land Day in 1976 and stretching to Land Day 1991
and beyond – have explicitly and implicitly challenged the creation of
this new regional geography. The following quotation from a leaflet
published before a Land Day demonstration in 1980 illustrates the
underpinning of the protest:

> The Arabs in Israel have demanded the allotment of land before it
> was appropriated for the purpose of housing, development and agri-
> culture ... instead of allocating our lands to the use of Arab villages
> which badly need them, they have been given by the government
> for the large number of *mitzpim* being currently built in the Galilee.
> These *mitzpim* are aimed at strangling our villages and preventing
> their free development (Lands Committee, March, 1980).

A less direct, yet still profound geographical influence is also evident
in Arab protest on national issues. Prior to 1948, Galilee was an integral part of the geographical unit of Palestine. The administrative division of the Palestinians between Israel and Jordan slowed, but did not

stop, the development of a collective political identity of an ethnic group living in its own homeland region. The protest on national issues documented above is therefore also influenced by the strong attachment of Arabs in Galilee to their land as a source of collective ethnic identity and pride.[73] In addition, Galilee is in close proximity to the main Palestinian concentrations in the West Bank (only 30–150 kilometers to the south), facilitating close contacts and the strengthening of common national identity, despite the existence of the 'green line' which officially separates the two communities into two administrative and political units.

Even the protest over social and economic issues is influenced by the geography of ethnic relations. In the main, the increasing mix between Arabs and Jews in the region has made the social and economic disparities between the two communities more visible. This has given Arab leaders potent 'ammunition' around which to mobilize protest, as illustrated by the following statement, given in an interview with the mayor of a large village in central Galilee:

> These new Jewish settlements all around us have brought home the double meaning of our discrimination in Israel. Not only don't we have a say in the planning of our own region, we also have to see the good-looking Jewish *mitzpim* every day through our windows, and thus see – and not only feel or hear – our pathetic existence in this society.

Ethnic regionalism

Juxtaposing the data presented above and theories of ethnic protest reviewed earlier, indicates that a process of ethnic regionalization is at work among Arabs in Galilee. The development of Arab protest in the region has been caused, as shown, by three relatively equal forces: national sentiments, socio-economic deprivation, and land issues. It is postulated here that the relatively equal impact of these three forces reflects a fledgling regional (rather than purely class or national) Palestinian identity in Galilee. This process is being shaped differently from the more open Palestinian nationalism in the occupied territories, demonstrating the difference between nationalism and regionalism spelt out earlier.[74]

As noted in the theoretical discussion, ethnic regionalism reflects a particular set of circumstances where ethno nationalism is geopolitically constrained, and full integration into the main state system is undesirable or structurally impossible. As such, it represents a compromise between opposing forces within the ethnic community. The process at work in Galilee resembles this constellation, with the Arabs appearing to head in the direction of other regional minorities 'trapped' in states controlled by dominant ethnic groups, such as the Tyroleaurs in Italy, the Basques in Spain, or the Scots in Britain.[75]

Although the data documented above relate only to Galilee, it should be noted that 79 per cent of all Arab protest events, and virtually all the important ones, have been staged jointly with Arabs from other regions, especially the 'Triangle' (see Figure 8.1). As such, the reading of Arab protest in Galilee as a surface reflection of ethnic regionalism can be extrapolated to the entire Palestinian-Arab community in Israel, despite some differences discussed below. This is necessary for the interpretation of the political mobilization process among Arabs in Israel, and is consistent with other political activity data.[76]

State-wide ethnic regionalism (that is, in the combined area of three main regional concentrations of Arabs in Israel) appears to be the main level on which the process of Arab regionalism is taking place. Supported by the findings of past research, and by the protest data analyzed above, it is argued that an 'Arab-Palestinian region' is emerging within Israel, with an 'enclave economy',[77] local and regional 'political enclosures', a distinct culture, and its own set of social and political institutions.[78] Recent calls by several leading Arab intellectuals and scholars to move towards a higher degree of cultural and political autonomy for Palestinian-Arabs in Israel are also examples of that process. The form of autonomy demanded is still vague, although it can mainly be expressed in Arab localities and regions.[79] I have elsewhere termed this reality 'fractured regionalism', which denotes the crystallization of group regional identity (between local and state) in a set of politically and culturally connected areas, but without geographical contiguity. A fractured region can be likened to a 'chain of beads', functioning as one unit internally and *vis-à-vis* the state or other such regions.[80]

The findings of other studies also confirm the emergence of 'fractured' Arab regionalism in Galilee and Israel, with patterns of increasingly cohesive emotional and functional links between Arab villages in the region, and a growing ability to mobilize support and participation on regional issues.[81] As Schnell observes when studying the territorial awareness of the Arabs in Israel: 'Israeli-Arab territoriality is developing from a newly evolving territorial awareness ... territorial awareness is reaching a higher level of generalization ... towards larger regional territorial units'.[82]

Paradoxically, in some respects Israel's attempts to de-territorialize the Arabs – which were supposed to stop the process of ethnic regionalization – have had the opposite effect. They provided Arab leaders with a strong rallying cause around which to mobilize political support. Further, the loss of land and regional cohesion raised Arab concerns about losing their ethnic identity, and spawned the development of survival strategies which strongly emphasized the bond to the land at local and regional levels.[83]

Significantly, this fledgling Arab regionalism draws on deep historical roots in the region, and on long-standing regional variations evident in Palestinian culture, in the fields of folk music, art, dress and speech dialects.[84] It has taken four decades for this regionalism to re-emerge, following the disaster inflicted on the Palestinians in 1948. The bond to the land and the political will associated with this movement are well illustrated by the late poet and politician Tuwafiq Ziyyad who wrote in 1989 as part of the 'Nazerath' trilogy:

> We guard the shades of our figs
> We guard the trunks of our olives
> We sow our hopes like the yeast of bread
> With ice in our fingers
> With red hell in our hearts ...
>
> If we are thirsty, we shall be quenched by the rocks
> And if we are hungry, we shall be fed by the dust ...
> And we shall not move
> Because here we have Past, Present
> And Future.

Notably, the growing regional awareness of Arabs in Galilee has not included any attempts to create an inter-ethnic regional movement in cooperation with the region's Jews. Jews in Galilee have well-established regional organizations of their own, and there is little, if any, common representation of regional issues by the two communities.[85] To be sure, the emergence of a regional Palestinian identity in Israel and in Galilee is still in its infancy, but the process has the potential to influence the relations between Arabs and Jews in Israel profoundly during the critical years to come.

Finally, it can be noted that the demonstrations staged by Arabs played a key symbolic role, not only in articulating their political grievances and aspirations, but also in shaping their nascent ethno-political identity. In that way Land Day – the first major protest event in the history of the Arab minority – has become an annual day of commemoration and celebration. The persistent campaign for rights and against dispossession by the state, has provided key dates, common memories and community practices as important foundations for a new Arab regional identity.

In general, then, a full understanding of the evolution of Arab protest in Galilee must take into account the role of geographical processes and factors, beyond the powerful national and socio-economic circumstances. Hence, the growing Arab-Jewish mix, the intensifying competition over ownership and use of land, the massive loss of Arab land to the state, the higher visibility of socio-economic inequalities, and the physical proximity to the core of Palestinian identity, have all exerted an influence on Arab protest. The combination of the above processes has spawned the emergence of Arab regionalism, around which a Palestinian-Arab identity in Israel and Galilee is being reconstructed.

Conclusions

We have seen above that Palestinian-Arab protest has become a notable force within the Israeli-Jewish 'ethnocracy'. With this protest, the minority has entered the Israeli extra-parliamentary political arena. In more detail, the analysis has highlighted the following:

1   The volume of protest has steadily increased between 1976 and 1991, with a notable increase of intensity after 1987.
2   In certain respects, the development of Arab protest has resembled patterns of Jewish protest and of other minorities around the world, with a general 5–10 year time-lag, and higher levels of protest intensity and violence.
3   There were three main issues around which Arab protest in Galilee evolved: national events, socio-economic deprivation and land and territorial issues.
4   National issues ignited the most intense protest, but there was a relatively even distribution in the overall magnitude of protest on all three key issues.
5   Israeli policies have had a pronounced impact on patterns of Arab protest: control policies have generally spawned protest, while conciliatory policies have had the opposite effect.
6   Geographical factors and processes have played a key role in shaping Arab protest, particularly the bond of Arabs to their land

(as a homeland minority); the changing ethnic spatial relations, and growing physical visibility of socio-economic inequalities.

7   The combined effect of the political and geographical factors outlined above, point to the emergence of Arab regionalism in Israel as a whole and in Galilee in particular, which is reflected in the nature of Arab protest.

In reference to the theories of ethnic protest discussed earlier, Arab protest in Galilee has demonstrated the saliency of *both* relative deprivation and ethnic nationalism. The national-Palestinian cause has illustrated the potency of the ethnic nationalism approach: Arabs have increasingly rallied around the national issue with growing intensity and militancy. This can be interpreted as a process of radicalization which may lead to demands for self-determination and possible ethnic separatism. However, the relative deprivation approach is also partially valid: Israeli public policy and subsequent socio-economic deprivations have formed a major cause for Arab protest, with changes in Israeli policy being mirrored by variations in protest levels.

The dual explanation of protest in Galilee reflects the dual process experienced by the Arabs there and in Israel as a whole, and links the findings of the present study to the politicization-radicalization dichotomy in the interpretation of Arab political behavior in Israel. As I have argued earlier,[86] the Palestinian-Arabs in Israel appear to be undergoing a process which strengthens both their political self-assertion within Israel and their potential for radical political action.

Therefore, our findings cannot fully support the leading 'politicization' explanation of Arab protest which claims that 'the Arabs fight independently, peacefully and rigorously to better their lot in Israeli society';[87] or that 'Arab protest has no intent of toppling the government in power, but rather demands equal treatment to that given to Jewish populations'.[88] These interpretations basically equate the Arab minority with an 'ethno-class', vying for a larger share of Israel's public resources.

The emergence of Arab regionalism in Galilee, and anti-governmental protest in this region, are early signs that material gains and even material equality with the region's Jews are not the main, let alone the only, purpose of Arab protest. Only a consideration of the total milieu of Arab existence in the region, which combines feelings of deprivation, bonds to their ancestors' land, group ambitions fueled by political mobilization, and reactions to a constantly changing regional geography, can provide an appropriate interpretation of Arab protest in the region to date.

It is therefore postulated that as a product of this regional milieu, the Arabs in Galilee are experiencing a process of ethnic regionalization, around which a refined ethnic identity is being reconstructed. That identity is born out of their politico-geographical situation within Israel – where the options of irredentism or separatism bear intolerable costs. It builds on the Arabs' unambiguous (but unfulfilled) Palestinian identity, on their involuntary but firm inclusion in the Israeli political system, and on their grievances generated by socio-economic deprivation. Our analysis has shown that neither national nor socio-economic issues have dominated Arab protest, and that regional territorial and land issues have been equally important. The nature of that protest points to the development of Arab regionalism which is able to build a new collective ethnic entity within the structural constraints of the Israeli ethnocracy, and locate this identity between the local and national levels.

That emerging collective identity combines issues of socio-economic and power disparities and national identification with specific protest over regional land and territorial issues. It differs from an ethno-class in its explicit territorial goals, and in the structural challenge it poses to the political status quo (which in Israel amounts to a persistent struggle against the state's Zionist character). It also differs from an ethnic national group (as evident in the West Bank and Gaza) by the lack of explicit separatist goals, rhetoric or action.

When returning to other explanations of Arab political orientation in Israel, the present regional interpretation – which was shown to be inconsistent with the 'ethno-class' (or politicization) explanation – is equally at odds with the ethno-nationalist (or radicalization) approach, which perceives the Arabs as steadily moving towards ethnic separatism.[89] A third explanation is proposed on the basis of our findings: Arab regionalism.

Accordingly, Arab political activity is likely to involve strengthening the campaign for land rights and territorial autonomy, as well as the closing of socio-economic gaps. It will neither accept the Zionist character of the Israeli ethnocracy nor confine its struggle merely to 'better terms of coexistence'.[90] It is not likely to attempt to separate the Arabs from the state, but rather struggle for Arab rights and identity in the specific and confined Arab spaces within Israel. The struggle for Arab regional rights within Israel is also likely to intensify if the peace process in the Middle East continues, with the focusing of attention on internal Israeli issues. Finally, it is hoped that these findings and assertions will assist students of ethnic minorities, and also help to form hypotheses for subsequent studies on the topic.

Notes

1 See: Horowitz, D.L., (1985); Gurr, T., (1970); Gurr, T.,(1993); Lichbach, M.I., (1989).
2 Lehman-Wilzig, (1992).
3 Yiftachel, O., (1992a), appendix 5.
4 Smith, A., (1992).
5 Lindblom, C.E., (1973).
6 Lane, J.E. and Ersson, S.O., (1991); Rabushka, A. and Sheples, K.A., (1972).
7 Manogaran, C., (1987); Douglas, J.N., (1983).
8 Grenier, C.E., (1988), p. 129.
9 Muller, E.N., (1977), p. 73.
10 Hibbs, D.A., (1973), pp. 11–16.
11 Grenier, (1988), p. 129; Hibbs, (1973), pp. 11–16.
12 Gurr, T., and Lichbach, M., (1986).
13 See Melucci, A., (1989); Tilly, C., (1984). The resource mobilization approach has been highly useful for explaining the emergence of 'new social movements', based on strong abstract ideologies and on educated, middle-class, membership (such as the feminist or Green movements). It is less appropriate for relatively large 'homeland' ethnic minorities whose membership is largely constructed as 'primordial'. The chapter thus focuses on the deprivation and nationalism theories as most relevant to our case.
14 Gurr and Lichbach, (1986), *op. cit.*
15 See Glazer, N., (1983); Gurr, (1970); Horowitz, (1985).
16 Gurr, (1993), p. 319.
17 Gurr, (1993), p. 319.
18 Connor, W., (1987); Gurr, (1993); Lichbach, (1989).
19 Van den Berghe, P.L., (1981).
20 Connor, W., (1992); Smith, A.D., (1981); Smith, (1992).
21 See also Mikesell, M., and Murphy, A., (1991); Yiftachel, O., (1994).
22 For notable exceptions, see: Keating, M., (1988); Murphy, A.B., (1989); Mikessel and Murphy, (1991).
23 See Friedmann, J., (1993).; Mikessel and Murphy, (1991); Yiftachel, O., (1992b).
24 Yiftachel, O., (1994).
25 See also Friedmann, J., (1992); Friedmann, J., (1993); Kellerman, A., (1993); Keating, (1988).
26 See, for example: Agnew, J., (1987); Coakley, J., (1990); Hechter, M., and Levi, M., (1979); Johnston, R., Knight, D., and Kofman, E., (eds), (1988); Markusen, A., (1987); Mikessel and Murphy, (1991); Schnell, Y., (1994); Williams, C., (1985).
27 See Boal, F., (1987); Eyles, J., (1990); Massey, D.S., (1985); Romann, M., and Weingrod, A., (1991).
28 Anderson, J., (1990); Coakely (1990); Gradus, Y., (1984); Rudolph, R.R.J. and Thompson, R.J., (1985); Murphy, (1989).
29 See Keating, (1988); Johnston, Knight and Kofman, (1988).
30 See Markusen, (1987), p. 16; McCrone, D., (1993), p. 507.
31 See Gurr, T. and Hanf, B., (1994).
32 See also Hechter and Levi, (1979); Markusen, (1987).

33 See Smith, (1981).
34 Mikessel and Murphy, (1991).
35 See Benziman, U., & Mansur, A., (1992); see: al Haj, (1988); Peled, (1992); Smooha, (1990); Waterman, (1990).
36 Newman, (1989); Portugali, (1993).
37 Khalidi, (1988); Zureik, (1979).
38 Smooha, (1989).
39 Al-Haj, M., (1988); Smooha, S., (1992); Rouhana, N., and Ghanem, A., (1993).
40 Haidar, (1991); Yiftachel, (1992a); Zureik, (1993).
41 This campaign was led by several bodies, including the National Committee of the Heads of Arab Councils (hereafter the 'National Committee'), the National Committee for the Defence of Arab Lands (hereafter 'the Lands Committee), and the Follow-up Committee (which is closely associated with the National Committee), the Druze Committee, the Association of the 40, and most recently the Islamic movement.
42 Smooha, (1992); Yiftachel, (1994); and Yiftachel, O., (1997).
43 Smooha, (1990, 1992); Ginat, (1989).
44 Regev, (1989); Soffer, (1983, 1988).
45 Yiftachel, (1992b).
46 Soffer and Finkel, (1989).
47 Carmon *et al.*, (1991); Kipnis, (1987); Soffer and Finkel, (1989).
48 Carmon *et al.*, (1991); Falah, (1990); Yiftachel, (1995).
49 Schnell, (1994).
50 Lehman-Wilzig, (1992); Rekhes, (1986); Reiter and Aharoni, (1992).
51 Lehman-Wilzig (1992), p. 4.
52 Grenier, (1988).
53 Gurr, (1993).
54 Hibbs, (1973).
55 Lehman-Wilzig, (1990).
56 Notably, at the time of finalizing this chapter, in mid-1998, it became clear that the level of Arab protest has been declining since 1992.
57 State-wide data is drawn from Lehman-Wilzig, (1990), pp. 34–41. It is compared with our data on Arab regional protest, which has been 'weighted' to account for the different size of the two populations.
58 Lehman-Wilzig, (1992), p. 18.
59 Smooha, (1992).
60 Rouhana and Ghanem, (1993).
61 Lehman-Wilzig, (1990), pp. 30–44.
62 Lehman-Wilzig, (1990), p. 44.
63 Peled, (1992).
64 Zureik and Haidar, (1991).
65 Gurr, (1993), pp. 101–112.
66 Gurr, (1993), p. 103.
67 Khameissi, (1992); Yiftachel, (1992a).
68 Al Haj and Rosenfeld, (1990).
69 Lewin Epstein and Semyonov, (1993); al Haj and Rosenfeld, (1990).
70 Al Haj and Rosenfeld, (1990).
71 Schnell, (1994).

72 See Rubinstein, (1991); Grossman, (1992).
73 Rubinstein, (1990); Schnell, (1994).
74 See Keating, (1988); McCrone, (1993).
75 Keating, (1988).
76 Al-Haj, (1993); Ghanem, (1995); Lehman-Wilzig, (1990); Smooha, (1992).
77 Khalidi, (1988); Schnell, (1996); al-Haj, (1993).
78 Ghanem, (1995).
79 See Bishara, (1993); Osatzki-Lazer and Ghanem, (1990).
80 See Yiftachel, O., (1997), 'Metropolitan Integration or "Fractured Regions"?' *Cities*, 14(6), pp. 371–80.
81 See Falah, (1989); Fenster, (1993); Schnell, (1994).
82 Schnell, (1994), p. 78.
83 See Rubinstein, (1990), pp. 60–1.
84 Rubinstein, (1990), pp. 55–69.
85 Peled, (1990); Yiftachel, (1994). Please note that another aspect of ethnic-spatial fragmentation in Galilee is between ashkenazi and mizrahi Jews (see Yiftachel, (1997)).
86 Yiftachel, (1992b).
87 Smooha, (1992), p. 11.
88 Lehman-Wilzig, (1990), p. 57.
89 Regev, (1989); Soffer, (1988).
90 Smooha, (1992)

References

Agnew, J. (1987), *Place and Politics* (London: Allen & Unwin).
Agnew, J. (1989), 'Is there a geography of nationalism? The case and place of nationalism in Scotland' in Johnston, R., Kofman, E. and Willimas, C., (eds), *Community conflict: Partition and Nationalism* (Routledge, London).
Al-Haj, M. (1988), 'The Socio-Political Structure of Arabs in Israel: External and Internal Orientations' in Jochanan Hofman *et al.* (eds), *Arab-Jewish Relations in Israel – a Quest in Human Understanding* (Bristol, Indiana: Wyndham Hall Press), pp. 92–122.
Al-Haj, M. (1993), 'The Changing Strategies of Mobilisation among the Arabs in Israel' in E. Ben Zadok (ed.), *Local Communities and the Israeli Polity* (SUNY Press, Albany), pp. 67–88.
Al-Haj, M. and Rosenfeld, H. (1990), *Arab Local Government in Israel* (Boulder: Westview).
Anderson, J. (1990), 'Separatism and Devolution: the Basques in Spain' in M. Chisholm and D. Smith (eds), *Shared Space, Divided Space: Essays on Conflict and Territorial Organization* (London: Unwin Hyman), pp. 135–156.
Benziman, U., & Mansur, A. (1992), *Subtenants: the Arabs in Israel: their Status and Government Policy Towards Them* (Jerusalem: Keter).
Bishara, A. (1993), 'On the Question of the Palestinian Minority in Israel' in *Theory and Criticism* [Teoria uvikkoret], 3, pp. 7–20 (Hebrew).
Boal, F. (1987), 'Segregation' in M. Pacione, (ed.), *Progress in Social Geography* (London: Croom Helm).

Carmon, N., Czamanski, D., Amir, S., Law Yone, H., Kipnis, B., and Lipshitz, G. (1991). *The New Jewish Settlement in the Galilee: an Evaluation* (Haifa: Center for Urban and Regional Research, Technion) (Hebrew).

Coakley, J. (1990), 'National Minorities and the Government of Divided Societies: a Comparative Analysis of Some European Evidence' *European Journal of Political Research*, 18, pp. 437–56.

Connor, W. (1987), 'Ethnonationalism' in M. Weiner and S. Huntington (eds), *Understanding Political Development* (Boston: Little Brown).

Connor, W. (1992), 'The National and Its Myth', *International Journal of Contemporary Sociology*, 33(1–2), pp. 48–57.

Douglas, J.N. (1983), 'Political, Integration and Division in Plural Societies – Problems, Measurements and Salience' in N.K. & S. Waterman, (eds), *Pluralism and Political Geography* (London: Croom Helm), pp. 47–68.

Eyles, J. (1990), 'Group identity and urban space: the North American Experience' in M. Chisholm and D. Smith (eds). *Shared Space, Divided Space: Essays on Conflict and Territorial Organization* (London: Unwin Hyman), pp. 46–66.

Falah, G. (1990), 'Arabs Versus Jews in Galilee: Competition over Resources', *Geojournal* 21, pp. 325–36.

Falah, R. (1989), 'Israeli Judaisation Policy in Galilee and its Impact on Local Arab Urbanization', *Political Geography Quarterly*, 8, pp. 229–53.

Fenster, T. (1993), 'Settlement Planning and Participation Under Principles of Pluralism', *Progress in Planning*, 39(3), pp. 169–242.

Friedmann, J. (1992), *Empowerment: the Politics of Alternative Development* (Cambridge: Blackwell).

Friedmann, J. (1993), 'Borders, Margins and Frontiers: Notes Towards a Political Economy of Regions' in *Regional Development: The Challenge of the Frontier* (Dead Sea, Israel: Negev Center for Regional Development, Ben Gurion University), pp. 1–20.

Ghanem, A. (1995), 'Political Mobilisation among the Arabs in Israel' in *The Arab Minority in Israel* (Dayan Center, Tel Aviv).

Ginat, Y. (1989), 'Voting Patterns and Political Behavior in the Arab Sector' in J.M. Landau, (ed.), *The Arab Vote in Israel's Parliamentary Elections, 1988* (Jerusalem: The Jerusalem Institute for Israel Studies), pp. 3–21, (Hebrew).

Glazer, N. (1983), *The Ethnic Dilemma: 1964–1982* (Cambridge: Harvard University Press).

Gradus, Y. (1984), 'The Emergence of Regionalism in a centralised system: the case of Israel', *Environment and Planning D: Society and Space*, 2, pp. 87–100.

Grenier, C.E. (1988), 'Violence, Inequality and Development at the National Level: a Comparative Analysis', *International Journal of Contemporary Sociology* 25, pp. 127–40.

Grossman, D. (1992), *Present Absentees* (Tel Aviv: Hakkibutz Hameuhad) (Hebrew).

Gurr, T. (1970), *Why Men Rebel* (New Jersey: Princeton University Press).

Gurr, T. (1993), *Minorities at Risk: the Global View of Ethnopolitical Conflict* (Arlington: Institute of Peace Press).

Gurr, T. and Lichbach, M. (1986), 'Forecasting Internal Conflict' *Comparative Political Studies*, 9, pp. 3–38.

Gurr, T. and Hanf, B. (1994), *Ethnic Conflict in World Politics* (Boulder: Westview Press).

Haidar, A. (1991), *Social Welfare Services for Israel's Arab Population* (Boulder, San Francisco, Oxford: Westview Press).

Hechter, M. and Levi, M. (1979), 'The Comparative Analysis of Ethnoregional Movements' *Ethnic and Racial Studies*, 2, pp. 260–74.

Hibbs, D.A. (1973), *Mass Political Violence: a Cross-National Causal Analysis* (New York: John Wiley and Sons).

Horowitz, D.L. (1985), *Ethnic Groups in Conflict* (Berkeley: University of California Press).

Johnston, R., Knight, D. and Kofman, E. (eds) (1988), *Nationalism, Self-Determination and Political Geography* (London: Croom Helm).

Keating, M. (1988), *State and Regional Nationalism* (New York: Harvester & Wheatsheaf).

Kellerman, A. (1993), 'Settlement Frontiers Revisited: the Case of Israel and the West Bank', *Tijdschrift voor Econ. en Soc. Geografie*, 84, pp. 27–39.

Khalidi, R. (1988), *The Arab Economy in Israel: the Dynamics of a Region's Development* (London: Croom Helm).

Khameissi, R. (1992), *Planning, Housing and the Arab Minority in Israel* (Boulder: Westview).

Kipmis, B. (1987), 'Geopolitical Ideologies and Regional Strategies', *Tijdchrift voon Economische en Sociale Geographie*, 78, pp. 125–38.

Lane, J.E. and Ersson, S.O. (1991), *Politics and Society in Western Europe* (London: Sage).

Lehman-Wiltzig, S. (1990), *Stiff-Necked People in a Bottled-Necked System: the Evolution and Roots of Israeli Public Protest, 1949–86* (Bloomington: University of Indiana Press).

Lehman-Wiltzig, S. (1992), 'Copying the Master? Patterns of Israeli-Arab Protest, 1950–1990' Paper presented at the conference: *Arab Politics in Israel*, University of Tel Aviv, Dayan Center.

Lewin-Epstein, N., & Semyonov, M. (1993), *The Arab Minority in Israel's Economy: Patterns of Ethnic Inequality* (Boulder: Westview).

Lichbach, M.I. (1989), 'An Evaluation of "Does Economic Inequality Breed Political Conflict?" Studies', *World Politics*, 61, pp. 431–70.

Lindblom, C.E. (1973), 'The Science of Muddling Through' in A. Faludi (ed.), *A Reader in Planning Theory* (Oxford: Pergamon), pp. 151–69.

Manogaran, C. (1987), *Ethnic Conflict and Reconciliation in Sri Lanka* (Honolulu: University of Hawaii Press).

Markusen, A. (1987), *Regions: the Economic and Politics of Territory* (Rowman & Littlefield, Totawa, New Jersey).

Massey, D.S. (1985), 'Ethnic Residential Segregation: a Theoretical Synthesis and Empirical Review', *Sociology and Social Research*, 69, pp. 315–50.

McCrone, D. (1993), 'Regionalism and Constitutional Change in Scotland' *Regional Studies*, 27, pp. 507–12.

Meir, A.(1994), 'Territoriality among Negev Bedouin in Transition: from nomadism to sedentarism' in U. Fabietti, U. and P. Zalzman (eds), *The Anthropology of Pastoral Societies* (Ibis, Como, Italy), pp. 159–81.

Melucci, A. (1989), *Nomads of the Present: Social Movements and Individual Needs and Contemporary Society* (Philadelphia: Temple University Press).

Mikesell, M. and Murphy, A. (1991), 'A Framework for Comparative Study of Minority Aspirations' in *Annals of the Association of American Geographers* 81, pp. 581–604.

Muller, E.N. (1977), 'Mass Politics: Focus of Participation', *American Behavioral Scientist*, 21, pp. 63–86.

Murphy, A.B. (1989), 'Territorial Policies in Multiethnic State', *Geographical Review*, 79, pp. 410–21.

Newman, D. (1989), 'Civilian Presence as Strategies of Territorial Control: the Arab-Israeli Conflict', *Political Geography Quarterly*, 8, pp. 215–27.

Ozacky-Lazar, S. and Ghanem, A. (1990), *Autonomy for the Arabs in Israel: the Beginning of a Debate* (Givaat Haviva: The Institute for Arab Studies) (Hebrew).

Peled, Y. (1990), 'Ethnic Exclusionism in the Periphery: the Case of Oriental Jews in Israel's Development Towns' *Ethnic and Racial Studies*, 13, pp. 345–67.

Peled, Y. (1992), 'Ethnic Democracy and the Legal Construction of Citizenship: Arab Citizens of the Jewish State', *American Political Science Review*, 86 (2), pp. 432–43.

Portugali, J. (1993), *Implicated Relations: Society and Space in the Israeli-Palestinian Conflict* (Dordrecht: Kulwer).

Rabushka, A. (1973), *Race and Politics in Urban Malaysia* (California: Hoover Institution Press, Stanford University).

Rabushka, A. and Sheples, K.A. (1972), *Politics in Plural Societies: a Theory of Democratic Instability* (Columbus: Merril Publishers Co.).

Regev, A. (1989), *The Arabs in Israel: Political Issues* (Jerusalem: Jerusalem Institute for Israel Studies) (Hebrew).

Reiter, Y. and Ahunoni, R. (1992), *The Political Life of Arabs in Israel* (Beit Berl: The Institute for Israeli Arabs Studies) (Hebrew).

Rekhes, E. (1986), 'The Arab Village in Israel: a Renewing National Political Center', *Ofakim Begeographia*, 17–18, pp. 145–60 (Hebrew).

Rekhes, E. (1991), *The Moslem Movement in Israel,* Paper Presented to a Conference – The Arab Minority in Israel: Dilemmas of Political Orientation and Social Change (Dayan Center, University of Tel Aviv).

Romann, M. and Weingrod, A. (1991), *Living Together and Apart: Arab-Jewish Relations in Jerusalem* (New Jersey: Princeton University Press).

Rouhana, N. and Ghanem, A. (1993), 'The Democratization of a Traditional Minority in an Ethnic Democracy: the Palestinians in Israel' in E. Kaufman & A. El Abed (eds), *Democracy and Peace in the Middle East* (Boulder: Westview).

Rubinstein, D. (1990), *The Fig Tree Embrace* (Jerusalem: Keter) (Hebrew).

Rudolph, R.R.J., & Thompson, R.J. (1985), 'Ethnoterritorial Movements and the Policy Process: Accommodating National Demands in the Developed World', *Comparative Politics*, 17, pp. 291–311.

Schnell, Y. (1994), *Perceptions of Israeli Arabs: Territoriality and Identity* (Aldershot: Avebury).

Schnell, Y. (1998), 'Arab Industrial Frontiers' in O. Yiftachel and A. Meir (eds), *Ethnic Frontiers and Peripheries: Landscapes of Development and Inequality in Israel* (Boulder, Westview Press).

Smith, A.D. (1981), *The Ethnic Revival* (Cambridge: Cambridge University Press).

Smith, A. (1992), 'Ethnicity and Nationalism', *International Journal of Contemporary Sociology*, 33(1–2), pp. 1–5.

Smooha, S. (1989), *Arabs and Jews in Israel: Conflicting and Shared Attitudes in a Divided Society* (Boulder: Westview Press).

Smooha, S. (1990), 'Minority Status in an Ethnic Democracy: the Status of the Arab Minority in Israel', *Ethnic and Racial Studies* 13(3), pp. 389–412.

Smooha, S. (1992), *Arabs and Jews in Israel: Change and Continuity in Mutual Intolerance* (Boulder, San Francisco, Oxford: West View Press).

Soffer, A. (1983), 'The Changing Situation of Minority and Majority and Its Spatial Expression' in A.S. Waterman and N. Kliot (eds), *Pluralism and Political Geography* (London: Croom Helm), pp. 80–99.

Soffer, A. (1988), *The Demographic and Geographic Situation in the Land of Israel: is it the End of the Zionist Vision?* (Haifa: University Press).

Soffer, A. and Finkel, R. (1989), *The Mitzpim Project – Interim Evaluation* (Rehovot: Center of Settlement Research) (Hebrew).

Tilly, C. (1984) 'Social Movements and National Politics' in C. Bright and S. Harding (eds), *Statemaking and Social Movements* (Ann Arbor: University of Michigan Press), pp. 297–317.

Van den Berghe, P.L. (1981), *The Ethnic Phenomenon* (New York: Elsevier).

Waterman, S. (1990), 'Involuntary Incorporation: the Case of Israel' in M. & S. Chisholm (eds), *Shared Space, Divided Space: Essays in Conflict and Territorial Organization* (London: Unwin Hyman) pp. 178–93.

Williams, C. (1985), 'Minority Groups in the Modern State' in M. Pacione (ed.), *Progress in Political Geography* (Croom Helm, London), pp. 111–57.

Yiftachel, O. (1992a), *Planning a Mixed Region in Israel: the Political Geography of Arab-Jewish Relations in the Galilee* (Aldershot: Avebury).

Yiftachel, O. (1992b), 'The Arab Minority in Israel and its relations with the Jewish Minority: A Review Essay', *Studies in Comparative International Development*, 27(2), pp. 57–83.

Yiftachel, O. (1994), 'Regional Mix and Ethnic Relations: Evidence from Israel', *Geoforum*, 25, pp. 1–55.

Yiftachel, O. (1995), 'The Dark Side of Modernism: Planning as Control of an Ethnic Minority' in S. Watson & K. Gibson (eds), *Postmodern Cities and Spaces* (Oxford: Basil Blackwell) pp. 216–42.

Yiftachel, O. (1997), 'Israel: Metropolitan Integration or "Fractured Regions"?, *Cities*, 14(6), pp. 371–80.

Zureik, E.T. (1979), *Palestinians in Israel: a Study of Internal Colonialism* (London: Routledge and Kegan Paul).

Zureik, E. (1993), 'Prospects of the Palestinians in Israel', *Journal of Palestine Studies*, 27(4), pp. 73–93.

Zureik, E., & Haider, A. (1991), 'The Impact of the Intifada on the Palestinians in Israel', *International Journal of the Sociology of Law*, 19, pp. 475–99.

Appendix 8.1 The Measurement of Arab Regional Protest

The measurement of Arab protest activity was based on the detailed documentation of all regional protest events, and the derivation of a 'regional protest intensity index'. Protest was considered 'regional' only if at least five of the region's villages participated in it. Only collective protest *activity* (not rhetoric) was included in the index calculations.

Table 8.1 The Quantitative Derivation of the Intensity Index

Protest activity	Value
National Arab general strike	10
Local authorities (national or) regional strike	
– 1 day or less	2
– 2–7 days	4
– 8–14 days	6
– 15 days or more	8
Peaceful demonstrations/rallies	
– under 2000 participants	2
– over 2000 participants	3
Violent demonstrations/riots/terror	
– no persons wounded	
but significant damage to property	
and/or up to 10 arrests	5
– under 20 wounded and/or	
10–20 arrests	10
– 20–40 wounded and/or arrested	15
or an incidence of death	20

Data were derived from a review of the records of the National and Lands Committees, personal archives of Arab leaders, a review of the daily newspapers *Ha'aretz*, and *Al Ittihad* and the local weekly newspapers *Kol Hatzfon* and *Hed Hatzfon* as well as the archives of the Jewish-Arab Centre of Haifa University and the Institute or Arab Studies Centre in Giva'at Haviva.

The quantitative derivation of the intensity index followed the methods used by Grenier (1988), Gurr (1993), and Hibbs (1973) (Table 8.1, page 181).

Table 8.2 summarizes collective regional protest, presented in six monthly periods, calculated according to the above index. The table specifies three types of protest activity: against the government's planning/land policy, against other government policies and on national-Palestinian issues.

Table 8.2   Arab Regional Protest in Galilee, 1975–91

Year	Half year No.	Event intensity	Total land policy	Planning/ policy (intensity)	Other issues (intensity)	National (intensity)
1975	1	0	0	0	0	0
	2	3	0	0	0	0
1976	1	8	48	48	0	0
	2	2	2	0	2	0
1977	1	2	3	3	0	0
	2	1	3	3	0	0
1978	1	1	3	3	0	0
	2	0	0	0	0	0
1979	1	3	12	12	0	0
	2	4	12	12	0	0
1980	1	3	17	12	5	0
	2	3	8	0	6	2
1981	1	2	4	4	0	0
	2	1	4	0	4	0
1982	1	3	22	3	0	19
	2	5	39	0	0	39
1983	1	7	16	16	0	0
	2	0	0	0	0	0
1984	1	5	14	6	8	0
	2	4	11	0	11	0
1985	1	4	15	3	12	0
	2	6	21	0	21	0
1986	1	3	11	9	2	0
	2	2	9	0	9	0
1987	1	7	37	13	24	0
	2	17	70	15	16	39
1988	1	7	33	12	16	5
	2	5	23	21	2	0
1989	1	10	57	22	13	22
	2	14	41	10	6	35
1990	1	15	103	9	58	26
	2	7	45	7	6	32
1991	1	7	40	0	27	13
	2	7	32	9	14	8
Total Event No.	168	168	69	78	21
Total Intensity:		762	267	262	233
Intensity/Event		4.5	3.8	3.3	11.1

Appendix 8.2   Key Events Impacting on Arab Protest in Galilee

On page 184 (Table 8.3) is a brief explanation of the main events influencing Arab protest in Galilee as marked in Figures 8.4 and 8.5. The events are listed chronologically and grouped into years. The dates in brackets are the periods during which Arab protest activity took place on the subject. Inevitably, the following list is abbreviated, with causes for minor protest not included. Details of *all* Arab protest in Galilee are available from the author. Arab perception of the impact of these events on the Arabs in Galilee is also marked next to each event.

Event/ Year	Impact	Description
1975	– –	Expropriation of Arab land for the expansion of Carmiel (6/75–6/76)
1976	+	Government promises to stop land expropriation and accommodate the Arabs' needs for further land resources in Galilee (4/76–4/77)
	–	Keonig Report: the publication of a policy strategy written by the Ministry of the Interior's Northern District Director, with harsh recommendations for treatment of Arabs in Galilee (9/76)
1977	–	Several demolitions of dwellings in Arab villages as part of an effort to stop Arab unauthorized construction, following the Kuberski Report of 1976 (9–12/1977)
1979	– –	Construction of 61 new Jewish settlements in Galilee ('Mitzpim'), in the heart of areas dominated by large Arab villages (5/79–3/81)
1980–1	–	Unrest in the occupied territories, which included the activities of the 'Jewish underground' and harsh Israeli treatment of Palestinians (7/80–3/81)
1982	– –	Lebanon War with direct Israeli attacks on Palestinian targets, and a Christian-led massacre of hundreds of Palestinians in Sabra and Shatila, Beirut (6–10/82)
	– –	The establishment of the (Jewish) Misgav regional council in central Galilee, incorporating large tracts of Arab-owned land, and spreading over land earmarked by Arab leaders for the development of their villages (11/82–7/83)
1983	+	Compromise on Misgav and the allocation of additional land to Arab villages
1984	–	On-going disparity between Arab and and Jewish municipal budgets. Arab municipalities have severe problems to ensure the provision of the most basic of services and infrastructure (roads, education, public health). The Israeli government is slow to close the Arab-Jewish gap (4/84–1/86)

+	positive impact	–	negative impact
++	highly positive impact	– –	highly negative impact

9
Nationalism and Non-racialism in South Africa

Gershon Shafir

At a time when ethnic and national struggles that were long thought extinct are burning out of control, this chapter will discuss a racial *cum* ethnic *cum* national conflict that was widely expected to lead to catastrophic bloodshed but, instead, has so far seen relatively peaceful accommodation. In a volume focused on 'challenges to the nation state', I wish to focus upon a phenomenon that seems to have something distinctly old-fashioned about it: an attempt to settle a potentially destructive racial conflict by framing it as a project of democratic nation-building. I will seek to show how it is that the African National Congress' policy of non-racialism, first conceived of in a much more rudimentary form in 1912, is a project of civic nationalism, in short, a venture in civility.

This paper is divided into three parts. First, I will present the different theoretical approaches to the national question in South Africa, which in most cases tended to fade into the ideological convictions of the various social forces. Second, I will examine two periods in which the ANC's non-racial approach was heavily contested: first in the 1940s by the Youth League from within; and later in the 1970s, when the Black Consciousness movement opposed the ANC from without. Finally, I will discuss non-racialism as the expression of social forces and processes that seem to have allowed it to survive and flourish, in spite of so many obstacles, and that, finally, give us hope that it will overcome the hurdles in its way.

Views of the nation

Four basic views of the nation have comprised the South African ideological spectrum, though these were rarely held in a pure form even by their most articulate spokespersons. Indeed, their mixture is one of the most distinct and significant dimensions of national consciousness in South Africa.

1   The National Party or Afrikaner nationalist view.

This states that South Africa is a multi-national state, composed of between 10 and 12 nations, each of which is entitled to the right of self-determination.[1] This view evolved out of the main thrust of apartheid – the doctrine of racial separation – adopted in 1948 by the National Party on the basis of the crude racial ideal of *baasskap*, or white 'boss-ship'.

Though the *verkrampte* (intransigent) elements remained satisfied with this version, by the 1960s the *verligte* (enlightened) wing of the National Party reformulated it by adopting the then-fashionable ideology of decolonization into South Africa. Under the new plan, the black majority population was assigned to tiny, impoverished, and non-contiguous tribal bantustans or 'homelands' (comprising 13 per cent of South Africa's land), where African tribes were allegedly free to pursue their own 'separate development' and, eventually, attain independence. Concurrently, Africans were denied any vestiges of citizenship in South Africa where, treated as 'immigrants', they were strictly regulated.[2] The disparity between the effective reservation of the modern framework of the nation for whites and the relegation of Africans to fragmented, frequently moribund, tribal frameworks reflected an approach to nationhood which, in spite of its ideological veneer, remained race-based. Though presented as a project of decolonization, the bantustans of the apartheid state amounted to continued maintenance of excessive privilege long associated with colonial states.

2   The liberal view

The view of South African liberals, originating in the Cape region, variously expressed by the old United Party, the Liberal Party, and the Progressive Party, is that in South Africa there are four nations: European, Indian, Colored, and black. From this point of view, a harmonious pluralist order could be attained through sound economic, political, and cultural policies.[3]

The liberal tradition did not, however, view the four nations as equal. Though its adherents 'always recognized one common human standard of measurement', this required the successful adoption, by the non-whites, of '"civilized" or modern, western ways'. South African liberals wished for 'equal rights for all civilized men', and not less significantly for 'equal opportunity for all men to become civilized',[4] but they did not expect it to be attained by all.

Those acquiring a 'civilized', or in practical terms a middle-class, existence, which would enable them to enjoy the rights, such as the franchise, already possessed by the members of the white nation, were expected to be no more than a minority of the Indian, Colored, and African nations. Given this limited view of progress, in which the white minority occupies a radically different place from the other three nations, it would seem appropriate, as Pierre van den Berghe has already done for nineteenth-century Cape liberalism, to recognize the conservative and paternalistic basis of this ideology. Even though liberals consented to permit individual members of the other nationalities or races social mobility, the latter could attain higher status only at the price of affirming that nationhood is reserved for the white minority.

3 The African nationalist view

The third view, associated with African, or Azanian (an African name for South Africa) nationalism, held, for example, by AZAPO, is that there are two nations in South Africa: an oppressing colonial, white nation, and a colonized and oppressed black nation. In this view, the white nation was expected to disintegrate as a result of the black nation's liberation struggle. Whites who refuse to remain in South Africa under its new rulers will emigrate, and those who stay will come to identify with the African nation. In the Africanist view Africans are the only true nation and, therefore, are entitled to rule South Africa.[5]

4 The non-racialist view

Finally, non-racialism, the creed of the South African Communist Party, the ANC, and the United Democratic Front claims that South Africa is a single nation, a nation in the making. In this view it is expected that the common fight of members of all races against the colonial structure of South African society will weld these groups together into a single nation.[6]

Though the goal is integrative, the motivating force of the struggle for a non-racial South African society was an African national struggle. The Africans, who are the majority, were expected to provide the leadership for the non-racialist society. Only at the Morogoro Conference in 1969 were whites admitted for first time as members to the ANC. Non-Africans were allowed to serve on the National Executive (which replaced the Revolutionary Council, a non-official ANC body, on which whites already served) only after the Kabwe Conference.

Non-racialism, therefore, was a movement that sought to win democratic rights for Africans and other non-whites, through cooperation with willing whites, and should be seen as a project of civic nationalism. But given the exclusion of Africans from South African citizenship, their struggle could not be limited to civil rights, but was at once a struggle for national liberation.[7] It is to the credit of the ANC and its allies that so far the potential contradiction between the two elements of the non-racialist struggle, between its means and goal, has been successfully contained.

Non-racialism and its African critiques

The establishment of the South African Union in 1910 and the construction of the apartheid regime in 1948 were two of the major turning points in the erosion of the liberal view of national development and the emergence of increasingly exclusivist forms of white and African nationalism.

The formation of the ANC (originally known as the South African Native National Congress) in 1912 was the African response to their legally enforced inferior status brought into being in the 1909 Act of Union by the newly formed South Africa. Though standing up for African rights, and seeking to weld all Africans into one group that could match the powers of the new Union,[8] the ANC was not nationalist in the traditional mold. The first generation of the ANC's leaders did not seek to create a state for its prospective nation, but remained under the influence of the Christian-liberal integrationist goal.

The first significant internal assault on this perspective originated with the ANC's Youth League, launched in April 1944. Its leaders, Tambo, Sisulu, Mandela, and its main ideologue Anton Lembede, challenged the old guard, and in 1949, a year after the victory of the National Party and the onset of apartheid, swept into some of the main leadership positions in the ANC. In the same year the ANC adopted its *Programme of Action*, which reflected Lembede's new national emphasis on 'Africanism'. Lembede rejected Communist influences and sought to employ the romantic inspiration of national pride and self-reliance. He evoked the metaphysical concept of the 'African spirit' to demonstrate that an African culture, different from European culture but equally valid in expressing human values, existed.[9]

Lembede's romantic perspective had a distinctively psychological and idealist bent. Though presented with particular urgency, it was akin to the nationalism of many other oppressed groups. In his view, under South African racial oppression national pride was indispensable for undoing the 'crippling complexes of inferiority and dependence imposed on Africans by their treatment at the hands of whites', including 'the stultifying evil' of the 'white paternalism' of well-meaning white liberals and communists.[10] The turn toward African nationalism which, in Lembede's view, could impart pride and self-reliance to the African masses, went hand in hand with a change in the ANC's strategy. Under the Youth League's influence the ANC abandoned its cautiousness and opted for the extra-legal tactics of mass action.

Lembede and the Youth League's concept of nationalism went beyond the original ANC project of seeking to eliminate divisive tribal loyalties, by endorsing a project of 'nation-building'. In the Africanist view,

> Africans comprised not *a* nation within the boundaries of South Africa, but in fact were, by right of indigenous origins and preponderant numbers, *the* nation, and the only nation, entitled to claim and to rule South Africa.[11]

The ANC's 1949 *Programme for Action* seemed to assert this goal by stating that the ANC would proceed 'under the banner of African nationalism', and by calling for 'national freedom' and 'self-determination'. It also advocated economic and cultural self-help to be attained by means of African business ventures, adult education, the establishment of an African press, and so on. In this nationalist phase, the ANC held that interracial cooperation would become possible only when Africans have reached a 'far higher degree of cohesion and self-confidence'. And yet the Youth League still held on to parts of the ANC's earlier heritage by rejecting the slogan, 'hurl the white man to the sea', and accepting that 'the different racial groups' of South Africa 'have come to stay'.[12]

> In 1949, the [ANC] had stood poised between conflicting interpretations of African nationalism, the Youth League pressing for the Lembedist conception of an all-African "nation", and others emphasizing the traditional ANC policy of a non-exclusive South African nationalism.[13]

By the mid-1950s, the traditional non-racial position not only regained pride of place in the ANC's ideology, but was advocated by the very same Youth League leaders – Sisulu and Mandela – who had earlier risen to prominence on the basis of their radical Africanist nationalism.

In 1959, under the leadership of an old-timer of the Youth League, Robert Sibukwe, a group formed the Pan African Congress and broke away from the ANC. The PAC opposed the abandonment of the nationalist principles of the *Programme of Action* and the adoption of the non-racial premises of the *Freedom Charter*. Within the PAC's ideology many of the Lembedist themes re-emerged. Mental conditioning for inferiority was viewed by Sibukwe, as by Lembede, as the root of South African race relations.[14] The PAC repudiated the possibility that whites can identify with the African cause in a racially divided society, and called on Africans to struggle by themselves for their freedom. The PAC called not just for universal suffrage, but also spelled out that this would mean African majority rule. Since by the late 1950s the African continent was undergoing decolonization and independent African states were springing up, new credence was given to African nationalist ideas.

Even the PAC did not intend to drive out or exclude whites and Indians from a free Africa, but it did reject the possibility of minority guarantees, because these were deemed contrary to the goals of a truly non-racial society. Instead, the PAC set itself the aim of assimilating minorities into a single African national identity, and making all citizens equal regardless of their color.[15] In fact, the PAC's commitment to non-racialism was even more single-minded than the ANC's. And yet its critics pointed out that an anti-white campaign could hardly lead to the establishment of a political order into which whites could be accepted as equals.[16]

In 1960, both the ANC and the PAC were suppressed, and their place was taken by the Black Consciousness Movement, under Steve Biko's leadership. Black Consciousness emerged among the black students who split from the multi-racial National Union of South African Students (NUSAS) to form their own South African Students Association (SASO) in 1969. The growing numbers of black students, mostly in black universities, created a desire to step out from the shadow of the white liberal student leaders. Mixing with white students, and with white liberals in general, was seen by Biko as artificial, since it is not possible to have 'black souls in white skins'. Whites, in his words, see the oppression of blacks as 'an eye-sore on an otherwise beautiful view', whereas blacks experience this situation as one from which they cannot escape for a single moment. Being opposed to apartheid, argued Biko, did not make one an ally of the black people.[17] The Black Consciousness Movement sought to replace the organizational consequences of this inferiority complex with self-sufficiency through separate organization. SASO's main focus was identity formation, first through psychological liberation and subsequently through opposition to physical oppression, which it expected in some vague way to lead to an overhaul of the socio-economic system and its replacement by a communal economic system.

The new body, in contrast to the PAC, did not restrict membership to blacks, but by defining Indians and Coloreds not only as oppressed but also as black, sought to integrate them into the movement. This ecumenical view led to a subjective, or political, definition of blackness. Instead of viewing it as skin pigmentation, the BCM comprehended blackness as 'a reflection of a mental attitude'. Consequently, its members agreed to describe as 'black' only a person committed to the liberation process. Africans who worked for the homelands and other apartheid institutions, and the Indian capitalist group in Durban, were viewed not as blacks but as 'non-whites'.[18] Whites, however, could not become black in this political sense.

Black Consciousness had a tremendous impact and, according to a poll conducted in 1978, half of all South Africans viewed themselves as its followers.[19] In one view, 'during the late 1960s and all of the 1970s, [African nationalism] was unquestionably the dominant view among black activists'.[20] It is also accepted wisdom that the 1976 uprising of Soweto's children against education in Afrikaans was inspired by Black Consciousness.[21] There are indications that in 1977, when Biko was caught by the security forces, he was involved in an effort to negotiate a pact for uniting the forces of the ANC, PAC and the BC movement on the basis of minimum consensus to be dictated by the latter (though some of the difficult questions had not yet been discussed).[22] Not surprisingly the BCM was also banned shortly after Biko was murdered in prison.

The basic framework of the BCM was retained by the Azanian Peoples Organization (or AZAPO) that was established in April 1978. AZAPO sought to evolve a new identity, signaled by its term 'Azania' as an African name for South Africa, in combination with a subordinate socialist explanation. AZAPO viewed blacks as 'a race of workers', thus excluding white workers from the purview of its organization.[23] Its influence, however, never regained the extent of the Black Consciousness Movement's authority.

The social foundations of non-racialism

The ANC's non-racialist program survived both the era of the Youth League, when the younger generation of African nationalists took it over from the inside, and the ascendance of the BCM, which operated in opposition to the ANC from the outside. The young nationalist leadership returned to the party's traditional non-racialist position with renewed vigor in the 1950s, and the BCM lost its prominence when the ANC made a spectacular comeback in the 1980s. This was not seen as self-evident, since the ANC that was in exile was only tangentially involved in the internal opposition and, consequently, for a decade was in 'relative dormancy'.[24]

The ANC re-emerged only after the Soweto uprising and the wave of suppression in the late 1970s, which led the newly exiled to join the ANC and reinvigorate its reputation through the attacks carried out by its military wing, the *Umkhonto we Sizwe* (known as the MK). On Robben Island, where the BCM leaders were now jailed with the old ANC leadership, the latter also succeeded in attracting many of the earlier BCM adherents to their viewpoint.

In addition the ANC 'tried to capitalize on the growing popular disillusionment by criticizing the BC movement's continued idealism, its "confusion" over economic issues, and its inability to organize large-scale resistance'.[25] In addition to pointing to the strategic weakness of translating consciousness to political organization, the ANC, in contrast to Africanist nationalists, also enjoyed the logistics and financial support of the Soviet Union and the South African Communist Party.

In spite of these resources and advantages, the ANC's continued adherence to a non-racialist approach cost the party the sympathy of Africans in the continent and many blacks in the US, for whom the Africanist response was seen as the 'natural' one, and also put it at grave risk of falling out with the masses of blacks in South Africa. In both periods that I examined, the nationalist approach seemed to gain the support of the majority of blacks, or at least of black activists, and in both periods, regardless of whether it operated from within or without the ANC, non-racialism was reduced to a minority. I would argue that neither the repressive policies of the South African state, nor the internal, cyclical, dynamics of the various resistance movements, are sufficient for explaining the persistence of non-racialism, its periodical comebacks, and its clear victory in the first South African democratic elections on 27 April 1994.

In 1990, Julie Frederikse published a book of interviews and documents entitled *The Unbreakable Thread,* in which she surveys the non-racialist approach and concludes on a triumphalist note that it was 'the most pervasive and enduring ideological tendency in South African history'.[26] But as we have seen, other forms of nationalism were also pervasive in South Africa, and non-racialism itself had been contested in the past on many occasions; I have merely presented two of the most dramatic, and temporarily successful, challenges.

The narrow interpretation given to non-racialism and the limits of its hold even among its supporters were recently confirmed in Shula Marks' sober, though temperately optimistic, assessment. None of the three major sources of inspiration behind the formation and preservation of the ANC's non-racialism – the Missionary Schools, which provided its early leaders with their education; the Cape Colony's tradition of non-racially qualified franchise (blacks were removed from the rolls only in 1936, and the Colored were moved to a separate roll in 1951); and the South African Communist Party's class analysis – held a view of non-racialism as it is understood today. For the founders of the SANNC, non-racialism frequently meant breaking down the barriers between the African groups themselves, and some of its important leaders were willing to entertain more equitable forms of racial segregation between whites and blacks. Liberal support shrank over time in the Cape, and even Suzman's Progressive Party only accepted the idea of universal non-racial franchise in 1978. The South African Communist Party had, at various times since its foundation in 1921, expressed hostility towards what it saw as the bourgeois nationalism of the ANC, and in the past worried that its defense of black workers would make it suspect in the eyes of white workers.[27]

But Marks points to sources of non-racialism in surprising places. The experience of the meeting on the South African frontier between white settlers and the African peoples they encountered had, at times, led to unexpected alliances and cooperation. A measure of intermarriage and interbreeding between them created a group that was set apart from the black Africans under the name Coloreds. Over its long history South African racism had remained unideological, and consequently contained a pragmatic dimension. In fact, the ideological tenor of the apartheid regime may be seen as a departure from this more general pattern.[28]

Yet the most important source of non-racialism is the recognition that the races in South Africa are interdependent, and that economic opportunity for blacks can only be had within a single economy. Africans in South Africa were not a separate group that could follow a path of separate development, nor could they replace the whites, who, in spite of their numerical weakness, were already viewed and accepted by the Congress in 1912 as a permanent part of the state. The pragmatic ANC was founded on the recognition that the colonial history of

South Africa may only be partially undone. Probably the best illustrations of the interdependence of blacks and whites are the internal contradictions of the apartheid regime: it was allegedly formed to segregate the races, but ended up establishing various institutions to ensure an ample and continuous supply of low-paid African labor to white employees, thus undermining much of apartheid's practicality and legitimacy. A common economy, then, seems to be the social foundation of non-racialism. And yet, that single economy is the site of continued inequality and, therefore, of ongoing conflict.

The South African non-racial accommodation is obviously threatened by the same kinds of pressures – if not worse ones, considering the continuing massive socio-economic gulf between whites and most blacks, and lesser gaps between whites, Indians and the so-called Coloreds – that led to tragic consequences elsewhere. For example, according to the UN's Human Development Index, were the whites in South Africa (12 per cent of the population) to constitute a separate country, it would occupy the 24th place in the world, only a smidgen behind Spain; black Africans, by contrast, would rank 123rd, just above impoverished Congo. Because of this disparity, there is no assurance that the South African non-racial project of civic nation-building will last, let alone succeed, in the terms in which it is being implemented.

The debate over 'affirmative action' provides a good illustration of the contradictions between narrowing the existing socio-economic gaps between the races within a reasonable time, and preserving the goal of non-racialism. The new South African government set up an affirmative action office in the Ministry of Labor which is authorized to guide and monitor the progress of voluntary hiring and promoting of blacks in the private sector. A backlash has already formed against this voluntary approach on the grounds that affirmative action requires the racial categorization of people by a government that is identified with the desire to break down such categories.

In seeking to address this debate, a new interpretation of non-racialism has begun to emerge within parts of the ANC. The view of Cyril Ramaphosa, the ANC's secretary-general, is that the deracialization of South African society – for people to stop looking at themselves in racial terms – requires that the country's institutions reflect the true character (or composition) of the country. In short, his interpretation is that the previous order, which is still in place in the economic sphere, is still a racial order. Affirmative action, in this view, is necessary to deracialize the economy.[29] It is not clear how far such a remedial program can go. The non-racialist perspective and program are far from coherent. As part of solving the conflict, non-racialism will probably find it harder to avoid employing racial distinctions than it expected.

The ability of the ANC to hold on to its non-racialism against harsh odds was probably due in large measure to its being so thoroughly opposed to the biological, and for that matter national, essentialism of the apartheid regime; in other words, it was due to its refusal to become apartheid's mirror image. With the end of apartheid, it might be more difficult for the ANC, and also less necessary, to insist on a visionary non-racial society. But the history of non-racialism in South Africa, which saw its repeated rebirths, and the ANC's skill in containing the mixed elements from which it was made up within one program, leaves the historical observer with a measure of guarded optimism in contemplating South Africa's future.

Notes

1 Alexander, Neville, 'Approaches to the National Question in South Africa', *Transformation*, No. 1, 1986 (pp. 63–95), p. 75.
2 Gerhart, Gail M., *Black Power in South Africa: the Evolution of an Ideology* (Berkeley, University of California Press, 1978), pp. 4–6.
3 Alexander, *op. cit.*, pp. 76–7.
4 Gerhart, *op. cit.*, p. 7.
5 Ibid., p. 67.
6 Slovo, Joe, 'The Working Class and Nation-Building', in van Diepen, Maria ed., *The National Question in South Africa* (London, Zed, 1988), p. 144; van Diepen, *op. cit.*, pp. 9–10; Hudson, Peter, 'The Freedom Charter and the Theory of National Democratic Revolution', *Transformation* No. 1, 1986 (pp. 6–38), pp. 6–11.
7 Meli, Francis, 'South Africa and the Rise of African Nationalism', in van Diepen, *op. cit.*, p. 69.
8 Ibid., p. 68.
9 Gerhart, *op. cit.*, pp. 63, 67.
10 Ibid., pp. 55, 59.
11 Ibid., p. 67.
12 Ibid., pp. 72, 75, 83–4.
13 Ibid., p. 119.
14 Ibid., p. 187.
15 Ibid., pp. 194–5.
16 Ibid., p. 198.
17 Buthelezi, Sipho, 'The Emergence of Black Consciousness: an Historical Appraisal', in Barney Pityama *et al.* (eds), *Bounds of Possibility: the Legacy of Steve Biko and Black Consciousness* (David Philip, Capetown, 1991), p. 119.
18 Ibid., p. 121.
19 Marx, Anthony W., *Lessons of Struggle: South African Internal Opposition, 1960–1990* (New York, Oxford University Press, 1992), p. 82.

20 Alexander, *op. cit.*, p. 82.
21 Buthelezi, *op cit.*, p. 128.
22 Marx, *op. cit.*, pp. 82–3.
23 Ibid., pp. 86–7.
24 Ibid., p. 93.
25 Ibid., p. 94.
26 Fredrikse, Julie, *The Unbreakable Thread: Non-Racialism in South Africa* (Johannesburg, 1990).
27 Marks, Shula, 'The Tradition of Non-Racism in South Africa', paper presented at the History Workshop, University of Witwatersrand, Johannesburg, 13–15 July, 1994, pp. 20–1.
28 Marks, *op. cit.*, p. 6.
29 *Economist*, 'A Survey of South Africa', 20 May 1995, pp. 19–20.

References

African National Congress, 'Strategy and Tactics of the South African Revolution', in La Guma, Lex, ed., *Apartheid: A Collection of Writings on South African Racism by South African* (N.Y., International Publishers, 1971), pp. 179–204.

Alexander, Neville, 'Approaches to the National Question in South Africa', *Transformation* (No. 1, 1986), pp. 63–95.

Fredrickson, George, 'Colonialism and Racism: The United States and South Africa in Comparative Perspective', in his *The Arrogance of Race* (Middletown, Wesleyan University Press, 1988), pp. 216–35.

Fredrikse, Julie *The Unbreakable Thread: Non-Racialism in South Africa* (Johannesburg, 1990).

Gerhart, Gail M., *Black Power in South Africa: the Evolution of an Ideology* (Berkeley, University of California Press, 1978).

Halisi, C.R.D., 'Racial Proletarization and Some Contemporary Dimensions of Black Consciousness Thought', in R. Hunt Davis Jr, ed., *Apartheid Unravels* (Gainesville, University of Florida Press, 1991), pp. 77–99.

Hudson, Peter, 'The Freedom Charter and the Theory of National Democratic Revolution', *Transformation* (No. 1, 1986), pp. 6–38.

Marks, Shula, 'The Tradition of Non-Racism in South Africa', paper presented at the History Workshop, University of Witwatersrand, Johannesburg, July 13–15, 1994.

Marks, Shula and Stanley Trapido, eds, *The Politics of Race, Class and Nationalism in Twentieth-Century South Africa* (London, Longman, 1987).

Marx, Anthony W., *Lessons of Struggle: South African Internal Opposition, 1960–1990* (New York, Oxford University Press, 1992).

Meli, Francis, 'South Africa and the Rise of African Nationalism', in van Diepen, pp. 66–76.

Pityana, Barney, Rauphele, Hamphela, Mpumlwana, Halusi and Wilson, Lindy, eds, *Bounds of Possibility: the Legacy of Steven Biko and Black Consciousness* (Cape Town, David Philip, 1991).

Price, Robert, 'Civic Versus Ethnic: Ethnicity and Political Community in Post-Apartheid South Africa', unpublished paper (1996a).

Prince, Robert, 'Race and Reconciliation in the New South Africa', unpublished paper (1996b).

Slovo, Joe, 'The Working Class and Nation-Building', in van Diepen, pp. 142–51.

Van Diepen, Maria, ed., *The National Question in South Africa* (London, Zed, 1988).

10

Rethinking Multinational Space: the Quebec Referendum and Beyond

Alain-G. Gagnon

> The present awakening of nationalities should serve as a warning of the terrible conflicts that have been launched within states that scorned nations, and attempted to replace them to the point of arbitrarily taking themselves for nations.
>
> Fernand Dumont[1]

Introduction

Political leaders, intellectuals and citizens have a moral obligation to re-evaluate and rethink political relationships in order to assist modern complex polities that face seemingly insurmountable challenges. The precarious political situations, not only in the Near and Middle East and the Balkans, but in Western liberal democracies such as Spain, Great Britain, Belgium, France and Canada, stand as effective reminders to these challenges.

There is also an urgent need to establish a new discourse that could assist in the legitimization of modern forms of liberal political expressions and bring new insight and vision into political deliberations.[2] Implicitly, the concepts of cultural pluralism, diversity, citizenship, and liberal nationalism provide some of the necessary tools that address issues of conflict management within modern democracies. The development of such a political discourse can increasingly contribute to a reassessment of the future of the nation-state and a reappraisal of the ever-increasing homogenizing currents. The Quebec referendum constitutes a major warning for anyone who would want to continue building a country without respect to the profound diversity that ought to characterize Canada.

This paper challenges the argument made by the late Ernest Gellner, that cultural and linguistic uniformity are essential for the efficient functioning of the modern state.[3] It is proposed that the political stability of Canada does not require cultural uniformity and homogenizing economic practices. Instead, it is argued that Canada must return urgently to the federal spirit[4] that characterized its creation if it wants to enter the new millennium with a sense of pride and purpose.

The intention of the present paper is to examine the Quebec/Canada conundrum, considering the following four axes:

(a) nationalism as a modern phenomenon;
(b) uniformity, continuity and the politics of recognition;
(c) the Quebec referendum of 30 October 1995; and
(d) the multinational state as an entry point into an advanced phase of modernity.

1   Nationalism: a modern phenomenon

Nationalism has become the most frequent expression of claims for political autonomy and self-realization in the modern world. It is significant to note that in territories as diverse as Canada and Spain, for example, nationalism has constituted simultaneously the struggle against a domineering view of the state imposed by central institutions and the attempt to establish democratic practices.[5]

The Quebec case challenges traditional modernization theory[6] since the merging of Quebec into the Canadian economic and political entity has not led to a decrease in the desire of its people to assert their differences and to elaborate innovative democratic practices. In fact, Quebec is often seen as a leader in many parts of the country. The passing of the Quebec Charter of Human Rights by the Quebec National Assembly in 1975 constitutes a good case in point. The 1982 Canadian Charter of Rights and Freedoms mirrors large segments of the Quebec Charter.[7] It is important to note, however, that Canada's pursuit of homogeneity has led to the mobilization of political forces in Quebec.

The dominant expression of nationalism in Quebec is an essentially modern one, as the most common claims for political rights are based on its existence as a nation and are inspired by well-ensconced democratic traditions and practices.[8]

To find a solution to, or at least understand, the Canadian conundrum, it is imperative to unravel the concepts of 'nation' and 'nation-state'. The concept of 'state' refers to a legal and political entity better known as a country. The concept of 'nation', in contrast, represents a socio-cultural entity whose frontiers often do not correspond to specific state boundaries.

In English Canada, the concepts of 'nation' and 'state'/'nation-state' are used interchangeably, collapsing the two to describe the same political reality. This fusion is interpreted by several English-Canadian spokespersons as a reflection of modernity, necessary for the establishment of the pillars of a new Canadian identity which neglects, and is intended to supersede, that of Quebec.[9] In sharp contrast, a vast majority of Quebecers tend to promote a very different understanding of themselves due, in part, to a Girondin legacy and to liberal nationalist influences which are rapidly taking hold and becoming an intrinsic part of the political discourse.

Peter Alter views this liberal nationalism, or Risorgimento nationalism, as 'a protest movement against an existing system of political domination, against a state which destroys the nation's traditions and prevents its flourishing. Its adherents stress the right of every nation, and with it the right of *each* and *every* member of a nation, to autonomous development, for in their minds, individual freedom and national independence are closely connected'.[10]

Among the best known proponents of liberal nationalism are the German, Johann Herder, the Italian, Giuseppe Mazzini, and the Frenchman, Ernest Renan, for whom nationalism is aimed at constructing a world based on human values of equality, fraternity, and liberty. The concept of nation as defined by Ernest Renan receives a favorable echo among most Quebecers:

> A nation is a soul, a spiritual principle. Only two things, actually, constitute this soul. ... One is the possession in common of a rich legacy of remembrances; the other is the actual consent, the desire to live together, the will to continue to value the heritage of which all hold in common. ... The existence of a nation ... is an everyday plebiscite.[11]

The concept of liberal nationalism has re-entered the political domain. One notable contribution is Yael Tamir's *Liberal Nationalism*, in which the author builds on the legacy of Herder and Mazzini to elaborating the view that 'personal autonomy' and 'communal belonging' are natural allies. Such 'concepts are viewed here as complementary rather than conflicting, suggesting that no individual can be context-free, but that all can be free within a context'.[12]

Nationalism, in particular liberal nationalism, constitutes a modern phenomenon[13] and represents a tool that can assist political communities seeking the establishment of just relations and pursuing mutual recognition.

Uniformity, continuity and recognition

The idea of historical continuity is central to the existence of nationalism. Recognition assumes continuity, a repeating argument in the recent literature on nationalism.[14] To quote Yael Tamir, 'nationalism is a theory about the eminence of national-cultural membership and historical continuity, and the importance of perceiving one's present life and one's future development as an experience shared with others'.[15]

In the aftermath of the failed Meech Lake Accord, the Quebec government on 4 September 1990 established the Commission on the Political and Constitutional Future of Quebec.[16] The problem, to quote the Report tabled by the Commissioners, is that:

> Theoretically, the Canadian federal union could have continued to change in constitutional and political terms while respecting both the aspirations of Quebecers and those of other Canadians. In practice, the overall conception of Canada and the federal regime which now predominates seems rigid and clearly oriented towards the quest for uniformity and the negation of differences.[17]

The failure to recognize Quebec as a 'distinct society' constitutes a rejection of 'deep diversity' or, if one prefers, of liberal communitarianism of the type expounded by my colleague Charles Taylor. This renowned political philosopher argues convincingly that

> Instead of pushing ourselves to the point of breakup in the name of the uniform model, we would do our own and some other peoples a favour by exploring the space of deep diversity. ... Europe-watchers have noticed how the development of the European Community has gone along with an increased breathing space for regional societies – Breton, Basque, Catalan – that were formerly threatened with the steamroller of the national state.[18]

Taylor's assessment is opening a very promising political space and challenges a homogenizing view of the concept of 'nation' that led to the break-up of several countries in Central and Eastern Europe. Taylor offers to Canadians an alternative to uniform federalism that requires the recognition of others. In a sense, this is why the notion of 'distinct society' has a very symbolic meaning for Quebec people; and the inability (if not the non-admission) on the part of the rest of Canada to accept this concept as a feature of the Constitution creates such a feeling of rejection among Quebecers.

According to Taylor, the politics of recognition (deep diversity) is essential for modern plural societies, as it appropriately identifies the desire to maintain the cultural difference between political communities as a fundamental fact of life. This approach to politics assists in attenuating the impact of 'procedural liberalism'[19] on the life of citizens. Taylor issues an important caveat as he challenges procedural liberalists:

> The claim is that the supposedly neutral set of difference-blind principles of the politics of equal dignity is in fact a reflection of one hegemonic culture. As it turns out, then, only the minority or suppressed cultures are being forced to take alien form. Consequently, the supposedly fair and difference-blind society is not only inhumane (because suppressing identities) but also, in a subtle and unconscious way, itself highly discriminatory.[20]

It is important to recognize that the state cannot claim cultural neutrality,[21] contrary to the discourse of procedural liberalists. For this reason, it is essential to recognize the multinational character of Canada. Such a course of action, it is suggested, would contribute to reconciling differences. Several Canadian authors are focusing their efforts in this direction: Guy Laforest (Laval University), Michel Seymour (University of Montreal), Charles Taylor, James Tully, and Jeremy Webber (McGill University), Joseph Carens and Frank Cunningham (University of Toronto) and Daniel Drache and Kenneth McRoberts (York University), John Conway (University of Regina), and Philip Resnick (University of British Columbia). No doubt, the more familiar one is with the Quebec milieu, the more one is inclined to appreciate the multinational nature of the country.

It is with this in mind that the 'politics of recognition' of the sort proposed by Taylor has a legitimate and crucial role in modern society. Taylor goes on to uphold Quebec's distinct society as a means to preserve and promote the cultural heritage of Quebec.[22]

The preservation of a language or a culture can be viewed as a public good and promoted by the state as a means of expressing 'collective distinctness'. In Canada, it rarely comes to the minds of our federal politicians that to defend Quebec's rights to be recognized as a nation within a multinational federation can be in the 'national interest'. The pursuit of such an objective does not mean that individual freedoms are abandoned, but simply that they should be juxtaposed with deep diversity. At stake is the place of federalism in the current debates on liberalism. Procedural liberalism tends to deny federal practices or, at least, territorial forms of federalism, while the concept of communitarian liberalism is considerably more suited to federalism. Webber, for one, argues that:

> Federalism necessarily assumes that there are good reasons for laws to differ from one province to another. Indeed, provincial governments exist precisely in order to permit that kind of variation. Federalism therefore recognizes, at least implicitly, that equality can be reconciled with the existence of different laws applicable to different people. ... If we accept that a federal structure of government makes sense, we cannot require that everyone be subject to precisely the same laws.[23]

There is a major current in liberalism that tends to undermine the necessity to recognize cultural diversity.[24] James Tully, a well-known communitarian political philosopher, feels that this condition constitutes one of the most destructive forces of modernity which needs to be rapidly identified and contained, reminding us that it was in the name of modernity that campaigns of colonization in North America, with the corresponding genocide of Aboriginal peoples, were justified.

The concept of modernity has too often served to rationalize the quest to eradicate cultural differences and to impose a uniform model of governance on all citizens residing in a given territory. In the Canadian case, initiatives pertaining to reforming the Canadian constitution without the consent of both Quebec and the Aboriginal nations represent both a denial of the federal spirit and a threat to the existence and further development of Canada's democratic practices.[25] To wish a long life to Canada is to encourage 'deep diversity' and to recognize the multinational nature of the country. The reluctance to do so on the part of many Canadians is incomprehensible to those whose federal vision is based on communitarian principles.

I submit that the key to Canada's constitutional crisis resides in the dismantling of a standardizing approach to federalism that does not allow Quebecers to feel at home in their own country. Some, but still too few, Canadian intellectuals are now exploring new forms of federalism to attend to the Canadian problem. To date, Taylor[26] and Tully[27] have provided the most innovative and persuasive arguments in favor of a revamped federalism. In his Austin and Hempel Lectures at Dalhousie University and the University of Prince Edward Island in March 1995, Tully reminded his audience that,

> When the Quebec Assembly seeks to preserve and enhance Quebec's character as a modern, predominantly French-speaking society, it finds that its traditional sovereign this area is capped by a [Canadian] Charter in terms of which all its legislation must be phrased and justified, but from which any recognition of Quebec's distinct character has been completely excluded. The effect of the Charter is thus to assimilate Quebec to a pan-Canadian national culture, exactly what the 1867 constitution, according to Lord Watson, was established to prevent. Hence, from this perspective, the Charter is 'imperial' in the precise sense of the term that has always been used to justify independence.[28]

From this viewpoint, Quebec's main objection to the Charter is that it is not sufficiently pluralistic and fails to recognize the multinational character of Canada. For most Quebecers there is an equilibrium that needs to be maintained between the rights of individuals and the rights of national communities that constitute a federal Canada.[29] For those Quebecers, the patriation of the Canadian Constitution from Britain in 1982 represents a breach of trust,[30] and constitutes a discontinuity with former constitutional practices as the rest of Canada 'embraced a kind of constitutional imperialism, thereby forcing Quebecers reluctantly to follow into the footsteps of American secessionists of 1776'.[31]

Attempts at reducing Quebecers to the status of one minority among others in Canada simply denies the fact that Quebec forms one of the main pillars upon which Canada was established in the Confederation agreement of 1867.[32] Over the years, several conventions have been broken by politicians in Ottawa as they pursued a policy based on uniformity and centralism. Contrary to what those politicians assumed, they were not entitled to change unilaterally what had been decided by the various parties to the original compact. Tully notes that:

> The acts of confederation did not discontinue the long-standing legal and political culture of the former colonies and impose a

uniform legal and political culture, but, rather, recognized and continued their constitutional cultures in a diverse federation in which
consent of each province was given.[33]

This observation leads Tully to assert that 'the imposition of *The
Charter* on Quebec in 1982, affecting its constitutional culture without
consultation and consent, appears as an anti-constitutional act of discontinuity and assimilation.'[34] One can also argue that such an act provided important ammunition to sovereignist forces during the
referendum of 30 October 1995.

3   The referendum of 30 October 1995[35]

On 30 October 1995, Quebecers came within a whisker of forcing a
reform of the Canadian federation and taking Canada closer to a
Maastricht-type political and economic arrangement. An impressive
turnout of 93.52 per cent confirmed the deep concern of Quebecers
from all linguistic groups, political allegiances, and regions. In the end,
only 54 288 votes in favor of the status quo demarcated the two
options. Opposition to the sovereignty-partnership project was registered within most non-francophone communities, with the exception
of the latino-Quebecers and, to a lesser extent, Haitian-Quebecers.
Youth, low- and middle-income earners, the unemployed, people on
welfare, francophones and intellectuals gave their overwhelming
support to the liberal nationalist cause. The changes advanced by the
Quebec government, under the leadership of *Parti Québécois'* Jacques
Parizeau, the *Bloc Québécois* official opposition in Ottawa, led by Lucien
Bouchard, and by the *Action démocratique du Qéubec*, an offshoot of the
Quebec Liberal Party, led by Mario Dumont, were quite ambitious. For
instance, these changes stressed the entrenchment of a Quebec Charter
of Human Rights (more encompassing than the Canadian Charter), a
decentralization of powers to the regions of Quebec, the elaboration of
a societal project more sensitive to the needs of the people and, among
other aspects, the maintenance and consolidation of free trade within
North America.

Pro-Canada political forces would have had difficulties challenging
such proposals, since Quebecers tend to be favorable to left-oriented
policies, entrenched rights at the provincial order of government, free
trade, and decentralization of powers at the regional level. There were
no forward-looking propositions initiated from the NO side, sure as it
was that Quebecers would not endorse the nationalist cause. Federalist

forces led by Jean Chrétien and Daniel Johnson waited until the very end of the campaign as polls started to confirm that the YES side could win the referendum before pointing to the possibility of change within existing institutions.

Figures from May 1980 and October 1995 reveal a significant increase in favor of sovereignty (see Table 10.1). When compared with the referendum results of 20 May 1980, the 30 October 1995 results show a significant increase of YES support in most ridings. In 1980, only 22 out of 110 ridings supported the sovereignty-association option, an alternative which would have only granted a mandate to negotiate a new political arrangement between the federal government (Ottawa) and Quebec. In 1995, the mood in Quebec was different: no less than 80 out of 125 ridings backed the stronger option of a declaration of sovereignty, accompanied by a proposal for economic partnership with the rest of Canada. All regions of Quebec were more in favour of the sovereignist option than the federalist one, with the exception of the Outaouais region, ridings of Western Montreal containing a high concentration of non-francophones, and ridings along the American, Ontario or New-Brunswick borders (see Table 10.2).

In the Montreal region, the breakdown reveals a deep division between the western end of the metropole, which is 41.9 per cent francophone, and the city's eastern side, which is 83.0 per cent francophone. An ecological analysis confirms that only 22.1 per cent of voters in Western Montreal and 55.3 per cent in Eastern Montreal backed the Quebec government's option. When aggregated along the French-

Table 10.1   Quebec's Referendum Results, 1980 and 1995

Referendum	*20 May 1980*	*30 October 1995*
Results		
Registered voters	4 367 584	5 087 009
Participation rate (%)	85.61	93.52
YES (% of valid votes)	40.44	49.42
NO (% of valid votes)	59.56	50.58
Spoiled ballots	1.74	1.82
(% of valid votes)		
Majority for NO	19.12%	1.16%
	(702 230 votes)	(54 288 votes)

Source: Quebec, Chief Electoral Officer, *Rapport préliminaire des résultats du dépouillement des votes le soir du scrutin: Référendum du 30 octobre 1995* (Quebec: Bibliothèque nationale du Quebec, 1995).

Table 10.2 Quebec's Referendum Results, by Regions, 30 October 1995

	YES	Francophones YES	%	Participation
Lower St-Lawrence				
Gaspé, North Shore	60.3	64.2	94.0	90.2
Saguenay Lac Saint-Jean	69.6	70.4	98.8	92.7
Quebec	54.4	56.3	96.6	93.5
Chaudières Appalachains	50.7	51.3	98.8	92.2
Mauricie Bois-Francs	57.2	58.3	98.0	93.0
Eastern townships	49.6	55.5	89.4	93.4
Montérégie				
Montreal South Shore	53.7	62.2	86.5	94.7
Laurentians				
Lanaudière	61.6	65.8	93.6	93.8
Outaouais	27.5	33.8	81.1	93.8
North West	55.8	63.9	87.4	89.8
Laval	46.7	59.6	78.4	95.3
Montreal	34.5	61.3	56.3	93.9
Total	49.4	60.0	82.4	93.5

Source: Pierre Drouilly, 'An Exemplary Referendum', *Canada Watch*, November–December 1995, p. 27.

English cleavage, the resulting data indicate that francophones favored the sovereignty option in the proportion of 52.6 per cent in the western part of Montreal and 66.7 per cent in eastern Montreal, the latter representing the second largest regional support of the sovereignist option by the francophone population after Saguenay/Lac St-Jean.[36]

The referendum of 30 October 1995 saw two societal projects competing with one another. Supporters of the YES side tended to back a social democratic vision of Quebec society that favored the maintenance and universality of social programmes, and that called upon the Quebec state to humanize capitalist initiatives. Advocates of the NO cause tended to undermine discussions of this sort, and argued for an unreformed Canada, assuming that no substantial change was necessary, and that nationalist forces would, in the end, lose the referendum by a significant margin.

The arrival of the *Parti Québécois* at the helm of the Quebec state in September 1994 suggested a desire among Quebecers to redress past injustices, as well as for a more progressive government. Several elected members associated with the social democratic wing of the *Parti Québécois* were appointed to the cabinet to pursue particular objectives, such as promoting greater equity between citizens and demonstrating to Quebecers the social advantages of sovereignty. Even the then-Premier, Jacques Parizeau, known for his more conservative approach to politics, started speaking in favor of a new societal project.[37]

Federal (*Bloc Québécois*) and Quebec (*Parti Québécois*) nationalist forces have constituted a common front in fighting the dismantlement of the social net by Ottawa. This trend led a Canadian observer to comment:

> What is our national [Canadian] project, the thing that binds our 30 million souls to a single, uplifting idea? Surely it isn't the quest to get by with 20 per cent fewer hospital beds, or the effort to boost productivity ratios, or clever ways to cut spending on social programs. That is an accountant's dream of national unity, and it shouldn't be any surprise that it appeals only to other accountants.[38]

Nationalist arguments stressed that sovereignty could make a significant difference, since in this debate the Quebec government could set its own priorities. Fewer subsidies to large corporations and more assistance to people in need were said to be policy initiatives conceivable in a sovereign Quebec. Quebecers started to believe that it was possible to be governed differently, to share common political and social goals, and to give a human face to economics.

The referendum of 30 October 1995 was essentially fought on two visions of society. It became obvious during the preceding hearings of both the regional and the national commissions, struck to study the political future of Quebec, that two models were clashing with one another. On one side, Quebec nationalists were proposing a social democratic image of the state; on the other, Quebec and Canadian federalists were simply advancing a neo-liberal project that would continue should the referendum be lost by the sovereignists.

Quebec sovereignists were particularly inspired by *Bloc Québécois* representatives in Ottawa, who brought to the floor of the House of Commons issues of equity and were demanding that social programmes be protected against repeated attacks. It can be added that *Bloc Québécois* members, with the near eradication of the New Democratic party at the last federal elections, have become Canada's social conscience. This is quite ironic considering that the *Bloc Québécois* wants to take Quebec out of the current Canadian federal system.

Federal Liberals, under the leadership of Jean Chrétien, have proposed a neo-liberal agenda for Canada, contrary to their platform during the electoral campaign of 1993. This objective is being achieved by the promotion of a pro-business agenda, cutting transfer payments to the provinces in the area of social programmes, imposing regressive measures to programs such as unemployment insurance, and, among other things, questioning the universality of income security programs.

During the last decade, central government policies have tended to support the dismantling of pan-Canadian institutions which had given a meaning to being Canadian. The undermining of old-age pensions, unemployment insurance, university education, research and production centers (National Film Board, Telefilm Canada, Canadian Broadcasting Corporation), the privatization of railways and airports, and the elimination of the government's arm's-length agencies, such as the Economic Council, have all contributed to a crisis of identity. Such moves have led many Quebecers to believe that Canada has outlived its useful existence.

Indeed, a Thatcherite vision has taken hold in Canada. The central government, led by Jean Chrétien, and the Premiers of Ontario, Alberta, New Brunswick, and Nova Scotia, have imposed a series of regressive social measures with a view to controlling the deficits and to reversing the expansion of the public debt. The welfare state is under serious threat, and all indications suggest that a concerted effort by Ottawa will be made to pursue this objective. The 1996 federal budget, released in early March, confirmed all these apprehensions. Contrary to the case of the 20 May 1980 referendum on sovereignty-association, at which time Ottawa stressed its role as a bulwark against attacks on the safety net, the referendum held on 30 October 1995 saw a reversal of these positions.

This shift of policy led many older citizens and women in Quebec, not natural supporters of the nationalists, to rally behind the secessionist/partnership cause. To quote former federal leader of the New Democratic party and current president of the Montreal-based International Centre for Human Rights and Democratic Development, Ed Broadbent:

> Increasing numbers of senior citizens came to think their benefits would more likely remain with a YES vote than if they relied on an Ottawa preoccupied with cutbacks. And Quebecois women, like other women voters all over the world, caring more for a fair society than for macho politics, moved in increasing numbers to the YES side with its emphasis on a more caring government.[39]

Class politics entered the political fray to a considerable extent. It was easier to mobilize women's organizations, unions and popular groups behind a nationalist project of the Left, willing to fight for a just and more caring society. Contrary to the 'critical' YES that labor organizations had given to the nationalist cause in May 1980, this time their support was unconditional. In addition, the Quebec Federation of Women challenged women from all walks of life to support the sovereignist project. A noted group of nuns also gave their support to the nationalist project, stressing that it was the only one that took to heart issues of social justice. Support came also from the leaders of the Hassidic community who felt sovereignty was not to their disadvantage.

Federalists attracted strong support from big business spokespersons and high income earners, to the point that a *Globe and Mail* reporter wrote: 'Referendum a battlefield for big business versus social democrats'.[40] Furthermore, speeches made by prominent Quebec business leaders, such as Laurent Beaudoin of Bombardier, who said on 4 October 1995 that the company would leave Quebec if the YES won on 30 October, created a great unease between workers and employers. Several business people were also unhappy with M. Beaudoin's statements, and decided to create their own group in favor of the YES option.

M. Beaudoin had no choice but to retract his comments few weeks later, on 25 October, by confirming that Bombardier would stay in Quebec regardless of the outcome of the referendum. Meanwhile, he accused M. Bouchard and M. Parizeau of transforming the constitutional debate into a class struggle. However, as the president of the Confédération des Syndicats Nationaux, M. Gérald Larose, wrote to the members of the union on the day after the referendum:

> From the middle of the first week of the referendum campaign, the debate was exposed as opposing wealthy capitalists in favor of federalism, system which serves their interests, against the workers and the majority of the Quebec population, in favor of change, who want to assume their own destiny and responsibilities.[41]

The language divide remained central during the referendum campaign. Francophones tended to vote to a greater extent in favor of sovereignty-partnership, while non-francophones were generally opposed to it. The YES side made significant progress among francophones, jumping from 49 per cent in 1980 to 60 per cent in 1995. Our data indicates that the largest support for the YES side came from francophone specialized workers, 72.2 per cent supporting the sovereignty-partnership project; non-specialized francophone workers and 60 per cent of professionals/administrators supported the YES side. Among the anglophone voters we observed the same phenomenon, even if our sample is relatively small: 27.8 per cent of the non-specialized anglophone workers voted for the YES side.[42] NO supporters were essentially middle-class voters. Therefore, even if we can observe an important language cleavage, the YES societal project seemed to have also attracted several lower-class anglophone voters.

We can also observe that the support for the YES option among francophone voters attracted citizens from different backgrounds. Cohorts of people between 18 and 54 years of age supported the YES alternative, while people over 55 voted more for the NO. The higher the education level, the higher the support for the YES option; the inverse holds true for the NO vote. The YES support among francophone voters came essentially from specialized workers and less from office employees. People searching for a job heavily supported the YES side; housekeepers were highly divided and retired people generally supported the NO cause. Although the YES side dominated in all income categories, the difference between the options is the least pronounced in the $10 000–19 999 category. Both men and women strongly supported sovereignty. Finally, the data demonstrates that support for the YES option was inversely related to attendance of religious services of the voter.[43]

When we look to the concerns of Quebecers during the referendum period, we see that the employment issue remained the key one. However, contrary to what the NO strategists thought during the referendum campaign, this issue surfaced primarily due to the major change to unemployment benefits proposed by the federal government. Indeed, the unemployment rate remained high in Quebec throughout 1995, but unemployed and seasonally unemployed workers (fishermen, and the like) were quite disappointed by the federal proposal. Ottawa postponed its reform until after the referendum because of its concern about losing votes because of an unpopular policy. Other economic issues, such as health care reforms and the increase in the cost of living, were among the top concerns of the electorate. Therefore, economic factors and the downturn of the economy brought advantage to the YES side, since the neo-liberal federal agenda left very few hopes for the Quebec middle and lower classes.

Social issues, such as education (increase in tuition fees for post-secondary students), social security reforms (pensions plan for older citizens) and the overall mismanagement by the federal government of the public finance (higher taxation) also favored the YES side. The language issue played a secondary role throughout the referendum campaign, with most public opinion polls indicating that Quebecers in general were relatively satisfied with Quebec government policy in this field. The election of the *Parti Québécois* in September 1994 reassured the Quebec population that Montreal will remain a francophone city, and that efforts would be made in that direction.[44] This only demonstrates that economic issues were more prevalent in 1995 than in 1980. Finally, concerns about the low birth rate of the francophone population were played down during the referendum campaign.

In contrast to the 1980 referendum, in which language and cultural issues were at the forefront, in 1995 the YES success can be attributed to the fact that this side responded to economic concerns, attracting support from all social classes.

4 Multinational state

With the advent of modernity, the concepts of nation and nationalism have not lost their relevance. Indeed, the word 'nation' has been utilized to support the claim for nationhood and to defend the legitimacy of existing or 'imagined' national communities.[45]

Lord Acton has made a significant contribution to the advancement of a modern theory of multinationalism in his seminal essay on 'nationality'. After juxtaposing the values inherent to a theory of unity and to a theory of liberty, Lord Acton concludes that the former leads to despotism and revolution while the latter flows to self-government. He then goes on to assert that:

> The presence of different nations under the same sovereignty ... provides against the servility which flourishes under the shadow of a single authority, by balancing interests, multiplying associations, and giving to the subject the restraint and support of a combined opinion. ... Liberty provokes diversity, and diversity preserves liberty by supplying the means of organization.[46]

Lord Acton exercised an early influence on Pierre Trudeau that waned over the years. Though he denounced narrow nationalism and national homogeneity, Acton supported the view of multinational states as the best guarantee for freedom. In Acton's view: 'a State which labours to neutralize, to absorb, or to expel them [different peoples and nationalities], destroys its own vitality; a State which does not include them is destitute of the chief basis of self-government'.[47]

Pierre Elliott Trudeau could never have been more perceptive, or more attuned to Acton's philosophical position, than when he wrote that 'it is necessary to divorce the concepts of the state and of the nation, and to make Canada a society truly pluralist and multi-national'.[48] It is therefore surprising that when he was Canada's prime minister he did not seek to attain this objective. Rather, Trudeau preferred to maintain and feed the same confusion which he had previously denounced as counter-productive. In addition, Trudeau admitted in the same text that in Canada 'there are two main ethnic and linguistic groups; each is strong, too well rooted in the past and too well supported by a mother culture, to be able to erase the other'.[49] This, however, had little influence on the way he attempted to settle the interminable constitutional crisis.

During the last twenty years expressions such as 'Canada national project', 'National television/radio Network', 'National community', 'National political parties', 'National Unity', 'National government', and 'National interest' have been used more frequently in Ottawa (the federal capital). This depiction of cultural, social and political reality suggests the undermining of any truly federal vision for the country, and discourages the expression of deep cultural diversity.

Different uses of the concepts of state and nation reveal profound divergences between Quebecers and English Canadians, which are nurtured by distinct political projects and agendas. As a result, Quebec ideologues and politicians tend to speak of a nation in order to describe their own political community while their English Canadian counterparts ignore the call for recognition of Canada's multinational entities with a view to claiming a stronger role for the Canadian state, acting on behalf of an imagined single Canadian nation.[50] Lord Acton issued an important caveat:

> The greatest adversary of the rights of nationality is the modern theory of nationality. By making the State and the nation commensurate with each other in theory, it reduces practically to a subject condition all other nationalities that may be within the boundary. It cannot admit them to an equality with the ruling nation which constitutes the State, because the State would then cease to be national.[51]

Of late, Canadian political scientist Philip Resnick has embraced the notion of a multinational state for Canada. This has led him to argue that '[t]he more willing we are to embrace sociological diversity in our understanding of nationality, the greater the possibility of making progress in resolving conflicts that national differences engender'.

Resnick further develops his argument by noting, 'As long as we operate under the assumption, as a majority of English Canadians do, that there is a single Canadian nation formed in 1867 of which Quebecois and aboriginal peoples are a constituent part, there is relatively little room for discussion'.[52]

This leads Resnick to conclude, as my colleague Guy Laforest and myself have done,[53] that Canada would benefit by establishing itself as a multinational federation. I believe that such a turn of events could go a long way in accommodating[54] both Quebecers and the Aboriginal nations to Canada's federal structure, and would also provide a culturally pluralist model to be emulated by other profoundly diverse societies in the world.

In the meantime, a significant number of Quebec intellectuals, and, to some extent, the Quebec government via its Draft Bill on Quebec sovereignty,[55] are proposing a view of the nation that builds on cultural pluralism and liberal nationalism to get out of the current political impasse.[56] Such a view rejects models based on ethnicity and builds on an inclusive, secular and multipolar notion of the nation in which all national communities are invited to build the emerging state and converge in establishing French as the language of a common political culture and as the foundation of a communitarian identity.

The dominant traits of Quebec nationalism revolve, first and foremost, around civic demands and obligations rather than ethnic aspirations.[57] Such an interpretation gains by being compared with Craig Calhoun's view, according to which 'nationalism is not simply a claim of ethnic similarity, but a claim that certain similarities should count as *the* definition of political community. For this reason, nationalism needs boundaries in a way premodern ethnicity does not.'[58] Hence, the importance for the Quebec state and leading intellectuals of providing a definition of the nation that is constructed on the principles of inclusion, liberal democratic practices and civic values.

Conclusion

The time has come in developed Western countries to decouple the notions of nation (political communities/identities) and citizenship. As we are reminded by Philip Resnick, political statehood and national communities/identities intersect but do not overlap perfectly.[59]

This chapter has argued that it is the lack of recognition of political communities as 'nations' that leads to political conflicts and to the quest of nations to secure nation-state status. Modernity calls for cultural diversity and invites political and social actors to encourage the respect of heterogeneity within states, not just between them.

The necessity to re-establish continuity is presently lost on most English-speaking Canadian spokespersons who do not even acknowledge the need to maintain a dialogue between the past and the present, and to reconcile Quebecers to the emerging Canadian state. English-speaking Canadians tend to feel that to pursue such a goal would simply lead to further political confrontations, and would cause various points of contention (that have been settled in their favor) to resurface.[60] Instead of facing reality, English Canadians' leaders prefer staying the course, ignorant of or insensitive to the fact that this could lead to Quebec's secession.

The fact that the existence of Quebec predates the establishment of the territorial state known as Canada gives the former the legitimacy of its own political claims in the public sphere and also provides, if such claims are denied, the moral justification for secession.[61]

In closing, I would argue that it is the failure of the dominant institutions and political actors in Canada to reflect the divergence of cultural, historical and political claims that has led to the present deadlock, and that the only way out of the current crisis is to enshrine multinational precepts in the process of democratic deliberations and governance.

Notes

1 'Le réveil actuel des nationalités suffit à nous avertir des terribles conflits déclenchés dans des états qui ont méprise les nations, tentant de se substituer elles au point de se donner eux-mémes arbitrairement pour des nations.' Fernand Dumont, *Raisons communes* (Montréal, Boréal, 1995), p. 55.
2 For an important work on the theme of 'deliberative democracy' see James S. Fishkin, *Democracy and Deliberation: New Directions for Democratic Reform* (New Haven, Yale University Press, 1991).
3 Ernest Gellner, *Nations and Nationalism* (Oxford, Blackwell, 1981), pp. 140–1.
4 For a similar point of view, see James Tully, 'The Crisis of Identification: the Case of Canada', *Political Studies*, vol. 42, special issue, 1994, pp. 77–96; and, for a closer examination of public policies during the Trudeau and Mulroney years, Hugh Donald Forbes, 'The Challenge of Ethnic Conflict/Canada: from Bilingualism to Multiculturalism', *Journal of*

Democracy, vol. 4, no. 3, 1993, pp. 69–84. For a general assessment of federal practices, see Marc Gjidara, 'La solution fédérale: bilan critique', *Pouvoirs*, no. 57, 1991, pp. 93–112.

5 Craig Calhoun, 'Nationalism and Ethnicity', *Annual Review of Sociology*, vol. 19, 1993, pp. 211–39. On the case of Japan, see J. White *et al.*, Michio Umegaki and Thomas R.H. Havens eds, *The Ambivalence of Nationalism: Modern Japan Between East and West* (Lanham, Md, University Press of America, 1990).

6 The case of the integration of the outlying regions of Great Britain into the British market is worth noting as it is this phenomenon which led to political mobilization in Wales and Scotland. Michael Hechter, *Internal Colonialism: the Celtic Fringe in British National Development, 1536–1966* (Berkeley, University of California Press, 1975); Tom Nairn, *Break-up of Britain: Crisis and Neo-Nationalism* (London, New Left Books, 1977). Nairn argued that nationalism should be conceptualized as an independent variable capable of 'unhinging the state' (1977), p. 89.

7 For a further development on this point, see Alain-G. Gagnon, 'Variations on a Theme', in James P. Bickerton and Alain-G. Gagnon, eds, *Canadian Politics*, 2nd. edition (Peterborough, Broadview Press, 1994), pp. 450–68.

8 Cf. Daniel Latouche, '"Quebec, see Under Canada": Quebec Nationalism in the New Global Age' and Louis Balthazar, 'The Faces of Quebec Nationalism' in Alain-G. Gagnon, ed., *Quebec: State and Society*, 2nd. edition (Toronto, Nelson Canada, 1993), respectively pp. 40–63 and 2–17.

9 See, Fernand Dumont, 'La fin d'un malentendu historique', in *Raisons communes* (Montréal, Boréal, 1995), pp. 31–48.

10 Peter Alter, *Nationalism* (London, E. Anorld, 1994), p. 29.

11 Renan Ernest, *Qu'est-ce qu'une nation* (Paris, Calmann-Levy, 1994 [1882]), p. 26.

12 Tamir, Yael, *Liberal Nationalism* (Princeton, NJ, Princeton University Press, 1993), p. 14.

13 For an important contribution to the literature on nationalism as a modern phenomenon, see Jacques Rupnick, ed., *Le déchirement des nations* (Paris, Le Seuil, 1995).

14 See, Benedict Anderson, *Imagined Communities* (London, Verso and New Left Books, 1983); Charles Taylor, 'The Politics of Recognition', in Amy Gutmann, ed., *Multiculturalism and 'The Politics of Recognitian'* (Princeton NJ, Princeton University Press) Fernand Dumont, *Genèse de la société québécoise*, *op. cit.*; and, Yael Tamir, *Liberal Nationalism*.

15 Yael Tamir, *Liberal Nationalism, op. cit.*, p. 79.

16 For an overview of the Commission's deliberations and report, see Alain-G. Gagnon and Daniel Latouche, *Allaire, Bélanger, Campeau et les autres: Les Québécois s'interrogent sur leur avenir* (Montréal, Quebec/Amérique, 1991).

17 Commission sur l'avenir politique et constitutionnel du Québec, *Report of the Commission on the Political and Constitutional Future of Quebec* (Quebec, March 1990), pp. 47–8.

18 Charles Taylor, 'The Deep Challenge of Dualism' in Alain-G. Gagnon, ed., *Quebec: State and Society*, 2nd. edition (Toronto, Nelson Canada, 1993), pp. 94–5. For Taylor, first-level diversity refers to the recognition of a multicultural Canada that adheres to the Canadian federation in a similar way,

while second-level or deep diversity refers to the different ways of belonging to, or of identifying with, a country.

19   For an important contribution on procedural liberalism, see Will Kymlicka, *Liberalism, Community and Culture* (New York, Oxford University Press, 1989).

20   Taylor, 'The Politics of Recognition', p. 43.

21   For an application to the case of Arab Minority in Israel, see Ahmad H. Sa'di, 'Israeli Social Sciences and Their Interpretation of the Arab Minority', paper presented at a conference on 'The New Politics of Ethnicity, Self-Determination and the Crisis of Modernity', Tel Aviv University, Tel Aviv, May 30–June 2, 1995. For an application to the Canadian case, see Jeremy Webber, *Reimagining Canada* (Montreal, McGill-Queen's University Press, 1993).

22   Taylor's analysis differs in part with that of Will Kymlicka in *Liberalism, Community and Culture, op. cit.* Kymlicka does not offer a corresponding justification for their promotion. Taylor argues that Kymlicka's approach goes some way in assisting cultural communities, but that the tendency to remain faithful to the fallacy of liberal neutrality could be fatal for their long-term cultural existence of these communities. One can also refer to Donald Lenihan, Gordon Robertson, Roger Tassé, *Reclaiming the Middle Ground* (Montreal, Institute for Research on Public Policy, 1994) for a critical interpretation of the doctrine of neutrality (see especially Chapters 5–6).

23   Jeremy Webber, *Reimagining Canada, op. cit.*, p. 225. See also, André Burelle, 'Les contrevérités de Pierre Elliott Trudeau, II-Pour une remise en question du fédéralisme unitaire', *Le Devoir*, 1–2 May 1993, p. A–13.

24   The work of Michael Ignatieff is a good illustration of this tendency, see his *Blood and Belonging: Journeys Into the New Nationalism* (London, Penguin Books, 1993).

25   James Tully, 'Un regard en arrière pour aller de l'avant', *Le Devoir*, 16 January 1995, p. B–1.

26   See especially Taylor, 'The Politics of Recognition', *op. cit.*, and *Reconciling the Solitudes: Essays on Canadian Federalism and Nationalism*, edited by Guy Laforest (Montreal, McGill-Queen's University Press, 1993).

27   James Tully, *Strange Multiplicity: Constitutionalism in the Age of Diversity* (Cambridge, Cambridge University Press, 1995) and James Tully and Daniel M. Weinstock, eds, *Philosophy in an Age of Pluralism: the Philosophy of Charles Taylor* (Cambridge, Cambridge University Press, 1994).

28   James Tully, 'Let's Talk: the Quebec referendum and the future of Canada', *The Austin and Hempel Lectures* (Dalhousie University and the University of Prince Edward Island, 23 and 27 March, 1995), p. 8.

29   For a well-argued interpretation, see André Burelle, *Le mal canadien: Essai de diagnostic et esquisse d'une thérapie* (Montréal, Fides, 1995); also, Michel Seymour, ed., *Une nation peut-elle se donner la constitution de son choix?* (Montréal, Bellarmin, 1995).

30   Guy Laforest, 'Le Quebec et l'éthique libérale de la sécession', dans *De la prudence: textes politiques* (Montréal, Boréal, 1993), p. 169; Alain-G. Gagnon and Guy Laforest, 'The Future of Federalism: Lessons from Quebec and Canada', *International Journal*, vol. 48, 1993, pp. 470–91.

31   James Tully, 'Let's Talk', *op. cit.*, p. 12. Tully argues also that this constitu-
     tional imperialism is based on a fraud of earlier political arrangements and
     maintained under the threats of force. This is bound to lead to additional
     confrontation and disunity, see p. 20.
32   See, Fernand Dumont, *Genèse de la soci été québécoise* (Montréal, Boréal,
     1993). One can also consult André Burelle, *Le mal canadien: Essai de diagnos-
     tic et esquisse d'une thérapie, op. cit.*, pp. 29–59.
33   James Tully, 'The Crisis of Identification: the Case of Canada',
     op. cit., pp. 84–5.
34   James Tully, 'The Crisis of Identification', *op. cit.*, p. 85.
35   For a more extensive treatment, see Alain-G. Gagnon and Guy Lachepelle,
     'Quebec Confronts Canada: Two Competing Societal Projects Searching for
     Legitimacy', *Publius*, forthcoming.
36   Pierre Drouilly, 'An Exemplary Referendum', *Canada Watch* (November-
     December 1995), p. 26. Pierre Drouilly, 'Un référendum exemplaire', *La
     Presse* (7 November 1995), B–3.
37   One should remember the warm reception Parizeau gave to the *Commission
     nationale sur l'avenir du Québec's* report in which solidarity and equity were
     two key pillars of Quebec's national project. See *Report* (Quebec,
     Bibliothèque nationale du Quebec, 1995).
38   David Olive, 'Listening to Quebec', *Report on Business Magazine* (February
     1996): 14.
39   Ed Broadbent, 'Why Bouchard succeeds, and where the federalists failed',
     the *Globe and Mail*, 19 January 1996.
40   Rhéal Séguin, 1995, 'YES, and the move to the left', the *Globe and Mail*, 20
     October 1995, p. D1 and D5.
41   Confédération des syndicats nationaux, Letter from Gérald Larose, 22
     November 1995.
42   See Alain-G. Gagnon and Guy Lachapelle, *op. cit.*, for tables.
43   See Gagnon and Lachapelle, *op. cit.*.
44   For an account of the 12 September 1994 Quebec provincial elections, cf.
     Alain-G. Gagnon., 'The Quebec General Elections of 12 September 1994',
     Regional and Federal Studies, 5 (1) (Spring 1995): 95–102.
45   See Rogers Brubaker, *Citizenship and Nationhood in France and Germany*
     (Cambridge, Mass., Harvard University Press, 1992) and G. Noiriel, 'La ques-
     tion nationale, comme objet de l'histoire sociale', *Gense*, vol. 4, 1991,
     pp. 72–94.
46   John Emerich Acton, 'Nationality' in *Essays on Freedom and Power*, ed.
     Gertrude Himmelfarb (Glencoe, Ill, The Free Press, 1949), p. 185.
47   John Emerich Acton, 'Nationality', in *Essays on Freedom and Power, op. cit.*,
     p. 193.
48   Pierre Elliott Trudeau, 'The Multi-National State in Canada': the Interaction
     of Nationalism in Canada', *Canadian Forum*, June, 1962, p. 53.
49   Pierre Elliott Trudeau, 'The Multi-National State in Canada' *op. cit.*, p. 53.
50   For an excellent analysis of nationalisms in Canada, cf. Jane Jenson,
     'Mapping, Naming, and Remembering: Globalization at the End of the
     Twentieth Century' in Guy Laforest and Douglas Brown, eds, *Integration and
     Fragmentation: the Paradox of the Late Twentieth Century* (Kingston, Institute
     of Intergovernmental Relations, 1994), pp. 25–51; see also Michael Burgess,

'Competing National Visions: Canada-Quebec Relations in Comparative Perspective', paper presented at the Conference on 'Cross-cultural and comparative approaches to Canadian Studies', Birmingham, University of Birmingham, 19–20 May 1995.

51 John Emerich Acton, 'Nationality', in *Essays on Freedom and Power, op. cit.,* pp. 192–3.

52 Philip Resnick, *Thinking English Canada* (Toronto, Stoddard, 1994), p. 7. See also John Meisel, 'Multinationalism and the Federal Idea' in Karen Knop ed., *Rethinking Federalism: Citizens, Markets, and Governments in a Changing World* (Vancouver, UBC Press, 1995), pp. 341–6, for a useful overview.

53 Alain-G. Gagnon and Guy Laforest, 'The Future of Federalism', *op. cit.,* pp. 470–91.

54 For an original contribution to the notion of accommodation and its utility in federal societies, see Daniel Latouche, *Plaidoyer pour le Quebec* (Montréal, Boréal, 1995).

55 Quebec National Assembly, *Draft Bill: an Act Respecting the Sovereignty of Quebec* (Quebec, Quebec Official Publisher, 1994); Daniel Turp, *L'Avant-projet de loi sur la souveraineté du Quebec: texte annoté* (Montéral, Les éditions Yvon Blais, 1995) for a legal and political interpretation of this Draft Bill on Quebec sovereignty. Also, Commission Nationale sur l'Avenir du Quebec, *Report* (Quebec, Bibliothéque Nationale du Quebec, 1995).

56 See, Groupe sur les Institutions et la Citoyenneté, 'The Case for a New Language Accord', *Inroads,* no. 3, Summer 1994, pp. 9–17 as well as Alain-G. Gagnon and Guy Laforest, 'The Future of Federalism', *op. cit.,* for a Quebec-centered liberal nationalist viewpoint and Donald Lenihan, Gordon Robertson, Roger Tassé, *Reclaiming the Middle Ground, op. cit.,* for a Canada-centered liberal nationalist point of view.

57 Several Aboriginal leaders, among whom Mary Ellen Turpel, Ovide Mercredi, and Matthew Coon-Come, state that Quebec cannot exercise its right of self-determination since it does not constitute a people. To exercise such a right, it is suggested by those leaders, Quebec would need to implement a racist policy and to present exclusivist claims of nationhood. For a similar interpretation of this aboriginal account, see Reginald Whitaker, 'Quebec's Self-Determination and Aboriginal Self-Government: Conflict and Reconciliation?', in Joseph Carens, ed., *Is Quebec Nationalism Just?: Perspectives from Anglophone Canada* (Montreal, McGill-Queen's University Press, 1995). To quote Whitaker: 'The important point lost in this legalistic objection is that Quebec's assertion of the right to national self-determination has been put in inclusionary, liberal democratic terms. Given guarantees of minority rights, a will of the majority on existing Quebec territory to seek sovereignty, expressed through a democratic mandate derived from a referendum, has legitimacy.' p. 212.

58 Craig Calhoun, 'Nationalism and Ethnicity', *op. cit.,* p. 229.

59 Philip Resnick, *Thinking English Canada, op. cit.,* p. 6.

60 This suggests a very interesting quotation from Petr Pithart which goes as follows: 'The "anationalism" of the dominating nation (as opposed to the nationalism of the dominated nation) cannot always be as innocent and powerless as it believes itself to be or would have itself believed, because it can leave others, who are weaker and forced to practice self-defense, to act

in its place. Czech "anationalism" which, feeling superior, flays the Slovak fervor, is far from an indifferent attitude. Rather, at stake is a temporary mutation of nationalism or, in other words, an implicit nationalism of the dominating nation.' The original French version reads: 'l'a-nationalisme de la nation dominante (par opposition au nationalisme de la nation dominée) peut ne pas être toujours aussi innocent et impuissant qu'il n'aime α le croire ou α le faire croire, et cela parce qu'il peut laisser les autres agir α sa place, ceux qui, plus faibles, se sentent obligés de pratiquer l'auto-défense. L'a-nationalisme tchéque qui, se sentant supérieur, fustige la ferveur nationale slovaque, est loin d'être une attitude désintéressée. Il s'agirait plutét d'une mutation temporaire du nationalisme, autrement dit d'un nationalisme implicite propre α la nation dominante.' 'L'identité tchéque: nationalisme réel ou séparatisme régional?', in Eric Philippart, ed., *Nations et frontières dans la nouvelle Europe* (Bruxelles, éditions complexes, 1993), p. 209.

61 Political philosopher James Tully denounces the current state of affairs in Canada when noting that 'imperial constitutionalism, based on the fraud of the 1980s and the threats of force of the 1990s, is the major cause of the disunity of Canada. The offensive words and deeds of "put up or shut up" federalists have provided secessionists with their main justifications .... Quebecers have no interest in a federation held together by fraud and force.' See, Tully, 'Let's Talk', *op. cit.*, p. 20. See, also, Guy Laforest, 'Le Quebec et l'éthique libérale de la sécession' in Michel Seymour, *Une Nation peut-elle se donner la constitution de son choix?*, *op. cit.*, pp. 215–33 and Laforest, 'Identit et pluralisme libéral au Quebec' in Simon Langlois, ed., *Identité et cultures nationales: L'Amérique française en mutation* (Sainte-Foy, Les Presses de l'Université Laval, 1995), pp. 313–27.

11
Modernity, Premodernity and the Political: the Neozapatistas of Southern Mexico[1]

Eric Herrán

> Only through time, time is conquered.
>
> T.S. Eliot

On 1 January 1994, an indigenous revolutionary movement under the name of the Zapatista Army of National Liberation (Ejército Zapatista de Liberación Nacional: EZLN) came to public notice in the southern Mexican state of Chiapas through a series of military actions. The most important of these actions consisted in temporarily seizing four towns in the state of Chiapas, among which San Cristóbal de las Casas, a city that since the colonial years has symbolized the domination exercised by the non-indigenous population over the *indios* of this state. Combats between the rebels and government troops began and went on for several days until peace talks were initiated. The first attempt to find a peaceful, bargained solution to the conflict, however, collapsed a few weeks later for several reasons, but mainly because of the government's attempt to limit the nation-wide political demands made by the EZLN (which had succeeded in making a majority of the Mexican people back these demands) to the local (state) level and merely to socio-economic issues. Fortunately, this and subsequent similar breaks in the peace talks which have recurrently occurred for over four years since the advent of the Chiapas affair, have not thus far meant the full re-enactment of military confrontations between the EZLN and the Mexican army. It is worth noting, however, that in February 1996 the EZLN and the Mexican government convened solemnly to sign the San Andrés Larráinzar Agreements which were supposed to represent an acceptable solution in principle to the Chiapas strife. The Comisión de Concordia y Pacificación (COCOPA), a congressional committee espe-cially created to assist – along with the Comisión Nacional de

Intermediación (CONAI) – in bringing about a peaceful end to the conflict, was charged with the task of rendering the Agreements into a law initiative, a task this committee accomplished by November of that year. But by the next month, none the less, the government unexpectedly felt compelled to revise the COCOPA initiative significantly, thereby providing no clear indication as to whether it would effectively abide by its own promise given at Larráinzar. At the moment of preparing this manuscript, the peace process undergoes yet another prolonged impasse, mainly as a result of the position taken by the government since the end of 1996 *vis-à-vis* the legal enactment of the Agreements.[2] Among other things, the emergence of the EZLN emphasized the systematic failure of Mexico's recent so-called neo-liberal administrations to confront significant problems of social justice adequately in a country where the gap between rich and poor is wide and keeps widening. In particular, it called attention powerfully to the miserable socio-economic situation which the majority of the Mexican rural population continues to endure, especially the indigenous communities.

In this way the Neozapatistas, just like other indigenous movements concerned with social justice in other parts of Latin America, vindicated the right of the communities they claim to represent to have land of their own along with better housing, food, health services, education, and so on. Moreover, and once again on the trail followed by similar Latin American minority-rights movements, the Neozapatistas linked this series of socio-economic demands with more political and cultural claims, such as the right of indigenous peoples to abide by a form of government they identify with, that is, one more faithful to their ethnic ideals of community life.[3] Finally, these political and cultural claims have been envisioned by the Neozapatistas as consonant with the main values and institutions of liberal democracy.[4] Put differently, the Neozapatistas strive to gain recognition for a form of self-government for indigenous communities that can be both accommodated with, and at least partially derived from, the liberal-democratic *intentions* that are believed to inform the general socio-political arrangements underlying the contemporary Mexican nation-state.[5]

A feature of the kind of indigenous movements to which the self-government demands made by the EZLN can be said to relate seems to be the perception of the primacy of the political sphere in envisioning solutions to pivotal cultural and socio-economic issues. At any rate, this feature is particularly salient in the case of the Neozapatistas.[6] In and of itself, the EZLN's strong recognition of the fundamental – and, literally, constitutional – character of the political might deservedly be the subject matter of an interesting study for the historian of political ideas with regard to contemporary revolutionary ideologies, especially after considering the leftist and, more precisely, Marxist origins of the Neozapatista non-indigenous leadership.[7] This study I cannot pursue here. I will instead, however, stress the Neozapatistas's perception of the primacy of the political in connection with their understanding of the *way* in which their ethnic ideals of community life are thought to relate consonantly to what can, in very general terms, be called the liberal-democratic culture.[8]

There clearly are a number of differences between these two broad types of cultures which cannot easily, if at all, be mitigated. But the fact remains that the Neozapatistas point, in their rhetoric, to an essential compatibility between the specific indigenous cultural forms they portray and defend, on one hand, and the most general cultural traits of liberal democracy on the other. Such essential compatibility has, from the outset, often been stressed by the Neozapatista communities when demanding recognition by the Mexican state of their rights to self-government.[9] In other words, I am making the point that when the EZLN claims for indigenous peoples the right to choose their own government 'freely and democratically', it frequently does so by resorting to an argument which presents itself as an internal reading of both the Neozapatista and the liberal-democratic communities.[10]

Let me be clear about where exactly the essential compatibility between the Neozapatista and the liberal-democratic cultures may lie. According to the particular interpretation of the Neozapatista discourse I will offer in this paper, what is essentially shared by these two broad types of cultures is a profound *political* commitment to equality. Thus, the Neozapatista internal-reading argument is ultimately meant to indicate:

(a) that the commitment to equality underlies the fundamental political arrangements pertaining to each of these cultural forms, and

(b) that these political arrangements should be seen as providing such cultural forms with their overall character.

In this paper I examine the validity of the Neozapatista belief in the existence of an essential agreement, in terms of a deep concern with political equality, between the traditional communities they stand for and liberal democracy. In doing so, I intend to offer an interpretation of the Neozapatista political rhetoric against the backdrop of the modernity/antimodernity debates. More precisely, I will try to show that, in so far as ideal types of political society are involved, the EZLN's essential identification of Neozapatista communities with democratic societies as regards the central importance of the value of political equality, is as much misleading as instructive.

It is misleading because each part of the equation refers to a distinct conception of equality which in turn refers to a distinct *figure of the political*. The figure of the political underlying the Neozapatista conception of equality is basically a *premodern* one, while the figure of the political sustaining liberal-democratic equality is *modern*. Nevertheless, the Neozapatista equivocation is instructive as well, since the deliberate (and often carefully crafted) premodern/modern mix we find at the basis of the Neozapatista discourse[11] may serve as a powerful reminder for the political theorist of the resilient nature of some problems inherent to political modernity which cannot discerningly be set aside. My perception is that these problems may even be so far-reaching as to suggest the need to rephrase our very idea of modernity, this time in terms of an insoluble tension between two distinct forms of the political, one modern, the other premodern.

It goes without saying that this interpretation of *neozapatismo* is intended to make full sense only within the framework of a particular understanding of what the political is about. The one I endorse here is indebted to the classical tradition as much as to the works of Claude Lefort, Pierre Clastres, and Marcel Gauchet. In the first section of this paper, then, I sketch out the main tenets of that particular interpretation of the political and in the second section, apply it as an analytical framework to the Neozapatista political rhetoric. In the final section I offer my conclusions.

The classical tradition

Claude Lefort's conception of the political is an interesting mixture of classical political philosophy and modern philosophical insights.[12] Like the classical philosophers, Lefort thinks that the political gives form and structure, or shapes human coexistence in a social space. The shaping *(mise en forme)* of society is 'at the same time a meaning-giving *[mise en sens]* and a staging *[mise en scène].*'[13] It is a *meaning-giving* process in that

> the social space unfolds as a space of intelligibility articulated in
> accordance with a specific mode of distinguishing between the real

and the imaginary, the true and the false, the just and the unjust, the permissible and the forbidden, the normal and the pathological.

But it is also a *staging* in the sense that 'this space contains within it a quasi-representation of itself' as being, say, aristocratic, monarchic, despotic, totalitarian or whatever.[14] It then seems that the political, according to Lefort, should be rendered as a paradox: on one hand, the political gives society its unity; on the other, such unity fundamentally presents itself through society's division. In other words, society's unity points to a *primary* division, that is, to the distance society takes *vis-à-vis* itself at the very moment it appears as a society. In Lefort's opinion, this sort of externality of society with regard to itself is enacted by the reference to what he calls 'the place of power', or the symbolic place, by reference to which society acquires the sense of its unity or the 'quasi-representation' of its being.[15]

It can fairly be said that, for Lefort, *the* political figure of modernity is liberal democracy.[16] What makes the modern democratic regime paradigmatically modern, he suggests, is that it is built on a certain view of power that recognizes the aforementioned separation between the symbolic and the real. According to the democratic view, power is an 'empty place' in the sense that power is meant to belong to no one (individual or party), that the actual exercise of power does not imply its appropriation in principle by the power-holders. This is so only because no individual or party can legitimately claim to *embody* power which, as I have noted, is the symbolic pole giving overall meaning to society. As a result, in the democratic regime the figures of authority cannot but be recurrently invented and reinvented as a result of this representation of power and the processes it involves.[17] A crucial implication of the nature of the modern democratic regime is that power, law, and knowledge are meant to remain separate from one another, thus making it impossible to provide society with any foundations whatsoever. According to Lefort, thus, political modernity (that is, liberal democracy) is characterized by the fact that 'the ultimate markers of certainty are destroyed'. Hence political modernity engenders a society 'without any positive determination'.[18]

Attention must be called to the radical novelty in Lefort's argument introduced by the modern democratic form of the political that conceives of power as an empty place. Unlike that of premodern societies, it implies that there can be no 'outside' (that is, any figure of the 'other' such as the gods or nature) which may serve as a foundation for power. Furthermore, the modern democratic figure of the political relies on the assumption that the substance of social life cannot be grounded (as, say, Marxism would attempt to do) in any kind of 'inside' either.[19] Put differently, political modernity understood as liberal democracy refuses in principle any form of heteronomy. In contrast, all premodern societies are fundamentally heteronomous to varying degrees and, consequently, reject in principle the kind of autonomy characteristic of modern democratic societies.

Pierre Clastres's and Marcel Gauchet's politico-anthropological works on so-called primitive societies throw further light on this comparison between premodern and modern figures of the political. In a nutshell, for Clastres, primitive societies are, ideally, societies that betray the sociological intention not to be divided into rulers and ruled, the intention that power must remain immanent to the group as a whole.[20] The worst thing that might happen to a primitive society would be to allow for the emergence inside itself of a centralized locus of decision different from the unified corpus of society. For such a centralized site of power would destroy the existing equality of condition among the members of the community and thus introduce, all by itself, a new form of social relations based on the separation between rulers and ruled.

Marcel Gauchet has built on Lefort's theory of the political and on Clastres's anthropological findings. In Gauchet's view, there is a 'debt of meaning' which is inherent to social life. There is, in other terms, 'the need for every society to think of itself as dependent on its outside and on its other in order to be able to think of itself. In order to exist, every society must decipher itself in something which is for it but not of it';[21] and there are several ways (in other words, different institutional arrangements) such a debt of meaning can take.[22] For our purposes we need only concentrate on the major difference between premodernity (as represented here by so-called primitive communities) and political modernity (understood as liberal democracy).

To Clastres's interpretation of primitive societies Gauchet adds the religious factor in order to show the way in which these societies relate to their outside. Briefly, if it is true that the primitive societies described by Clastres are almost perfectly egalitarian (the group as a whole being the only entity authorized to exercise power over its members), this is so, Gauchet notes, *because these societies stand in a relation of complete subordination to their gods (their outside) to whom they owe all of their meaning.* Thus, in primitive societies, 'the separation between the lords of meaning and ordinary mortals is not meant to take place *amongst men'* (italics in the original). Rather, this separation is fully projected into the outside of society, over the division into the living and the gods, so that all men can be equally subjected to the same invisible forces. Moreover, this subjection is so pervasive that it may explain why primitive societies do not tolerate the existence at their core of any division into rulers and ruled: for no man is allowed to emulate the gods by relating to another man in the way these gods relate to the group as such.[23] The sort of political egalitarianism which is supposed to characterize primitives societies cannot, therefore, exist apart from the absolutely heteronomous relationship these societies entertain with their gods (as their outside or other).

Modern democracy, on the other hand, relates differently to its outside. As I noted earlier when discussing Lefort, the uniqueness of the modern democratic regime consists in its referring to an outside or another as an 'empty place'. Power (the symbolic figure indicating that outside) appears here, so to speak, without a face. I have already hinted that the major consequence of this view of power (that is, of this form of the relationship of society to itself) is that there can be no ultimate (no determinate) foundations for social meaning. Everything here moves and changes. Modern democracy, therefore, is the only kind of society which may be capable of recognizing its self-instituting power, or in other words, of audaciously recognizing the power which society ultimately possesses to re-create itself. Only a modern democratic society, by virtue of placing such recognition at the very core of its being, can have a sense of autonomy *vis-à-vis* itself as well as other societies.

The tradition as an analytical framework

Let us now direct our attention back to the Neozapatistas. I have argued that the EZLN stands for indigenous cultural ideals that are taken in conjunction with chief liberal-democratic values. In other words, the Neozapatista indigenous communities by no means regard their claims to self-government as inimical to the basic political framework of liberal democracy.[24] I think that the Neozapatistas are right in making this point, at least at the most general, theoretical level: the recognition of some group (cultural) rights for unfairly disadvantaged national minorities (such as the Mexican indigenous communities) can plausibly be made congruent with liberal-democratic fundamental rights, practices and institutions.[25] It should then be kept in mind, when considering my arguments below, that I do not object to this.

My concern is, rather, with the fact that the EZLN – in its legitimate attempt to bring indigenous communities and liberal democracy together as the main constituents of its political discourse – confuses two distinct figures of the political. Such confusion is in turn at the basis of the Neozapatista's unwarranted identification of modern democratic equality with premodern political egalitarianism. Nonetheless, this mistake turns out to be as misleading as it is instructive about what it means to effect an internal reading of liberal democracy today.

It is misleading because it points to a fundamental affinity between the politico-egalitarian practices of the indigenous communities the EZLN stands for, on one hand, and modern democratic ways and institutions on the other. In the preceding section I think I have substantiated the argument that these two forms of egalitarianism are by no means interchangeable, since each refers to a distinct broad conception of political community.

Yet such unfounded identification envisioned by the Neozapatistas is instructive, too. It sheds light, I believe, on the nature of modernity's current predicament, if I may use this expression. For it can be interpreted as an indication that the Neozapatista attempt to identify, say, indigenous councils with modern parliaments not so much betrays their own theoretical limitations or ideological maneuvering as forcefully exhibits our contemporary paradoxical situation. I mean that the Neozapatista *mélange* of two distinct figures of the political may lead one, under certain reflecting conditions, to the idea that *some* normative criticism of modernity undertaken from outside it must at present be considered as part of both our understanding and our defense of modernity itself. But in order to appreciate this paradoxical situation fully, we must first be able to distinguish, as I did in the previous section, between premodern and modern figures of the political.

The Neozapatistas refuse in principle to make such a distinction by merging instead two different primary views of political equality. In the next section I will reflect briefly on what we are supposed to make of the Neozapatista equivocation in this respect, in light of the particular understanding both of the political itself, and of the uniquely political nature of modernity that I have presented in this chapter.

Throughout my argumentation I have hinted that, according to the EZLN, the fundamental political vision of the indigenous groups it stands for can (and should) be reconciled with that of modern democracy in a degree, I venture, much higher than would be expected. But, while finding this effort at reconciliation justifiable and commendable in general, I have also said that the *way* in which it has often been made presents some major theoretical flaws. Yet the latter, if they are properly elucidated, can provide us with some insights into the nature of political modernity. Consider the following discussion.

On several occasions, the EZLN has argued that the political egalitarianism, say, of the Tzotzil communities of southern Mexico can be made to coincide essentially with modern democratic equality. 'Marcos', by far the most relevant public leader of the EZLN, has characteristically called attention to the way a *rencontre* like this must be interpreted. The indigenous communities making up the Neozapatista movement, he notes, have long since practiced what we moderns call democracy. In fact, he emphasizes, these communities have practiced it from their very foundation and, consequently, well before the term was coined in Western culture.[26] Yet when read against the particular interpretation of both premodernity and modernity I have set forth above, this claim cannot be sustained.

To be sure, there can be little doubt that the indigenous communities of the Mexican state of Chiapas which the EZLN is said to represent are, ideally at least, politically shaped by a profound commitment to equality. What is more, some recent anthropological work makes one immediately think of Clastres's ideal type of primitive society (as amended by Gauchet). In a short but instructive essay, for instance, Taciato Arias makes a claim which is meant to be valid not only for the indigenous communities of Chiapas but for other Mexican *indios* (and even for indigenous groups in other parts of the Americas). The claim is this: in conformity with the socio-political self-definition of these communities, the only relation of subjection considered to be legitimate is the one between the community as a whole and the gods who are the creators of everything that exists.[27] No relation of subjection of one man to another (or one people to another) can then be legitimate. Hence for these indigenous communities, 'a man cannot be another man's lord'. This is also the reason why 'a *pueblo* – the men's abode – can be possessed – that is, cared for, guarded – only by its own inhabitants', for no other *pueblo* nor any stranger must intervene in its affairs.[28]

It should be evident here, as Clastres would claim, the extent to which the entire cultural life of these communities can be said to be shaped by what appears as their principal political aim, namely to create and maintain the necessary conditions for the group as a whole to be the only entity capable of effectively holding and exercising power over its members.[29] At the same time, though, as Gauchet would note, it is likewise evident that the political egalitarianism underlying these societies simply cannot be detached from the absolutely *heteronomous* relation they bear in principle to the forces of the religious invisible (as their outside or other).

Therefore, as we have seen, the Neozapatista attempt to bridge the gap between premodernity and modernity through the political egalitarianism which is the hallmark of both simply does not hold sway. As already indicated, premodern egalitarianism cannot be separated from the complete deprivation of meaning which the community experiences *vis-à-vis* the gods who have created the world. Premodern egalitarianism, thus, cannot be conceived of in isolation from the belief that it is impossible for human society to be the source for its own meaning. Modern (democratic) egalitarianism, in contrast, relates to the historically unique experience that society's meaning is grounded neither in an outside (such as the gods or nature) nor in an inside (such as the economy). This type of society is consequently traversed by the sense of being always on the brink of re-inventing itself, by what Lefort called, following de Tocqueville, the 'democratic revolution'.[30] In short, modern democratic egalitarianism is based on the perception that society cannot be truly grounded at all. In this light, thus, and in spite of *prima facie* similarities between the two, premodern and modern egalitarianism ultimately differ as to their own socio-political conditions of possibility.

Conclusion

I have suggested that the analysis of the EZLN's political discourse from the viewpoint of a certain reading of the political may throw light on the nature of what I called modernity's current predicament. I think this predicament cannot finally be overcome, since it originates in the very nature of liberal democracy as the only kind of political regime in which 'the ultimate markers of certainty are destroyed' and in which power – and consequently the contours of society – cannot rest on 'any positive determination'. In other words, if liberal democracy is the only kind of regime that attempts seriously to take account of the otherness of others when conceiving of general social arrangements from an egalitarian perspective, then the following conclusion obtains. It is only too natural that an *internal* interpretation of liberal democracy has normatively to hint, as entailed by such internal reading itself, at other interpretations of it which may paradoxically be perceived as *external* from the standpoint of what might pass as 'liberal-democratic' at a certain point in time. This is not to imply that any external reading of modern democracy will *per se* qualify as internal. It rather implies, in regard to liberal democracy, that every internal interpretation, if it is truly such, must constitutionally be open to other (external) interpretations. As regards the Neozapatistas, it is easy to see that their potential resilience to modernity is but the result of the socio-politically imaginary (to employ Castoriadis's expression[31]) in which the egalitarianism of the indigenous communities they stand for is embedded. It is evident, thus, that the Neozapatista endorsement of what we may – broadly yet distinctly – call modern culture cannot be a radical one. At the same time, however, as has already been noted, the EZLN's cultural criticism (potential, and tacit) of modernity attempts to leave intact the legitimacy and centrality of liberal-democratic political ideals. Consequently, the intrinsically antimodern penchant of the Neozapatistas cannot be a radical one either.

Such an in-between situation is not in itself unfortunate. For, in the first place, this ambiguity reminds us that the present crisis of modernity is such that the full restoration of the ideals of the Enlightenment (that is, our unqualified belief in reason and progress, on one hand, and a too-optimistic reference to the universal on the other) does not seem to be any longer possible (nor even, perhaps, desirable.) In the kind of pluralist social contexts made possible by post-Enlightenment critical reasoning, therefore, it will always be reasonable to expect a legitimate (that is, friendly) critique of modernity to be carried out, to a certain extent, from what may appear, *prima facie* at least, as a normative standpoint outside of modernity itself.[32]

But then, if the discussion of *neozapatismo* here presented has some plausibility, modernity's current predicament may be calling for nothing less than a revision of our very idea of modernity in terms of an insoluble tension – a tension that is normatively implied by modernity itself – between two major figures of the political, one typically modern (liberal democracy), and the other always, to a certain extent – and only to a certain extent – premodern. To conclude, that this tension should be seen as insoluble means that no one term of it ('modern', 'premodern') must ever be ignored lest we renounce a comprehensive grasp of our present.

Notes

1 I thank the editors of this volume for helpful suggestions made on an earlier draft of this chapter. I am especially grateful to Alberto Spektorowski who first encouraged me to write on the issue. I also acknowledge Mónica Maccise for cheerfully helping with research work and manuscript preparation.

2 It should be noted in passing that the EZLN does not count as the first outbreak of the Zapatista ideology (whose name comes from Emiliano Zapata, who represented the peasant side of the 1910 Mexican Revolution) in the state of Chiapas. This is by no means surprising about a region chiefly devoted to agrarian activities and with a strong colonial, almost feudal, heritage of land exploitation. A good introduction to the role played by *zapatismo* in the Mexican Revolution is still John Womack, Jr's, *Zapata and the Mexican Revolution* (New York: Vintage, 1970). For an account of the early history of Zapatista movements in the state of Chiapas, see Antonio García de León, *Resistencia y Utopía. Memorial de agravios y crónica de revueltas y profecías acaecidas en la provincia de Chiapas durante los últimos quinientos años de su historia* (Mexico City: Era, 1985), vol. 2, pp. 101–33.

3 See EZLN, *Documentos y comunicados 1* (Mexico City: Era, 1994), esp. pp. 33–5, hereafter *EZLN1*; *Documentos y comunicados 2* (Mexico City: Era, 1995), esp. pp. 93–6, hereafter *EZLN2*. For specific accounts of minority-rights issues involving indigenous populations in Mexico, see Jorge Alberto González Galván, *El estado y las etnias nacionales en México. La relación entre el derecho estatal y el derecho consuetudinario* (Mexico City: Universidad Nacional Autónoma de México, 1995); Héctor Díaz-Polanco, *La rebelión zapatista y la autonomía* (Mexico City: Siglo XXI, 1997). On the bearing of these issues in the wider Latin-American context, see Héctor Díaz-Polanco, *Indigenous Peoples in Latin America: the Quest for Self-Determination* (Boulder: Westview Press, 1997); Pablo González Casanova and Marcos Roitman, eds, *Democracia y estado multiétnico en América Latina* (Mexico City: La Jornada/Centro de Investigaciones Interdisciplinarias en Ciencias y Humanidades, UNAM, 1996).

4 See, for instance, *EZLN1*, pp. 295–300; *EZLN2*, pp. 100–4, 358–9, 441–4; EZLN, *Documentos y comunicados 3* (Mexico City: Era, 1997), pp, 79–86, 161–4, 278–92, 359, hereafter *EZLN3*; *Crónicas intergalácticas* (Mexico City: Planeta Tierra, 1997), pp. 215–20, 225–6, hereafter *Crónicas*. See Díaz-Polanco, *La rebelión zapatista y la autonomía,* pp. 127–224.

5 *EZLN3*, pp. 42–5, 77–155.

6 See, for instance, *EZLN1*, pp. 272–4, 277.

7 It is no secret that the Latin American left (especially in its Marxist variants) has been – and, in general, still is – much less willing than its European counterpart to confront the horrors related to the real socialist experience and to strike the due balance. However, it is precisely one of the most notable features of the EZLN's rhetoric that, in its acceptance of the centrality of liberal-democratic values in envisioning political and social reform, it departs greatly from the authoritarian practices characteristic of the old, Stalinist kind of left. And this, so it seems, despite the EZLN's own hard-line revolutionary Marxist origins. About the way in which the radical social

project initially envisioned by the non-indigenous leaders of the EZLN may have been substantially moderated through the latter's gradual integration into the indigenous communities they claim to represent, see Subcomandante Marcos, *El sueño zapatista,* interview with Yvon Le Bot, trans. Ari Cazés (Mexico City: Plaza & Janés, 1997), pp. 123–52; *EZLN3,* pp. 319–24; *Crónicas,* pp. 52–5, 65–71; Antonio García de León's foreword to *EZLN1,* especially pp. 20–1.

8 This, of course, relies on the premise that we can speak of a 'liberal-democratic culture' in the same way as when we speak of the Maori or the mid-nineteenth-century Japanese cultures. One of the most challenging recent critiques of the idea of the cultural unity of liberal democracy, is Jeremy Waldron's 'Minority Cultures and the Cosmopolitan Alternative', in Will Kymlicka, ed., *The Rights of Minority Cultures* (Oxford: Oxford University Press, 1995), pp. 93–119. For a rejection of Waldron's 'cosmopolitan' view in terms that I would basically endorse, see Will Kymlicka, introduction to ibid., pp. 7–9; and Will Kymlicka, *Multicultural Citizenship: a Liberal Theory of Minority Rights* (Oxford: Clarendon Press, 1995), pp. 84–6, 101–5.

9 See *EZLN1,* pp. 175–7; *EZLN3,* pp. 92. For a full discussion of this point, see below.

10 One might be tempted to resort to Walzerian language here and say that the EZLN's intention is to present itself as a 'connected critic' for *both* the indigenous communities it claims to represent *and* liberal democracy. See Michael Walzer, *Interpretation and Social Criticism* (Cambridge, Mass.: Harvard University Press, 1987).

11 Needless to say, thus, and contrary to what is sometimes considered to be the case, this compounded political intention on the part of the Neozapatistas clearly shows not only how far they are from upholding leftist orthodox revolutionary programs but also from staging a radical critique of political modernity in favour of a full restoration of archaic views of society. See, for instance, *EZLN1,* pp. 97–9, 102–4, 295–300, 310; *Crónicas,* pp. 43–4, 49–55.

12 To be sure, a thorough account of Lefort's theory of the political should first lay out the intellectual and political context in which it originated and developed. It then should make clear whether (and how) it could be regarded as a better alternative to other major conceptions of the political and, finally, consider the kind of problems it may not have adequately dealt with. I have made a first attempt at providing such an account elsewhere. See my *Between Revolution and Deconstruction: Ferry and Renaut's Juridical Humanism* (PhD Dissertation, Yale University, 1995), Chapter 1. In presenting here Lefort's idea of the political I draw on this previous work of mine.

13 Claude Lefort, 'The Question of Democracy', in *Democracy and Political Theory,* trans. David Macey (Minneapolis: University of Minnesota Press, 1988), p. 11; translation modified.

14 Ibid., pp. 11–12.

15 Claude Lefort, 'Permanence of the Theologico-Political?', *Democracy and Political Theory,* p. 225.

16 Needless to say, this does not mean that Lefort considers liberal democracy to be the sole modern political form but rather that liberal democracy is

one way or another at the source of the main political transformations which are characteristic of modernity.

17 Lefort, 'Permanence of the Theologico-Political?', p. 225.
18 Ibid., pp. 228, 226.
19 Ibid., p. 226.
20 Pierre Clastres, *Society Against the State: Essays in Political Anthropology*, trans. Robert Hurley and Abe Stein (New York: Zone Books, 1987); *Recherches d'anthropologie politique* (Paris: Seuil, 1980).
21 Marcel Gauchet, 'La dette du sens et les racines de l'Éetat. Politique de la religion primitive', *Libre*, no. 2 (1977), p. 29.
22 Ibid., p. 31.
23 Ibid., p. 7.
24 In this light, as has already been noted, it makes no sense to say that *neozapatismo* calls for a full restoration of the way of life of premodern, traditional indigenous communities. Nor does it make sense to regard the EZLN as a straightforward continuation (into the 1990s) of politico-military utopias such as those associated with leftist revolutionary programs that, at least since the mid-1970s, began to be clearly perceived by the left itself as adding many more problems to those they were meant to solve.

It is true that the critique of leftist revolutionary ideals that was carried out by the left itself in the aftermath of 1968, was initially a phenomenon peculiar to Western Europe, and more concretely, to French intellectuals. There is a wealth of literature on the subject too copious to cite here. For the significance of such self-criticism to what is known as the 'return of the political' in French political theory, see my *Between Revolution and Deconstruction*, Chapter 1, first section.

25 There is, of course, a heated debate currently going on in political theory about whether or not this should be the case. I cannot enter into this debate here. I will just assert that I side with those who think that such group rights not only *can* be accommodated with liberal-democratic justice but are in fact strongly (internally) dictated by it. Two of the most interesting contemporary discussions that follow on this line come from somewhat different philosophical persuasions. See Charles Taylor, 'The Politics of Recognition, in Amy Gutmann, ed., Multiculturalism: Examining the Politics of Recognition' (Princeton: Princeton University Press, 1994), pp. 25–73; Kymlicka, *Multicultural Citizenship*.

For a glimpse at some of the main issues involved in the many-sided subject of group-rights in regard to contemporary debates in political theory, see Gutmann, *op. cit.*; John Horton, ed., *Liberalism, Multiculturalism and Toleration* (New York: St. Martin's Press, 1993); Will Kymlicka, *Liberalism, Community, and Culture* (Oxford: Oxford University Press, 1989); *Multicultural Citizenship*; Kymlicka, ed., *The Rights of Minority Cultures*; Chandran Kukathas, ed., *Multicultural Citizens: the Philosophy and Politics of Identity* (St Leonards: Centre for Independent Studies, 1993); Ian Shapiro and Will Kymlicka, eds, *Ethnicity and Group Rights* (New York: New York University Press, 1997); James Tully, *Strange Multiplicity: Constitutionalism in an Age of Diversity* (Cambridge: Cambridge University Press, 1995).

For a useful hint at how multifarious and overdetermined the theory and practice of multiculturalism can be, see Avery F. Gordon and Christopher

Newfield, eds, *Mapping Multiculturalism* (Minneapolis: University of Minnesota Press, 1997).

26 *EZLN1*, pp. 175–7; *EZLN3*, p. 92.

27 Jacinto Arias, 'Nuestra batalla para pertenecernos a nosotros mismos', in María Luisa Armendáriz, ed., *Chiapas, una radiografía* (Mexico City: Fondo de Cultura Económica, 1994), pp. 198–210.

28 Ibid., p. 201.

29 We would thus make a gross mistake, as Will Kymlicka does, if we were to interpret the fact that 'indigenous cultures display a profound antipathy to the idea that one person can be another's master' as suggesting that such cultures 'are often quite individualistic in their internal organization'; Kymlicka, *Multicultural Citizenship*, p. 172. This mistake, moreover, is linked to another, more fundamental misunderstanding: the confusion of premodern and modern forms of political egalitarianism. For, just as is the case with the Neozapatistas's intimation at the essential compatibility of the indigenous communities they stand for with liberal-democratic societies, such confusion underlies Kymlicka's overall assessment that these and other minority cultures 'are often just as liberal as the majority culture'; ibid.

30 See Claude Lefort, *L'invention démocratique. Les limites de la domination totalitaire* (Paris: Fayard, 1981), Introduction. See, naturally, Alexis de Tocqueville, *Democracy in America*, ed. J.-P. Mayer, trans. George Lawrence (New York: Harper & Row, 1966), Introduction.

31 Cornelius Castoriadis, *The Imaginary Institution of Society*, trans. Kathleen Blamey (Cambridge: Polity Press, 1987).

32 As an indication of what 'friendly' and 'to a certain extent' are supposed to mean in this context, the least one can say about the Neozapatista ambivalent (premodern/modern) rhetoric is that it represents no more, but also no less, than a carefully crafted token of the now trendy belief – yet a fashionable belief which, fortunately, touches deeply on some of the most important lessons we are to learn from recent revolutionary history – that a radical, *sans reste* critique of political modernity, such as the one set forth by totalitarianism whether red or brown, can only lead to horror and stupidity.

12
Control and Resistance: Two Dimensions of Palestinians' Existence in Israel

Ahmad H. Sa'di

Introduction

Many believe that a political agreement between the Palestine Liberation Organization and the state of Israel will bring about a permanent solution to the troubled relations between Jews and Palestinians. Yet, as this article will show, such a compromise will leave many fundamental issues unresolved. The question regarding the nature of the Israeli state and its relation to the Palestinians inside the 1967 border will not fade away. The majority-minority relations in Israel are not merely a reflection of regional development, they are, rather, influenced by a variety of changes and transformations such as globalization, the declining socio-economic role of the state, the re-emergence of civil society as an opposing force to the state, and so on. Furthermore, recent scholarship has drawn attention to the subordinate groups' culture as a viable venue of resistance. These insights will be used to promote a new outlook on the relationships between the Israeli state and the Palestinian minority. It is argued that the Palestinians should be viewed as a self-conscious national minority that has endeavored in various ways to retain control over its life within formidable constraints, rather than as a passive agent whose history is determined by outside forces. The first section of the chapter describes the institution by the state of a control system to subdue the Palestinians. The second briefly discusses the nature of the Israeli state, while the third shows the implications of the nature of the Israeli state for its socio-economic policies towards the Palestinian minority. The following sections analyse the research on the Palestinians as citizens in a Jewish state. These studies are classified into two categories according to the perspective used: research that used top-down method of research versus that which used bottom-up methodology. The chapter concludes by summing-up what has been achieved and pointing to issues that should be further explored and analysed.

Palestinians in Israel: the foundation of political control

In 1948 the State of Israel was established over 77 per cent of Palestine's territory – a much larger area than the territory allotted to the Jewish state by the 1947 UN Partition Resolution. During the 1948 War, Israel occupied wide territories in Galilee, the Triangle and the Negev, which were designated to the Arab Palestinian State envisaged by the UN resolution.[1] Inside Israel's boundaries, only about 160 000 out of the 900 000[2] (according to the other estimates, 750 000[3]) Palestinian inhabitants remained, to become citizens of the Jewish state. Their existence created disappointment and concern among leading Israeli politicians. During the initial discussions on the fate of the Palestinian minority, some politicians inquired into the plausibility of expulsion,[4] while Ben-Gurion, the long standing leader of the Zionist movement and the first Prime Minister of Israel, asked his aides about the possibility of converting Palestinian youth to Judaism.[5] However, it soon became clear that this minority would stay for the foreseeable future. Two policy lines have consequently emerged. The first stems from Israel's international obligations and the self-image it has endeavored to project, of a democratic enlightened nation amidst a region that lacks progressive civilized values. In accordance with the 1947 UN Partition Resolution (article 181 [11]), the Palestinian minority was promised equal rights. On various occasions Israeli and Zionist leaders expressed their commitment to grant the non-Jewish population equal rights. For example, in his testimony before the Anglo-American Committee of Inquiry on Palestine (1946), Ben-Gurion commented that in the future Jewish State,

> We will have to treat our Arab and other non-Jewish neighbors on the basis of absolute equality as if they were Jews, but make every effort that they should preserve their Arab characteristics .... . while making every effort to make all the citizens of the country equal civilly, socially, economically, politically, intellectually, and gradually raise the standard of life of everyone, Jews and others.[6]

These promises were also expressed in Israel's Declaration of Independence, which pledged 'complete equality of social and political rights ... without distinction of creed, race or sex'. Yet, according to the second policy line, the new reality was viewed in terms drawn from the near past: the Palestinians were conceived as an enemy that should be marginalized, excluded and disenfranchised. The pursuit of this policy seemed quite natural for the new leaders, who until 1948 had headed Jewish organizations and led the struggle against the Palestinians militarily, politically, economically and in the labor market.[7] The result was the adoption of these two policy directions simultaneously.

The Palestinians were granted Israeli citizenship and formal political rights to vote and be elected. However, these rights were emptied of their content. With the Declaration of Independence, the Knesset adopted the Mandatory Defense (Emergency) Regulations, except those which limited Jewish immigration. These regulations, which were enacted to fight (mainly Jewish) terrorism and were condemned by leading Jewish and Zionist figures, have become a main tool of governance by Israel. Until recently, they have been used almost exclusively against Palestinians. These regulations had constituted the legal basis for the military government which was imposed over the Palestinian populated areas until 1966.[8] The military government was initially established to achieve three goals:

1 To prevent the return of Palestinian refugees and expel those who succeeded in returning.
2 To relocate (and occasionally to transfer) the population of partly empty villages and neighborhoods, and Palestinian villagers residing adjacent to the new borders, and transfer Palestinian-owned lands to Jewish settlements.
3 To establish political control over the Palestinians and segregate them from the Jewish majority.[9]

By the mid 1950s it became clear that the initial objectives has been achieved, and that new aims should be defined. A top-secret memorandum from 1959 included one major goal which was entrusted to the military government:

The government's policy ... has sought to divide the Arab population into diverse communities and regions ... The municipality status of Arab villages, and the competitive spirit of local elections, deepened the divisions inside the villages themselves.[10]

Three additional objectives were revealed later on.
4   To prevent the establishment of Arab nationalist organizations.
5   To prevent internal refugees (Palestinian refugees inside Israel) from
    returning to their villages and to stop Palestinians whose land had
    been confiscated from trying to re-establish their holding over it.
6   To confine Palestinian workers to their villages, and prevent them
    from competing with Jewish immigrants in the labor market.[11]

Mapai, then the major political force, sought to use the military government in the interest of 'the state and the party'. The party's political committee and secretariat, in their meeting in 1952, outlined Mapai's policy as follows:

1   The expulsion of the Arabs is not possible.
2   The activities of the Party and the government must be increased
    (among this population).
3   The existing separate institutional frameworks ... should be
    strengthened in the interest of the state and the party.[12]

Under the Emergency Regulations, the Military Governors were given sweeping powers. These included the ability to restrict the movement of any citizen, to forbid him/her from entering certain places, to compel him/her to notify the authorities about his/her whereabouts, to prohibit him/her from using or possessing certain articles, and to impose restrictions on his/her employment, associations and communications with others. Moreover the Military Governors could place any person under the supervision of the security forces, deny him/her free movement outside certain boundaries without written permission, or exile him/her from one part of the country to another. They could also impose night curfews and declare the closure of any area.[13] These regulations had been used extensively, giving the military government total control over the Palestinians' life. The Palestinians were dependent upon the good will of the military commanders in getting a travel permit for a few days of work in the cities, working their fields which were outside the village boundaries, visiting relatives, or receiving a permit to set up a business, open a shop or be employed in the local educational system. This good will was usually achieved in return for various acts of collaboration: voting (they and their families) for Mapai, informing the authorities about relatives who had expressed criticism of the state, showing public support for the state, defending its policies, and so on. In contrast, dissidents were subjected to punishment ranging in severity from surveillance to banishment; they were black-listed and denied (both they and their families) any fair treatment. Palestinians' endeavors to address state offices directly did not bear fruit. In February 1950, the influential foreign minister Sharet warned his fellow ministers against the growing tendency among Palestinians of approaching the official bodies directly and asked them not to reply to such applications before discussing them with the military government, through which the replies should be given.[14]

Now, after more than three decades have passed since the abolition of the military government, its impact has not vanished. During the military government era a whole set of structures, procedures, attitudes and ideologies that governed the majority-minority relations were laid down. This included the establishment of official bodies for dealing with the Palestinians such as an office that cordinates the state's activities in the Arab sector (the Prime Minister's Adviser on Arab Affairs or a minister who fulfils this function), discrimination against the Palestinians in the entitlement for social benefits and in awarding public funds, the establishment of particular departments in various ministries for dealing with the Arabs, the emergence of negative attitudes towards the Palestinians, and an ideology that legitimizes their status as second-class citizens. As to the Palestinians, this gave rise to relations of patronage and co-option, the emergence of new causes for conflict, and strong feelings of alienation towards official bodies.

An Israeli dilemma

Students of Israeli society frequently refer to the contradiction inherent in the state structure. Israel is declared to be both a Jewish and a democratic state. In the wording of the Declaration of Independence, Meir Wilner, the representative of the Communist party, suggested defining Israel as a sovereign independent Jewish state, thus limiting the boundaries of the concept 'the Jewish people' to those residing in Israel.[15] Yet the nebulous term 'the Jewish people' continues to define the collective that the state serves. Consequently, three collectives represented by the state were created: the Jewish citizens of Israel, the Jews all over the world and the Palestinian citizens of Israel. This categorization reflects also a set of legal rights. The Jewish nature of Israel has been articulated through a variety of laws, regulations and policies. Not only do Jews world wide enjoy the right to immigrate freely to Israel and receive citizenship (and substantial material benefits) upon their arrival, but also international Jewish organizations (the World Zionist

Organization, the Jewish Agency and the Jewish National Fund) were assigned state functions. Two acts epitomize the meaning of 'Jewish state'. The first concerns the High Court ruling in 1972 regarding the concept of nationality: 'There is no Israeli nation apart from the Jewish people, and the Jewish people consists not only of the people residing in Israel but also of the Jews in the Diaspora.'[16] Accordingly, the Palestinians were excluded from the 'nation' which the state represents and for which it acts. This exclusion is manifested in the second act – Basic Law: Israel Lands (1960). According to this law the ownership of the state's land (more than 93 per cent of Israel's surface) is entrusted to the Jewish people, and cannot be transferred to another party by sale or any other method.[17] This conception of the Jewish state was canonized in Basic Law: the Knesset (1985) in which questioning the Jewish nature of Israel is equated with racism.[18]

Although Israel has incorporated the Palestinians, due to its exclusionary foundation it will never be able to integrate them as equal citizens. Put differently, Israel, in its current legal, ideological, organizational and procedural structures, will never employ universalistic criteria with regard to all its citizens. Until the late 1970s, this shortcoming had not received any critical examination in mainstream Israeli social science. Israel was portrayed as a democratic state, and the impact of its structure on the Palestinian minority was either played down or regarded as a non-issue. Since then, however, a series of sociological studies have tried to grapple with this dilemma: their characterization of the state – minority relations – will be discussed in a coming section.

Socio-economic conditions

The Jewish nature of Israel has a great impact on its social policies. Voluminous research has documented discriminatory policies and practices against the Palestinians in various fields of life including education, health, entitlements for social benefits, the labor market, state's awards for local authorities, housing and regional planning, agriculture and so on. For example, the State's Comptroller Report of 1992 indicates that state funding for the Palestinian educational system per pupil did not exceed one third of the amount allocated to its Jewish counterpart.[19] Likewise, a study on Arab local governments has revealed that in 1975 state awards for Jewish localities in relation to Palestinian localities with similar size stood at the ratio of 14:1. In 1984, the ratio was 35:1.[20] And the areas under their jurisdiction were at the ratio of 8.5 *dunums* per person versus one *dunum* per person respectively. Palestinians are also the poorest population and have received the lowest level of social support. In 1994, 34.5 per cent of Israeli children were classified as poor; however 34 per cent of them received some alleviation from poverty due to state support – this in relation to a poverty level of more than 58 per cent among the Palestinians children of whom only 26 per cent were taken out of poverty.[21] Palestinian farmers receive a negligible portion of the irrigation water, and they cannot lease or sub-lease state land.[22] These are only scattered examples of the way in which the state structure has influenced its policies towards the minority.

Scholarly presentation

1 Viewpoints from the center

Until the mid-1970s, mainstream scholarship on the Palestinians in Israel had been produced by Israeli social scientists, journalists and state officials who identified with and represented the ruling power. Any critical inquiry into the structure of the Israeli state and its relation to the Palestinian minority was fiercely attacked or silenced. The anti-intellectual attack launched by Kimmerling – a leading sociologist at the Hebrew University – on Zureik's book *Palestinian in Israel: a Study of Internal Colonialism* is illuminating:

> While reading Zureik's book, the impression that comes out is that it represents a continuation of the war by other means (in this case an academic publication). The fate of the Palestinians (whether in Israel, under Israeli occupation, or those who live in different Arab countries) is difficult, and the blackening of their prospects does not bear [positive] contribution either to them or to the accumulation of social science knowledge on conflict management and the motivations and obstacles that the processes of nation-building entail.[23]

Kimmerling's critique is interesting because it contains various ideological presentations which prevail in mainstream Israeli sociology.

1 He leaves the second clause of the first sentence without a subject, '... the impression that comes out'; whose impression? Kimmerling's? That of the Israeli social scientists who have to respond to Zureik's aggression? Or the impression of the fair-minded reader, who must reach similar conclusions to those of

Kimmerling? The question is not linguistic, for through this linguistic exercise Kimmerling tries to present his arguments as reasonable and even benign.

2   Why does he mention the fate of the Palestinian refugees in the Arab countries? Is it more than an ideological device of universalization? Instead of dealing with Zureik's specific arguments regarding the existential conditions of the Palestinians in Israel, he contends that the fate of the Palestinians everywhere is regrettable and the status of those living in Israel is part of this general reality.

3   If at the beginning of the cited quotation we were warned about Zureik's aggressive intentions, at the end of it we are assured that (like all the acts of aggression that the Arabs committed against Israel) it is futile and would only aggravate the predicament of the Palestinians.

Ian Lustick, in his book *Arabs in the Jewish State: Israel's Control of a National Minority*, began by presenting his background as a credible alibi for the sincerity of his intentions.

All my life I have been involved, as a participant, leader, and resource person, in Jewish and Zionist organizations. Because of my upbringing, my emotional commitments, and my involvement in Jewish affairs, I know from the inside – from inside myself and from inside the Jewish community – the painful issues which serious consideration of Jewish-Arab relations in Israel raises … . Published material can always be misused and quoted out of context. This book may indeed provide ammunition for groups with which I strongly disagree. But this should not deprive those genuinely concerned for the welfare of Jews and Arabs in Israel of analysis which clarifies the basic issues, provides the facts necessary to clear the air of myth …[24]

Although the environment of bullying and intimidation of those who dare to criticize the official (Zionist) version of history is slowly passing, it has not yet disappeared. During the last decade a group of Israeli scholars 'new historians and sociologists', who are revising Israel's history by analyzing declassified archival material and bringing to the forefront subjects that had been considered non-issues, were accused by mainstream scholars of not being patriotic.[25] In the next section I shall discuss the presentation of state-minority relations by the official sociology.

Modernization

Modernization theory is one of the late models that the evolutionary thinking of the late-nineteenth and early-twentieth centuries produced. Two central themes run through this perspective. According to the first, modernization represents a project of integrating the various ethnic groups into the mainstream of society in order to achieve consensus and social harmony. The second describes an evolutionary development of societies and collectivities from traditionalism to modernity. In Israel, this theory has formed the basis for analyzing 'ethnic relations', and S.N. Eisenstadt, the founder of Israeli sociology, has been a prominent theoretician of modernization. Modernization theory has been applied to analyzing the absorption of Oriental Jewish immigrants by the established European Jewish community, through a policy of 'melting pot' (*Kur Hituch*). They were diagnosed as a traditional population (backward, primitive, childlike, and so on) which has been led to modernity by the state and the European Jewish community. Their integration has been evolving through the functioning of various institutions, most notably the army. Thus an Israeli nation with a European orientation began its crystallization.[26]

This model could not be fully applied to the analysis of the status of the Palestinian minority, owing to the absence of a secular Israeli nation that encompasses all citizens regardless of their religious affiliation. In the absence of a process of nation formation as occured in many post-colonial states, the research has dealt solely with the 'development' of the minorities. It has described the progress that has taken place in the minority's various aspects of life: education, the stratification system, health, political behavior, changing social attitudes, agriculture, social organization and so on.[27] Even in its structure the research is designed to mirror the unfolding evolutionary process of modernization. It begins by describing the degenerate conditions of the minority when the state was established. Then it presents indeces of comparisons between the past and the present which always 'reveal' that a change for the better was achieved; these changes are attributed to the modernizing role of the state, and the Jewish majority who act as modernizing agents. Finally, it briefly dwells on the 'gaps' which continue to exist between the majority and the minority; these gaps are explained by the different levels of modernization when the state was established as well as the barriers to modernization that the traditional values and institutions in the Arab communities pose. In the light of its premises and methodology, can this research accomplish anything more than self-fulfilling prophecies?

To get a closer look at this research I will briefly discuss a representative study of it, the book written by Issac Arnon and Michael Raviv, *From Fellah to Farmer: a Study of Change in Arab Villages.* The study begins by describing the helpless condition of Palestinian agriculture when the State of Israel was established: 'The basic characteristics of traditional agriculture ... have remained practically unchanged since biblical times ...'[28] However, thanks to the state's modernizing efforts the situation has dramatically improved:

> The use of animals for work on the farm had ceased completely by 1963. Agriculture in all the villages, including the hill villages, is fully mechanized ... The use of sickles for the harvesting of cereals ceased in 1964; the entire cereal crop is at present combine-harvested.[29]

After describing this 'monumental' progress, the authors report that: 'Arab agriculture in Israel has reached a high level of achievement, and of this *the state of Israel can be justifiably proud* ...'.[30] The rosy picture that this book presents contradicts all available data. When it was published, the state had already completed the confiscation of more than 70 per cent of Palestinian-owned lands and their transfer to Jewish ownership and use.[31] This policy of land expropriation resulted in bloody clashes between the security forces and Palestinians in 1976 – four years before the study's publication – but in the book there is no mention of that. Additionally, the authors ignored the fact that Palestinian farmers receive a negligible portion of the irrigation water (about 2 per cent), and that they have suffered from a systematic policy of discrimination by the Ministry of Agriculture in the awarding of subsidies.[32] Palestinian farmers were also excluded from the advisory, marketing and planning bodies which have a great influence on national agricultural policies.[33]

If, methodologically, this research is designed to express the official version of politics and history, its ideological underpinnings are more far reaching.

1   By accrediting the state and the Jewish majority with the role of modernizing agents it undermines the legitimacy of any struggle waged by Palestinians. Indeed, criticisms of the state or its policies are described by this research as signs of traditionalism, radicalism, alienation, or even of a terrorist orientation.

2   By defining the Palestinians as a 'traditional' community, it determines that their frameworks of identification are primordial or religious, and therefore they are devoid of nationalist consciousness. Jews are presented as the sole national group, and voluminous research, designed to negate Palestinian identity, has been published.[34]

3   This research confines the discussion of the state to its public policy functions, leaving the structure of the state and its affinity to the various social groups unanalysed. The fact that the state behaves as a sectarian structure, rather than as a neutral arena, is left without consideration.

4   By presenting the Palestinians as an object of modernization, their role – as a collectivity with specific cultural, national, class and regional characteristics – in influencing their history is eliminated.

Citizenship rights and democracy

Endeavoring to present a novel solution to the Israeli dilemma, Sammy Smooha argues that Israel represents a new type of democratic regime. It has not adopted the principles of liberal democracy, where citizens have equal rights and direct affinity to the state. Nor is it a consociational democracy, where state/citizen relations are mediated by representative institutions of the various ethnic groups, or a *Herronvolk* democracy (democracy of the master race), since the Palestinians enjoy formal political rights. Thus, he argues that a new type of democracy exists in Israel, which he labels 'Ethnic Democracy'. For him, this regime: 'Combine[s] the extension of political and civil rights to individuals and certain collective rights to minorities with institutional dominance over the state by one of the ethnic groups.'[35] As to the minorities, this model suggests that they will be 'disadvantaged but they can avail themselves of democratic means to negotiate better terms of coexistence'.[36]

Practically this means that the majority controls the state, defines its objectives and sets up its priorities; what is left for the minority is to try, through the politics of wheeling and dealing, to improve the socio-economic conditions of its members. Put simply, the Palestinians can struggle to achieve better housing, education, and so on, but they should be denied any say in the state's prime goals. Recently Smooha has been trying to present this model as the best way for the establishment of democracies in East European and various Third World countries.[37]

Theoretically, this model has many pitfalls.

1 The control of the state by one national group is at odds with the principle of equality. It is for this reason that political theorists such as Aristotle and Rousseau emphasized the importance of denying any group in society control over the state.

2 The dimensions of democracy are confined to the formal level. However, as research on countries with long-standing liberal traditions has revealed, various groups in society, although they may formally enjoy full citizenship rights, are in practice marginalized or excluded.[38] The history of the Palestinians in Israel clearly shows that despite their enjoying formal rights they have been marginalized and disadvantaged by selective imposition of laws and by legal manipulations.

3 Smooha failed to explain why ethnic democracy is essentially different from the dictatorship of the majority. It is understandable that most ruling groups try to achieve legitimacy and international recognition by abiding by fair rules as long as these rules serve their interests. But does this mean that the whole difference between majoritarian regime and democracy is circumstantial or stylistic?

4 Various students of democratic regimes emphasized the involvement of citizens and their experience of participation as the essence of democracy, processes which they call active citizenship. Can minorities under the suggested model enjoy active citizenship?

Beyond the theoretical debate, it is essential to look at the ideological aspects of the model. It is obvious that the model came to justify the existing regime. Smooha does that through two well-known ideological devices: normalization and universalization. According to the principle of normalization, abnormal or distorted reality is described as normal and even as desirable. Meanwhile, the universalization principle legitimizes reality by emphasizing its prevalence. Smooha not only tells us that the denial of equal rights to a group of citizens is compatible with democracy, he goes as far as suggesting the Israeli model to other nations. Furthermore, it is essential to take into account the state of debate in the Israeli academic circles when the model was presented. A heated debate between the 'establishment' and the 'new' scholars concerning the state's structure and the Zionist historiography had been taking place.[39] The model of ethnic democracy could be regarded as the author's position in this contention.

Political control

Ian Lustick tries to present a critical analysis of majority-minority relations in Israel by analyzing the control system that the state has imposed on the Palestinians. According to Lustick, an elaborate system of control was established during the formative stage of the state, through which the Palestinians were subdued, disadvantaged and many of their resources were confiscated and/or used for the benefit of the Jewish majority. Composed of three mutually reinforcing components – segmentation, co-optation and dependency[40] – this system had operated successfully until the early 1970s. The first Palestinian defiance against state policy, on 30 March 1976 – known as Land Day – signaled the erosion of the control system and called for the development of new tools of governance. Faced with the options of modernizing the control system – an option that entails the allocation of ever-increasing resources – or introducing new measures of democratization, the state seems to have opted for the second alternative, thus paving the road for 'creeping bi-nationalism within the Green Line'.[41]

Lustick's critical account of the control system points to the limits of the criticism that could be conducted by looking through the vantage point of the center. Neither in his dwelling on the erosion of the control system nor in his analysis of the venues for change, did Lustick pay attention to the role of Palestinians in influencing their history. For him, state-minority relations are determined by the trickle-down of state power. Thus, Lustick's model of political control could not incorporate an analysis of the ways through which minorities could resist the ruling power without reaching a frontal confrontation with it.

2   From democracy to ethnocracy

Critical theorization of the Israeli state's structure and detailed descriptions of the Palestinians' existential conditions are quite recent. Not before the late 1970s, almost three decades after the establishment of Israel, did critical research begin to be published and gain currency in academic circles. Prior to that, only a few such books had appeared, most notably Jiryis's pioneering work, *The Arabs in Israel,* first published in 1966 in Hebrew,[42] and El-Asmar's personal account, *To Be An Arab in Israel* (1975).[43] Since then a growing body of literature has appeared. Elia Zureik, a Palestinian sociologist, employed a Marxist version of dependency theory to analyse state-minority relations.[44] Contrary to the modernization perspective, which describes the Zionist project in terms of idealism, ideological commitment, humane endeavor, and so on, Zureik treats it as a project of colonization, and state-minority relations as reflecting a situation of internal colonialism. The treatment of Israeli reality in terms drawn from models and practices of colonialism has been recently gaining ground. Shaifr's book, *Land, Labor, and the Origins of the Israeli-Palestinian Conflict*,[45] represents an essential contribution in this direction. In his study, Shafir argues that Zionism began as an ethnic nationalist movement,[46] but that it shares the practices of the late phase of European overseas colonialism. As an incarnation of colonialism, Israeli society was created through the combinations of various degrees, of military control, colonization, territorial dispossession, and exploitation of the natives.[47] The practices of territorial dispossession, exploitation, control and marginalization were analysed by various scholars through further exploration of the nature of Israeli state and society. For example, Yiftachel [48] shows how the state confiscation of Palestinian-owned lands in Galilee, and its regional policy of 'Judaization of the Galilee', derives from its conception of the region as an internal frontier. The characterization of Israeli society as a frontier society with a drive to take over the land in Palestinian-populated regions inside Israel and in the occupied territories, along with the Jewish nature of the state, led, according to various scholars, to the creation of a hierarchy of citizenships. In their theorization of citizenship discourse, Peled and Shafir[49] argue that through the allocation of different types of citizenship to various collectives, Israel created a social entity which lacks clear-cut boundaries. The liberal conception of citizenship which guarantees basic human rights, formal political participation and basic welfare entitlements was granted to both Jewish and Palestinian citizens of Israel, thus separating the latter from the Palestinians in the occupied territories. The ethno-nationalist discourse, which expresses individual membership in a homogeneous community of descent, has been employed to separate Jews from Palestinians (both citizens and those in the occupied territories). Meanwhile the republican discourse – where citizenship is practiced through an involvement in the definition, formulation and pursuit of the common good – has been used to legitimize the hierarchical order between European and Oriental Jews. Such conceptualizations shed light on the complexity of social, political, economic and legal aspects that the unfolding of the colonization process has created. In short, the characterization of the Israeli political and social system has been shifting from enlightened, democratic, western, modern, and so on, to frontier society, ethnocracy and the like.

3 Viewpoints from the periphery

Although a large body of literature on the Palestinian minority in Israel has been published during the last three decades, very few studies have analysed the ways that the Palestinians survived and handled the conditions of control and marginalization. The bulk of existing studies describe either their disadvantagement or their modernization by the state. In both perspectives the Palestinians are treated as passive agents who have negligible influence on the shaping of their life. Expressing the need to consider the Palestinians as a self-conscious national group that has been endeavoring, in various ways, to influence its fate, Kamen wrote:

> The components of the system of control over the Arabs in Israel have been described elsewhere, as have the consequences of this system for the Arab population. But no one has yet tried to see how the Arabs themselves attempted to overcome the conditions which have been imposed on them in order to rebuild their lives despite the limitations and restrictions under which they lived.
>
> It is no exaggeration to say that after 1948 the Arabs in Israel, as a national community, had to begin their communal life afresh on the national level, and in many cases on the local level as well. The history of the Arabs in Israel is in large measure the story of their reconstruction of their society.[50]

Since the writing of these words, very little has been done to rectify the situation. And the history of the Palestinians in Israel is still awaiting reconstruction, particularly as the cohort of Palestinians who survived the tragic events of the 1948 war and the years of harsh oppression during the 1950s, 1960s and early 1970s is passing away. What has been written so far can be divided into three main categories. The first included few studies which analysed empirical data, either ethnographic or statistical, regarding specific cases. The second category includes studies which viewed the revival of Palestinian collective action through the establishment and functioning of various community-based and nation-wide NGOs (Non-Governmental Organizations) and coordinating institutions. The third line views Palestinian history in terms of what J. Scott called 'weapons of the weak',[51] meaning that a culture resisting the political control was created. This culture stems from both the historical experience of the Palestinians and their negation of the dominant ideology.

1.   Empirical studies

In various studies Yiftachel[52] analysed the ways used by Palestinian inhabitants of Galilee to resist the state's planning policies of 'Judaizing' the region. The acts of protest that he studied – demonstrations and strikes, voting for Arab parties, and the establishment of NGOs – centered around three issues: national demands, socio-economic deprivation, and land use and territorial issues. Each of these factors influenced the Arab protest differently:

> ... the national issues ignited the most intense protest but there was a relatively even distribution in the overall magnitude of protest on all three key issues; ... Israeli spatial and socio-economic policies have had a pronounced impact on patterns of Arab protest; and the geographical factors, particularly the emergence of ethnic regionalism, have played a key role in shaping Arab protest.[53]

As a geographer whose interest is in the intermingling of socio-political and spatial factors, Yiftachel characterized the Palestinians in Galilee as 'a "homeland" regional minority within a unitary "ethnic (Jewish) state"'. Bearing this definition in mind, the state's public policies, particularly planning, are not presented as expressing modernization, rationality, effectiveness, and so on – as modernizational researchers would have argued – but rather as an instrument of control.[54] Additionally, Palestinian protest is treated as legitimate, although not always legal.

Another characterization of the Palestinian minority that radically departed from the mainstream conception was presented by Rabinowitz in his study of the political mobilization among Palestinian residents of the predominantly Jewish city of Nazareth Illit:

> Palestinian citizens of Israel and Palestinians in the occupied territories, in exile in the Arab countries, and abroad, share a basic historical narrative which portrays them as victims of events imposed on them by the powers, wills, and predicaments of others. Their very identity as Palestinians hinges on the experience of dispossessions and exile ...[55]

Rabinowitz analyses a main paradox faced by Palestinian political activists and candidates at local and national levels. Campaigning and successful political mobilization of Palestinians touch upon issues that evoke deep national sentiments of dispossession, heritage of loss, and so on. Being faithful to one's political platform and presenting his voters at the center of power, the politician would be denied the ability to deliver tangible resources for his constituents. However, the achievement of material benefits (no matter how small) entails co-option by the establishment, and consequently would tarnish the politician's image in the community. This small margin of maneuvering made Palestinians both politically involved and at the same time disillusioned with politicians. In the case of Nazareth Illit, the candidate for the municipality that Rabinowitz described (Abu 'ata) made the shift after his election from stressing national identity and an agenda of nationalist character, to trying in 'pragmatic' ways to secure material gains for his voters. In contrast to Smooha's favorable treatment of the Israeli political system, Rabinowitz's anthropological study unveiled one tragic implication of the system's functioning for the Palestinian minority.

A key area that the regime uses to subdue the Palestinian minority is the employment of Palestinians in the public sector, particularly the Arab educational system. Lustick described the methods of blacklisting, promotion in exchange for collaboration, patronage, and so on, that the officials in charge of Arab affairs use.[56] He also analysed the damaging effects of these methods on the educational process. However, he did not account for the actions of those who were disadvantaged because of their political attitudes or behaviors. One venue of action that became increasingly accessible to such individuals after 1974, and particularly since the 1980s, is the appeal to the courts. Mazawi studied the appeals that Palestinian teachers filed to the High Court of Justice against alleged misconduct in the promotion of candidates to management positions.[57] It was found that in 40 per cent of the 28 cases reviewed, the selection processes were found improper and inadequate candidates were chosen. Moreover, in various cases the court criticized high officials in the Ministry of Education for disreputable practices.

2. *Palestinian civil society*

The second category of research includes studies that view Palestinian collective activity through the NGOs and other coordinating bodies they established. According to Doron, these organizations represent the basis for the emerging Palestinian civil society in Israel.[58] This civil society began its ascendance, along with its Jewish counterpart, in the mid-1970s, as a result of the state's diminishing role in the socio-economic sphere. Palestinian organizations are of two types: political coordinating committees, and the voluntary and non-profit sector.

The first type includes organizations such as *The Follow-Up Committee on Arab Affairs*, an umbrella organization comprised of mayors, Knesset members and representatives of all Palestinian political and social movements, *The National Committee of Chairmen of Arab Local Authorities*, and *The Committee of Defense of Arab Lands*. Under the auspices of these organizations various sub-committees were established to monitor the development of the Palestinian sector and to document the gaps which exist between Jews and Palestinians.[59] The second type includes non-profit organizations. The mushrooming of non-profit Palestinian organizations has been impressive: their number in 1990 reached 186. Their areas of activities include: the preservation of Palestinian heritage and culture, the provision of preventive health services for residents in small remote villages, defense of Bedouin rights, the establishment of preschool settings, and the provision of legal assistance on issues of significance for the whole community.[60]

Could these organizations be regarded as a proper basis for an emerging civil society? For Doron the answer is self-evident: such wide-ranging organizations represent the action of associations of free individuals who act for the benefit of the community. However, I think that one should not jump quickly to conclusions. The reservation is twofold. Firstly, the state, since its establishment, has endeavored to stir rivalries among Palestinians, and has actively promoted non-national identities and loyalties among them. This policy has been particularly successful in influencing voting patterns – most mayors and Knesset members are elected on the basis of primordial or religious affiliation. Could the coordinating bodies, which they established, be regarded as components of civil society? Edward Shils tells us that the associations of the civil society are established around common interests, beliefs, attitudes, and so on, and that the person joins them as an individual and not as a bearer of a specific identity.[61] This conception contradicts the essence of primodiality, where the person is treated according to the nature of the group to which he or she belongs. Secondly, has the state so easily given up its policy of subjecting the Palestinians to political control and preventing them from establishing worthwhile autonomous bases? I think that the answer is negative. These organizations could be almost effortlessly monitored and manipulated. In addition, they are dependent for their existence on resources from overseas donors (mainly European NGOs), which makes them accountable to the foreign donors, and not to the community in whose name they act.

3.   *Resistance through culture*

The third category of research includes my own theorization of Palestinian resistance.[62] Following propositions made by Gramsci[63] and developed by Scott,[64] I argued that control and resistance are part of everyday life of the regime and the minority. In their daily life Palestinians are disadvantaged, and experience discrimination, harassment, verbal abuse and other forms of domination. The strategies that they have developed to survive these conditions were presented as a promising area of research, particularly as the Palestinians' position seems to be permanent. For one thing they are a stable minority in the population. Despite the dramatic demographic fluctuations in Israel, they still compose about 16 per cent of the population within the 1967 borders. This constancy does not underpin demands for a radical change in majority-minority relations. Another reason is that the diplomatic efforts being made to solve the long-standing conflict in the Middle East peacefully will not bear any direct impact on their position. They are not and will not be part of any political deal – their problem is considered an internal Israeli affair. Thirdly, because of the Jewish nature of the state, and subsequently the national antagonism in Israel, Palestinians have not been nearly as successful (and are not expected to be so in the future) in occupying strategic positions in the decision-making bodies as are religious Jews or the new immigrants from the ex-Soviet republics.

Given these realities, Palestinians face two options. The first amounts to submission, and implies an acceptance of the Zionist narrative, the system of control and its far-reaching consequences for their marginalization and alienation from their history and culture. The second embodies a persistent effort to try, within these limitations, to influence their life. These alternatives have found their expression in the prevailing ideologies. Three ideologies describe the status of the Palestinians in Israel and their conditions.

The Zionist ideology.   Although its main interests are the promotion of Jewish migration to the country, the establishment of a modern Jewish state, the integration of the various ethnic groups into one nation, and so on, it justifies the development of the Zionist project, and portrays it not only as legitimate, but also as moral and progressive.

The ideology of modernization.   The second ideology is used by the regime in order to subdue the Palestinians intellectually and morally. It emphasizes the state's role in guiding the Palestinians from backwardness to modernity. Furthermore, it aims at increasing the admiration of Palestinians for the state and the Jewish majority, and at the same time, enhancing their feelings of inferiority regarding their Arab culture and Palestinian identity. These ideas have been vigorously promoted by the educational system and the media.

The ideology of resistance The frame of reference of this ideology is the historical experience of the Palestinian people, the shattering experience of the destruction of their society in the 1948 war, and the harsh reality of land expropriation, discrimination and marginalization which they have experienced under the Israeli regime. Unlike the first two ideologies, the ideology of resistance is promoted through informal education, proverbs, folk songs, and so on. Its main focus is the rejection of collaboration and co-optation, and the promotion of steadfastness. As reality unfolds on the ground it is grasped, understood and explained differently. Thus, the resistance takes place in both the realm of day-to-day life as well as in the domain of ideas. The struggle of Palestinians in Israel has evolved around various key issues, including land ownership and control, the demolition of houses, the right of the refugees living inside Israel to return to their localities, and so on.

To illustrate this understanding of the Palestinians' evolving reality, I will use the struggle over land as an example. Conflicts over land ownership and use date back to the beginning of Jewish immigration. Mandel,[65] who studied Jewish-Palestinian relations during their early period, reported on clashes that took place between settlers of the first colonies and adjacent Palestinian villages during the 1880s. During the British Mandate, the struggle over the land was one major issue of conflict between Jews and Palestinians. After the establishment of Israel, the state took over the lands of the refugees and the property of the Muslim endowments (*Waqf*), in addition to about 70 per cent of the lands owned by Palestinian citizens. The struggle of Palestinians throughout this period to prevent Zionist takeover of the land created a tradition of resistance. One famous proverb reflecting that is '*Al-Arad Mithl Al-Ard*' – land is as significant as honor. Those who lose their land cannot be regarded as honorable men. Therefore, the vast majority of Palestinians whose lands were confiscated, refused to accept the compensations that the state offered. This is not because the amount of the compensations were far below market prices, but because they considered the act of expropriation itself unjust and immoral. By their refusal they indicated that the state can take their land by force, but it will never gain the moral legitimacy of ownership. Palestinians who acted as middlemen and bought lands for Zionist organizations were the most despised in their communities. They were labeled '*Smaserah*', a description of greedy individuals who are ready to defile their honor for the sake of money. This attachment to the land was behind the first massive protest on 30 March 1976 – known as Land Day – which led to violent clashes with the security forces, and resulted in the death of six Palestinians and the injury of many more. Since then this occasion has become a day of national remembrance.

This ideology of resistance gains its vitality by its continual reproduction at the local level; it composes part of the everyday life of ordinary women and men. In each neighborhood, village and city, people define and relate to each other on the basis of categories derived from the culture of resistance. Thus, this ideology has become the main component in the construction of local, as well as national historiography.

Various scholars criticized such ideologies of resistance,[66] arguing that they promote passivity and legitimize the reconciling of subordinate groups with their harsh realities. This criticism seems to be valid only for situations where direct action that could bring about a change for the better, is possible. Given the structural constraints under which the Palestinians live and act, I think that the ideology of resistance was essential for the development of Palestinian national identity, communal solidarity, and the promotion of collective goals.

Conclusion

In this chapter an attempt has been made to analyse both the conditions of the Palestinian minority in Israel, and their conceptualization in the main perspectives in social science. Looking at this interplay between reality and the way it was conceived and theorized, a main conclusion emerges: there has been a steady departure, during the last decade and a half, from a unitary conception towards a state of pluralism. The pluralism has been manifested in two ways: the viewpoint through which reality is viewed, and the theoretical models employed. As the discussion in the last two sections shows, there has been a growing tendency to view the conditions of the Palestinians in Israel not only through the vantage point of the state and the Jewish majority, but also through Palestinian perspectives.

This was accompanied by a diversity in the theoretical perspectives used. The modernization paradigm, with its Eurocentric assumptions, has been losing ground as an explanatory model for analysing 'ethnic relations in Israel', both for Jewish-Palestinian and for Ashkenazi-Oriental relations. The diversity of the models and perspectives used highlights the complexity of the political, socio-economic and legal conditions of the Palestinian minority. Some of the studies reviewed in the last section remind us of the importance of the efforts of human actors in influencing their fate. Regardless of the power of the modern state, minorities can influence their fate, and state power has its limits. I believe that this human endeavor should be the focus of the research on the Palestinian minority, as well as other subordinate groups, instead of the over-development of general formulas and abstract models.

Despite this significant change, the employment of the same standards for all is not accepted yet by many (Israeli) social scientists who study the Palestinian minority. For example, would those who endorse the use of religion as a basis for citizenship in Israel accept discrimination against Jews in other countries due to their religious affiliation? In 'establishment' social science, the use of double standards in the treatment of Jews and Palestinians is justified by 'the uniqueness of the Israeli case', security reasons, and so on. Every case has its peculiarities, but does this vindicate unequal treatment of different groups on the basis of socially constructed definitions? Relating to this point, although indirectly, is the use of cultural relativism as a justification for discrimination. Indeed, the principle of enabling minorities to keep their culture has paradoxically been championed by both outright racists and liberals. While for the first group cultural relativism means the segregation of ethnic/racial groups from the rest of society, for the second cultural differences imply a diversity in outlooks, visions, ways of life, and so on, that enriches social life. In many cases, concepts such as 'culture' and 'mentality' have been used to disadvantage the Palestinians, and to discriminate against them. This suggests that the question of genuine equality would be posed forcefully in the future. I think this will be an essential issue not only for Palestinians, but particularly for them.

Notes

1 S. Hadawi, *Bitter Harvest: Palestine Between 1914–1967* (New-York, New World Press, 1967), pp. 79–81.
2 J. Abu-Lughod, 'The Demographic Transformation of Palestine' in A. Abu-Lughod (ed.), *The Transformation of Palestine* (Evanston, Northwestern University Press, 1971), pp. 139–63.
3 B. Morris, *The Birth of the Palestinian Refugee Problem* (New York: Cambridge University Press, 1987).

4   T. Segev, *1949 – The First Israelis* (Jerusalem, Domino, 1984) (in Hebrew), p. 59. A broader outlook is found, among others, in Y. Melman and D. Raviv 'A Final Solution of the Palestinian Problem?', *Guardian Weekly*, 21 February 1988, also in I. Shahak, 'A History of the Concept of "Transfer" in Zionism', *Journal of Palestine Studies*, 18, (1983) pp. 22–37, and in N. Masalha, *Expulsion of the Palestinians: the Concept of Transfer in Zionist Political Thought, 1882–1948* (Washington DC, Institute for Palestine Studies, 1992).

5   U. Benziman and A. Mansour, *Subtenants: Israeli Arabs, Their Status and State Policy Toward Them* (Jerusalem, Keter, 1992), (in Hebrew) p. 59.

6   Quoted in I. Lustick, *Arabs in the Jewish State: Israel's Control of a National Minority* (Austin, University of Texas Press, 1980), pp. 37–8.

7   Ibid., Chapter 2.

8   Jiryis, *The Arabs in Israel* (New York, *Monthly Review*, 1976), D. Kretzmer, *The Legal Status of the Arabs in Israel* (Tel-Aviv, The International Center for Peace in the Middle-East, 1987), and I. Lustick, *Arabs in the Jewish State*.

9   T. Segev, *1940 – The First Israelis*, pp. 64–5.

10 Ibid., p. 70.

11 Z. Schiff, 'The Pros and Cons of the Military Government', *New Outlook*, 5 (1962). pp. 70–1; regarding the last point see A. Sa'di, 'Incorporation Without Integration: Palestinian Citizens in Israel's Labor Market, *Sociology*, 28 (1995), pp. 432–3.

12 R. Wiemer, 'Zionism and the Arabs after the Establishment of the State of Israel', in A. Sholch (ed.), *Palestinians Over the Green Line* (London, Ithaca Press, 1983), p. 37.

13 D. Kretzmer, *The Legal Status of the Arabs in Israel*; I. Lustick, *Arabs in the Jewish State*; S. Jiryis, *The Arabs in Israel*; Z. Schiff, 'The Pros and Cons of the Military Government'.

14 T. Segev, *1949 – The First Israelis*, p. 77.

15 U. Davis and W. Lehn, 'Land Ownership, Citizenship and Racial Policy in Israel' in T. Asad and R. Owen (eds), *Developing Societies, the Middle-East*, (London, Macmillan Press, 1983), pp. 145–6.

16 Quoted in N. Chomsky, *Peace in the Middle East*, (Glasgow, Collins, 1975), p. 111.

17 U. Davis and W. Lehn, 'Land Ownership, Citizenship and Racial Policy in Israel', pp. 156–7; D. Kretzmer, *The Legal Status of the Arabs in Israel*, pp. 74–6.

18 D. Kretzmer, *The Legal Status of the Arabs in Israel*, p. 41.

19 The State's Comptroller Office, the State of Israel, *Annual Report – 42* (Jerusalem, 1992).

20 M. Al-Haj and H. Rosenfeld, *Arab Local Government in Israel* (Tel-Aviv, the International Center for Peace in the Middle East, 1988), pp. 123–8.

21 A. Sa'di, 'Poverty Among Arab Children in Israel: a Question of Citizenship' in J. Gal (ed.), *Poor Children in Israel* (Hamo'azah Leshlom Hayeled, 1997) (in Hebrew), pp. 35–6.

22 R. Khalidi, *The Arab Economy in Israel* (London, Croom Helm,1988), Chapter 3.

23 B. Kimmerling, 'The Palestinians From Two Research Perspectives', in *State, Government and International Relations*, 16 (1980) (in Hebrew), p. 77. Zureik's book was published by Routledge and Kegan Paul in 1979.

24 I. Lustick, *Arabs in the Jewish State* (Austin: University of Texas, 1980) p. XI.

25 I. Lustick, 'To Build and to Be Built By: Israel and the Hidden Logic of the Iron Wall', *Israel Studies*, 1, (1996), pp. 196–7.

26 For such arguments see for example S.N. Eisenstadt, *Israeli Society* (London: Weidenfeld and Nicolson, 1968) A review of this literature is found in S. Smooha, *Israel: Pluralism and Conflict* (University of California Press, 1978), and a critical review was presented in U. Ram, *The Changing Agenda of Israeli Sociology* (New York, 1995).

27 See for example S. N. Eisenstadt, *Israeli Society*; O. Sttendel, *The Minorities in Israel: Trends in the Development of Arab and Druze Communities 1948–1973* (Jerusalem, the Israeli Economist, 1973); J. Landau, *The Arabs in Israel* (Oxford University Press, 1969), and his more recent book *The Arab Minority in Israel 1967–1991: Political Aspects* (Tel-Aviv, Am-Oved, 1992) (in Hebrew); R. Cohen, *Complexity of Loyalties: Society and Politics – The Arabs in Israel* (Tel-Aviv, Am-Oved, 1990) (in Hebrew). For a similar analysis but with a different vocabulary see E. Rekhess, *Israeli Arabs Since 1967: the Issue of Identity* (Tel-Aviv, University, 1976), and A. Soffer, 'Geographical Aspects of Change Within the Arab Communities in Northern Israel', *Middle-Eastern Studies*, 19 (1983), pp. 213–43. These are only representative works – a huge amount of literature is found on this issue; the bibliography that Landau (1992) supplies is useful.

28 I. Arnon & M. Raviv, *From Fellah to Farmer: a Study of Change in Arab Villages* (Rehovot: the Settlement Study Center, 1980), p. 9.

29 Ibid., p. 54.

30 Ibid., p. 222, italics added.

31 B. Abu-Kishk, 'Arab Land and Israeli Policy', *Journal of Palestine Studies*, 11 (1981), pp. 124–35.

32 R. Khalidi, *The Arab Economy in Israel* (London, Croom Helm, 1988), p. 76; A. Sa'di, *The Palestinians in Israel: a Study of a Subordinate National Minority* (University of Manchester, PhD thesis, 1992), pp. 195–201.

33 A. Sa'di, *The Palestinians in Israel* pp. 199–200.

34 I discuss this research in my article 'Between State Ideology and Minority National Identity: Palestinians in Israel and Israeli Social Science Research', *Review of Middle East Studies*, 5 (1992), pp. 110–30.

35 S. Smooha, 'Minority Status in an Ethnic Democracy: the Status of the Arabs in Israel', *Ethnic and Racial Studies*, 13 (1990), p. 391.

36 Ibid., p. 410.

37 S. Smooha, 'Ethnic Democracy as a Mode of Conflict Regulation in Deeply Divided Societies', a paper presented at the conference on 'The New Politics of Ethnicity', held in Morris E. Couriel Centre for International Studies, Tel-Aviv University, 1 June 1995; also S. Smooha, 'The Status of Minority in an Ethnic Democracy: The Arab Minority in Israel', *Readings in the Revival of Israel*, 6 (1996), and S. Smooha and T. Hanf, 'The Diverse Modes of Conflict Regulation in Deeply Divided Societies', *International Journal of Comparative Sociology*, 33 (1992), pp. 26–47.

38 For example, R. Lister, *The Exclusive Society* (London, CPAG, 1990); F. Twine, *Citizenship and Social Rights* (London, Sage, 1994).

39 See, for example, *Israel Studies* 1, 1&2 (1996).

40 He defines these components as follows:

'Segmentation' refers to the isolation of the Arab minority from the Jewish population and the Arab minority's internal fragmentation. 'Dependence' refers to the reliance of Arabs on the Jewish majority for important economic and political resources. 'Co-optation' refers to the use of side payments to Arab elites or potential elites for purposes of surveillance and resource extraction'. I. Lustick, *Arabs in the Jewish State*, p. 77.

41 I. Lustick, 'Creeping Bi-nationalism within the Green Line', *New Outlook* 31, 7 (1988), pp. 14–9; and 'The Changing Political Role of Israeli Arabs' in A. Arian and M. Shamir (eds), *The Elections in Israel – 1988* (Boulder, Westview, 1990).

42 In this chapter the English version is cited.

43 F. El-Asmar, *To Be an Arab in Israel*, (London, Frances Pinter, 1975).

44 E. Zureik, *The Palestinians in Israel: a Study in Internal Colonialism* (London: Routhledge & Kegan Paul, 1979).

45 G. Shafir, *Land, Labor, and the Origins of the Israeli-Palestinian Conflict* (Cambridge, 1989).

46 Ibid., p. 8.

47 G. Shafir, 'Israeli Society: a Counterview', *Israel Studies*, 1, 2 (1996), p. 193.

48 O. Yiftachel, 'The Internal Frontier: Territorial Control and Ethnic Relations in Israel', *Regional Studies*, vol. 30 No. 3 (1996), pp. 49–508.

49 Y. Peled and G. Shafir, 'The Roots of Peacemaking: the Dynamics of Citizenship in Israel, 1948–93', *International Journal of Middle East Studies*, 28 (1996), pp. 391–413.

50 C. Kamen, 'After the Catastrophe II: the Arabs in Israel, 1948–1951', *Middle Eastern Studies*, 24 (1988), p. 107.

51 J. Scott, *Weapons of the Weak: Everyday Forms of Peasant Resistance* (New-York, Yale University Press, 1985). Further elaboration of his main thesis is found in his book *Domination and the Art of Resistance: Hidden Transcripts* (New Haven, Yale University Press, 1990).

52 O. Yiftachel, 'Planning as Control: Policy and Resistance in a Deeply Divided Society', *Progress in Planning*, 44 (1995), pp. 119–84; O. Yiftachel and L. Yone, 'Regional Policy and Minority Attitudes in Israel', *Environment and Planning A*, 27 (1995), pp. 1281–301; O. Yiftachel 'The Internal Frontier: Territorial Control and Ethnic Relations in Israel', *Regional Studies*, 30,3 (1996), pp. 493–508, and see Chapter 8 in this volume.

53 O. Yiftachel, Chapter 8 of this volume pp. 171–2.

54 O. Yiftachel, 'Planning as Control'.

55 D. Rabinowitz, 'Common Memory of Loss: Political Mobilization among Palestinian Citizens of Israel', *Journal of Anthropological Research*, 50 (1994), pp. 27–8.

56 I. Lustick, *Arabs in the Jewish State*.

57 A. Mazawi, 'Patterns of Competition over School Management Positions and the Mediation of Social Inequalities: a Case Study of High Court of Justice Petitions against the Appointment of Principals in Public Arab Schools in Israel', *Israel Social Science Research*, 11, 1 (1996), pp. 87–114.

58 G. Doron, 'Two Civil Societies and One State: Jews and Arabs in the State of Israel', in A. Norton, (ed.), *Civil Society in the Middle-East* (New-York, E.J.Brill, 1994), Vol. 2, pp. 193–220.

59 For a discussion of these organizations see M. Al-Haj and H. Rosenfeld, *Arab Local Government in Israel* (Tel-Aviv: The International Center for Peace in the Middle-East, 1988); M. Al-Haj and H. Rosenfeld, 'The Emergence of an Indigenous Political Framework in Israel: the National Committee of Chairmen of Arab Local Authorities', *Asian and African Studies*, 23 (1989), pp. 205–44; A. Sa'di, *The Palestinians in Israel: a Study of a Subordinate National Minority*, (University of Manchester, PhD thesis, 1992), pp. 358–9.

60 Jaffa Research Center, *A Guide to Arab Community Associations and Institutions in Israel* (Nazareth, Jaffa Research Center, 1990) (Arabic).

61 E. Shils, 'The Virtue of Civil Society', *Government and Opposition*, 26, 2 (1991), pp. 3–20.

62 A. Sa'di, 'Minority Resistance to State Control: Towards a Re-analysis of Palestinian Political Activity in Israel', *Social Identities*, 2, (1996), pp. 395–412.

63 A. Gramsci, *Selections from the Prison Notebooks*, ed. Q. Hoare and G.H. Smith (London, Lawrence and Wishart, 1986), Chapter 2.

64 J. Scott, *Weapons of the Weak*, and *Domination and the Art of Resistance*.

65 N. Mandel, *The Arabs and Zionism Before World War I* (Berkeley: University of California Press, 1976).

66 G. Matthew, 'Rituals of Resistance: a Critique of the Theory of Everyday Forms of Resistance', *Latin American Perspectives*, 20 (1993), pp. 74–92; also C. White, 'Everyday Resistance, Socialist Revolution and Rural Development: the Vietnamese Case', *Journal of Peasant Studies*, 13, 2 (1986), pp. 49–63.

References

Abu-Kishk, Bakir, 'Arab Land and Israeli Policy', *Journal of Palestine Studies*, 11, 1981, pp. 124–35.

Abu-Lughod, Janet, 'The Demographic Transformation of Palestine', in Ibrahim Abu-Lughod (ed.), *The Transformation of Palestine* (Evanston: Northwestern University Press, 1971), pp. 139–63.

Al-Haj, Majid and Rosenfeld, Henry, *Arab Local Government in Israel* (Tel-Aviv: The International Center for Peace in the Middle East, 1988).

Al-Haj, Majid and Rosenfeld, Henry, 'The Emergence of an Indigenous Political Framework in Israel: the National Committee of Chairmen of Arab Local Authorities', *Asian and African Studies*, 23, 1989, pp. 205–44.

Arnon, Issac and Raviv, Michael, *From Fellah to Farmer: a Study of Change in Arab Villages* (Rehovot: Settlement Study Center, 1980).

Benziman, Uri and Mansour, Atallah, *Subtenants: Israeli Arabs, Their Status and State Policy Toward Them* (Jerusalem: Keter, 1992) (Hebrew).

Chomsky, Noam, *Peace in the Middle East* (Glasgow: Collins, 1975), p. 111.

Cohen, Ra'anan, *Complexity of Loyalties: Society and Politics – The Arabs in Israel* (Tel-Aviv: Am-Oved, 1990) (Hebrew).

Davis, Uri and Lehn, Walter, 'Landownership, Citizenship and Racial Policy in Israel', in Talal Asad and Roger Owen (eds) *Sociology of Developing Societies: The Middle East* (London: Macmillan Press, 1983), pp. 145–58.

Doron, Gideon, 'Two Civil Societies and One State: Jews and Arabs in the State of Israel' in Audusts Norton (ed.), *Civil Society in the Middle East* (New-York: E.J. Brill, Vol. 2, 1994), pp. 193–220.

Eisenstadt, S.N. *Israeli Society* (London: Weidenfeld and Nicolson, 1967).

El-Asmar, Fouzi, *To Be An Arab in Israel* (London: Frances Pinter, 1975).

Gramsci, Antonio, *Selections From Prison Notebooks* Q. Hoare and Geoffrey H. Smith (eds) (London: Lawrence & Wishart, 1986).

Gutmann, Matthew, 'Rituals of Resistance: a Critique of the Theory of Everyday Forms of Resistance', *Latin American Perspectives*, 20, 1993, 74–92.

Hadawi, Sami, *Bitter Harvest: Palestine Between 1914–1967* (New York: New World Press, 1967).

Jaffa Research Center, *A Guide to Arab Community Associations and Institutions in Israel* (Nazareth: Jaffa Research Center, 1990) (in Arabic).

Jiryis, Sabri, *The Arabs in Israel* (New-York and London: Monthly Review Press, 1976).

Kamen, Charles, 'After the Catastrophe II: the Arabs in Israel 1948–1951', *Middle Eastern Studies*, 24, 1988.

Khalidi, Raja, *The Arab Economy in Israel* (London: Croom Helm, 1988).

Kimmerling, Baruch, 'The Palestinians From Two Research Perspectives', *State, Government and International Relations*, 16, 1980, p. 77. (in Hebrew).

Kretzmer, David, *The Legal Status of the Arabs in Israel* (Tel-Aviv: The International Center for Peace in the Middle-East, 1987).

Landau, Jacob, *The Arabs in Israel* (Oxford: Oxford University Press, 1969).

Landau, Jacob, *The Arab Minority in Israel: Political Aspects* (Oxford: Clarendon Press, 1993).

Lister, Ruth, *The Exclusive Society* (London: CPAG, 1990).

Lustick, Ian, *Arabs in the Jewish State: Israel's Control of a National Minority* (Austin: Texas University Press, 1980).

Lustick, Ian, 'Creeping Bi-nationalism Within the Green Line', *New Outlook*, 31, 7, 1988.

Lustick, Ian, 'The Changing Political Role of Israeli Arabs' in Asher Arian and Michal Shamir (eds), *The Elections in Israel – 1988*; (Boulder: Westview, 1990), pp. 115–31.

Lustick, Ian, 'To Build and to Be Built By: Israel and Hidden Logic of the Iron Wall, *Israel Studies*, 1, 1996, pp. 196–223.

Mandel, Neville, *Arabs and Zionism Before World War I* (Berkeley: University of California Press, 1976).

Masalha, Nur, *Expulsion of the Palestinians: the Concept of Transfer in Zionist Political Thought, 1882–1948* (Washington, D.C: Institute for Palestine Studies, 1992).

Mazawi, Andre, 'Patterns of Competition over School Management Positions and the Mediation of Social Inequalities: a Case Study of High Court of Justice Petitions Against the Appointment of Principals in Public Arab Schools in Israel', *Israel Social Science Research*, 11, 1, 1996, pp. 87–114.

Melman, Yossi and Raviv, Daniel, 'A Final Solution of the Palestinian Problem', *Guardian Weekly*, 21 February, 1988.

Morris, Benny, *The Birth of the Palestinian Refugee Problem, 1947–1949* (Cambridge: Cambridge University Press, 1987).

Peled, Yoav, and Shafir, Gershon, 'The Roots of Peacemaking: the Dynamics of Citizenship in Israel', *International Journal of Middle East Studies*, 28, 1996, pp. 391–414.

Rabinowitz, Dan, 'Common Memory of Loss: Political Mobilization among Palestinian Citizens of Israel', *Journal of Anthropological Research*, 50, 1994, pp. 27–49.

Ram, Uri, *The Changing Agenda of Israeli Sociology: Theory, Ideology and Identity* (New York: New York University Press, 1995).

Rekhess, Elie, *Israeli Arabs Since 1967: the Issue of Identity* (Tel-Aviv: Tel-Aviv University, 1976) (Hebrew).

Sa'di, Ahmad, *The Palestinians in Israel: a Study of a Subordinate National Minority* (University of Manchester, unpublished PhD thesis, 1992).

Sa'di, Ahmad, 'Between State Ideology and Minority National Identity: Palestinians in Israel and Israeli Social Science Research', *Review of Middle East Studies*, 5, 1992, pp. 110–30.

Sa'di, Ahmad, 'Incorporation Without Integration: Palestinian Citizens in Israel's Labor Market', *Sociology*, 28, 1995.

Sa'di, Ahmad, 'Minority Resistance to State Control: Towards a Re-analysis of Palestinian Political Activity in Israel', *Social Identities*, 2, 1996, pp. 395–412.

Sa'di, Ahmad, 'Poverty Among Arab Children in Israel: a Question of Citizenship' in John Gal (ed.) *Poor Children in Israel* (Hamo'azah Leshlom Hayeled, 1997) (Hebrew).

Schiff, Zeev, 'The Prose and Cones of the Military Government', *New Outlook*, 5, 1962.

Scott, James, *Weapons of the Weak: Everyday Forms of Peasants' Resistance* (New-York: Yale University Press, 1985).

Scott, James, *Domination and the Art of Resistance: Hidden Transcripts* (New Haven: Yale University Press, 1990).

Segev, Tom, *1949–First Israelis* (Jerusalem: Domino, 1984) (in Hebrew).

Shafir, Gershon, *Land, Labor and the Origins of the Israeli Palestinian Conflict* (Cambridge: Cambridge University Press, 1989).

Shafir, Gershon, 'Israeli Society: a Counterview', *Israel Studies*, 1, 2, 1996, pp.189–213.

Shahak, Israel, 'A History of the Concept of "Transfer" in Zionism', *Journal of Palestine Studies*, 18, 1983, pp. 22–37.

Shils, Edward, 'The Virtue of Civil Society', *Government & Opposition*, 26, 2, 1991, pp. 3–20.

Smooha, Sammy, *Israel: Pluralism and Conflict* (Berkeley: University of California Press, 1978).

Smooha, Sammy, 'Minority Status in an Ethnic Democracy: the Status of the Arabs in Israel', *Ethnic and Racial Studies*, 13, 1990, pp. 389–413.

Smooha, Sammy, *Ethnic Democracy as a Mode of Conflict Regulation in Deeply Divided Societies*. A paper presented in the conference on 'The New Politics of Ethnicity, Self-Determination and the Crisis of Modernity', held in Morris E. Couriel Centre for International Studies, Tel-Aviv University, 30 May–1 June, 1995.

Smooha, Sammy, 'The Status of Minority in an Ethnic Democracy: the Arab Minority in Israel', *Reading in the Revival of Israel*, 6, 1996, pp. 277–311 (Hebrew).

Smooha, Sammy and Hanf, Theodor, 'The Diverse Modes of Conflict Regulation in Deeply Divided Societies', *International Journal of Comparative Sociology*, 33, 1992, pp. 26–47.

Soffer, Arnon, 'Geographical Aspects of Change Within the Arab Communities in Northern Israel', *Middle Eastern Studies*, 19, 1983, pp. 213–43.

Stendel, Ori, *The Minorities in Israel: Trends in the Development of Arab and Druze Communities 1948–1973* (Jerusalem: the Israel Economist, 1973).

The State's Comptroller Office, The State of Israel, *Annual Report*-42 (Jerusalem, 1992).

Twine, Fred, *Citizenship and Social Rights* (London: Sage, 1994).

White, Christine, 'Everyday Resistance, Socialist Revolution and Rural Development: the Vietnamese Case', *Journal of Peasant Studies*, 13, 2, 1986, pp. 49–63.

Wiemer, Reinhard, 'Zionism and the Arabs After the Establishment of the State of Israel', *Palestinians Over the Green Line*, Alexander Scholch (ed.) (London: Ithaca Press, 1983), pp. 26–63.

Yiftachel, Oren, *Planning as Control: Policy and Resistance in a Deeply Divided Society*, Progress in Planning, 1995.

Yiftachel, Oren, 'The Internal Frontier: Territorial Control and Ethnic Relations in Israel', *Regional Studies*, 30, 3, 1996, pp. 493–508.

Yiftachel, Oren, 'The Political Geography of Ethnic Protest: Nationalism, Deprivation and Regionalism Among Arabs in Israel', *Transaction*, 22, 1, 1997, pp. 91–110.

Yiftachel, Oren and Yone, Law, H, 'Regional Policy and Minority Attitudes in Israel', *Environment and Planning A*, 27, 1995, pp. 1281–1301.

Zureik, Elia, *The Palestinians in Israel: a Study in Internal Colonialism* (London: Routhledge & Kegan Paul, 1979).

PART FOUR

Ethnic Conflict in Post-colonial Societies

13
The Resurgence of 'EthnoHinduism' – a Theoretical Perspective

Ornit Shani

Introduction

The resurgence of communalism (Hindu-Muslim antagonism) in India since the 1980s presents a serious challenge to secular Indian democracy and to the stability of the subcontinent. The striking feature of this phenomenon is not only the prominence, growth and popularity of informal, militant, extremist Hindu organizations such as the Rashtriya Swayamsevak Sangh (RSS), the Vishwa Hindu Parishad (VHP) and the Bajrang Dal,[1] but also the rise to power of the Bharatiya Janata Party (BJP), the Hindu nationalist party, at the center of national politics.[2] In the main, it defines itself as in opposition to Islam and Muslims, attacks 'the government policy of appeasing the Muslim minority', and seeks to establish India as a primarily Hindu country. This rhetoric has also been associated with an increasing degree of violence. Throughout the 1980s and early 1990s, severe communal riots took place all over the country, in which at least 10 000 people lost their lives. This chapter attempts to set out an outline for an analysis that would trace the origins of the rise of Hindu nationalism in this period, in order to understand why it became so important, popular and persuasive, and, in particular, to find out why it developed when it did.

The key issue I examine in this chapter is the process by which a collective 'Hindu identity' was crystallized and large numbers of people mobilized in its name. The notion of a single uniform Hindu identity is, in fact, inherently implausible – as implausible as that of a singular Muslim identity. There are good reasons to question the coherence of the claim that Hinduism has ever offered a singular monolithic identity. Moreover, the idea that in India there are two homogenous communities of Hindus and Muslims is not borne out by historical evidence, least of all, perhaps, in the partition of India in 1947.[3] Commonly, the rise of Hindu militancy in the 1980s has been ascribed to an 'already existing' religious Hindu identity. The claim that the rise of Hindu nationalism can be explained in terms of the realization of a latent consciousness among Hindus, of a pre-existing 'Hindu identity', assumes that this identity is natural, 'given' and, therefore, compelling. However, this assumption is belied by the evidence that such a 'Hindu identity' often appears as contingent upon different social circumstances, at times playing a prominent role, or at others disappearing altogether.[4] Even recent ideologies and movements of 'ethnoHinduism' have proved to be mutable. The Ram Mandir question, for example, was not an equally important issue in all regions of India, and, since 1993, it has become less prominent. Moreover, if a Hindu identity is latent and natural, why was its appeal limited almost exclusively to upper castes and urban middle-class Hindus?

An alternative explanation, almost as widespread, sees the 'Hindu turn' in Indian politics as the effect of strategies adopted by politicians and political parties for their own particular purposes. But this argument, in terms of political manipulation, cannot satisfactorily explain why the masses do what their leaders tell them. Indeed, it is limited by its own mechanistic and instrumentalist logic, and usually reaches a point where it falls back upon cultural explanations: as, for instance, when writers who stress the effects of political maneuvers as a catalyst in the Hindu upsurge often point to the popular mood created by the telecasting of the Ramayana television series.

In a third, more recent approach, scholars have sought a 'golden mean', by combining both these lines of argument. They allow the assumption of a Hindu mentality to stand, but reject the notion that it is natural or given. Rather, they contend, it is produced, expressed, or accelerated by political or religious processes and discourses. The proposition that Hindu militancy can be explained (even partly) by the character of a collective Hindu consciousness and its psychological complexes (such as a sense of vulnerability) in response to other defined collectives, still assumes that such an 'organic' collective exists in the first place. However, it is scarcely credible to speak of a homogenous community psyche that is cut off from its sociogenesis, or to assume, rather than explain, the 'Freudian short cut' that some of these scholars take from the individual to the society. Moreover, although this approach gives due recognition to the 'material' aspects of the question, it takes the cultural traits of large social collectives for granted, and in this respect becomes indistinguishable from the culturalist argument. Consequently, the 'golden mean', no less than the dichotomous explanations, which emphasized either cultural or material factors, has a limited value in explaining the ascent of Hindu militancy, and appears inadequate for the theoretical and empirical understanding of ethnic (Hindu) identity formation.

In general theoretical terms, aside from theories that view national or ethnic identity as a genetic 'given',[5] these analyses are based on three underpinnings aiming to understand conflicts that involve questions of ethnic or national identity: essentialist approaches that view identity as prior to the conflict – as its essence – and approaches that ascribe the formation of national or ethnic identities to economic, social and political factors.[6] For the former, the reasons behind religious, ethnic or national conflicts are quite obvious, for they stem from the very reality of cultural difference. The chances of resolving such conflicts are very low; at best we can hope to mitigate them somewhat. For the latter, contextual approaches, collective identity is crystallized in the context of social, economic and political conflict and serves as an instrument of political mobilization within that conflict. According to this perception, changes in socio-economic structures and relations can increase the likelihood of ethnic and national conflicts either breaking out or being resolved. Finally, contemporary studies, which adopt the 'golden mean' approach, attempt to transcend the pitfalls of the dichotomous explanations. These studies deny religious passion as a 'given' or natural attribute, on the one hand, and reject it as a mechanism by which elites hide the 'real' material clashes in society on the other. In order to explain the rise of ethnic nationalism, they 'locate' an 'ethnic identity' facing an external ('threatening') Other, through which ethnic identity is in turn more clearly defined.[7]

My aim in this chapter is not to present a complete solution to the limitations of the existing theoretical approaches, but to move beyond these approaches. Taking my point of departure from the contextual approach, I propose to examine other significant social processes, which coincided in time with the rise of Hindu nationalism, and see if they can bring more light to the understanding of this phenomenon. I propose to examine, primarily, the growth of caste conflicts, and the social and political mobilization of lower castes that coincided with the startling rise in support for Hindu militancy in India in the 1980s. It is important that these two processes took place together, particularly because they appeared to represent contradictory trends. Militant Hinduism assumes the principle of a 'unitary' Hindu identity as the 'anchor' of society, while caste conflicts demonstrate deep divisions in Hindu society. In fact, they are usually perceived as a barrier to further growth of Hindu militancy.[8] I argue that the two phenomena, which seem contradictory, manifest, in different ways, the same conflict and social struggle.

Since the growth in caste and communal conflicts occurred coincidentally, it would seem important to investigate the dynamic processes by which caste conflicts, which are exclusive to Hindu society and revolve usually around policies for the benefit of backward Hindus, translated into a controversy between Hindus and Muslims. I propose to investigate how far antagonism between Hindus and Muslims might be, in fact, an expression of deep divisions and conflicts among Hindus themselves. I intend to pursue the hypothesis that the Hindu-Muslim conflict, in its post-independence phase, derives some of its venom from conflicts between Hindus, in which the threat which Hindu militants claim is posed by 'external' others – the Muslims – is actually the peril of violating the Hindu 'sacred' order from within.

Central to the rhetoric of Hindutva is the notion of the appeasement of Muslims by the state. This rhetoric has appealed especially to upper-caste and urban middle-class Hindus, anxious about compensatory policies for the lower and backward castes. These groups have found new opportunities for social mobility over the past two or three decades, but have often felt that they did not benefit from them sufficiently, while at the same time other people of lesser status were able to exploit them equally or even more fully. They found the cause of their own limited mobility in the favors which government policies appeared to bestow on minorities, for instance, through the reservation of college and university places and government jobs. Muslims were lumped together with these minorities, even though religion was excluded as a category qualifying a candidate for positive discrimination.

For this reason, it would seem important to focus on societal changes within Hindu society, and therefore to examine the interaction between caste, class and Hindu identity, that is at the core of this conflict. This might reveal the origins, or clarify our understanding, of the rise of Hindu nationalism. As an initial guideline I propose to examine the conflict itself, at least in its present form, in the framework of the 'cultural' division of labor that exists in the Indian labor market.[9]

The resurgence of Hindu nationalism

The latest, and, thus far, most extreme manifestation of Hindu militancy was the destruction of the Babri Masjid mosque in the northern city of Ayodhya, an event that plunged India into the worst outbreak of communal violence since the partition of the subcontinent in 1947. This outburst was followed by communal riots across the country, in December 1992 and January 1993. The sixteenth-century Muslim mosque, built by the first Mughal, Babur, on the ruins of a Hindu Ram temple, was destroyed by members of the two extremist nationalist Hindu organizations – the militant Hindu paramilitary organization, Rashtriya Swayamsevak Sangh (RSS), and the World Hindu Council, Vishwa Hindu Parishad (VHP). Both are connected to the right-wing Hindu nationalist party, Bharatiya Janata – Party of the Indian People (BJP).[10]

Claiming to bring back their god-king Lord Ram to his birthplace, and wanting to put the foundations for a Ram temple, tens of thousands of activist Hindus assembled around the mosque on 6 December 1992. They subdued the line of policemen who tried to hold them back, and shattered the mosque using axes, hammers and their bare hands. Turmoil spread across the country, as a result of which 3000 people or more died – a majority of whom were Muslims – and thousands more were wounded. The government proclaimed the disputed place a closed area and promised to build both a mosque and a Hindu temple there.[11]

Although the issue of the Ram Mandir (temple) itself lost its force after 1993 as the axis around which Hindutva propagators rallied, the destruction of the Babri Masjid at Ayodhya is a watershed in the reality (and study) of communalism. As the apex of a violent decade, the Ayodhya riots brought into India's national agenda the debate over secular statehood and the future of the state. Hindu extremists demanded an end to Indian secularism and recognition of India as a Hindu state. The outrageous events severely damaged the authority of the Indian state and raised doubts about the democratic secular nature of the Indian polity.[12]

As a matter of fact, such doubts can be dated back to 1989. The results of elections since 1989 indicate that Hindutva – the combination of a monolithic Hindu identity and an anti-minority stance – has become a significant force in Indian politics. The BJP represents this growing force and the new perception of 'Hindu Rashtra', a Hindu nation based on Hindu ethos, values and religion. The performance of the BJP in the Lok Sabha elections shows a phenomenal growth: in 1984 the party won two seats (7.4 per cent of the vote); in 1989 it won 86 seats (11.5 per cent); and in 1991 it won 119 seats (19.9 per cent). In 1996 the party won 160 seats; including its allies, it formed a block of

194 seats, only 72 seats short of a clear majority in parliament; and it actually formed a government for two weeks.[13] A similar pattern of growth is evident in state elections. In Gujarat, for example, the BJP legislators in the state assembly increased from 11 in 1985 to 67 (about one third) in 1990. In 1989, the BJP won 30.4 per cent of the votes in Gujarat constituencies for the Lok Sabha; by 1990, it won 51.4 per cent of the votes in this state assembly elections. Similarly, in February 1997, an alliance of the Akali-Dal and the BJP won 93 seats out of a total of 117 seats in the Punjab legislative assembly. Finally, in the 1998 Lok Sabha election, the BJP emerged as the largest party, winning 177 seats (25 per cent of the votes) (250 seats with its allies).

Militant Hinduism seeks to capture the ethos of Hindu religion and culture and demands that 'Hinduism become the anchor of Indian inheritance and civilization'.[14] It stirs the winds of historical resentment against the Islamic rulers, especially, the Mughals, who governed the subcontinent from the thirteenth to the eighteenth century. Moreover, Hindu activists fight what they see as the government policy of appeasing the Muslims.[15] Since the mid-1980s, the BJP has begun to present new kinds of '*satyagrahas*'[16] for the mobilization of the masses, and invoked religious symbols through forms such as *Yatras*, to create the sentiment of an Hindu identity. On the face of it, the rise of Hindu nationalism seems to be a religious movement, the outcome of 'religious' politics, or a combination of both. Yet, the question is whether we should understand it as a process of 'religious nationalism', or see it as a move in a new set of negotiations for political, social and economic power and status in Hindu society.

Theoretical considerations

It has already been suggested that the explanations for the rise of Hindu nationalism since the 1980s have either stressed its primordial roots and cultural identity, adopted a more instrumentalist approach, or tried to reconcile both these approaches in search of a 'golden mean'. This last set of arguments tries to elucidate the role of religious and cultural symbols in the construction of a Hindu identity by emphasizing the significance of an external Other, or more precisely, a 'threatening Other'.

For the culturalists, communalism is observed 'as a religious phenomenon, [which] in all its manifestations derives strength from irrational forces of religious identity, which are magnified in India through individuals' traditional awareness of themselves as members of the largest groups'.[17] In this view, militant Hinduism reflects what Geertz has called the 'tension between primordial sentiments and civil politics' which do not respect traditional codes and the power of the 'given,' rooted in the non-rational foundation of personality.[18] Some works within the culturalist position deny the relevance of secularism for India, and claim that the increase in communal violence is a result of the limits and foreignness of that (Western) notion for Indian society.[19] In their view, secularism has little to say about the substance of cultures which are of immense importance in that society, and therefore, cannot sufficiently guide moral or political action. Conversely, they aspire to a society which expresses 'a "modern" national culture that is nevertheless not Western'.[20] Some scholars suggest that 'the traditional ways of life have, over the centuries, developed internal principles of tolerance ... [which] must have a play in contemporary politics'.[21] In this perspective, religious neutrality and policies derived from it seem irrelevant to Indian politics, precisely because they ignore religion, whose authentic tradition is believed to lead naturally towards benign tolerance. In this emphasis on an authentic indigenous tradition and its natural religious tolerance, these arguments legitimize, sometimes unintentionally, the 'politics of religious identity' and consequently play into the hands of Hindutva forces.

The proponents of Hindutva have not been slow to derive arguments from similar 'culturalist' positions. They look back, for instance, to the 'real' traditions of a Hindu Golden Age, which declined under Muslim rule and which they seek to revive. Similarly, they assert the persistence of historical disputes dating back to the period of the 'tyrant' Mughal Aurangzeb, who began the 'tradition' of destroying Hindu temples in the seventeenth century. They have also stressed the historical friction between the two communities by presenting cases of Hindu conversion to Islam as a large-scale phenomenon threatening Hinduism.[22] In the 'culturalist' analysis, the communal conflict will continue to beset India, since the state underestimates the strength of these almost 'immanent' religious and cultural identities.

Among 'materialist' explanations, many writers give primacy to the political process as a factor in the formation of communal identities and focus on the Hindu turn of the Congress party, from which the BJP profited.[23] They view the rise of Hindu militancy as a result of the transformation of secular politics in India by a process of communal polarization. They emphasize the effects of the tactics of Indira Gandhi and her followers and rivals in the 1980s, to play the communal card in order to create 'vote banks'.[24] However, this view is limited by its concentration on high-level politics and its neglect of the wider social meaning and implications of political processes.

Other scholars look at the socio-economic aspects of communalism. To some extent, this view coincides with explanations which rely upon political and elite manipulation. Generally, this perspective suggests that Hindutva's social backbone is the urban, educated middle-class, or the upper-caste component of the urban petty bourgeoisie. Both groups feel threatened by political and economic mobilization of the lower castes and by policies of positive discrimination.[25] Amiya Bagchi, examining the situation of the poor, suggests, by contrast, to look at the predatory commercialization and capitalism that have developed in India, and their effects upon the impoverished Muslims and Hindus, in order to understand their 'proneness' to communal violence.[26] He contends that the insecurity of the poor (as a result of unemployment, disease, and so on), the overcrowded conditions of most cities, and the competition for valuable urban space, which can be divided and re-divided for profit, create a fertile ground for 'major communal conflagration'.[27]

One more line of demarcation within the 'materialist' framework of analysis is represented by scholars like Sheldon Pollock who show how Hindu nationalists invoked a specific set of religious symbols for the purpose of political mobilization, in contrast to 'communalist arguments' which identify the symbols they use with what they claim is a 'true history' – notably about the warrior-god Rama and his birthplace temple in Ayodhya.[28]

More recent studies, adopt a 'golden mean' approach as an attempt to negotiate the shortcomings of these explanations. They reject the notion that Hindu identity is natural, and give due recognition to the political or religious processes that produce it. They place emphasis on the emergence of a 'Hindu identity' facing an external ('threatening') Other, through which it is defined.

Peter van der Veer's basic assumption is that religious identities form the premise of politics in South Asia, yet 'their naturalness is produced by a political process'.[29] Religious identity, he argues, is constructed in ritual discourse and practice, and is a specific product of changing forms of religious organization and communication. Hindu and Muslim nationalisms need one another to draw symbolic boundaries between them. Since the coherence of the (religious) 'nation is never entirely secure, it is always threatened by forces from the outside'.[30]

From a different viewpoint, Christophe Jaffrelot suggests a 'hybrid' combination of instrumental and idealistic-psychological approaches. Jaffrelot analyses the formation of a Hindu identity through a combination of three 'strategies': The first is a process of stigmatization and emulation based on the 'threatening Other', and on stereotypes of Muslims and Hindu feelings of inferiority and vulnerability.[31] In this part of the argument, Hindus imitated and assimilated those cultural traits from which the Other, the Muslims, were believed to have gained their strength (the task, for instance, to build immense temples that would function as common meeting places like the mosques), in order to resist the Other, to re-discover those traits in their own culture, and to regain the self-esteem they had lost with the passing of the Golden Age.[32] In addition, Hindu nationalism is also, in his view, an instrument in the hands of elites who manipulate Hindu symbols, and its growth is also the result of party-building and organization of the Hindu forces. According to this theory, these three interactive strategies found the right conditions to prosper in the 1980s.[33]

Neither the culturalist nor the materialist explanations are satisfactory in themselves for a theoretical and empirical understanding of ethnic (Hindu) identity formation. For 'culturalists', it is hard to explain why identity is almost never mobilized contrary to lines of material stratification in society; for 'materialists', it is difficult to explain the role religion does play in these processes, especially when there is some gap between the economic and political 'causes', and the final results.

Contemporary attempts to find the theoretical 'golden mean' are problematic too. Either they try to indicate mechanisms by which the 'naturalness' of religion is produced by political processes,[34] or they claim that religion plays a role in the formation of nationalist identities 'only after passing through a process of reinterpretation'.[35]

1   These analyses have not, in fact, transcended the boundaries of 'culturalist' and 'materialist' discussions, and most of them are tied at their center to cultural arguments, as they assume the prior existence of a Hindu religious identity, or a specific Hindu mentality. Consequently, these explanations, despite their claim to the contrary, remain ahistorical.[36]

2   It is not clear why and how Muslims came to be seen as the 'Threatening Other', when, in reality, they constitute a generally impoverished community, that poses little threat to the 'majority'.

3   Some of these analyses disclose the Achilles' heel of instrumental material approaches, for they overlook the part played by the

masses and almost exclusively stress the role of political and intellectual elites.

4   Finally, the attempt to synthesize the cultural and material explanations sometimes brings together contradictory assumptions.

An alternative point of departure

As I have already mentioned, the rise of Hindu nationalism in the 1980s coincided with the growth of caste conflicts, and although these two social processes appear to represent conflicting trends, and delineate incompatible political agendas, I propose that the seeming 'contradiction' between these processes reveals at their core the overlapping concerns shared by both Hindu nationalism and caste conflicts. Therefore, by investigating the relations and interactions between the two, or by combining them in the analysis, emphasizing the interdependence of political rivalries and economic pressures, on the one hand, and social context and identities on the other, I seek to obtain a better understanding of the nature of communalism in India in the last two decades. I wish to argue that what appears to be a religious conflict between Hindus and Muslims is, in fact, an expression of *ethnic* conflicts within Hindu society and is generated mainly by Hindus' recent experience of caste and its changing character. This position rejects the idea of an enduring Hindu culture, and, although it emphasizes the importance of an 'Other', it claims that the *significant other* is another among us: not an outsider to Hindu society, but an insider. As a preliminary guideline for trying to examine the intricate links between caste, class and Hindutva, I would like to work through Michael Hechter's theory of internal colonialism.[37]

The key concept of Hechter's theory is the 'cultural division of labor', that is a stratification system which 'assigns individuals to specific roles in the social structure on the basis of [perceived] objective cultural distinctions' such that those roles commonly defined as having high status are generally reserved for ... members of the 'core' group, while members of 'peripheral' or backward groups are at the bottom of the socio-economic ladder. The central argument of this model, focusing on political conflicts between core and peripheral groups, is that the 'cultural division of labor between core and periphery contributes to the development of ethnic identification'.[38]

A stratification system based on a cultural division of labor has two defining characteristics: 'segmentation' and 'hierarchy'. Segmentation is a vertical distinction, categorizing groups by occupational status, while hierarchy refers to a horizontal or class distinction between the different groups. 'The more hierarchical and segmental the cultural division of labor, the more likely are the groups comprising it to display ethnic rather than class consciousness.' Since, in such a system, 'objective' cultural distinctions are superimposed upon social roles, they become increasingly important as a basis, and are even regarded as a weapon, for social solidarity and political mobilization.[39] In that context, as Hechter points out, 'the (very) slowness of actual economic integration, in the face of larger expectations, will most likely insure that more militant groups will rise'.[40]

The cultural division of labor in India is segmental and hierarchical, as is commonly inferred from the structure of the 'caste system', usually considered to be the pillar of India's social structure. Although the occupational norms attributed by the caste order have weakened during the last few decades, the division of labor tied to hierarchy and separation has not disappeared and is still central to social existence in India. This structure has endured, to some extent, because labor is frequently recruited through caste connections, and because the division of labor has proceeded to spheres of life beyond the work place. Castes that shared the same occupation, mainly in factories and industry, shared also, in many cases, the same neighborhoods, social life and life style.[41] Moreover, to the extent that caste as *Jati*[42] has coincided with occupational clusters and broadly with a pattern of class differentiation, then under certain circumstances, often in towns, class differences have overlaid sub-caste distinctions.

Although, traditionally, there is a four-caste hierarchy in Hinduism (the *Varna* order),[43] this is only a symbolic simplification of a much more complex reality. The perception of caste as an unchanging rigid system of hierarchies, predominantly established by religious and cultural principles of purity and pollution, that left no room for social mobility has been challenged. Recent studies illustrate how Indian society and the caste system itself have been shaped by political processes and struggles.[44]

Caste identities and conflicts are an important influence on the perception and politics of communalism. I propose to avoid an understanding of caste as a purely cultural-religious order, which encompasses the idea of purity and pollution of the *Varna* theory. Conversely, we should also not look at caste as a purely economic mechanism. Caste is crucial to social existence in India, and serves to reinforce social practice and social position. It is an ideological-wrapped and vigorous mechanism which serves to exchange structures of social power and to control and regulate labor, property and gender, and therefore constantly attains new meaning in changing circumstances. This fact helps to explain its resilience. However, its very flexibility means that it is subject to change and adaptation according to social and political circumstances. Although caste represents relations between dominant and subordinate, between those who have power and those who are powerless, it seems to me that caste makes incarnate a dialectical and reciprocal form of power, as power is not derived from caste alone. The changing relationships between dominant and subordinate castes has acted on the 'caste system' as a whole and helped to reproduce it. Its integrative operation produces a more complex pattern of caste and class relations within Indian society.

By focusing on the political and economic aspects of castes, and particularly on their demands for political recognition in the post-independence period and their location in the labor market, it is possible to think about castes as ethnic groups. This is because caste can be given an ethnic character in politics and thus work through the prism of ethnicity. And precisely because castes are politically malleable, their interests as social groups were formed and reformed within changing historical states of affairs. Moreover, castes can be referred to as ethnic groups because of the socio-cultural practices which differentiate them: endogamy, language, dialect, occupation, life style, region and other aspects.[45] In some situations, one may even notice a sense of caste 'patriotism'.

Observers of Indian society claim that, since independence, as they expected, castes have been weakened through the course of modernization and industrialization, or split into opposing classes through the process of class differentiation. However, class fissures take place within castes themselves, and, consequently, reproduce 'caste' mechanisms again and again. Paradoxically, the path of various caste groups towards 'modernization' and social mobility was overlaid upon their caste status, which consequently, in most cases, remained as their barrier to social acceptance within the social hierarchy. Thus, caste and class categories are not simply interchangeable, but bound to each other, not least as long as the state and the whole political structure (going back to its colonial roots) exist on the presupposition of these distinctions.

After independence, the Indian constitution accorded specific recognition to both the scheduled castes (former untouchables) and the scheduled tribes. These groups were granted reservation rights of 14 per cent and 7 per cent, respectively, in educational institutions and governmental posts. Additionally, a Backward Classes Commission was nominated in 1953 to define and identify Other Backward Castes, or Socially and Educationally Backward Castes/Classes. However, in the absence of acceptable criteria for defining backwardness at the national level, it was open to different state governments to initiate their own policies (subject to some Supreme Court decisions). These policies of positive discrimination led to political, educational and economic mobilization of sections of these groups, who used reservations to obtain positions in social domains which were formerly the exclusive territory of upper castes. Moreover, the introduction of universal suffrage created new opportunities for the backward castes to assert mobility. Correspondingly, in an era of growing electoral politics, the large backward castes provided fertile ground for vote gathering. Thus, as they became more politically conscious and more politically important, some castes obtained a new lease of life.

The opportunities for mobilization were enhanced by modernization processes – the green revolution in agriculture, industrialization and rapid urbanization, and the land reforms, which, where conscientiously implemented, advantaged certain low-caste groups that had previously been tenants. Concurrently, modern technology diminished geographical distances, broadened communications, and in so doing raised further the consciousness and expectations of the distinctive groups. In the wake of these processes, backward and lower castes began to demand recognition and rights, and new socio-economic layers were formed. Some groups achieved greater prosperity, became more politically active, while remaining lower caste by status. Pressed between the middle and lower castes, upwardly mobile castes are a potential source for political recruitment. Other groups were also able to achieve a higher caste status as well.[46] Yet, socio-economic developments in India tended to be the purview of certain castes, sub-castes and regions, consequently creating social tensions – groups that stayed behind failed and felt ostracized.

The assertiveness of the backward class became more prevalent towards the beginning of the 1980s, when growing numbers among them were graduating universities, entering governmental posts and beginning to play an important role in politics. In Gujarat state, for example, in the 1980 elections, a Congress KHAM[47] (caste) coalition – an alliance of backward Hindus and Muslims – came to power, 'pushing out' the upper castes, mainly Patels, from the political center. In other states too, backward castes emerged, or began to establish a political presence through newly formed regional parties.[48] The upper castes, especially those belonging to the old middle class, became apprehensive of losing their dominance as a result of these developments. In some areas, such as Gujurat, Brahmins, the highest in the caste hierarchy but not well-established economically, became concerned about lower castes' mobility in education, as it is the Brahmins' main source of livelihood. In addition, they became fearful that the government would go too far in accommodating the backward castes and that these rising social forces would see in them, justifiably, the source of the gigantic economic gaps between the different groups in Indian society, and of governmental indifference to this reality.[49]

In response to these developments, the upper castes/classes adopted a strategy of erecting a monolithic, uniform Hinduism, glossing over the internal ethnic and cultural divisions within the Hindu community. They sought to consolidate common Hindu grievances by pointing to external 'Others' – the Muslims – as the source of economic difficulties and poverty. Thus they sought to divert attention from a conflict internal to the Hindu community. The rhetorical claim that the 'state' tended to appease minorities has been utilized for that purpose. This call enchanted some lower-caste Hindus, since the sense of Hindu unity gives them the illusion of an equal stand within the society; the possibility of overcoming their (status) barrier to social acceptance. The new multi-layered medium for the creation of a Hindu sentiment was the rhetoric of Hindutva, which has offered a convenient dialogue between the individual, his affinity to the wider community of Hindus, 'Hindu culture,' and his difference from the 'Others'. Hindutva is offering a new kind of patronage within Hindu social hierarchy, but precludes any changes in its structure. In fact, some of its propagators have launched a 'holy' war for a 'sacred' social order.

Conflicts between forward and backward castes over policies of positive discrimination have often been inextricably linked to communal tension between Hindus and Muslims. In 1985, anti-reservation riots in Ahmedabad transmogrified into communal ones. In this case the riots that erupted were not an immediate response to significant religious issues, but rather a reaction to the government announcement that it would raise the reserved quotas in educational and governmental institutions for the Socially and Educationally Backward Classes to 28 per cent. By the end of the decade, communal riots erupted all over the subcontinent, following the decision of V.P. Singh's government to implement, at the national level, the recommendation of the Mandal Commission to increase reservations for the (Hindu) Other Backward Castes. In these cases, a struggle by upper-caste Hindus against reservations for backward-caste Hindus turned into conflicts between Hindus and Muslims. During the early and mid-1980s, Hindu militancy and communal riots were devoid of the image of a mass movement in search of Hindu identity, and were quite distinct from religion.[50] 'Communal' conflicts were born out of caste conflicts rather than religious ones. In 1981, over the issue of reservation, severe clashes between high-caste Hindus and Dalits erupted in Ahmedabad and spread all over the state of Gujarat. By 1985, anti-reservation agitation in the city had transformed into communal riots. The Muslims became the target, while significant numbers of the Dalits joined the Sangh Parivar fold. Referring to the 1990 riots, Peter van der Veer commented, 'since the agitation around the reservation issue imperiled the Hindu agenda of the VHP/BJP/RSS, Lal Krishna Advani, the leader of the BJP, decided to start a ritual procession ...'[51] This kind explanation of the critical turning point in the dynamics of 'communal' riots is common. Yet it only serves to obscure our ignorance of the real reasons behind communal hatred and violence.

Conclusion

Hindu sentiments are constructed and fostered within political processes and discourse, but these processes are set in socio-economic circumstances, which are crucial for the political processes to occur in the first place. As I have tried to delineate, ethnoHinduism is 'located' between caste and class: it involves bringing together into tension the courses through which different groups and social categories were formed and reformed within historical experience and power struggles, in a rapidly changing landscape.

If, as claimed by the theory of the cultural division of labor, ethnic conflicts are indeed created in the context of labor market relations, then if relations in the labor market were to change, or if groups in the labor market were to form class solidarity, distinctions between groups with similar occupations would become politically irrelevant, and it might become possible to mitigate communal hostility. This point can be illustrated by recent developments in Uttar Pradesh (UP). After the demolition of the mosque in Ayodhya, the central government dismissed the four elected state governments held by the BJP and replaced them with administrations run directly from New Delhi. One of these states was UP – the most populated state in India, with a very large Muslim population, where Ayodhya, the disputed city, is located.

Historically, UP has been the arena for severe communal clashes. However, in November 1993, a year after the events in Ayodhya, new elections were held in which groups of backward Hindus and lower-class Muslims formed the SP-BSP coalition (Samajwadi Party; Bahujan Samaj Party). Competing with the BJP, they won the elections. The government they formed – a coalition of Hindus and Muslims – fell apart after a few months due to internal quarrels within the backward Hindu groups themselves. Thereafter, a minority government of the BSP (composed of Dalits and Muslims), headed by the first ever Dalit Chief Minister, Mayawati, continued to govern, backed from outside the government by the BJP. Mayawati promoted pro-Dalit policies, trying to impose their hegemony over the state. Consequently, the BJP (an upper caste-dominated party), withdrew its support from the government, and in October 1995 the assembly was dissolved and the state was placed under presidential rule. The results of the 1996 elections again brought about another coalition of the BSP and BJP, based on an agreement that the two parties would rotate the office of Chief Minister. The state still suffers from political instability, but there have not been any communal riots in UP since 1993.

In this case, then, social alliances were rapidly changing. This was manifested in the form of changing political blocs, but it is the reflection of inter-caste/class struggles (in UP, mainly between the backward Yadavs, Dalits and Upper castes). At first, class solidarity between economically backward Hindus and Muslims overpowered the 'cultural-religious' solidarity offered by the BJP. Subsequently, the ongoing political struggle has not been drawn along religious boundaries, but along class boundaries among the Hindus themselves. Therefore, it is clear that the foundation of Hindutva identities can be fluid, and it is too early to tell where the most important political fault lines will be drawn.

Thus, militant ethnic and nationalist movements may be counter-poised by the crystallization of class solidarity, or by efforts at redistributing economic goods, resources and well-being. In West Bengal, where despite the apparent existence of some hopeful conditions, such as the migration of Muslims from Bangladesh and a refugee memory, conducive to Hindu militancy, Hindu groups have not been able to gain power and popularity. In that state, many years of local communist party government by the CPI(M) succeeded in fostering land and economic reforms. Although land redistribution never reached its original objectives, the party was able to mobilize and bring about the inclusion of previously excluded groups by bypassing the bureaucracy, which was allied with the high-classes' establishment.[52] The CPI(M) put efforts into establishing and spreading democratic practices at local levels, and beyond narrow 'material' benefits, provided the lower classes with a sense of well-being. Social conflicts were contained thus impeding Hindutva's forces and rhetoric.

Acknowledgement

I am much indebted to Dr Rajnarayan Chandavarkar for many helpful discussions and comments on the issues raised in this paper. For their generous financial support I am grateful to the Wingate Scholarships. Finally, and especially, this paper would not have been written in the first place without the support and encouragement given to me by Dr Yoav Peled.

Notes

For full citations of the works mentioned, see references on page 289.

1 These organizations are known as the 'Sangh Parivar', or 'Sangh Family'. Together with the BJP (Bharatiya Janata Party), they form the foreground of the Hindu nationalist movement, propagating 'Hindutva' – the idea of a recognition of an all-Hindu identity.

2 Although communal questions were present in the background of Indian politics since (and before) the partition of the subcontinent into India and Pakistan, no Hindu political force gained substantial power or legitimacy during the first three decades after independence.

3 Romila Thapar has refuted the idea of a historically well-defined Hinduism and a singular and coherent Hindu community, which, she argues, is in part the creation of 'a modern search for an imagined Hindu identity'. It does not have as long an ancestry as is often presumed. Geography, caste and languages, she suggests, acted as a deterrent to the formation of a single Hindu community, while even the 'kaleidoscopic change in the constitution of religious sects precluded [its] emergence'. See Thapar, 'Imagined Religious Communities? Ancient History and the Modern Search for a Hindu Identity', in *Interpreting Early India*, pp. 60–88. Gyanendra Pandey has also questioned the category of 'Hindu' in modern times, see Pandey, 'Which of us are Hindus?'.

4 In the 1960s, for example, identities in the subcontinent were shaped around the divisive category of language and not along Hindu lines.

5 See van den Berghe, 'Race and Ethnicity: a Sociobiological Perspective'.

6 Approaches that view identity as prior to national or ethnic conflicts base their stance especially on Clifford Geertz. See Geertz, 'The Integrative Revolution: Primordial Sentiments and Civil Politics in the new States', in *The Interpretation of Culture*, pp. 255–310. The discussion in this paper (from a contextual point of view) is anchored in the reactive model of nationalism, see, Hechter, *Internal Colonialism* pp. 30–43; 1976: 214–24; 1978: 293–318.

7   The shift in the new writings can be attributed, at least partly, to the appearance of postcolonial discourse and the cultural turn in the study of Indian society (and ethnicity and nationalism in general). The theoretical framework on which these discussions are based deals with the processes of identity formation and definition through association with 'other', by identification with it, or a struggle in the way that it recognizes the self. To some extent, this discourse is a part, or continuation of, the realization of Foucault's perspicacious view of Western 'truth' as 'another rule of knowledge'. Edward Said's study of orientalism began the application of this view (see Said, *Orientalism* . Other works that form the intellectual base for these writings are: Bhabha, *The Location of Culture* and Young, *Colonial Desire*, pp. 1–28, 159–82 – both mainly add Freudian and Lacanian psychoanalytical applications (see also Slavoj Zizek, 'Eastern Europe's Republic of Gilead', in Chantal Mouffe (ed.), *Dimensions of Radical Democracy: Pluralism, Citizenship, Community* (Verso, London, 1993). For other discussions of identity see Taylor, *Multiculturalism and 'The Politics of Recognition'* (Princeton University Press, Princeton, New Jersey), pp. 25–73; Hall, 'Ethnicity Identity and Difference', and 'Who Needs identity?'.

8   See, for example, Kaviraj, 'Religion and Identity in India'.

9   This theory is anchored in the reactive model of nationalism. See Hechter, *Internal Colonialism:* pp. 22–43 esp. pp. 37–40; 'Group Formation and the Cultural Division of Labor'.

10 For additional information about the roots of the BJP and its connection with the RSS and the VHP see Graham, *Hindu Nationalism and Indian Politics*; Basu *et. al*, *Khaki Shorts Saffron Flags*; Anderson and Damle, *The Brotherhood of Saffron*; Frykenberg, 'Hindu Fundamentalism and the Structural Stability of India'; Yogendra K. Malik, and Dhirendra K. Vajpeyi, 'The Rise Of Hindu Militancy: India's Secular Democracy at Risk', *Asian Survey*, Vol. xxix, No. 3, 1989, pp. 311–4; Thakur, 'Ayodhya and the Politics of India's Secularism'.

11 Other sources for the events during the Ayodhya riots, see *India Today,* 31 January 1993; 15 February 1993; Newsweek, 21 December 1992. (I have also benefited from personal experience, since I was in India – in Uttar Pradesh – between December 1992 and February 1993).

12 These issues are represented clearly in Vanaik Achin, *The Furies of Indian Communalism* (Verso, London, 1997), pp. 3–24, 65–117.

13 Sources: *Data Hand Book On Lok Sabha Elections 1952–1990* (Sage Publications); *Election Commission of India statistical 1990 election; India Today*, 15 July 1991, pp. 40–8, and 31 May 1996.

14 That declaration was made by L.K. Advani, the leader of the BJP, in *India Today,* 31 March 1990: 27.

15 A major example of accusations about the government's policy of appeasing Muslims concerns the 'Shah-Bano case'. Mrs Shah-Bano, an elderly Muslim divorcee, applied to court for maintenance allowance, though according to the Muslim religion a woman is not allowed any compensation or maintenance when divorced. However, the Supreme Court decided that the provisions of the Indian penal code on maintenance take precedence over the *Sharia* and allowed her maintenance. The court maintained that 'traditional interpretation of the *Sharia* had become outdated and that

the court's judgment was closer to the original intent of the Koran'. However, Rajiv Gandhi's government yielded to the organized pressure mounted by the Muslim community and legislatively overturned the court's decision.

16 *Satyagraha*: truth-force; quest for truth.

17 Gold, 'Organized Hinduism', p. 582.

18 Geertz, *The Interpretation of Culture*, pp. 276–7. This view, in fact, reflects the colonial perception of communalism, see Pandey, *The Construction of Communalism*, pp. 2–3. However the idea of religious communities as the fundamental social units of the Indian milieu is also shared by Chandra, *Communalism in Modern India*; Dumont, *Homo Hierarchicus*, Appendix D, pp. 314–34, especially his definitions pp. 314–16. Both the colonial view and the set of positions posed by Gold and Chandra perceive communalism as a pathology which might be corrected by the 'enlightened' state, in contrast to, for example, Ashish Nandy, who observes communalism as a result of the homogenizing pressures of the modern state. See Nandy, 'The Politics of Secularism and the Recovery of Religious Tolerance'. Other works within the culturalist approach have discussed the meaning of Hindu heritage and the message it communicates in the great epic *Ramayana*. Stanley Wolpert, for example, draws an analogy between the demon-king Ravana, which the demi-god Lord Rama fights in the story of the Ramayana, and 'demons' like the mughal Babur, who is believed to be the destroyer of Ayodhya's Hindu temple (Wolpert, 'Resurgent Hindu Fundamentalism', pp. 10–11). He concludes that, 'far below the surface patina and gloss of the Nehru-Gandhi family and their friends, the ancient Epic heart of Bharat continued to beat and bubble its mantras on high, "*Ram-Ram, Hari! Om!*"' (Ibid.: 10–17). Moreover, books and articles that have been published lately by Indian presses attribute the rise of the BJP. and Hindu militancy to the telecasting of *the Ramayana* and *the Mahabharata* on national television. See 'Rajiv Gandhi and Rama's Kingdom' by Ved Mehta, in *India Today*, 30 November 1995. Within this framework, I would also include idealistic-psychological discussions as presented, for example, by Sudhir Kakar, who adapts a kind of Durkheimian perspective (very similar to Dumont's) by discussing the continuity of collective memory; however, he mainly focuses on the unconscious Hindu psyche. See Sudhir Kakar, 'Some unconscious Aspects of Ethnic Violence in India', in Das (ed.), *Mirrors of Violence*, pp. 135–45.

19 See Nandy, 'The Politics of Secularism'; Chatterjee, *The Nation and its Fragments*, and 'Secularism and Tolerance'; Madan, 'Whither Indian Secularism'.

20 Chatterjee, *The Nation and its Fragments*.

21 Works cited by Nandy, Chatterjee and Madan in note 19 above. These scholars are also labeled neo-Gandhians. Madan, for example observes that Nehru's perception of secularism, which dominated after independence, is alien to Indian society, as a rational and modern notion, derived from Western Enlightenment. See Madan, 'Whither Indian Secularism?' Also see Nandy, 'The Politics of Secularism'. For critiques of these positions see Vanaik, 'Reflections on Communalism', p. 56 and *The Furies of Indian Communalism*, pp. 130–62, 180–205; Ahmad, 'Fascism and National

Culture; and Mark Juergensmeyer, 'The Debate Over Hindu Nationalism, pp. 216–9.

22   This perspective is usually referred to as communal discourse, according to which, communalism has nothing to do with British colonialism. For discussions that review these lines of argument see, Amartya Sen, 'The Threats to Secular India'. This ideology, or version of Indian history, is dispensed through the RSS and the other members of the *Sangh Parivar* (family of Hindu organizations). See, for example, the discussion in Basu *et al.*, *Khaki Shorts and Saffron Flags*, Chapter 3.

23   Within this instrumentalist view, Paul Brass was among the first to suggest looking at the manipulations by elites within ethnic groups that 'select aspects of the group's culture … and use them as symbols to mobilize the group' for their own end' (Brass, 'Elite Groups', p. 41). More recently, he points to 'specific policies pursued by the central and state governments' as a cause for communal conflict (Brass, *The Politics of India* 147).

24   See Kothari, *Politics and the People*, Vol. II, pp. 440–79. Similarly, Atul Kohli suggests that 'communal conflicts are more profitably conceived of as the result of acquired cultural suspicions (which in turn are intensified by the political elite for their political goals)' – Kohli, *Democracy and Discontent* , p. 195. Other works that share this viewpoint claim that Indira Gandhi was the first leader to use this tactic when she had gathered around her Hindu clerics and 'sacred sadhus' during the campaign of the 1984 general elections. Thus, she became 'an orthodox Hindu' in her attempt to conquer the Hindu vote. See Frykenberg, 'Hindu Fundamentalism'.

25   Alvi, 'Politics of Ethinicity', pp. 232–4; Cayachandri, 'Predatory Commercialization and Communalism', p. 154; Lal, 'Shadows of the Swastika', p. 170.

26   Baghi, 'Hindu "Fundamentalism" Revisited', pp. 193–218.

27   Ibid., 210–11.

28   Pollock, 'Ramayana', p. 261–93. See also Lal, 'Hindu "Fundamentalism" Revisited', p. 169. Before I proceed to the 'golden mean' approach, it is worth mentioning that another leading viewpoint, which is not directly applied to the emergence of communalism since the 1980s, perceives the Indian communal conflict as the end product of the colonial era, and particularly as the outcome of the British policy of divide and rule. In these arguments, the colonial policies and their assumptions on the nature of the society in purely communal or religious terms, created, constructed and promoted an imperative of animosity between Hindus and Muslims. Gyanendra Pandey, for example, illustrates this dynamic by focusing on the British 'communal riot narrative' in nineteenth-century Banaras (Gyanendra Pandey, 'The Colonial Construction of "Communalism" in Das (ed.), *Mirrors of Violence*, pp. 94–132). For a discussion of the various ways in which communalism was promoted by the colonial government see, Aditya Mukherjee, 'Colonialism and Communalism', in Sarvepalli Gopal (ed.), *Anatomy of a Confrontation* (Zed Books, London, 1991), pp. 164–78. This kind of argument is sometimes entitled 'nationalist discourse' as opposed to the colonial view of communalism. For a broader discussion of the 'nationalist stance' see Pandey, 'The Construction of Communalism' 6–22; Partha Chatterjee, *Nationalist Thought and the Colonial World*, pp. 1–35. This

discussion of communalism and colonialism involves scholars like Chatterjee and Nandy, whom I have classified in the 'culturalist' category, since their analyses give primacy to an 'existing' Hindu culture and consciousness. However, contrary to the colonialist understanding, they perceive traditional identities as a factor for communal, harmonious relations. Additionally, some studies within the weave of discussions on communalism and colonialism try to understand the effects of the British rule on communalism, yet without denying agency to Indian society. Peter van der Veer, for example, asserts that the 'essentialization of difference between Hindus and Muslims is certainly not a colonial invention since it depends on the essentializing features of Hindu discourses about Muslim "others"' (Van der Veer, 'The Foreign Hand' 24). Although he acknowledges the colonial influence on the division between the two communities, and particularly emphasizes the effects of colonial discourses, which drew an image of a Hindu decline with the Muslim invasion of the subcontinent, he claims that nationalist politics are, to a significant degree, 'indigenous'. Other analyses suggest looking at the consequences of the processes produced by modernity (i.e. processes that were introduced to the societies of the subcontinent with colonialism) to the traditional, or pre-colonial societies. Sudipta Kaviraj, for instance, looks at the logic of modernity's reconstitution of identities in order to understand the relations between religion and political processes in India, through a form of historical sociology. In his view, 'modernity not only makes new identities possible, it does not leave older ones alone' (Kaviraj, 'Religion, Politics and Modernity' pp. 299–300).

29 Van der Veer, *Religious Nationalism*, p. 7.
30 Ibid., 193.
31 Jaffrelot, *The Hindu Nationalist Movement*, pp. 1–10, 17–75.
32 At the beginning of the century, this process transpired by India emulating certain aspects of Western society. In the 1980s, according to Jaffrelot, identity-building played upon the sense of Hindu vulnerability 'while stigmatizing their [Muslim] opponents and emulating those aspects of their beliefs and behavior which were believed to be a source of strength' (Jaffrelot, *The Hindu Nationalist Movement*, p. 410).
33 Ibid., pp 1–10, 193–221, 358.
34 Van der Veer, *Religious Nationalism*.
35 Jaffrelot, *The Hindu Nationalist Movement*.
36 There is a great deal of similarity, for example, between Jaffrelot's analysis of the process of stigmatization and emulation that is based on the 'threatening Other' and arguments presented by Ashish Nandy in his discussion on British colonialism. While telling the story of the meeting between East and West, or between modern and non-modern types of awareness, Nandy draws, in a psychoanalytic mode, the way colonialism produced the Oriental and the Occidental 'selves' through their existence as 'threatening external others' for each other. See Nandy, *The Intimate Enemy*. In his more recent work on the Ramjanmabhumi movement, he extends this line of analysis. See Nandy *et al.*, *Creating a Nationality*.
37 Hechter, *Internal Colonialism*, pp 22–43, 'Ethnicity and Industrialisation', and 'Group Formation'.

38   Hechter, *Internal Colonialism*, pp 39–40. See also the discussion by Yoav Peled on the theory of internal colonialism in Peled, *Class and Ethnicity in the Pale*, pp. 7–9.

39   Peled, *Class and Ethnicity in the Pale*, p. 8.

40   Hechter, *Internal Colonialism*, p. 41.

41   This situation prevailed mainly in the cities, in the developing industries. See, Rajnarayan Chandavarkar, 'Workers' Politics and the Mill Districts in Bombay between the Wars', *Modern Asian Studies*, 15, 3, 1981, pp. 603–47; and *The Origins of Industrial Capitalism in India. Business Strategies and the Working Classes in Bombay, 1900–1940* (Cambridge University Press, Cambridge, 1994).

42   *Jati*: an endogamous unit of caste; a sub-caste.

43   From the top downwards: the *Brahmins* – priests; *Kshatriyas* – warriors; *Vaishayas* – traders; *Shudras* – cultivators and laborers. Beyond the pale of this hierarchical caste system are the Scheduled Castes and Scheduled Tribes – the former Untouchables.

44   For the perception of a 'timeless caste system of unknowlegable past' see Dumont, *Homo Hierarchicus*. Studies which examine the political, economic and constructed aspects of caste: Nicholas B. Dirks, *The Hollow Crown* (Cambridge University Press, Cambridge, 1987); 'The Invention of Caste: Civil Society in Colonial India', *Social Analysis*, No. 25, pp. 42–52; Bernard S. Cohn, *Anthropologist Among the Historians and Other Essays* Washbrook, 'The Development of Caste Organisation', pp. 150–203; Frankel and Rao, *Dominance and State Power*, Vol. I, pp 204–64; Carroll, 'Colonial Perceptions'.

45   This point of departure for analysis would 'release' Indian society and its 'caste system' from the 'unique' position it has obtained in academic studies. I would also like to mention at this point, that the term 'communalism' is used in the Indian context to describe hostility between communities based on religion, especially with regard to the Hindu-Muslim conflict. Yet, it may be more usefully considered in terms of what elsewhere is regarded as ethnic relations and conflict, which even associatively encompasses more than religious affiliations alone.

46   The Patidars (known today as Patels), of Gujarat, for example, are considered Shudras (Kanbi) by the *Varna* law. But they were able to become members of the high castes of Gujarat (pursued their *Savarna*. See Nandy, *et. al.*, *Creating a Nationality*, pp. 102–22). However, some sub-castes among them, Kedva Patels, are still considered to be lower Patels. Similar patterns of mobility and hierarchy developed also among sub-castes of Dalits (the former untouchables).

47   KHAM stands for Kshatriya (backward caste in Gujarat), Harijans (former untouchables), Adivasis (scheduled tribes) and Muslims. For a comprehensive study of the KHAM strategy see John R. Wood, 'Congress restored?'.

48   The Yadavs (Other Backward Castes) in Uttar Pradesh are an example for such a group.

49   It is notable that the circumstances of communal riots in India were linked to Upper Castes' fears of losing their advantages. For instance, when V.P. Singh's government decided to carry out the Mandel commission recommendation for affirmative action for members of the Backward

Castes, upper-castes students violently disturbed urban areas in the country.
50 The Ramjanmabhumi movement began to take shape in October 1984, but did not gain any mass support.
51 Peter van der Veer, *Religious Nationalism*, p. 5.
52 See Ruud, 'Land and Power pp. 357–80, and Bhattacharyya, *Agrarian Reforms and the Politics of the Left.*

References

Books and journal articles

Ahmad, Aijaz, 'Fascism and National Culture: Reading Gramsci in days of Hindutva' in *Social Scientist*, Vol. 21, Nos. 3–4, March–April, 1993, pp. 32–68.

Ahmad, Aijaz, 'Culture, Community, Nation: On the Ruins of Ayodhya', *Social Scientist*, Vol. 21, Nos. 7–8, July–August, 1993, pp. 17–48.

Alvi, Hamza, 'Politics of Ethnicity in India and Pakistan', in H. Alvi and H. John (eds), *Sociology of Developing Societies, South Asia* (Macmillan, London, 1989), pp. 222–46.

Anderson, W.K., and Damle, S.P., *The Brotherhood in Saffron* (Vistaar Publication, New Delhi, 1987).

Bagchi, Amiya Kumar, 'Predatory Commercialization and Communalism in India', in Sarvepalli Gopal (ed.), *Anatomy of a Confrontation. Ayodhya and the Rise of Communal Politics in India* (Zed Books, London, 1991), pp. 193–218.

Basu, Tapan Datta, Pradig, Sarkar, Sumit, Satkar, Tanika, and Sen Sambuddha, Kaaki, *Khaki Shorts and Saffron Flages* (Orient Longman, Delhi, 1993).

Bayly, C.A., 'The Pre-History of 'Communalism'? Religious Conflict In India, 1700–1860', *Modern Asian Studies*, 19, 1985, pp. 177–203.

Bayly, Susan, '"Caste" and "Race" in Colonial Ethnography', in Peter Robb (ed.), *Concept of Race in South Asia* (Oxford University Press, Oxford, 1995), pp. 165–218.

Bhabha, Homi K., *The Location of Culture* (Routledge, London, 1994).

Bhattacharyya, D., *Agrarian Reforms and the Politics of the Left in West Bengal*, Unpublished PhD thesis, (University of Cambridge, March, 1993).

Bougle, C., *Essays on the Caste System* (Cambridge University Press, Cambridge, 1971), pp. 29–40.

Brass, R. Paul, *Language, Religion and Politics in North India* (Cambridge University Press, Cambridge, 1974).

Brass, R. Paul, 'Elite Groups Symbol Manipulation and Ethnic Identity Among the Muslims of South Asia', in David Taylor and Malcolm Yapp (eds), *Political Identity in South Asia* (Curzon Press Humanities Press, 1979), pp. 35–77.

Brass, R. Paul, *The Politics of India Since Independence* (Cambridge University Press, Delhi, 1992).

Carroll, Lucy, 'Colonial perceptions of Indian Society and the emergence of Caste(s) Associations', *Journal of Asian Studies*, Vol.xxxviii, No. 3, 1978.

Chakravarti, Uma, and Haksar, Nandita, *The Delhi Riots. Three Days in the Life of a Nation* (Lancer International, Delhi, 1987).

Chandavarkar, Rajnarayan, 'Workers' Politics and the Mill Districts in Bombay between the Wars', *Modern Asian Studies* 15, 3, 1981, pp. 603–47.

Chandavarkar, Rajnarayan, *The Origins of Industrial Capitalism in India. Business Strategies and the Working Classes in Bombay, 1900–1940* (Cambridge University Press, Cambridge, 1994).

Chandra, Bipan, *Communalism in Modern India* (Vikas, New Delhi, 1984).

Chatterjee, Partha, 'Caste and Subaltern Consciousness', Subaltern Studies VI, (Oxford University Press, Delhi, 1989), pp. 169–209.

Chatterjee, Partha, *Nationalist Thought and the Colonial World: a Derivative Discourse?* (University of Minnesota Press, Minneapolis, 1986).

Chatterjee, Partha, *The Nation and its Fragments* (Princeton University Press, Princeton, New Jersey, 1993).

Chatterjee, Partha, 'Secularism and Tolerance', *Economic and Political Weekly*, 9 July, 1994.

Chatterji, Joya, *Bengal Divided* (Cambridge University Press, Delhi, 1995).

Clifford, James, *The Predicament of Culture, 'On Orientalism'* (Harvard University Press, London, 1988), pp. 255–76.

Cohn, Bernard S., *An Anthropologist among the Historians and Other Essays* (Oxford University Press, Oxford, 1987).

Connor, Walker, *Ethnonationalism the Quest for Understanding* (Princeton University Press, Princeton, New Jersey, 1994).

Das, Veena, (ed.), *Mirrors of Violence. Communities, Riots and Survivors* (Oxford University Press, Delhi, 1990).

Davis, Natalie Zemon, 'The Rites of Violence', in *Society and Culture in Early Modern France* (Polity Press, 1987), pp. 152–87.

Dipanikar, Gupta (ed.), *Social Stratification* (Oxford University Press, Delhi, 1992).

Dirks, Nicholas B., *The Hollow Crown* (Cambridge University Press, Cambridge, 1987).

Dirks, Nicholas B., 'The Invention of Caste: Civil Society in Colonial India', *Social Analysis*, No. 25, September, 1989, pp. 42–52.

Dirks, Nicholas B., *Colonialism and Culture* (University of Michigan Press, Ann Arbuor, 1992).

Dumont, Louis, *Homo Hierarchicus* (University of Chicago Press, Chicago, 1980).

Frankel, Francine R., *India's Political Economy, 1947–77: the Gradual Revolution*, (Oxford University Press, New Delhi, 1978).

Frankel, Francine R., 'Decline of Social Order', in Francine R. Frankel and M.S.A. Rao (eds), *Dominance and State Power in Modern India*, Vol. II, (Oxford University Press, Delhi, 1990), pp. 482–517.

Frankel, Francine R., and Rao, M.S.A., *Dominance and State Power in Modern India*, Vol. I (Oxford University Press, Dehli, 1989), pp 204–64.

Frykenberg, Robert Eric, 'Hindu Fundamentalism and the Structural Stability of India', in Martin Marty and R, Scott Appleby (eds), *Fundamentalism and the State. Remaking Politics, Economies and Millitance* (University of Chicago Press, Chicago, 1993), pp. 233–55.

Geertz, Clifford, *The Interpretation of Culture* (Fontana Press, London, 1973 (1993 edition)).

Gellner, Ernest, *Nations and Nationalism* (Cornell University Press, 1983).

Gold, Daniel, 'Organized Hinduism: From Vedic Truth to Hindu Nation', in Martin Marty and R, Scott Appleby (eds), *Fundamentalism Observed* (University of Chicago Press, Chicago, 1991), pp. 531–93.

Graham, Bruce, *Hindu Nationalism and Hindu Politics* Cambridge University Press, Cambridge, 1993.

Hall, Stuart, 'Ethnicity Identity and Difference', in *Radical America*, 23, 4, Oct–Dec, 1989.

Hall, Stuart, 'Who Needs "identity"', in Stuart Hall and Paul Du Gay (eds), *Questions of Cultural Identity* (Sage Publication, London, 1996), pp. 1–17.

Hasan, Mushirul, 'Indian Muslims Since Independence in Search of Integration and Identity', *Third World Quarterly*, Vol. 10, No. 2, April, 1989, pp. 818–42.

Hawthorn, Geoffrey, 'Caste and Politics in India Since 1947', in Dennis B. McGilvray (ed.), *Caste Ideology and Interaction* (Cambridge University Press, Cambridge, 1982), pp. 204–20.

Hechter, Michael, *Internal Colonialism: the Celtic Fringe In British National Development 1536–1966* (University of California Press, L.A., 1975), pp. 22–43.

Hechter, Michael, 'Ethnicity and Industrialization: On the Proliferation of the Cultural Division of Labor', *Ethnicity*, 3, 1976, pp. 214–24.

Hechter, Michael, 'Group Formation and the Cultural Division of Labor', *American Journal of Sociology*, 84, 1978, pp. 293–318.

Hechter, Michael, 'Nationalism as Group Solidarity', *Ethnic and Racial Studies*, Vol. 10, No. 4, 1987, pp. 415–26.

Inden, Ronald, *Imagining India* (Basil Blackwell, Oxford, 1990).

Jaffrelot, Christophe, *The Hindu Nationalist Movement and the Indian Politics 1925–1990s* (Viking, Delhi, 1996).

Jalali, Rita, 'Preferential Policies and the Movement of the Disadvantaged: the Case of the Scheduled Castes in India', *Ethnic and Racial Studies*, Vol. 16, No. 1, 1993.

Juergensmeyer, Mark, 'The Debate Over Hindu Nationalism', *Contention*, Vol. 4, No. 3, Spring 1995, pp. 211–21.

Kakar, Sudhir, 'Some Unconscious Aspects of Ethnic Violence in India', in Veena Das (ed.), *Mirrors of Violence* (Oxford University Press, Delhi, 1990), pp. 135–15.

Kakar, Sudhir, 'When Saffron Speaks', *Sunday Times of India*, July 19, 1992, pp. 12–13.

Kaviraj, Sudipta, 'Religion, Politics and Modernity', in U. Baxi and B. Parekh. (eds), *Crisis and Change in Contemporary India* New Delhi, 1995, pp. 295–316.

Kaviraj, Sudipta, 'Religion and Identity in India', *Ethnic and Racial Studies*, Vol. 20, No. 2, April, 1997, pp. 325–44.

Keppley, Mahmood, Cynthia, 'Rethinking Indian CommunCulture and Counter Culture' *Asian Survey*, Vol. xxxiii, No. 7, pp. 722–37.

Kohli, Atul, *Democracy and Discontent* (Cambridge University Press, Cambridge, 1990).

Kothari, Rajni, *Caste in Indian Politics* (Gordon and Breach, Science Publishers, London, 1970), pp. 3–25.

Kothari, Rajni, *Politics and the People*, Vol. II (Ajanta Publication, Delhi, 1990).

Krishna, Gopal, 'Communal Violence in India. A Study of Communal Disturbances in Delhi', *Economic and Political Weekly*, January 12, 1995, pp. 117–31.

Lal, Deepak, 'The Economic Impact of Hindu Revivalism', in Martin Marty and R. Scott Appleby (eds), *Fundamentalism and the State. Remaking Politics, Economies and Militance* (University of Chicago Press, Chicago, 1993), pp. 410–26.

Lal, Vinay, 'Hindu "Fundamentalism" Revisited', *Contention*, Vol. 4, No. 2, Winter, 1995, pp. 165–73.

Madan, T.N., 'Whither Indian Secularism?' *Modern Asian Studies*, 27, 3, 1993, pp. 667–97.

Nandy, Ashish, 'The Politics of Secularism and the Recovery of Religious Tolerance', in Veena Das (ed.), *Mirrors of Violence* (Oxford University Press, Delhi, 1990), pp. 69–93.

Nandy, Ashish, *The Intimate Enemy, Loss and Recovery of Self under Colonialism* (Oxford University Press, Delhi, 1993).

Nandy, Ashish, Trivedy, Shika, Mayaram, Shail and Yagnik, Achyut, *Creating a Nationality. The Ramjanmabhumi Movement and Fear of the Self* (Oxford University Press, Delhi, 1995).

Pandey, Gyanendra, *The Construction of Communalism in Colonial North India* (Oxford University Press, Delhi, 1990).

Pandey, Gyanendra, 'The Colonial Construction of "Communalism": British Writings on Banaras in the Nineteenth-Century', in Veena Das (ed.), *Mirrors of Violence* (1990) pp. 94–132.

Pandey, Gyanendra, 'Which of Us Are Hindus?', in Gyanendra Pandey (ed.), *Hindus and Others* (Viking, Delhi, 1993), pp. 238–72.

Peled, Yoav, *Class and Ethnicity in the Pale: the Political Economy of Jewish Workers' Nationalism in Late Imperial Russia* (Macmillan, London, 1989).

Pollock, Sheldon, 'Ramayana and Political Imagination in India', *Journal of Asian Studies*, 52, No. 2, May, 1993, pp. 261–97.

Raychaudhuri, Tapan, 'Shadows of the Swastika: Historical Reflection on the Politics of Hindu Communalism', *Contention*, Vol. 4, No. 2, 1995, pp. 141–62.

Robinson, Francis, 'Nation Formation: the Brass Thesis and Muslim Separatism', *Journal of Commonwealth and Comparative Politics*, Vol. XV, No. 3, November, 1977, pp. 215–30.

Robinson, Francis, 'Islam and Muslim Separatism', in David Taylor and Malcolm Yapp (eds), *Political Identity in South Asia* (Curzon Press/Humanities Press, 1979), pp. 78–112.

Roy, Ajit, 'Caste and Class: an Interlinked View', *Economic and Political Weekly*, Vol. XIV, Nos. 7–8, 1979, pp. 297–301.

Rudolph, Loyd I., and Rudolph Hoeber, Susanne, *In Pursuit of Lakshmi* (University of Chicago Press, London, 1987).

Ruud, Arild Engelson, 'Land and Power: the Marxist Conquest of Rural Bengal' *Modern Asian Studies*, 28, 2, 1994, pp. 357–80.

Said, Edward W., *Orientalism* (Vintage Books, New York, 1978 (1979 edition)).

Sarkar, Sumit, 'Orientalism Revisited: Saidian Framework in the Writing of Modern Indian History', *Oxford Literary Review*, Vol. 16, 1–2, 1994, pp. 205–24.

Sen, Amartya, 'The Threats to Secular India', *New York Review of Books*, April 8, 1993, pp. 26–32.

Stern, Robert W., *Changing India* (Cambridge University Press, Cambridge, 1993).

Thakur, Ramesh, 'Ayodhya and the Politics of India's Secularism: a Double-Standards Discourse', *Asian Survey*, Vol. XXXIII, No. 7, July, 1993, pp. 645–63.

Thapar, Romila, *Interpreting Early India* (Oxford University Press, Delhi, 1992).

Taylor, Charles, 'The Politics of Recognition' in Amy Gutman, ed. *Multiculturalism and 'The Politics of Recognition'* (Princeton University Press, Princeton, New Jersey, 1992).

Van der Veer, Peter, 'God Must be Liberated! A Hindu Liberation Movement in Ayodhya', *Modern Asian Studies*, 21, 2, 1987, pp. 283–301.

Van der Veer, Peter, 'The Foreign Hand. Orientalist Discourse in Sociology and Communalism', in Carol A. Reckenbridge and Peter van der Veer (eds), *Orientalism and the Post Colonial Predicament* (University of Pennsylvania Press, Philadelphia, 1993), pp. 23–44.

Van der Veer, Peter, *Religious Nationalism, Hindus and Muslims in India*, (University of California Press, London, 1994).

Vanaik, Achin, 'Reflections on Communalism and Nationalism in India', *New Left Review*, No. 196, Nov/Dec, 1992), pp. 43–63.

Vanaik, Achin, *The Furies of Indian Communalism* (Verso, London, 1997).

Van den Berghe, Pierre, 'Race and Ethnicity: a Sociobiological Perspective', *Ethnic and Racial Studies*, Vol. 1, No. 4, 1978).

Washbrook, David, 'The Development of Caste Organisation in South India 1880–1925', in C.J. Baker and D. A. Washbrook (eds), South India: Political Institutions and Political Change 1880–1940 (The Macmillan Company of India Ltd, Dehli, 1975), pp. 150–203.

Wolpert, Stanley, 'Resurgent Hindu Fundamentalism', *Contention*, Vol. 2, No. 3, Spring, 1995, pp. 9–18.

Wood, John R., 'Congress Restored? The 'KHAM' Strategy and Congress(I) Recruitment in Gujarat', in John R. Wood (ed.), *State Politics in Contemporary India: Crisis or Continuity?* (Westvies Press, Boulder and London, 1984), pp. 197–227.

Young, Robert J.C., *Colonial Desire. Hybridity in Theory, Culture and Race* (Routledge, London, 1995).

Newspapers

India Today 1993–1996.

14

Ethnic Groups and the State in Africa

Benyamin Neuberger

Contemporary Africa abounds with problems related to ethnicity or 'tribalism' ('if one disapproves of the phenomenon it is tribalism and if one is less judgemental it is ethnicity'[1]). Throughout Africa – in Angola, Ethiopia, Sudan, Rwanda, Burundi, Liberia, Chad and Niger – ethnic wars are waged. In nearly all African states that are multi-ethnic we see ethnic politics in action – ethnic governments and coalitions, ethnic *coups d'etats*, ethnic parties and elections. Lately, mainly in the 1990s, the age of democratization with its successes and failures, an old debate has been revived in Africa. Does multi-ethnicity constitute a solid base or an obstacle for liberal democracy? Can ethnic groups become building stones of a pluralist society?

This chapter deals with the interrelationship between state and ethnic groups in Africa. Because almost all states in Africa are multi-ethnic and have borders which cut through ethnic groups the analysis of the connection between state and ethnic groups is vital for anybody who wants to understand the internal and external politics of the African states. In order to deal with this question we have first to define what we mean by ethnic groups (or 'tribes' in colonial parlance). An ethnic group is first of all a group with a name, an identity, a solidarity, common sentiments, mutual interests and shared goals and visions. This 'subjective' dimension of ethnicity is grounded in some 'objective' characteristics and markers – language, culture, religion, customs, folklore, traditional political and social institutions. Ethnic groups share also a myth of common descent and a sense of common history which may be either 'objective' and grounded in 'real' history or 'subjective' – a sheer 'invention' of recent times. We certainly agree with the dictum that 'ethnicity is a specific form of historically grounded relationship'.[2]

We know of too many 'new' ethnic groups in Africa – for example, Congo's Bangala, Kenya's Kalenjin, Nigeria's Yoruba, Zimbabwe's Shona and Tanzania's Nyakyusa and Sukuma – to accept the primordialist-essentialist view of ethnicity. Whether ethnic groups (or 'tribes') are, as the instrumentalist-constructionalist school claims, sheer 'inventions' or manipulations by elites or whether they are products of dynamic historical processes, one may certainly distinguish between pre-colonial 'natural' groups and newly created 'artificial' groups that were 'invented' by colonialism or formed in the colonial era. We must however keep in mind that the 'natural' groups were at one point of pre-colonial history as 'artificial' and new as the 'artificial' ethnic groups of the colonial era.

In general the ethnic groups are closer to most people than the new states which lack ethno-cultural and historical depth. In Joseph Rothschild's words 'the ethnic group [and not the state!] is somewhat analogous to Robert Frost's definition of home – the place where, when you have to go there, they may have to take you in'.[3]

Most African ethnic groups are not nations because they do not strive for independent statehood and most African states are not nation-states because their population consists of a host of ethnic groups who have very few common objective (for example, language, religion, culture) or subjective (for example, emotions, patriotism, ideology) characteristics.

African anti-colonialism was principally a kind of political and territorial nationalism and had no ethno-cultural goals and aspirations. Some of the nationalist movements (for example, the Mau Mau, SWAPO, FRELIMO, MPLA, FNLA, UNITA, ZANU, ZAPU, ANC) had very clearly an ethnic base but even they aspired to independence within the colonial boundaries and rejected ethno-cultural 'separatism'. For the same reason that certain ethnic groups dominated the 'non-ethnic' nationalist movements a host of ethnic groups in Africa (for example, Hausa-Fulani in Nigeria, Ashanti in Ghana, Hutu in Rwanda, Africans in Zanzibar, Kalenjin in Kenya, Makua in Mozambique, Dinka in the Sudan) did not participate in decolonization and even preferred the continuation of colonial rule as the lesser evil. Donald Horowitz explained this phenomenon with one concise sentence: 'For everyone it was a question ... who would rule over them.'[4]

Those ethnic groups which did not come to power after independence did not necessarily feel 'independent'. For them 'national self-determination' was in fact 'other-determination' because they were forced by numbers, power and diplomacy to go 'independent' within a state which they regarded as 'foreign' and sometimes even hostile.

What we have in post-colonial Africa is a situation in which there is no congruence between states and nations. We have states which contain a multiplicity of ethno-cultural groups, borders which cut through ethnic groups and competition between a nationalism which is territorial, statist, integrative and conservative and a nationalism which is ethnic, secessionist and revisionist. One kind of nationalism is governmental and status-quo oriented while the other is opposed to the established government and revisionist in its goals. The classical literature on nationalism in Africa which lumps together all forms of nationalism is irrelevant in the post-colonial context.[5]

In most African states there are numerous ethnic groups. Many of these groups are small and weak and thus will never rise to become 'nationalist', or aspire to take over the state or to secede in order to have 'their' state. Most African states are not divided between majority and minority ethnic groups. In Africa, in almost all states all ethnic groups are larger or smaller minorities. The struggle is not one of minority versus majority but between the various minorities (although in parts of the country a majority-minorities situation may very well exist as, for instance, in some of the Nigerian states). In Africa the overarching identity is relatively weak. Nigerian, Kenyan, or Angolan identity has not much historical strength and depth. Identities which cut across ethno-cultural groups, such as religion and class-consciousness are also much less pronounced in Africa than in other parts of the world.

While many African states have many things in common with regard to the 'Ethnic Problem', there are also important differences. States which have a few major ethnic groups who compete for power (for example, Nigeria, Kenya or Zimbabwe), are very different from states which have a 'dispersed system' of dozens of ethnic groups none of which has the power to rule or to secede (for example, Tanzania, the Ivory Coast or Liberia). Some states have a clearly dominant ethnic group which may be a majority (Shona in Zimbabwe or Ovambo in Namibia) or a minority (Kikuyu in Kenyatta's Kenya and Amhara in Haile Selassie's and Mengistu's Ethiopia) while others have no clearly dominant group although they may be ruled by alternating ethnic coalitions. In the same way we have to differentiate between states which have an historical-cultural 'ethnic center' (for example, Mali and Ethiopia) and states which lack such a center (for example, the Ivory Coast). States with a dominant group or an ethnic center may follow a policy of ethno-cultural integration while those without will put their emphasis on economic, political, legal and administrative integration.

Africa abounds with ethnic conflicts. Almost all governments are in one way or another based on ethnic groups, ethnic coalitions and ethnic arithmacy. In the early years of independence ethnic rivalries were regarded as 'tribal' remnants of a primitive traditional past which would be washed away by the modern economy, city, school and state. What occurred was very often the opposite. Modernization brought about increased ethnic tensions because it created 'modernization gaps' between ethnic groups. Competition broke out between groups for the scarce goods of modernization (such as jobs, schools, clinics, investments, monetary income and standard of living). This competition was 'objective' and real where the ethnic groups were on a similar level of modernization. Where there were large modernization gaps between the ethnic groups[6] the competition was 'subjective' in the sense that the less modernized groups felt that they could not compete because they were discriminated and unfairly treated by the more modernized. Increased mobility and urbanization did not bring about a 'melting-pot' expected by the optimists of the 1950s, but increased conflicts between groups which were territorially separated and non-competing and became now territorially inter-mixed and competing. Modernization made the different groups more similar but Donald Horowitz had explained that 'men enter into conflict not because they are different but because they are essentially the same'. Modernization makes them more alike 'in the sense of possessing the same wants'.[7] Modernization has increased ethnic conflict not only for 'material' but also for 'ideal' reasons. Modernization is very often linked to an open or latent policy of cultural assimilation which frequently threatens or is thought to threaten the very identity of ethnic groups. This threat to the very existence and survival of ethnic groups may trigger as a response an ethnic movement of differentiation. Horowitz is right to reject economic determinism for every ethnic conflict. In addition to threats to ethnic identity posed by modernization, fears of subordination to another ethnic group in the new state and hostility towards an influx of foreigners into the ethnic homeland create 'new' ethnic conflicts in the context of modernization. Horowitz is right in defining ethnic conflict as a 'bloody phenomenon' which cannot be explained by a purely 'material', 'bloodless theory'.[8] That does not mean that material conditions are not part of the explanation of ethnicity. In Africa, indeed, secessionist movements developed either in relatively developed regions (such as Katanga, Biafra and Eritrea) or in poor regions; but in the latter case they were led by modernizing elites (for example, Southern Sudan, Ogaden and Northern Chad). We may very well generalize that ethnic nationalism has been at least as much a product of modernization as territorial nationalism.

African governments have followed three basic strategies in dealing with ethnic groups and ethnic conflict. We may differentiate between strategies to impose ethnic domination, strategies to mitigate ethnic conflict and strategies of 'nation-building'.

Strategies of ethnic domination include:

- legal inequality (for example, in apartheid South Africa or Haile Selassie's Ethiopia)
- ethnic slaughter (for example, Amin's Uganda, Micombero's Burundi and Habyarimana's Rwanda)
- ethnic expulsions or 'displacement' (for example, Mauritania and Moi's Kenya)
- a policy of forced assimilation (for example, Sudan and Imperial Ethiopia)
- the institutionalization of ethnic rule by an ethnic dictatorship which prohibits any ethnic opposition (for example, Toure's Guinea, Doe's Liberia and Babangida's and Abacha's Nigeria) and
- a divide-and-rule strategy by the dominant ethnic group (for example, Habre's Chad, Kaunda's Zambia and Banda's Malawi).

Strategies to mitigate ethnic conflict occur when the ruling ethnic group or groups engage in negotiations and 'deals' with the non-dominant groups in order to reduce ethnic conflict and stabilize the political system. These strategies – called by Donald Rothchild 'hegemonic exchange' – include co-optation of leaders, ethnic arithmacy in government, proportionality in civil service appointments and allocations, power-sharing in central, regional and local government and even a federal system which is enabled to 'compensate' ethnic groups out of power at the center by giving them a role in regional politics and administration. Kenya, the Ivory Coast, Nigeria, Tanzania, Ghana and Cameroun are states which have very often employed some of these strategies to ameliorate ethnic conflicts.[9]

Nation-building strategies are intended in the long run to overcome ethnic conflict and to create real 'nations' within the statist shell and thus to create a 'nation-state' of the European type. Basically there are three nation-building strategies followed by African leaders and governments.

One strategy, which in the short run combines with a strategy to mitigate ethnic conflict, aims to build 'pluralist nations', by institutionalizing pluralism which is equal to all. The vision of 'pluralist nations' in Africa was propagated in the 1940s by the Nigerians Nnamdi Azikiwe and Obafemi Awolowo,[10] and indeed Nigeria is the closest example of a country following such a policy.

A different strategy is to encourage a slow gradual process of nation-building which aims in the long run to create a homogenous nation. For this very reason leaders who followed such a strategy were vehemently opposed to federalism, autonomy or any other form of institutionalized pluralism. In Africa, Kenyatta's Kenya and Senghor's Senegal are prime examples for such a strategy.

The most radical strategy of nation-building is the Jacobin one which aims to assimilate – by force if necessary – the non-dominant ethnic groups in order to achieve in the shortest possible time a homogenous nation-state. Such a policy may (as in the Sudan and in Haile Selassie's and Mengistu's Ethiopia) go together with a strategy to impose ethnic domination. The vision holds the ruling ethnic group as the nucleus of the future nation, a nucleus to which all other groups have to assimilate. Jacobinism may also be followed by a government (for example, Tanzania) innocent of any intention to assure ethnic domination.

As well as the policies of governments on the 'Ethnic Problem' it is important to analyse what the ethnic groups themselves aim to achieve. In general we may differentiate between the few ethnic groups who want secession and the many whose aim is more power and influence at the center. Secession is largely regarded as exceptional, illegitimate, threatening, destructive and non-negotiable while ethnic power politics within the system is tacitly if not openly accepted as normal, legitimate, manageable and negotiable. In between the two basic currents are those ethnic groups who strive for regional autonomy or a federal state. They may do so for the 'negative' reason that they do not have the power to secede or for the 'positive' reason that they believe – as some governments do – in the vision of a pluralist nation-state. In general we agree with Donald Horowitz who defined the goal of ethnic groups as either 'control of the state, control of a state' or 'exemption from control by others'.[11] As we see, the goals and policies followed by ethnic groups have an impact on the structure and politics of the state, on inter-state relations and on the whole African state system. It should be clear that there is nothing permanent in the politics followed by the leadership of the ethnic groups. For example, in the 1960s the Lunda in Zaire and the Ibo in Nigeria followed a policy which shifted from power politics to separation and back to power politics. One way or the other this has been true for the Somalis, Oromo and Afar in Ethiopia, the Tigrineans in Eritrea, the Dinka, Zande and Nuer in the Sudan, the Toubous and Sara in Chad, the Tuareg in Mali and the Baganda in Uganda.

Those ethnic groups which followed a secessionist or irredentist policy engaged in ethnic revisionism but in almost all cases the seceding area was not homogeneous. In almost all cases the secessionists and irredentists who denied the legitimacy of one set of colonial boundaries insisted on another set of colonial boundaries, whether 'older' colonial boundaries (as in the irredentisms of Togo, Cameroun and Libya) or internal provincial (but non-ethnic!) boundaries (as in Eritrea, Katanga, Biafra, Southern Sudan and Northern Somalia). Revisionism is very often an intriguing 'mix' of an ethnic core (Ibo in Biafra, Lunda in Katanga, Diula in Casamance, Issak in Northern Somalia, Tigrinean in Eritrea, Sara in Southern Chad or Somali in the NFD of Kenya) within a 'state' or province which possesses non-ethnic 'historical' borders of one sort or the other.[12] In Katanga and Biafra the ethnic heterogeneity of the seceding regions even created a civil-war situation in the seceding province which very much weakened the secessionists. In Eritrea and the Southern Sudan the ethnic heterogeneity has made it also very difficult to unite all ethnic groups for the common secessionist goal.

In Africa hundreds of ethnic groups which preserved a sense of community have been cut by the colonial boundaries. The potential for irredentism is very great but in the last forty years there have been only relatively few irredentist movements of importance (the major irredentist states were Morocco, Somalia, Ethiopia and Togo). One may ask why so few cases of irredentism exist in Africa and why most of the irredentists have up to now failed to achieve their goals.

In Black Africa there are very few nation-states and *quasi* nation-states, and the likelihood for a state's active involvement in irredentism is therefore greatly diminished. Most ethnic groups, divided between two states by an international boundary, are not candidates for irredentism for the very reason that they do not regard the two states as 'theirs'. In that sense we agree with Phiri that 'partitioned ethnic groups are often bound by community feeling but they "belong" to neither one state or the other ... they "belong" to themselves'.[13] African ethnic minorities who feel dominated and oppressed in one plural state have no incentive to become irredentist and join another plural state in which they may be equally dominated and oppressed. That is why the Toubous in Chad did not strive to join Libya in the

1960s and 1970s, why the Kenyan Oromos have no wish to join their brothers in Ethiopia (or vice versa), and why the Sudanese Zande do not have the inclination to be annexed by what used to be called Zaire or by the Central African Republic.

Horowitz's rule that 'if the retrieving group does not have a strong position in the putative irredentist state, its claims will be ignored or suppressed'[14] clearly applies to most partitioned groups in Black Africa because 'only rarely did partitioned groups wield much influence within a state identified with their ethos, thus becoming virtually a nation-state'.[15] The exceptions to this African rule (Somalia, Swaziland and Togo) did indeed produce irredentist movements and aspirations. Another factor that should not be ignored is that most partitioned groups are small, weak and peripheral, compared to the size of the population and the power of the state to which they belong; therefore, their chances of successfully breaking away from the state are slim.

Another reason for the relative absence of ethnic irredenta is the processes of integration that occured in the colonial and post-colonial periods and that weakened the emotional-ethnic ties to such an extent that the different sections of the partitioned groups developed differential interests, feelings and identities. Their exposure to different administrations, educational systems, colonial languages, markets, currencies, economic policies, mass media and political orientations quite often led to the emergence of different identities. Some examples of these processes of gradual estrangement were researched by Miles, Morton, and Vail who studied the Hausas of Nigeria and Niger, the Bakgatla baga Kgafela of Botswana and South Africa, and the Swazi of Swaziland and South Africa, respectively.[16] Sometimes different names were given to the various parts of the divided groups (for example, the Yoruba of Nigeria are called Nago in Benin, the Toubou of Chad are Goranes in Niger, and the Liberian Kpelle are known as Guerze in Guinea).

The surprising paucity of irredenta in Africa is partly due to the plural 'softness' of the African post-colonial state. In most states the central government has neither the will nor the capacity to turn 'Jacobin' – to force the partitioned and peripheral groups to assimilate, to conform, or to adapt to the center. Most states are plural, multiethnic states, which have developed informal mechanisms to make life at least bearable for most ethnic groups. This adjustment is made easier by the fact that the post-colonial state is not a nation-state in which the partitioned group is the only minority. The state is a state of minorities, and a group that is left out of power and its amenities is more likely to seek redress within the same state than to look for salvation across the border. The softness of the African state also means that partitioned groups may ignore the border at will. Such a liberal partition mitigates their 'unhappiness' and diminishes the pressure on 'their' government to adopt an irredentist policy on their behalf. *Realpolitik* and utilitarian calculations on the part of the potentially redeeming states are the reasons for the relatively small number of African irredenta and their failure to change the post-colonial map dramatically. The multi-ethnic character of most African states and their internal lack of cohesion and stability are the prime reasons for their unwillingness to go irredentist, as they could easily fall victim to irredentist retaliation. Suhrke and Noble rightly claim that the feelings of vulnerability of the multi-ethnic states 'lead to a restrained policy toward boundary disputes',[17] and irredentism is certainly a kind of boundary dispute. A state that has to worry about lack of cohesion and possible disintegration will indeed act according to a 'calculus of vulnerability'.[18] It will hesitate to support irredentism in another state when this could serve as a precedent for irredentism within its own borders. The Kenyan Masinde Muliro vividly evoked the fear of disintegration by irredentism when he rhetorically asked, 'What would remain of Kenya if the Somalis unite with Somalia, the Luo and the Abeluhya with their brothers in Uganda and the coastal Nyika and inland Masai break away to be together with their people in Tanzania?'[19]

Other 'rational' calculations may dampen the enthusiasm for irredentism. Touval observed that 'the delicate balancing of tribal interests in each state has apparently exercised a moderating influence, restraining governments from embracing open irredentist policies which might upset the existing tribal balance'.[20] We should also bear in mind that 'not all the ethnic constituents of such a state will be equally enthusiastic at the prospect of incurring costs and risks on behalf of the ethnic brethren of only one of them'.[21]

The pursuit of irredentism also runs counter to the prevailing status-quo ideology of the OAU and the African political establishment. Clause III of the OAU Charter (1963) talks about the obligation of the member states to respect 'the sovereignty of territorial integrity of each state',[22] and the Cairo Resolution of 1964 declares 'the borders of the African states on the day of independence constituted a tangible reality' and that 'the member states pledge themselves to respect the borders existing on their achievement of independence'.[23] The OAU as an organization has indeed opposed all irredentist movements, and this consistent position, shared by most African governments, certainly strengthened the status quo forces in Africa and weakened the case for revisionism, whether separatist, irredentist or expansive. Although Tolstoy's statement that divided peoples are unhappy is certainly true, in reality

> the sword of self-determination is sharp when severing the colony from its metropole. However, its reverse side is blunt and unavailable when minorities within the former colonies seek either their own independent state or union with more desirable brothers across the frontier.[24]

The more 'legitimate' role of ethnic groups in the politics of African states assumes various forms. In most African states ethnic groups are involved in ethnic power politics as they strive for power and influence in the government. While few governments are pure 'ethnocracies', almost all of them can be identified with a dominant ethnic group (for example, Moi's Kenya with the Kalenjin, Kaunda's and Chiluba's Zambia with the Bemba, Toure's Guinea with the Malinke, Obote's Uganda with the Lango, Meles Zenawi's Ethiopia with the Tigrineans, Mugabe's Zimbabwe with the Shona, Eyadema's Togo with the Kabre, and so on). Busia's statement that 'no African president or prime minister can keep his place without the backing of large tribes'[25] is certainly true. All major parties in Africa, whether in one-party systems or in competitive multi-party systems, are identified with ethnic groups. Some define themselves openly as parties of one or some ethnic groups. Others regard themselves as non-ethnic, territorial and nationalist but in fact they too have an 'ethnic base' and are not equally supported by all ethnic groups. Ethnicity played a crucial role in elections in Africa whether in the decolonization era in the 1950s or in the re-democratization era in the late 1980s and in the 1990s. Ethnic groups are also involved with the military which has ruled a good part of Africa during the post-colonial era. Armies, military *coups d'etats*, the officer corps, military leaders and military governments are very well identified with ethnic groups. We may generalize that much of the army in politics and the politics in the army is in fact ethnic politics.

The end of the Cold War and recent events in Eastern Europe have had an impact on the role of ethnicity in Africa. The explosions of ethnic nationalism in Eastern Europe and the break-up of the Soviet Union and Yugoslavia have weakened the delegitimization of ethnicity and separatism also in Africa. It is not accidental that the first two successful secessions in Africa – that of the Tigrinean Eritrean People's Liberation Front (EPLF) in Eritrea and that of the Issak Somali National

Movement (SNM) in Northern Somalia – occurred simultaneously with the ethnic upheavals in Eastern Europe. In the early 1990s we have indeed seen a resurgence of separatism in Africa. The Southern Sudanese SPLF which strove for autonomy throughout the 1980s became all-out secessionist. Bakongo's FLEC in the Cabinda enclave which belongs to Angola became again very active. The same is true with Zambia's Lozi, Ethiopia's Afar and Oromo and the Tuareg in Mali and Niger. In Sengal, the Diula-led Mouvement des Forces Democratiques de la Casamance (MFDC) seriously threatens the state's territorial integrity. Strong separatist rumblings are also heard in Tanzania's Zanzibar and Zaire's Shaba Province (the former Katanga). During the Cold War era the involvement of the super-powers did not give separatists much of a chance to succeed. The withdrawal of the Soviet Union from Africa and the end of global competition creates a new situation also in the sense that any future struggle between a central government and a secessionist movement will be decided by the local balance of power and not by big power interventions (as was the case in the past in Katanga, Biafra, Eritrea, the Ogaden and Southern Sudan).

In addition to separatism, violent clashes between ethnic groups for control of the state have occurred in the 1990s in Liberia, Rwanda, Burundi, Togo, Chad, Ethiopia, Angola, Mozambique and South Africa.

The democratization 'wave' of the 1990s has also brought about more and not less ethnic politics. Results from multi-party elections in many African countries have shown that the elections have been heavily ethnic. The new party formations and alignments have in many instances revived the 'old' ethnic cleavages of the 1950s and 1960s. A few examples will suffice:

- In **Kenya** the ruling KANU won in the 1992 elections less than 2 per cent of the vote of the two largest Kenyan ethnic groups – the Kikuyu and the Luo.
- In **Ghana** the results of the 1993 elections confirm the old ethnic polarization between the Southern ethnic groups (for example, Ewe, Fanti) and the Ashanti to the north.
- In **Malawi** there was in the 1994 elections a clear-cut electoral division of the country into the three major ethnic groups – Chewa, Tonga and Tumbuka.
- In **Namibia** SWAPO received overwhelming support among the Ovambo while the opposition DTA remained strong among the Herero, Damara, Hottentotes and other minorities.

- In **South Africa** in addition to the Whites, the majority of three other racial-ethnic groups (Indians, Coloreds and Zulu) also did not vote for the ANC in the 1994 elections.

Democratization and elections pose a threat of ethnic majoritization and ethnic defeat and can thus be a major reason for heightened ethnic tensions. In many cases ethnicity has been a major problem for any meaningful progress towards democratization. A few examples will make this point:

- In **Togo** the northern Kabre (14 per cent in the country but 75 per cent in the army), base their power on the army. Any real democratization will sweep them from power and lead to the formation of a government led by the Ewe – the leading southern ethnic group. The military Kabre leaders led by President Eyadema fear that in that case they will have to stand trial for the many crimes committed by their regime. For that reason they expelled hundreds of thousands of Ewe across the borders and conducted fake elections boycotted by the Ewe-led opposition.
- In **Ethiopia** the tiny Tigrinean ethnic groups (4 per cent in the country) had taken power in 1991 while the major ethnic groups of the country (the Amhara who ruled Ethiopia during Haile Selassie's and Megistu Haile Mariam's rule and comprise 20 per cent of the population and the Oromo who are Ethiopia's largest group with 40 per cent of the population) were (and are) in fierce opposition. The elections held in 1995 were boycotted by the major Amhara and Oromo parties and manipulated by the ruling TPLF. It is clear that any free elections will throw the TPLF out of power and knowing that, the TPLF will do everything possible to thwart such a development.
- In **Nigeria** all the military governments of the 1980s and 1990s were led by Muslim Northerners, mainly Hausa-Fulani. The election victory of a Muslim Yoruba Southerner in June 1993 was immediately declared null and void by the ruling Northern generals. The winner of the elections was imprisoned and the military government has become since then more and more authoritarian.
- In **Djibouti** the 1993 elections were won by the ruling Issa Somalis and boycotted by the Danakil. Both groups regard politics in the tiny country as a zero-sum game. The Danakil have continued their struggle for power by guerrilla warfare led by the Front pour la Restauration et l'Unite de la Democratie (FRUD).

- In **Burundi** free elections in 1993 resulted in a first Hutu president elected by the Hutu majority. Within months he (and later also his successor) were assassinated by the Tutsi-led army.

Ethnicity is a stumbling block to successful democratization for the following reasons:

1   In the absence of an overriding national identity there is no minimal consensus – even not on the elite level – which is vital for any functioning democracy. Without a consensus the rules of the democratic game cannot be agreed upon. The basic trust between ethnic groups which will enable losing groups to accept the verdict of elections is very often missing.
2   Ethnic bloc voting means that statistics and demography are deciding elections. In such a situation the losers have no chance to come to power and will therefore have no motivation to see the electoral decision as legitimate and final.
3   In a polarized ethnic party system the role is fixed and no votes change from one side to the other. Such ethnic voting rigidity does not allow change of governments as a result of elections.
4   Dictatorships based on ethnic minorities will not democratize for fear of being swept out of power by the larger ethnic groups who possess larger voting blocs.
5   An army based on an ethnic group put out of power through democratization will pose a constant threat to the newly elected government.

The question will remain whether multi-ethnicity will make it in the long run easier or more difficult for African states to go democratic. Again the old debate between John Stuart Mill who thought that 'free institutions are next to impossible in a country made up of different nationalities'[26] and Lord Acton for whom 'the coexistence of several nations under the same state is ... the best security of freedom'[27] will be tested – this time under the rough conditions of the African continent.

Notes

1   L. Vail, 'Introduction: Ethnicity in Southern African History' in Vail, L. ed., *The Creation of Tribalism in Southern Africa* (Berkeley, University of California Press 1989), p. 1.
2   B. Jewswiecki, 'The Formation of the Political Culture of Ethnicity in the Belgian Congo 1920–1959' in Vail, L., *op. cit.*, p. 325.

3   J. Rothschild, *Ethnopolitcs: a Conceptual Framework* (New York, Columbia University Press, 1981), p. 6.

4   D. Horowitz, *Ethnic Groups in Conflict* (Berkeley, University of California Press, 1985), p. 189.

5   See for example, J. Kautsky, *Political Change in Underdeveloped Countries* (New York, John Diley, 1962), K. Minogue, *Nationalism* (London, Batsford, 1967), J. Coleman, *Nigeria – Background to Nationalism* (Berkeley, University of California Press, 1965), T. Hodgkin, *Nationalism in Colonial Africa* (New York, New York University Press, 1965).

6   R. Melson and H. Wolpe 'Modernization and the Politics of Communalism', *American Political Science Review*, Vol. 64, No. 4, (1970), pp. 1012–30.

7   Horowitz, *op. cit.* p. 100.

8   Ibid, p. 140.

9   D. Rothchild, 'State and Ethnicity in Africa: a Policy Perspective' in N. Nevitte and H. Kennedy, eds, *Ethnic Preference and Public Policy in Developing States* (Boulder Lynne Rienner, 1986), pp. 15–62. 'An Interactive Model for State-Ethnic Relations' in F. Deng and W. Zartmann, eds, *Conflict Resolution in Africa* (Washington, Brookings, 1991) pp. 190–215. D. Rothchild and V. Oluronsola, 'African Public Policies on Ethnic Autonomy and State Control' in D. Rothchild and V. Oluronsola, eds, *State Versus Ethnic Claims: African Policy Dilemmas* (Boulder, Westview, 1983), pp. 233–50.

10 N. Azikiwe, *Zik: a Selection from the Speeches of Nnamdi Azikiwe* (Cambridge, Cambridge University Press, 1961). O. Awolowo, *Path to Nigerian Freedom* (London, Faber and Faber, 1947).

11 Horowitz, *op. cit.* p. 5.

12 B. Neuberger, 'What is the Self?' in *National Self-Determination in Post-Colonial Africa* (Boulder, Lynne Rienner, 1986), pp. 19–60.

13 H. Phiri, 'The Chewa and Ngoni' in A.I. Asiwaju, ed., *Partitioned Africans* (New York, St. Martin's Press, 1985), p. 117.

14 Horowitz, p. 282.

15 S. Touval, 'Partitioned Groups and Inter-State Relations' in Asiwaju, *op. cit.* pp. 223–32.

16 W.F.S. Miles, 'Self-Identity, Ethnic Affinity and National Consciousness: an Example from Rural Hausaland', *Ethnic and Racial Studies*, Vol. 9, No. 4, (October 1986) pp. 427–44. R.F. Morton, 'The Bakgatla Baga Kgafela of Bechuanaland' in Asiwaju, *op. cit.* pp. 127–54. H. Macmillan, 'A Nation Divided-The Swazi in Swaziland and Transvaal 1865–1986', in Vail, L., ed., *The Creation of Tribalism in Southern Africa*, pp. 289–323.

17 A. Suhrke and L.G. Noble, eds, *Ethnic Conflict in International Relations* (New York, Praeger, 1977), p. 13.

18 Ibid, p. 17.

19 V. Matthies, *Der Grenzkonflikt Somalias mit Athiopien und Kenya* (Hamburg, Institute für Afrika-Kunde, 1977), pp. 244–5.

20 S. Touval, 'The Sources of the Status Quo and Irredentist Policies' in C.G. Widstrand ed., *African Boundary Problems* (Uppsala, Scandinavian Institute of African Studies 1969), p. 69.

21 J. Rothschild, *op. cit.* p. 183.

22 S. Chime, 'The Organization of African Unity and African Boundaries' in Widstrand, *op. cit.* p. 66.

23 J. Mayall, 'Self-Determination and the OAU' in I.M. Lewis, ed, *Nationalism and Self-Determination in the Horn of Africa* (London, Ithaca Press, 1983), p. 91.

24 R. Emerson, 'The Problem of Identity, Self-hood and Image in New Nations', *Comparative Politics*, Vol. I, No. 3 (April 1969), pp. 297–312.

25 K. Busia, *Africa in Search of Democracy* (London, Routledge and Kegan Paul, 1967), p. 32.

26 J.S. Mill, *Considerations on Representative Government* (Indianapolis, Library of Liberal Arts Press, 1958), p. 232.

27 Lord Acton, 'Nationality' in *Essays on Freedom and Power* (New York, Meridian, 1965), p. 160.

15
Islamism and Democracy in Algeria

Gema Martin Muñoz

Six years after the interruption of the electoral process in Algeria in January 1992, we now know that this historic turn of the screw was ineffective: it neither saved the people from terror and indiscriminate massacres, nor protected stability in the Maghreb, nor freed this vast North African country from political authoritarianism.

The dominant ideological orientation in the presentation of the Algerian conflict has been based on culturalist analyses and socio-cultural antagonism: a sort of 'crusade' against what is monolithically called 'Islamic Fundamentalism'. The official presentation of the crisis tends to limit the problem of violence to the existence of a terrorist phenomenon, and the regime is presented as representing 'authentic' and 'enlightened' Islam against Islamism, which is interpreted monolithically as a fundamentalist movement that can engender only violence and extremism.

This is a false presentation of the conflict aimed at turning 'their' war (unleashed by those responsible for the coup of January 1992) into 'our' war and 'their' political enemy into 'our' enemy of civilization. Investing strongly in western cultural fears and prejudices about Islam, the Algerian government elites have demonized, without great difficulty, their Islamist political opponents to the extent that their authoritarianism has become the 'lesser evil' for the West against the 'shared Islamic enemy'. This perspective has become the ideological alibi thanks to which they find support for their autocratic systems which they would not achieve so easily if the actors in the conflict were not translated into Islamic code.

This 'ideological packaging' has prevented western societies from rationally assessing the Algerian conflict: a war for the perpetuation in power of a dominant group confronting an opposition that offers a social alternative. However, this general perception that the conflict is cultural, between a social model similar to ours (secular) and a different, unacceptable, social model framed by religious rules derived from the Koran, prevents the conflict from being analysed with the use of social sciences, rather than negative western images about Islam.

No one represents this secular model, and none, except a few crazy radicals who do not know very well who they represent, are demanding an Islamic state. Rather, what is demanded is a democratic transition with the other political forces, including the ruling powers.

Hence, the representations in this war are inverted and confused: the authoritarian powers become defenders of modern and republican values; the phenomenon of violence is interpreted as solely a pathology of Islam; a Manichean polarization is presented between Republic and Islamic State; and it is questionable whether the bulk of those actors recognized and elevated in the West as democrats should be defined as such, given their scant resistance to the authoritarian state and their lack of enthusiasm for the democratic pact;[1] meanwhile, the credibility of those who demand a government by the ballot box in a free and democratic framework remains under suspicion.

A socio-political reading of the conflict

The military action of January 1992, far from defending the world from the Islamist cultural threat, was carried out to protect the political order that had prevailed in Algeria since its creation as an independent state: to prevent the sharing of power with a new political elite so that power and authority could continue to be exercised mostly outside the framework of the state without those really responsible for the government of the country being known. To bolster this principle and this political culture, an undeclared civil war started in 1992, and since 1995 a political-electoral process has developed aimed at guaranteeing the continuity of the country's traditional political-military elite.

After the electoral interruption of January 1992, Algeria was governed by decree-laws via a High Committee of State that marginalized political parties and devoted itself to elaborating ideological, military and security strategies against the Islamic Salvation Front (FIS), the Islamist party whose electoral victory was defeated by the *coup d'etat* and which was subsequently made illegal.

In January 1995 a political event modified the status quo of the conflict: a representative group of opposition Algerian parties including the FIS[2] publicly elaborated and presented a statement of principles and offered it to the government in the form of a democratic pact. Meeting in the Rome headquarters of the Community of Sant Egidio, this group, henceforth known as the Rome Platform, comprising Islamists and non-Islamists, agreed to develop a legal and institutional framework that would enable the pacification of Algeria and lead the country towards democratization.

This group questioned the official view of the conflict, which had been presented up to then as a Manichean war between Islamists and non-Islamists, and posed a political challenge to the Algerian regime. It was a challenge not because it signified a project with chance of real success (given that the regime with a single refusal was able to short-circuit the Rome proposal of dialogue and national reconciliation), but because it showed that the official representation of the conflict did not match the real situation. It showed that other non-Islamic political forces existed that together with the FIS sought peace through a democratic transition without political exclusions.[3]

The Algerian authorities refused to accept a framework of dialogue based on consent rather than rigid rules imposed and orchestrated exclusively by the regime (a conception that has characterized the framework of dialogue proposed by the government). But they were constrained to offer an alternative in order to justify to the international community their rejection of a democratic pact offered by the opposition. They also sought to cause dissent among the political parties of the Rome Platform, between those who would participate in the political arena even under the government's rigid rules, and maximalists whose political strategy was to maintain the group's unity.

This government response took the form of the establishment, from November 1995, of a 'made-to-measure' process of parliamentary restoration that suited government interests. As well as seeking, by means of this process, the neutralization of the Rome Platform, the Algerian authorities were attempting to free themselves from the 'millstone' of the aborted elections in December 1991 that were supposed to instal Algeria's first pluralist parliament. Instead, in 1995 the regime started a new political process which was considered pluralist, but in which the influence of parliament was nullified, the opposition was weakened and, most importantly, the main opposition force, the Islamic Salvation Front (FIS), was marginalized.

The 1991 elections took place in a juridico-political framework established by the Constitution of February 1989 that amended a text of 1976 to eliminate the socialist model, withdraw the political prerogatives of the army and establish a multi-party system with the separation of powers. The drafting of this Constitution did not embody the idea of consensus, and the opposition was not invited to participate. But it did establish a framework of liberties and wide-ranging democratic advances that were acknowledged by all those involved.

This Constitution went into hibernation with the *coup d'etat* of January 1992, since the juridical regime that prevailed in Algeria from then on ruled by decree, sometimes endorsed by a National Transition Council, whose members were all nominated, and which had replaced the parliament.[4] In November 1996 a new constitutional text emerged that installed a juridico-political framework that reinforced what was in effect a presidential system of rule. According to the new text, the president could govern by decree in situations where he had formerly not been allowed to do so, such as during parliamentary recess or between sessions. Similarly, his ability to nominate key institutional figures was broadened to include magistrates, provincial governors and the governor of the Central Bank. Particularly important was the virtual power of veto that the president obtained over parliament: the National Assembly, converted into a Lower Chamber, had to share legislative power with an Upper Chamber (National Council), elected by indirect suffrage, in which all the sectors closest to the regime were congregated.[5] Proposed legislation must win a three-quarters majority in the National Council in order to be enacted. This meant that the parliament barely functioned, and in political terms, MPs had the representative function of a parliament, but without its full legislative powers. However, the new constitution did not define the role of the army which, in practice, permitted the Algerian military elite to rule the country as it had in the past. Hence, Berbers' linguistic claims were not recognized; and Islam, being the official religion of the state, could not be claimed by political parties. The state imposed on its citizens what it does not impose upon itself. Hence, rather than depoliticize religion, it has established a government monopoly on its political utilization.

A new law on the formation of political parties also established restrictive measures, including the prohibition of political parties based on 'religious, linguistic, racial, sexual, corporativist foundations, or with links to, dependence on or control of a trade union or association or any other civil organization' (articles. 5 and 8).[6]

Power and oppositions

From 1995, the various political forces started to define themselves more clearly than before. On one hand, the regime surrounded itself by the 'revolutionary family', the politico-ideological sub-stratum that had always dominated the Algerian political scene. This socio-political group traditionally based its loyalty to the regime on historical legitimacy, the legacy of the independence generation and its successors: the ex-combatants' association, sons of martyrs, veterans of the National Liberation Army, the Algerian General Workers' Union (UGTA – the union of the former single party), and so on. All these formed a social base formerly included within the National Liberation Front (FLN), and are currently divided mainly between it and the National Democratic Regroupment (RND), a new party created in March 1997 aimed at 'renovating' the image of the president's party, given that the FLN is associated with the failure of the system. The youth of the party and the vagueness of the RND's political message ('build a strong Algeria, resistent, self-confident and serene about the future ... without renouncing its cultural patrimony'), do not help to explain how, in only a few months, it achieved 40.78 per cent of parliamentary seats in the legislative elections of 5 June 1997, and 55 per cent of the vote in the municipal elections of 23 October 1997.[7]

The FLN is the best expression of the fragmentation into clans that has always characterized the Algerian political system. Since 1992, it has undergone wide-ranging changes according to the predominance within it of one power group or another. At the beginning of the crisis, the dominant sector in the party was the reformist sector, led by Mulud Hamrouche and Abdelhamid Mehri, close to the ousted president Chadli Bendjedid, who opposed the electoral interruption unleashed by the coup of 2 January 1992. They led FLN, for the first time in its history, to distance itself from the government, and to a critique that culminated in the signing of the Rome Platform. However, the relation of forces changed, so that in January 1996, at the meeting of the FLN's central committee, the party's general secretary who supported this political line, Abdelhamid Mehri, was dropped. At the same time, Mulud Hamrouche was replaced by Bualem Benhamuda,[8] who was elected the new general secretary by 89 votes to 82 and re-established the party's traditional loyalty to the government. With the creation of the RND, the FLN has suffered numerous defections, but neither this, nor its progressive political decline during 30 years of authoritarian political rule, have prevented its surprising 'renaissance' to win 16.8 per cent of parliamentary seats and 21.8 per cent in the localities.

Alongside this group is another pole of political forces who represent divergent ideologies but have in common their reluctance to put the regime directly into question. They form an opposition that has accepted the framework of dialogue proposed by the regime and its rules of the game,[9] and are represented in the National Transition Council. There are two main parties, the Regroupment for Culture and Democracy (RCD) and Hamas. The first is the leading party of the Islamist eradication ideology led by Sa'adi, who not only supported the *coup* in 1992 but, along with the Algerian communist party Ettehadi, called on the army to stage it. The RCD concentrates the bulk of its criticisms of the government on everything that refers to the acceptance of the Hamas party, given that its particular and exclusive vision of democracy implies the annihilation of the adversary. The leaders of this party, whose influence is much greater abroad than in Algeria,[10] have received much media coverage in Europe, particularly in France, where they are wrongly believed to be democratic simply because they are secular.

Hamas and the Algerian regime

When the FIS existed as a legal party, Hamas had a fairly narrow social base,[11] but in the current political framework, both the regime and Mahfuz Nahnah, the movement's leader, have sought to benefit from the absence of the FIS. This has permitted the development, albeit closely watched, of an Islamic-leaning party that is not politically dissident and which accepts what the regime offers, aware that in a more pluralist framework, like that of 1990–1, it would not obtain the representation it currently enjoys. With this strategy, the Algerian military hopes to neutralize a good part of FIS supporters, reabsorbing them through Hamas.

Hamas has assumed its vocation of FIS's substitute that it had from the start. It was the electoral success of the FIS in the municipal elections of June 1990 that prompted government forces in the FLN to create Hamas, with the aim of weakening the FIS.[12] The 'Movement for Islamic Society' (Hamas) was formed on 5 December 1990, led by Shaykh Mahfuz Nahnah, then director of the influential Islamic cultural association, Al-Islah wa-l-Irshad, which urged the progressive re-islamization of society, but without political aims.

The political role that Nahnah fulfilled in Algeria, after earlier militancy that landed him in jail, was the fundamentalism of 'constructive opposition' that often neared agreement with the regime after he was freed from prison in 1981 by Bendjedid. He thus dissociated himself from the confrontational line of his colleagues Madani, Sahnun,

Benhadj, which is why Nahnah refused to participate in the creation of the FIS. Tensions between Nahnah and the FIS, especially with Abbasi Madani, were constant after 1989, and increased when Nahnah refused to back the FIS in the municipal elections of 1990.

Hamas had a deeper and more elaborate doctrine than that of the FIS, but its moderate attitude towards the regime softened its image as an opposition force, from which the FIS derived most of its success. Nahnah's argument, which is that of Hamas, is that there are two kinds of *ulemas* (doctors in Islamic law): one written into the traditional current that forms the consciousness of the Muslim community towards its government, without giving prominence to the question of political power; and the other seeking the direct exercise of power. Hamas belongs to the first current, the only one acceptable to the regime, and the FIS to the second.[13] The question arose because of the Algerian people's emphatic rejection of the established power and the overwhelming search for political leaders able to replace it: this was the message that the FIS, but not Hamas, put across. And this is the main difference between an Islamist movement that represented the sociological change experienced in Algeria since the 1980s, with which a large new generation of young people identified, and an Islamic tendency based more on the preservation of traditional Muslim values than on promoting a new generation of leaders.

However, even though the Algerian political system absorbed Hamas, it did not allow it to play an important political role. On the contrary, in the framework designed by the military regime, Hamas seemed entrusted with instruments for the Islamic management of society in moral and social terms, but not with those that could make the group capable of presenting an alternative or a renewal of ruling elites, which was what the FIS's victory in 1992 implied. So the results of the legislative elections fitted in with the regime's strategy, against the expectations of Hamas, which under a new law had to change from a Movement into a Peace Society (MSP-Silm).[14] This party suffered a significant decline in votes for its leader, Shaykh Nahnah, in the presidential elections of 1995, and won only half of its previous vote.[15] In an interview with the *Al-Sharq al-Awsat* newspaper (14 September 1997), Shaykh Nahnah said he was a victim of fraud in some constituencies and thought that some of his votes 'had gone to the RND and the FLN, especially in the west of the country and the capital ... . while others had been "assigned" to Ennahda in the eastern region'. This fact, if true, strengthened the idea that the MSP was boosted by the regime to weaken the FIS, and that Ennahda (a very small Islamist party led by Abdallah Djaballah) would also be encouraged to prevent the MSP from becoming a political threat. In any case, Ennahda's ability to win 34 seats made it a surprisingly powerful political force, given its very localized base in the Constantina region.[16] However, the MSP's reduced parliamentary presence was compensated by obtaining seven ministers, although none with important posts.

The third pole of the political scene was the group of signatories of the Rome Platform, with the Front of Socialist Forces (FFS) and the FIS at its head. The FFS has the great symbolic resource of its charismatic leader, Ait Ahmed, and is a social democratic party well placed in the international community as a member of the Socialist International. Its social implantation is very uneven since, despite national aspirations, its Berber origins mean its social base is concentrated in Cabilia and Algiers where it is a rival of the RCD.

Ever since it joined the Rome Platform, the FFS has been increasingly criticized by a sector that disapproved of its acceptance of the FIS and which urged the party to participle in elections rather than boycott them. This situation, used by the regime to destabilize the Front, prompted a dissident faction led by Sa'id Khelil to form a new party, the Movement for Democracy and Citizenship (MDC), which wants to be 'distant from the regime and the Islamists' (*La Tribune*, 9 March 1997), but which in practice contributes to the fragmentation, and hence the weakening, of the opposition.

For this reason, the FFS has had to confront the internal current of opinion that believes the boycott policy marginalizes it and prevents it from being 'present in society'. It finally opted to participate in the elections of 1997 and to be represented in parliament, but without its leader, Ait Ahmed, who did not stand for election.

The FFS would have preferred to create a joint united opposition list, including some FIS candidates, or independents close to them. But the MDA (Movement for Democracy in Algeria) of Ben Bella refused to participate in the electoral process, the FLN 'reformists' did not feel able to take this step because of pressures from orthodox members (who none the less exluded them from their lists), and the FIS refused in the end to take part obliquely in a process that did not recognize them and kept them illegal.

Some clarifications about the FIS and Algerian Islamism

The emergence of Islamism as a socio-political force in Algeria occurred when sectors of the Islamic establishment 'became politicized' and, consequently, were perceived by the regime as a political threat. The regime was thus brought into political confrontation with the Islamists, a development that took place throughout the 1980s.

Until then, dissident fundamentalism, which was loosely structured, manifested itself mainly through the emergence of preachers who criticized from the mosques, with greater or lesser virulence, the non-Islamic orientations of the regime. Further, Shaykh Soltani's virulent criticism of Algerian socialism did not necessarily represent everyone's opinion,[17] and was in broad terms a mainly socio-cultural mobilization, comprising moralizing, arabization and personal laws. During the 1960s these were the aims of the Al-Qiyam al-Islamiyya (Islamic Values) association founded in 1963 by El-Hachemi Tidjani, which was well represented in the state apparatus by those close to Ben Bella. It included the 'imams' who would become the country's religious personalities of the coming years: Ahmed Sahnun, Abd al-Latif Soltani, Mesbah Houidek, Abbasi Madani.[18]

The regime never confronted this tendency politically, but sporadically issued 'warnings' against some 'dissident preachers'. This was mainly because these 'preachers' were simply the expression of a religious ideology to which state institutions adhered with pride. Further, the state created points of interpenetration between 'official' fundamentalism and 'dissident' fundamentalism through the overwhelming social importance of the mosque. It created a separate educational system parallel to the general one (specializing in Arab language and Islamic sciences) and Islamic cultural activity was sponsored by the Ministry of Religious Affairs through Islamic centres, the organization of annual Seminars of Islamic Thought, and various publications, mainly the magazines *Al-Asala* and *Al-Risala*.[19]

This broad religious infrastructure in a country where no social space existed, except for the mosque, meant that dissident voices could arise without being crushed. The discrediting of the *langue de bois* of the official imams occurred alongside the increase in the prestige of a generation of confrontational preachers, indissolubly identified with the mosques from which they preached. Mesbak Houidek will always be remembered for his links with the mosque in the Al-Harrak neighbourhood, where Boumedienne could not ban him because of the strong popular support movement that emerged when the government tried to dismiss him as imam. The intellectual Malek Bennabi is historically linked to the creation in 1968 of the mosque at the main university in Algiers, where he played an important role in the 'Islamization' of the student community and the Algerian intelligentsia, which gave rise to the Al-Djazara branch of Algerian Islamism. Similarly, from the mid-1960s the mosque at Bayt al-Arkam was the mosque of Ahmad Sahnun, Abdelatif Soltani and Abbasi Madani, considered the master thinkers of Algerian Islamism, and later Bab al-Oued was the mosque that symbolized the discourse of Ali Benhadj.

The regime was aware of the proliferation and influence of these 'dissident centres', but it sought to control them through individual actions of repression. Further, for fear of being accused of going 'against Islam', and because a regime that contained a religious lobby in its own FLN ranks perceived no real threat, the government could not, or did not know how to, prevent Islamist dissidence increasing around 'free mosques' that escaped state control, and where an 'emir' was put in charge together with an imam, a treasurer, a representative for cultural affairs and another for social questions.

In the years 1978–82, two trends interacted: the radicalization of fundamentalism linked to the state, and the beginnings of an Islamist current around the mosques of some urban centres. Several factors explain this interaction. On the one hand, within the ruling class, the perception of the Isof society was not unanimously welcomed, especially since the move to the left of the regime in 1972 established a rapprochement between itself and the Socialist Vanguard Party (PAGS)' communist ideology. In 1977, Algerian education was unified and *l'enseignement originel* (Islamic education system), dependent on the Ministry of Religious Affairs, disappeared. This prompted great disquiet within the Ministry and amongst those supporting the Islamization of Algeria. The president of the Islamic Superior Council, Shaykh Hammani, in the IV Congress of the FLN that was to appoint a successor to Boumedienne, denounced the previous period and demanded measures of re-Islamization.[20]

On the other hand, the Iranian Islamic revolution of 1979 had great influence, not only through its reading of liberation through Islam but also for its revolutionary character in a country that had built the phenomenon of popular revolution into myth. Hence, in 1982 Algeria produced a radical Islamic movement led by Mustafa Buyali, preacher of the Al-'Ashure mosque, that took the road of armed conflict with the 'impious' Algerian state. This group, the 'Algerian Islamic Movement' (MIA), made a big national impact with some spectacular armed actions carried out in 1982. Linked with Islamic movements from abroad, and with a limited ideological base, the MIA was subjected to a permanent military offensive till February 1987, when Buyali was killed in a police ambush and 207 of its militants detained.[21]

At the same time, events that shook the Algerian university in November 1982, as part of the continuous confrontations between Arab-speakers and leftists, enabled Islamists to gauge the large audience they had in the university. A strike organized by Arab-speaking students against social and employment discrimination was taken over by the Islamists after the government closed the mosque in the central faculty of Algiers following the death of a student in confrontations.

For the first time, Abbasi Madani decided to challenge the regime by calling a demonstration on 7 November 1982, which Sahnun and Soltani also supported. However, Shaykh Mahfud Nahnah, head of the Muslim Brothers in Algeria, preaching the values of prudence, dissociated himself from the action and has already revealed himself as a representative of an Islamism close to the regime, which he became in the coming decade when he created the Hamas party to confront the FIS.

At the end of the march on 7 November, Madani read a 14-point manifesto which demanded, among other things, more effective Arabization, greater respect for Islamic values, an alcohol ban and the drafting of a personal statute that respected the spirit of the Koran. Soltani, Sahnun and Madani were arrested, and Madani remained in jail until 1984. These events triggered the non-violent political confrontation of Algerian Islamism and the start of the sociological change mentioned earlier.

This process of debate within Algerian society was not the only one at that time. The gradual process of delegitimization of the regime, caused by its failure to fulfil the hopes it had raised, prompted the emergence of other political actors that sought to escape from state tutelage: the Berber cultural movement blossomed in 1980, the movement of women against sex discrimination appeared in 1981, and the human rights movement emerged in 1983. A wave of strikes after 1977, together with a series of social movements (demonstrations in Cabilia in 1980, revolts in Constantina and Setif in 1986) also expressed this process of delegitimization.

These dissident movements arose at the same time as the collapse of what we may define as the political component of the Algerian nation. That is, instead of the cultural comprehension of an Algerian nationality that resorted to Islam as a control mechanism (to legitimate the established order), and as a sign of identity (to reaffirm indigenous cultural values)[22] the nation's political understanding was based on the promise to the people to achieve national independence, modernization and economic development.

In the 1980s this national project collapsed, revealing an authoritarian state with neither democratic legitimacy nor the counter-weight of a welfare system that could, with the cult of nation-building, maintain a social contract with the people.

At this point the regime had to strengthen its sources of legitimacy, either by investing in the 'political nation' (by reinforcing democratic legitimacy) or in the 'cultural nation' (by intensifying Islamic legitimacy). It chose the second. Hence, the government's 'Islamizing' strategy, represented by the presidency of Chadli Bendjedid in the 1980s. In this way, when the petroleum crisis unleashed an economic crisis, Algeria's rulers, isolated from society and living off the pillaging of petroleum income, opted for Islamism as the way to bolster the reforms of economic liberalization. Their criticisms of socialism and their opposition to land reform converted the Islamists into the supposed defenders of a liberal reform that met serious resistance in the state apparatus. It was significant that 1984 saw the first reformist laws and the approval of the ultra-traditionalist Family Code (at the same time as the first family planning programme began in Algeria!).

Berber claims were crushed by tanks in 1980; Communist activity was restricted by the revival in 1981 of Clause 120 of FLN statutes that banned non-FLN activists from any post in trade unions or mass organizations (where the Algerian Communist party (PAGS) had its social base); the human rights movement was reabsorbed by the regime through the creation of an Algerian Human Rights League close to the government; and the women's movement saw parliament approve the Family Code in 1984, which was more backward-looking than a project they had succeeded in blocking some years before. Faced with this, the regime sought tactical support from the most radical sector of fundamentalism then operating in the state, in which the nascent Islamism, as long as it did not manifest itself violently, could enjoy official sympathy and tacit support.

Thus, the regime of Chadli Bendjedid persecuted Buyali's group, but as part of its strategy of broadening the religious ambit absorbed within 'official Islam' many of 'dissident Islam's' socio-cultural demands.

- religious teaching was established at all levels of education, compulsory for examinations;
- Islamic sections were created in secondary schools and the baccalaureat, with the possibility of continuing studies at the Institut Superieur des Sciences Sociales Islamiques de Constantina;

- the five-year plan of 1980–4 proposed the construction of 160 mosques and Koranic schools, the creation of 5 000 teaching posts for the Koran and of 26 new Islamic centres;
- TV and radio programmes increased their religious programming, including, after 1981, the speeches of the Egyptian Shaykh al-Ghazali, close to the Muslim Brothers, who was proposed as the first rector of the Islamic University of Constantina in 1984;
- after 1979, flourishing campaigns of moralisation and Islamic demands were sponsored by the Ministry of the Interior, which was run from 1980 by the traditionalist Abderahman Chibane.

Until the popular revolts of October 1988, the Islamist current adopted a strategy of 'entryism' in the spaces that state fundamentalism assigned to it (Madani and Sahnun wrote in official magazines such as *Al-Asala* and *Al-Risala* and Mahfuz Nahnah considered Bendjedid 'a servant of Islam'). Within the mosques they created study and action groups that eluded the direct control of the Ministry of Religious Affairs. They also conducted effective social action that was amply revealed in the economic crisis that followed the petroleum crisis of 1986.

The profound changes experienced by Algeria in 1988–9 opened the political arena to multi-partyism, and this gave birth to the FIS when various religious leaders decided to regroup their forces and take collective action within a legal framework.

Once formed and legalized, the movement's leaders promptly gave the FIS an efficient and centralized organization, designed to control radical initiatives, which linked political impact (in its forms of mobilization) with the cultural-religious (a swearing-in ceremony to establish group loyalty, the importance of the mosque as medium, the use of religious language and a Muslim style of dress).

After the crisis of June 1991 when Abbasi Madani and 'Ali Banhadj were imprisoned, Abdelqader Hachani took over the movement and, in a meeting in Batna at the end of July 1991, decided to expand its ruling committee, the Majlis al-Shura, and encouraged it to support the al-Djazara tendency (the organizing and negotiating current of the FIS). Abdelqader Hachani's campaign for the legislative elections in 1991 took a prudent and correct attitude towards the regime and the electoral rules. The FIS represented well the Islamist political sector that favoured integration into the institutional framework, and which was certainly a majority compared with radical and revolutionary groups. Hence, the strategy adopted between 1989 and 1992 of political integration logically prompted Islamism to make compromises, which weakened its radical sectors – in a minority up to 1992. By contrast, the strategy of frontal repression adopted that year allowed the radical Islamist sectors to dominate the scene as they had never done before. The phenomenon of violence coincided with the halt of political liberalization in 1992 and the government's strategy of energetic repression of Islamism that followed.

In the last seven years since it was banned, and as a result of pragmatism, the FIS seems to have experienced a notable process of political maturation. This is shown in its proposals for a negotiated solution, its democratic commitments derived from the Rome Platform and its statements proposing dialogue and the acceptance of a multi-party system. However, it has great difficulty convincing western political opinion that it is not a violent and radical movement.

What are the reasons for its failure to put across its position in a credible way? There are two main explanations. On the one hand, Islamists find it enormously difficult to communicate with the western world, which has formed a demonized cultural perception of them: unable to see them as a new political generation, it considers them a malignant deviation. However, although they do contain fanatic and violent elements, there are also sectors with whom dialogue is possible, and what is really needed is to isolate the first in favour of the second, and to favour their access to government jointly with other parties in a pluralist transition.

This lack of communication is partly because there have been no common intellectual bridges between Islamists and the western world (comparable to those that formerly ideologically linked third-world or nationalist movements with the European left), and so they need intermediaries among non-Islamist democratic forces that have a voice in the western world, and are hence able to understand the real causes of the problem and how to solve it. This is one of the values of the group around the Rome Platform.

On the other hand, in Algeria the strategy of the armed forces, which keep an iron grip on security information, has imposed a Manichean vision that conceals the diversity of Islamist actors in the conflict. There is certainly a very radical revolutionary guerrilla movement, represented by the Islamic Armed Group (GIA) and the Movement for the Islamic State (MEI), that uses terror against the people in its aim of overthrowing the regime. And these groups assassinate journalists, women, foreigners, and so on. But, independently of these groups, and in no way deriving from them, the FIS has an armed wing, the Islamic

Salvation Army (EIS), which is 'militarily correct',[23] and fights for the rehabilitation of the FIS by attacking military and security targets.

Military strategy towards the guerrillas is to give maximum publicity to the revolutionary guerrillas and even occasionally let them flourish, while discrediting and concealing the FIS guerrillas. Hence, the virtually hegemonic appearance of the GIA, whose importance is less than it seems, because it feeds the international community's fear of seeing Algeria ruled by extremist emirs. So, in reaction, it guarantees external support for the regime, which is considered the 'lesser evil'. The Interior Ministry's control of information through a ministerial decree that bans 'the diffusion of all information about security that is not contained in an official communique or the public press' means that the Algerian conflict is conducted 'behind closed doors', without images or witnesses.

Political understanding of economic factors

Algeria and the European Union opened negotiations on the Free Trade Association Agreement which, in the framework of Euro-Mediterranean dialogue, must be signed in the near future, producing an enormous new financial inflow.[24] These accords establish in their article 2, as an essential element, that all relations among participants must be based on 'the respect for human rights and democratic principles'. However, they also include a 'security clause' that allows governments to apply 'measures' that may be necessary to protect national security and maintain law and order.

Human rights groups have urged the European Parliament to use the signing of these accords to improve the human rights situation and encourage democratization so that, contrary to what has happened up to now, article 2 takes precedence over the security clause.[25]

Hence, the principal aims of Algeria's politico-juridical reform carried out since 1995 are to win political recognition for the regime, and to obtain the economic aid that derives from that. However, although the huge financial resources received by Algeria to promote economic liberalization have certainly improved macro-economic indices,[26] the people do not experience any economic progress and their social conditions deteriorate daily.

The transition from the socialist to the liberal model has not modified the behaviour patterns of the elites that dominate the world of finance in Algeria, and the closed nature of the system means that the country operates as a market reserved for those in the know with large networks of contacts at their disposal.

Large financial flows supplied by the International Monetary Fund (IMF), which rose from US$14 000m between 1994 and 1996 to more than US$20 000m in 1998, have served to cover the great deficit in the state coffers, external debt and the public deficit, to the massive importation of consumer goods (US$10 000 m in 1995 and 1996), and to pay for the war (the security sector increased its budget by 150 per cent in 1995). But the funds have not helped education, health, housing or investment in enterprises. Of the 1 350 public companies considered viable for sale, only 26 have actually been sold; begging and unemployment have grown to unprecedented levels (around 30 per cent of the working population, but up to 75 per cent of people aged between 16 and 24[27]); construction of public housing fell by 70.9 per cent between 1995 and 1996; and malnutrition and the progressive deterioration of Algerians' health is causing the emergence of infectious diseases.[28]

The only economic reforms carried out inflict great suffering on the majority of the population (price adjustment, wage freezes, destruction of public companies and often mass dismissals). And the external debt, far from declining, has grown under the impact of rescheduled interest payments (from US$32 000m in 1995 to US$36 000m in 1996).[29] Hence the great dependence on the hydrocarbon sector, which produces 95 per cent of the country's foreign exchanges, interacts with an economic model based on financial wealth that the country does not produce and which brought the regime to financial disaster in the mid-1980s as a consequence of the 'petroleum crisis'.

Is Algeria then on the point of social explosion that could imperil the regime in a way beyond the reach of the guerrillas? The threat of social explosion is a spectre that undoubtedly hovers over the country, but this risk is neutralized partly by psychological factors – given that people are paralysed by the daily experience of violence and terror – and because the authorities devote part of the financial resources now at their disposal to economic investment in social sectors essential to the maintenance of the status quo: civil servants have been the only beneficiaries, through a wage increase of more than 10 per cent directed at ensuring their loyalty; unproductive jobs have been created to absorb some of the youth who might be tempted to join the 'undergound'; unrestricted trade liberalization established since 1994 has produced flourishing import-export businesses and speculation benefiting an urban bourgeoisie formerly tempted to provide economic support to the FIS.

In addition, the government realized that the police and the army were unable to contain the violence and in 1995 began to finance a civilian militia of 'patriots'. These forces began occupying territory by carrying out raids against Islamist guerrillas with a brutality that incited even greater violence in the regions where they were active – something that is not unrelated to lamentably frequent rural massacres.

Security or politics

The Algerian regime insists the conflict is a security problem, not a political one. Hence it persists with its schedule of elections, as if the concomitent violence and massacres have nothing to do with them; or it prefers to negotiate with the Islamist armed wing (the Islamic Salvation Army–EIS) instead of the political leadership of the FIS (which was blocked again at the end of 1997).

By contrast, for the FIS and for the opposition in general, the political predominates over the military, because they insist there will be no solution to the problem until the political dimension and the question of power-sharing is addressed. The problem is that for the present regime to accept a transition, its elite would need to feel vulnerable and conceive its own survival as capable of being guaranteed only by a pact. At the moment, however, the regime does not seem to feel the need to open the system to any new political elite, because the opposition is atomized and unable to present itself as an alternative, and because of the political and economic external support that it receives.

Beyond the Rome project of January 1995, which unfortunately did not gain the necessary momentum either inside or outside the country, the Algerian opposition has been unable to generate a strategy to express itself by consensus. The 'twin enemies', RCD and FFS, are far from reaching an understanding, given the distance between them about whether FIS should participate in a political transition. FIS is an essential actor in any political process that seeks to end Algeria's civil confrontation. But it neither convinces Europe that it is a credible interlocutor nor is it accepted by 'eradicator' sectors and parties.

Furthermore, the Algerian regime is grateful for the international community's fearful resistance to the conflict, which it translates in its favour. The policy of the European Union towards Algeria has implied a discreet support for the regime without ever making explicit condemnations of the repression it practises. Hence, while municipal and regional elections were denounced by the whole opposition, and even by groups from within the system, the EU foreign ministers supported the process of political reform promoted by the Algerian government and said they were waiting for its initiatives and projects to finance. According to the 'Eurocrats', this is the only option, given the absence of other political interlocutors. And this is how they explain the opening of negotiations for signing the Free Trade Association between the EU and Algeria. The economic explanation is also a justification: it will help stabilization, democratization and economic diversification.

However, if we take into account that the export of hydrocarbons constitutes 95 per cent of Algerian exports, and that imports, despite existing in a juridical framework of almost complete liberalization, are in the hands of cliques and speculators, we can gauge the extent to which a blind eye is being turned, as well as western governments' vulnerability to the policies of force and their lack of initiative to confront the Algerian government's authoritarianism. This all tends to a conservatism towards the interlocutors because a conflict of such complex violence creates unease and paralysis.

However, the Algerian situation of recent years shows that militarist and repressive policies are incapable of resolving the country's bloody civil conflict: on the contrary, they favour national disintegration and obstruct civil reconciliation and democratization.

Notes

1 This so-called 'eradicator' sector supports the hardest sector of the Algerian army and favours a military solution to the conflict, whatever the consequences, in order to annihilate the Islamic electorate. This sector is a small minority in Algeria, but nonetheless, is highly regarded in Europe, and especially in France, where it manipulates the language of democracy to appear as respectable defenders of 'our' Western ideal.

2 Signed by the FIS, the FFS and the FLN (led at the time by Abdelhamid Mehri), the MDA, the Trotskyist party of Louisa Hamoun, the al-Nahda party and the Algerian League for the Defence of Human Rights led by the lawyer Yahya Abdennour.

3 On the origins and development of the Algerian conflict see Gema Martin Muñoz, 'Le regime algerien face aux Islamistes' in B. Kodmani and M. Chartouni (eds), *Les Etats Arabes face à la contestation Islamiste*, (Paris, Armand Colin/Ifri, 1997), pp. 41–7.

4 The CNT mission has concluded and its 'deputies' received a special subsidy equivalent to a year's salary (*La Tribune*, 13 May 1997).

5 Article 101: Two-thirds of National Council members are elected indirectly by members of municipal and regional Popular Assemblies. The third third is appointed by the president of the Republic from national personalities of

the world of science, culture, the economy and society. *Journal Officiel (JORA)*, 8 December 1996.

6 *JORA*, 6 March 1997.

7 The general election results were: with a turnout of 65.5 per cent, of the 380 seats of the National Assembly, 57.6 per cent were won by the RND (155 deputies) and the FLN (64 deputies), to whom some of the 11 seats occupied by independents could give their support. The second political group was the Islamic tendency with 69 seats for the MSP (plus 4 independents) and 34 for Ennahda. To these two blocs were added 19 FFS deputies, 19 of the RCD, 4 of the Workers' Party and 5 of other minority parties. In the municipal elections the results, challenged by all the opposition, were: RND and its ally the National Liberation Front (FLN), 7 242 and 2 864 seats respectively, of the 13 123 in the municipal assemblies. Far behind came the Movement for an Islamic Society (MSP/exHamas) with 890 seats, the Socialist Forces Front (FFS) with 645, independents with 508, the Regroupment for Culture and Democracy (RCD) with 444 and the al-Nahda party with 290 seats. In the regional assemblies the RND won 986 of the 1880 seats, followed by the FLN (373) and the MSP (260). See Gema Martin Muñoz, 'Algérie, des élections sur mesure', *Confluences Méditerranée*, no. 23, 1997, pp. 89–103.

8 Former leader of the war of liberation, he occupied various ministerial posts from the Boumedienne era to 1987. He is considered an ultra-conservative with few liberal convictions. *Al-Watan*, 21 January 95 and *Liberté*, 18 January 1996.

9 In Algeria, 'political dialogue with the opposition and associations' has experienced various stages since the High Committee of State launched it on 13 March 1993, but essentially it has legitimized the nomination of the president of the Republic in January 1994 and of the National Transition Council (CNT) in May 1994. See Gema Martin Muñoz, 'Egypte et Algérie. Convergences et divergences', *Politique Etrangère*, IFRI.Paris, 2/1995, pp. 403–15.

10 In the 1991 elections, the RCD won no more than 2.9 per cent of votes cast (200 267) and 4.2 per cent in 1997.

11 In the 1991 elections, Hamas won 5.3 per cent of votes cast (368 697), without winning a single seat in the first and only electoral round that took place. The FIS won 47.3 per cent (3 260 359) with 188 seats won, and with 171 constituencies still to vote.

12 The same motive prompted the emergence of the Islamic tendency party Ennahda in October 1990, heir of the Islamic Association that existed clandestinely from 1974 led by Chaikh Abdallah Djabballah.

13 Fawsi Oussedik ben al-Hachimi, *The Attitudes of Sheikh Mafouz Regarding Vocation and Religious Movement*. Argel, Dar al-Intifada li-l-nachr wa-l-tawzi', s.d. (1991?) (Arabic).

14 This party is usually called Silm, the Algerian pronunciation of the Arab word *Salam* (Peace).

15 Hamas was permitted visibility in the presidential poll, and invited to take two ministerial posts in the government that followed. This constituted the main basis for its cooptation by the regime, although Hamas still criticized it on several occasions, albeit with great prudence.

16   In 1991 only two of its candidates stood in the cancelled second round.
17   *Le Mazdaqisme est a l'origine du socialisme*, published in Morocco in 1974.
     M. Al-Ahnaf, B.Botiveau and F. Fregosi, *L'Algerie par ses Islamistes*, (Paris,
     Karthala, 1991).M. Bormans, 'Le Ministere de l'enseignement originel et des
     Affaires Religieuses en Algerie', *Oriente Moderno*, LVII, 1972, pp. 467–81.
18   The speech was published in *Al-Asala*, No. 65–6, 1979, pp. 56–7. Extracts
     appear in L.-W. Deheuvels, *Islam et Pensée Contemporaine en Algérie. La revue
     Al-Asala, 1971–1981*, (Paris CNRS, 1991), pp. 25–6.
19   H. 'Ayyachi, *Al-Islamiyyun al-djaza'irun, bayna el-sulta wa-l-rasas [Moslem
     Fundamentalists between the Authority and the Bullets]* (Argel, Dar al-Hikma),
     1991 (Arabic); Francois Burgat, *L'Islamisme au Maghrab, la voix du sud* (Paris,
     Khartala, 1988).
20   Henri Sanson, *La?cita islamique en Algérie*, (Paris CRESM/CNRS, 1983).
21   The expression was used by Luis Martinez in *Confluences Mediterrannée*,
     no. 20, Winter 1996–7. According to this Algerian political specialist in vio-
     lence, 'when the pro-government militias were sent to carry out an
     extremely brutal guerrilla campaign against the AIS, the AIS combatants felt
     compelled to respond with the same methods and this created a gulf
     between their political aspirations and their practice in combat.'
22   It must be borne in mind that, after the CIS (the former Soviet Union),
     Algeria is the second supplier of gas to Europe, their best clients being Italy,
     France, Belgium and Spain. Thus, Algeria is very important for the EU in its
     search to diversify its energy sources and avoid excessive dependence on
     Russia.
23   Free Trade Association Agreements have already been signed with Morocco,
     Tunisia and Israel, and negotiations are in an advanced stage with Egypt,
     Lebanon and Jordan, and more recently with Algeria. Human Rights Watch,
     Amnesty International and the Center for International Human Rights
     Enforcement of Jerusalem consider that, of the agreements already signed,
     those with Tunisia and Israel should be reconsidered in accordance with
     article 2. *Financial Times*, 11 February 1997.
24   The growth of Gross Domestic Product will reach 5 per cent in 1997 (com-
     pared with 4 per cent in 1996); inflation will fall to 9 per cent compared
     with 18 per cent in 1996 and the balance of trade for the first time in 10
     years showed a surplus of US$42 000m in 1996. The reasons for these good
     indicators are the continuing high price of petroleum and the direct effects
     of various reschedulings of the foreign debt.
25   70 per cent of the population is under the age of 30 and, according to
     World Bank estimates, Algeria needs US$25 bn in investment to create
     enough jobs. See World Bank report 'Claiming the Future: Choosing
     Prosperity in the Middle East and North Africa', Washington, 1995, p. 80.
26   'Rapport de conjoncture du CNES', *Liberté*, 28 April 1997.
27   IMF report of November 1996. Algeria has rescheduled its public debt twice,
     in 1994 and 1995, with the Paris Club, for US$10 000 m (milliards); and
     rescheduled its private debt in 1995, conceded by the London Club
     for US$32 000 m. Thanks to this, Algeria was able to delay payment of
     US$13 000 m of credits obtained, when debt servicing accounts for 35 per
     cent of total external incomes instead of 90 per cent in 1993. But from 1998

debt servicing will become 50 per cent, and 75 per cent in the year 2000 – a situation similar to that of 1993.

28 After A. Madani and A. Hachani were freed in July 1997, it seemed that dialogue was taking place beteen the government and the FIS political leadership, but unexpectedly, the army was apparently negotiating a unilateral truce with the AIS, which caused confusion, divisions and finally, once again, the collapse of political dialogue and military truce.

29 *El Pais*, 27 October 1997.

Index

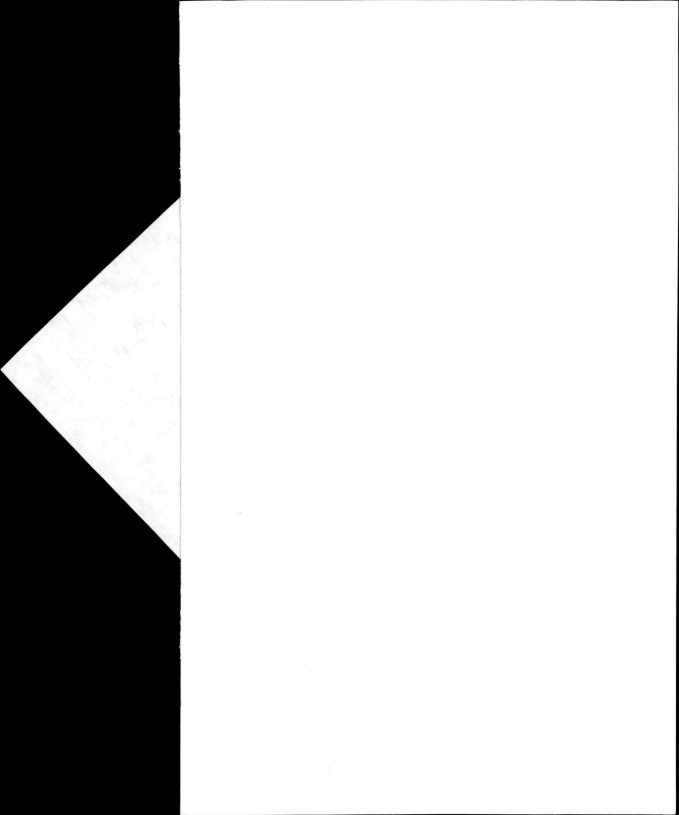

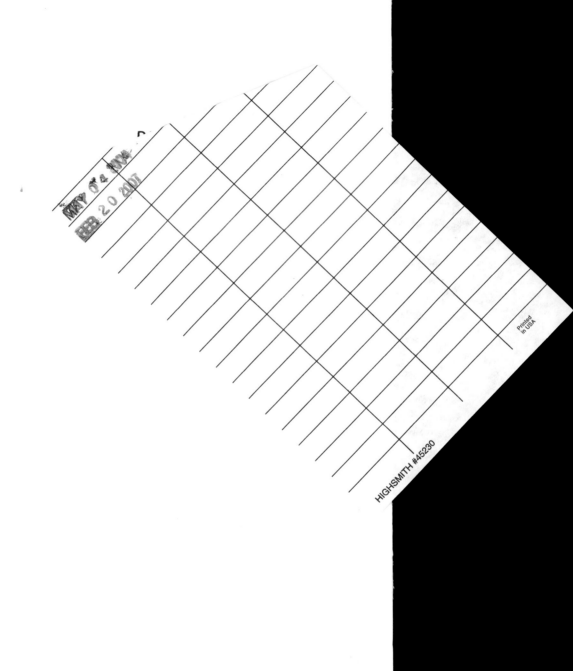

HIGHSMITH #45230

Printed
in USA